# Consumption and Culture in Sixteenth-Century Ireland

Irish Historical Monograph Series
ISSN 1740-1097



**Previous titles in this series**

I. Ruling Ireland 1685–1742: Politics, Politicians and Parties, *D. W. Hayton*, 2004

II. Lord Broghill and the Cromwellian Union with Ireland and Scotland, *Patrick Little*, 2004

III. Irish Migrants in New Zealand, 1840–1937: 'The Desired Haven', *Angela McCarthy*, 2005

IV. The Fenian Ideal and Irish Nationalism, 1882–1916, *M. J. Kelly*, 2006

V. Loyalism in Ireland, 1789–1829, *Allan Blackstock*, 2007

VI. Constructing the Past: Writing Irish History, 1600–1800, *edited by Mark Williams and Stephen Forrest*, 2010

VII. The Making of the Irish Protestant Ascendancy: The Life of William Conolly, 1662–1729, *Patrick Walsh*, 2010

VIII. The Militia in Eighteenth-Century Ireland: In Defence of the Protestant Interest, *Neal Garnham*, 2012

IX. The Anglo-Irish Experience, 1680–1730: Religion, Identity and Patriotism, *D. W. Hayton*, 2012

X. The Presbyterians of Ulster, 1680–1730, *Robert Whan*, 2013

XI. The Welsh and the Shaping of Early Modern Ireland, 1558–1641, Rhys Morgan, 2014

XII. The Irish in the Spanish Armies in the Seventeenth Century, Eduardo de Mesa, 2014

# Consumption and Culture in Sixteenth-Century Ireland

## Saffron, Stockings and Silk

*Susan Flavin*

THE BOYDELL PRESS

First published 2014
The Boydell Press, Woodbridge

ISBN 978-1-84383-950-7

The Boydell Press is an imprint of Boydell & Brewer Ltd
PO Box 9, Woodbridge, Suffolk IP12 3DF, UK
and of Boydell & Brewer Inc.
668 Mt Hope Avenue, Rochester, NY 14620–2731, USA
website: www.boydellandbrewer.com

A CIP catalogue record for this title is available from the British Library



This publication is printed on acid-free paper

To Peter and Brenna

# Contents

# *Illustrations*

**Plates**

**Figures**



**Maps**

## Tables

# Acknowledgements

This book developed from my University of Bristol Ph.D. thesis, and my first and greatest debt is to my former supervisor, Dr Evan Jones, who provided guidance, support and encouragement throughout the process, and whose outstanding academic professionalism and generosity to his students I continue to admire and respect.

I am immensely grateful to Dr Brendan Smith and Professor Raymond Gillespie, co-investigators on the 'Ireland–Bristol' project, for their advice and guidance. Thanks are also due to Dr Josie McLellan, Dr Fernando Cervantes and Dr Richard Sheldon, at the University of Bristol, all of whom provided valuable feedback on particular chapters and on the general direction of my research.

I am also much indebted to those who provided positive and encouraging responses to conference and seminar papers based on my developing research, in particular Nuala Zahedieh, Stuart Jenks and Wendy Childs and also to the anonymous referees for the Irish Research Council for the Humanities and Social Sciences (IRCHSS), the *Economic History Review* and Boydell & Brewer, all of whom provided very valuable comments on various aspects of my research and methodology. I would particularly like to thank Professor David Hayton for his detailed comments on a draft of the book and also Peter Sowden at Boydell & Brewer for his help and guidance. My thanks are also due to Dr Toby Barnard, my Ph.D. examiner, for his ongoing support and encouragement and to Professor Howard Clarke, whose teaching and mentorship inspired me as an undergraduate. Thanks also to Sue Vaughan for compiling the index.

I wish to acknowledge the support of the Economic and Social Research Council (ESRC), who funded the 'Ireland–Bristol project', which generated the quantitative data for this book, and also the Arts and Humanities Research Council (AHRC), without whose financial support this research would have been impossible.

I am also grateful to the National Archives at Kew; the Wellcome Library; the Governors and Guardians of Marsh's Library, Dublin; Edinburgh University Library; the Ashmolean Museum; and the British Library for permission to reproduce copyright material.

Finally, I would like to thank my husband and family for their encouragement and for not losing patience with my endeavours. This book is dedicated to you.

# *Abbreviations and Measures*

## Abbreviations

| | |
|---|---|
| AFM | *Annals of the Four Masters* |
| Cal. Carew MSS. | *Calendar of the Carew Manuscripts* |
| C.S.P. Ire. | *Calendar of State Papers Ireland* |
| DIER | Database of Irish Excavation Reports |
| EEBO | Early English Books Online |
| GPB | *The Great Parchment Book of Waterford* |
| HCA | *High Court of Admiralty Examinations* |
| IPMAG | Irish Post Medieval Archaeology Group |
| JRSAI | *Journal of the Royal Society of Antiquaries of Ireland* |
| OED | *Oxford English Dictionary* |
| OT | *Optometry Today* |
| TNA | The National Archives (Kew) |

## Measures

**Bale** A package of woad, alum, almonds etc., capacity varying with the commodity.

**Barrel** A cask; a measure of capacity that varies with the commodity. There are 12 barrels of herring to a last and 8 barrels of wine and oil to a tun.

**Burden** A load, a varying measure of quantity.

**Butt** Measure of wine, fish etc., equal to a pipe.

**C** (Lat. centum, centenarium):

**(a)** a hundredweight; according to Carus-Wilson, when reckoning 'great wares' (i.e. woad, alum etc.) C equals 112lb and when reckoning 'subtle wares' (i.e. saffron) it equals 100lb.

**(b)** C can also mean a 'long hundred' of 120 pieces, for example with fish and sheep skins or a hundred of 100 ells when looking at certain cloths.

**In** practice it is often possible to work out how many pieces (or lb) to the C for various commodities, based on a comparative study of values over the course of the century.

**Chest** Variable measurement of sugar. In the pre-1558 accounts a chest equals 120lb; later, the accounts specify that a chest contains 3C.

**Dimidium** (Text Di') Half.

**Ell** Measurement of cloth, varying in different countries. The Flemish ell equalled threee-quarters of an English yard, and five Flemish ells was equal to an English ell.

**Hogshead** Measure of capacity of wine etc., equal to one-quarter of a tun.

**Kilderkin** (Text kinderkin) A cask for liquids or fish etc. It is usually equal to half a barrel.

**M** A thousandweight or ten hundreds or hundredweights. See C.

**ob** Obol, or halfpenny.

**Pipe** A cask; hence a measure. A pipe of wine is equal to half a tun (this measure varies with other commodities).

**Quintal** (Text kindal) Equal to a hundredweight.

**Stone** (petra) A weight varying locally and for different commodities; from 8lb to 24lb.

**Tierce** Measure of capacity equivalent to one-third of a pipe, usually of wine but also means a cask or vessel holding this quantity, and can be of various other kinds of provisions such as honey.

**Tun** A cask of definite capacity; hence, a measure of capacity for wine and other liquids, usually equivalent to 2 pipes or 4 hogsheads, containing 252 old wine-gallons.

**Tunnage** The space occupied by a tun cask of wine, which was the unit used in measuring the carrying capacity or burden of a ship.

**Wey** Measure of salt, coal, wheat etc., varying locally and for different commodities. A wey of wheat, for example, equals 6 quarters, which equals 48 bushels.

**Yard** A measurement for cloth. The statute yard is 36in.

# Part I

# *The Irish Import Trade, 1503–1601*

... for the trade and enterdeale of seacoste nacons one with another worketh more civility and good fashions, all sea men being naturally desirous of new fashions, than the Inland dwellers which are seldome seene of forreyners; yet some of them as I have noted, I will recounte unto you.

Edmund Spenser
*View of the Present State of Ireland* (1596)

# Introduction

## Subject and Sources

### I. Consumption and material culture

In the past three decades, there has been a proliferation in historical studies of consumption. These include explorations of changing attitudes towards acquisition and ownership as well as ways in which consumer goods were interpreted. This new work is rooted both in the use of previously neglected sources and in the development of a multidisciplinary approach to consumption studies. Together, these have transformed our knowledge of early modern society and culture.[1] Despite such historiographical developments, in Ireland, the history of consumption and, indeed, the study of material culture in general have been slow to excite the interest of historians. Until recently, work in the area of Irish consumption was limited largely to attempts to chart the development of distinctive expressions of Irish culture.[2]

[1] For example: N. McKendrick, J. Brewer and J.H. Plumb (eds), *The Birth of a Consumer Society: The Commercialization of Eighteenth-Century England* (Indiana, 1985); J. Brewer and R. Porter (eds) *Consumption and the World of Goods* (London, 1993); M. Berg and H. Clifford, *Consumers and Luxury: Consumer Culture in Europ. 1650-1850* (Manchester and New York, 1999); M. Berg, *Luxury and Pleasure in Eighteenth-Century Britain*, (Oxford, 2005); L. Jardine, *Worldly Goods: A New History of the Renaissance* (London, 1996); T. H. Breen, 'An empire of goods: the Anglicisation of colonial America, 1690–1776', *Journal of British Studies*, 25 (1986) pp. 468–99; T. H. Breen, '"Baubles of Britain": the American and consumer revolutions of the eighteenth century', *Past and Present*, 119 (1988), pp. 73–104; C. Shammas, *The Pre-Industrial Consumer in England and America* (Oxford, 1990); C. Shammas, 'Changes in English and Anglo-American consumption from 1550 to 1800', in Brewer, J. and Porter, R. (eds), *Consumption and the World of Goods* (1993), pp. 177–205; L. Weatherill, 'The meaning of consumer behaviour in late seventeenth and early eighteenth-century England' in Brewer and Porter, *Consumption*, pp. 206–27. For a discussion of the current historiographical problems in this field see: S. Pennell, 'Consumption and consumerism in early-modern England', *Historical Journal*, xlii (1999), pp. 549–64; J. Brewer, 'The error of our ways: historians and the birth of a consumer society', Lecture to the Cultures of Consumption Programme, The Royal Society, 23 September 2003, working paper no. 12. Available from: http://www.consume.bbk.ac.uk/publications.html [accessed 2 December 2008].

[2] M. S. Dudley Westropp, *Irish Glass, an Account of Glass-Making in Ireland from the XVI Century to the Present Day* (London, 1920); H. F. McClintock, *Old Irish and Highland Dress* (Dundalk, 1950); A. Longfield, *Irish Lace* (Dublin, 1978); C. Kinmonth, *Irish Country Furniture, 1700–1950* (Yale, 1995); P. Francis, *Irish Delftware* (London, 2000); J. Sheehy, *The Rediscovery of Ireland's Past: The Celtic Revival 1830–1930* (London, 1980); K. Danaher, *Foirgneamh na nDaoine: Ireland's Vernacular Architecture* (Cork, 1975); K. Ticher, *A Guide to Irish Silver* (Dublin, 1868); R. Elliott, *Art and Ireland* (2008); L. Mitchell, *Irish Spinning Dyeing and Weaving* (Chester Springs, 1978). An important

Lately, however, a number of influential works have emerged that have done much to develop interest in this field. Of particular importance are two books by Toby Barnard: *Making the Grand Figure: Lives and Possessions in Ireland, 1641–1770*, and *A Guide to the Sources for the History of Material Culture in Ireland, 1500–2000*. The former considered the ways in which Irish Protestant elites adopted the fashions of empire and of the Continent, while the latter, taking a multidisciplinary approach to material culture, explored the range of sources available for the study of this field in Irish history, including: family histories, wills, inventories, letters, diaries, account books, estate records, advertisements and manuscript sources.[3] Other recent studies include Martyn Powell's *The Politics of Consumption in Eighteenth-Century Ireland*, which considered the politicisation of the consumer goods of the Protestant Ascendancy in eighteenth-century Ireland along with the consumption of display, leisure activities and entertainment; Helen Burke's study of the politics of Anglo-Irish cross-dressing in the eighteenth century and Robert Mahony's discussion of ideas of 'dependence' and 'consumption' in Swift's Irish pamphlets.[4] These works tend to mirror historiographical trends in studies of British and American consumption in terms of both methodology and chronological focus. In particular, they reflect the increasing tendency to represent consumption primarily as a cultural activity rather than as an economic or social one and, with this, in some cases, a distinct wariness of research that seeks to measure consumption in quantitative terms.[5] They also tend to focus predominantly on the long eighteenth century.

Of late, a number of British historians, particularly those interested in specialised areas of consumption and material culture, have sought to extend the chronological focus of consumption analysis, and recent studies have revealed significant changes in consumption in the sixteenth century and indeed earlier.[6] Historians of dress, in

exception to this was Louis Cullen's *The Emergence of Modern Ireland* (1981), which was the first work to apply *Annales* approaches to Irish issues, including housing and diet.

[3] T. Barnard, *Making the Grand Figure: Lives and Possessions in Ireland, 1641–1770* (New Haven, 2004); and *A Guide to the Sources for the History of Material Culture in Ireland, 1500–2000* (Dublin, 2005).

[4] M. Powell, *The Politics of Consumption in Eighteenth-Century Ireland* (Hampshire, 2005); H. Burke, 'Putting on Irish "stuff": the politics of Irish cross-dressing', in J. Munns and P. Richards (eds), *The Cloths that Wear Us: Essays on Dressing and Transgressing in Eighteenth-Century Culture* (Newark, 1999) pp. 217–32; R. Mahony, 'Protestant dependence and consumption in Swift's Irish Writings' in S. J. Connolly (ed.), *Political Ideas in Eighteenth-Century Ireland* (Dublin, 2000), pp. 83–104.

[5] Powell, *Politics*, p. 2.

[6] M. Koweleski, 'A consumer economy', in R. Horrox and W. Ormrod (eds), *The Social History of England 1200–1500* (Cambridge, 2006), pp. 238–59; J. Thirsk, *Economic Policy and Projects* (Oxford, 1978); J. Thirsk, *Food in Early Modern England: Phases, Fads, Fashions 1500–1760* (London, 2007); A. Jones and P. Stallybrass, *Renaissance Clothing and the Materials of Memory* (Cambridge, 2001); C. Richardson, *Clothing Culture 1350–1650* (Hampshire, 2004); S. Vincent, *Dressing the Elite: Clothing, Culture and Identity in Early Modern England* (Oxford, 2003); I. Archer, *History of the Haberdashers' Company* (Chichester, 1991); M. Dawson, *Plenti and Grase, Food and Drink in a Sixteenth-Century Household* (Totnes, 2009).

particular, have acknowledged the sixteenth century as a period of very significant change across Europe. Developing markets and production methods made available new types of fabrics and dress to societies, while the Reformation changed the material culture of religion and added a significant moral dimension to the accepted modes of dress. Indeed, according to Stallybrass and Jones, 'it was in the sixteenth century that the word "fashion" first took on the sense of restless change'.[7] Likewise, important developments have been identified in food consumption in this period. Joan Thirsk's study of the 'widening world of food' between 1550 and 1600, for example, showed the impact of growing domestic and overseas trade on the availability of new ranges of foodstuffs and domestic utensils and on changing attitudes to food and health in England.[8]

In Ireland, however, studies of sixteenth-century consumption have been slow to emerge and, indeed, archaeologists, rather than historians, have been the more proactive in this regard. The Irish Post-Medieval Archaeology Group, which was established in order to raise the profile of post-medieval archaeology, history and material culture within Ireland, has had a significant and continuing impact on this field. Recent publications include volumes of multidisciplinary papers on settlement and material culture in Plantation Ireland and on the changing material culture of Britain and Ireland from a comparative 'Atlantic World' perspective.[9]

In terms of historical studies, a recent examination of diet and nutrition in Ireland between 1500 and 1920, undertaken by Clarkson and Crawford, considered changes in patterns of consumption over time among different social classes; the impact of new agricultural techniques and cultural values on Irish diet; and the relationship between food, nutrition, health and demography.[10] This study included a single chapter on changing patterns of dietary consumption in the sixteenth and seventeenth centuries, utilising evidence from contemporary writings, army purveyancing records and a small number of elite household accounts. Also of note, and inspired in part by Felicity Heal's work on hospitality in early modern England, is Catherine O'Sullivan's work on the practice of hospitality in Gaelic Irish society, including guesting, feasting and gift giving, which has shed significant light on key aspects of Ireland's medieval material culture.[11]

[7] Jones and Stallybrass, *Renaissance Clothing*, p. 1. See also, L. Levy Peck, *Consuming Splendour, Society and Culture in Seventeenth-Century England* (Cambridge and New York, 2005).

[8] Thirsk, *Food*, pp. 27–57.

[9] A. Horning and N. Brannon (eds), *Ireland and Britain in the Atlantic World. Irish Post Medieval Group Proceedings 2* (Dublin, 2010); J. Lyttleton and C. Rynne (eds), *Plantation Ireland, Settlement and Material Culture, c.1550–c.1700* (Dublin, 2009); A. Horning and M. Palmer (eds), *Crossing Paths or Sharing Tracks? Future Directions in the Archaeological Study of Post-1550 Britain and Ireland* (Woodbridge, 1995); A. Horning *et al.* (eds), *The Post-Medieval Archaeology of Ireland, 1550–1850, Irish Post-Medieval Archaeology Group Proceedings* (Dublin, 2007).

[10] L. A. Clarkson and E. M. Crawford, *Feast and Famine: A History of Food and Nutrition in Ireland 1500–1920* (Oxford, 2001).

[11] C. M. O'Sullivan, *Hospitality in Medieval Ireland, 900–1500* (Dublin, 2004); F. Heal, *Hospitality in Early Modern England* (Oxford, 1990).

There are a number of reasons, beyond the influence of wider historiographical trends, as to why sixteenth-century Ireland has been slow to generate interest amongst historians of consumption and material culture. One of these is the persistent belief that the Irish economy remained fundamentally underdeveloped during this period. Opinions vary as to why this was the case. Recent interpretations, for example, have downplayed the impact of English policies on Ireland's economic growth, explaining Irish underdevelopment in terms of economic factors such as lack of skill specialisation and the high cost of capital.[12] Whatever the validity of such arguments, the standard narrative of Irish economic and political development portrays a chronically underdeveloped sixteenth-century economy that regressed even further at the end of the century due to the disastrous effects of the Nine Years' War (1594–1603).[13] Indeed, the basis for Louis Cullen's pioneering work on the emergence of modern Ireland was the assumption that Ireland was 'the last western European country to abandon the medieval world'. Cullen assumed that in 'anthropological terms, sixteenth-century Ireland had affinities with Europe two centuries previously'.[14] Given such perceptions, in addition to the overriding fact that the 'birth of a consumer society' in Britain is still widely accepted as having occurred in the eighteenth century, in line with growing industrialisation and commercialisation, it is unsurprising that sixteenth-century Ireland is not perceived as the most likely place to find significant changes in consumption. The topic, therefore, has not been seen by historians as one that would repay the arduous task of pursuing it.

Another significant deterrent is the severe lack of documentary evidence for this period in Irish history. The destruction by fire of the Public Record Office in Dublin in 1922 means that documentary source material, particularly for the period 1485–1641, covering the years of Kildare ascendancy, the Tudor re-conquest and the plantations, is very sparse overall.[15] It is not possible to calculate population figures with any accuracy, nor is there significant evidence of price or wage movements during this period.[16] The sorts of sources considered by Barnard for Irish material culture from the seventeenth century are usually rare survivals for the sixteenth century. Wills, even those of Irish people proved in England, are scarce, as are inventories, including those that list the stock of shopkeepers and traders.[17] The lack of inventories is particularly unfortunate, since despite their limitations, these have been used for the systematic study of changing patterns of early modern consumption

[12] R. Gillespie, *The Transformation of the Irish Economy, 1500–1700* (Dundalk, 1991), p. 9.

[13] Ibid., p. 31.

[14] L. M. Cullen, *The Emergence of Modern Ireland 1600–1900* (London, 1981), pp. 25, 107.

[15] A guide to sources for Irish history known to be kept in the British archives, although not exhaustive, has been produced. B. C. Donovan and D. Edwards (eds), *British Sources for Irish History, 1485–1641* (Dublin, 1997).

[16] Gillespie, *Transformation*, pp. 9–10; L. M. Cullen, T. C. Smout and A. Gibson, 'Wages and comparative development in Ireland and Scotland, 1565–1780', in L. M. Cullen, T. C. Smout and A. Gibson (eds), *Economy and Society in Scotland and Ireland, 1500–1939* (Edinburgh, 1988), p. 105.

[17] Barnard, *Guide*, p. 82.

in Britain, Europe and America.[18] Business records, such as letters between Irish merchants and their correspondents elsewhere, do not survive. Pictorial sources, including maps and surveys, are more plentiful, but overall, the lack of documentary material, along with the poor survival, recovery and recording of the physical evidence from this period makes any serious consideration of changing consumption patterns very onerous.

Nevertheless, evidence does exist that can be used to examine trends in Irish social and economic development and, in particular, changing consumption patterns. The focus of this book is on the English exchequer customs accounts and their use as a quantitative framework for examining changing consumption patterns and material culture in sixteenth-century Ireland.

## II. The exchequer customs accounts

The English exchequer customs accounts are an outstandingly detailed record of overseas trade in the pre-modern period. Both the 'particular' accounts, which were produced until 1565, and the 'port books' series thereafter, list every item of the recorded trade that entered or left the country, regardless of its value or size, with most accounts including information about the volume, the unit of measurement, the nominal value of the goods and their ownership. The port books also detail how items were packaged, and include the domicile of the merchants, along with the exact port of arrival or departure of the shipments. Survival of the accounts is piecemeal, but of those that are extant, only a fragment have been analysed in any detail and those almost entirely by economic historians interested in distinct branches of overseas trade.[19] Initial work, on the 'particular' accounts for example, included Ada Longfield's *Anglo-Irish Trade in the Sixteenth Century* and Eleanor Carus-Wilson's *The Overseas Trade of Bristol in the Later Middle Ages*, both of which were based on

[18] For example: Shammas, 'Changes'; J. de Vries, 'Purchasing power and the world of goods' in J. Brewer and R. Porter (eds), *Consumption and the World of Goods* (Routledge, 1993); Weatherill, 'Meaning'.

[19] A. K. Longfield, *Anglo-Irish Trade in the Sixteenth Century* (London, 1929); E. M. Carus-Wilson (ed.), *The Overseas Trade of Bristol in the Later Middle Ages* (Bristol Record Society publications, 7, 1937); E. M. Carus-Wilson, 'The overseas trade of Bristol', in E. E. Power and M. M. Postan (eds), *Studies in English Trade in the Fifteenth Century* (London, 1933); A. M. Millard, 'The import trade of London, 1600–40' (London University, Ph.D. thesis, 1956); A. P. Hinton, *The Port Books of Boston, 1601–1640* (Lincoln Record Society, 1956); W. B. Stephens, *Seventeenth-Century Exeter* (Exeter, 1958); D. Woodward, *The Trade of Elizabethan Chester* (Hull, 1970); W. R. Childs, 'Ireland's trade with England in the later Middle Ages', *Irish Economic & Social History*, 9 (1982); D. H. Sacks, *Trade, Society and Politics in Bristol, 1500–1640*, 2 vols (New York, 1985); H. S. Cobb (ed.), *The Overseas Trade of London: Exchequer Customs Accounts: 1480-1* (1990); E. T. Jones, 'The Bristol shipping industry in the sixteenth century' (University of Edinburgh Ph.D. thesis, 1998); E. T. Jones, *Inside the Illicit Economy: Reconstructing the Smugglers' Trade of Sixteenth-Century Bristol* (Farnham, 2012); S. Flavin, 'The development of Anglo-Irish trade in the sixteenth century' (University of Bristol MA thesis, 2004); N. Zahedieh, *The Capital and the Colonies: London and the Atlantic Economy 1660–1700* (Cambridge, 2010).

the Bristol accounts, although Longfield also made use of one Bridgwater and one Chester account from the later sixteenth century. Since then, a number of economic historians have examined both sets of records but, owing to the massive amount of detail in the accounts, studies have tended to be based on a limited number of accounts.

The exception to this is a recent three-year ESRC-funded project (2006–08), undertaken to examine changes in the size and structure of Ireland's trade with Bristol during the sixteenth century and to shed light overall on the economic development of southern Ireland during this period. This entailed the digital capture and computerisation of full import and export accounts for 11 individual fiscal years over the course of the century, which have been published in a volume entitled: *Bristol's Trade with Ireland and the Continent 1503–1601: The Evidence of the Exchequer Customs Accounts* and are also available, along with detailed glossaries, as online datasets.[20] The data, which in large part constitutes the quantitative framework of this study, revealed major changes in the nature of Anglo-Irish trade over the course of the century, most notably showing the unanticipated collapse of the gross value of trade between Ireland and Bristol in the second half of the century. The project also highlighted the potential to expand the methodology for future customs-account-based studies. Of particular significance is the fact that the Bristol port books of the late sixteenth century were found to include details regarding the exact port of arrival or departure of ships and also the domicile of the merchants that laded goods on them, making it possible for the first time to examine where the owners of the recorded commodities came from, a factor of particular significance to this study.

Apart from the increasing general economic interest of the customs accounts, however, their use as a source for trends in consumption and material culture has been very limited to date. Certainly, in the context of English consumption studies there are a number of significant limitations to their use. For the sixteenth century, the main problem is survival. Only two accounts survive for London's Elizabethan import trade, covering the fiscal years 1567/8 and 1587/8. Neither of these records the imports of alien merchants and, to date, only the 1567/8 account has been published.[21] Fragments of surveys of London imports exist for 1558 and 1565 but these appear to omit many commodities. Nor is it possible to examine English consumption patterns in any detail by analysing data from the other ports. As will be discussed in chapter 2, a comparison of the range of goods exported from Bristol to Ireland with the goods arriving into Bristol from the Continent shows major disparities, and suggests that many types of manufactured goods and luxury consumer items were not shipped directly from the Continent to Bristol but were obtained via the

[20] For a detailed discussion of the aims of the project and the value of the Bristol customs accounts as a source for Irish economic history see: http://www.bris.ac.uk/Depts/History/Ireland/ See also S. Flavin and E. T. Jones (eds), *Bristol's Trade with Ireland and the Continent 1503-1601: The Evidence of the Exchequer Customs Accounts* (Dublin, 2009). Electronic data available from: http://rose.bris.ac.uk/dspace/handle/1983/594/browse-title.

[21] B. Dietz (ed.), *The Port and Trade of Early Elizabethan London: Documents* (London, 1972).

London market and transported to Bristol overland. Another issue is that England became increasingly less dependent on imported manufactured goods from the late sixteenth century and a large proportion of consumer durables were manufactured at home rather than imported from the Continent, and therefore would not turn up consistently in the customs records.[22]

Nevertheless, some use has been made of customs data to examine changes in early modern English consumption patterns. Joan Thirsk recently used the London, Southampton and Boston port books to shed light on changes in the consumption of food in early modern England between 1500 and 1760.[23] Also, Carole Shammas used the London port books to examine consumer demand by the English and colonial Americans from the late seventeenth century, but only with regard to trends in the consumption of groceries, notably sugar products, tea, coffee and tobacco. This limitation was imposed because, as noted above, while most groceries were imported and could be examined in the port books, many consumer durables – both in England and in the American colonies – were manufactured at home rather than imported. Shammas' study therefore combined the use of probate inventories to analyse the consumption of durables with the use of the port books to examine the consumption of groceries.[24] More recently, Maxine Berg demonstrated the potential to use customs data and other quantitative data, including probate inventory analysis, alongside qualitative material, to explore developments in the consumption and domestic production of luxury goods in eighteenth-century England. Berg made particular use of customs data taken from studies by N. Steensgaard and K. N. Chaudhuri to examine the importation of goods from the East, including chinaware, textiles and porcelain.[25]

While customs data has not been used specifically for the study of Irish consumption patterns, a number of studies have touched on the changing nature of Irish imports during this period. Longfield's groundbreaking study of Anglo-Irish trade in the sixteenth century, although not specifically a study of Irish consumption or material culture, showed the potential to use the accounts in this manner by considering changing trends over the course of the century in the Irish importation of various groups of commodities, including wine, drapery, salt, iron and coal. This work, however, relied very heavily on the quantitative analysis of just three customs accounts, all from different ports: a 'particular' Bristol customs account from 1503/4, a Bridgwater account from 1560/1 and a Chester account from 1588/9. The limited coverage was no doubt influenced to a large extent by technological constraints, which until very recently made both the transcription and analysis of such large quantities

[22] Shammas, 'Changes', p. 178.

[23] Thirsk, *Food*.

[24] Shammas, 'Changes', p. 178; and *The Pre-Industrial Consumer*, p. 76.

[25] M. Berg, *Luxury and Pleasure in Eighteenth-Century Britain* (Oxford, 2005), pp. 46–84; N. Steensgaard, 'The growth and composition of the long-distance trade of England and the Dutch before 1750', in J. D. Tracy (ed.), *The Rise of Merchant Empires* (Cambridge, 1990); K. N. Chaudhuri, *The Trading World of Asia and the English East India Company1660-1760* (Cambridge, 1978).

of data extremely difficult and time-consuming. Also important is Wendy Childs, who also undertook some statistical analysis of Anglo-Irish trade in the late Middle Ages, based on the Bristol 'particular' accounts.[26] More recently, Donald Woodward noted changes in the nature of Dublin's late sixteenth-century imports using data from the Chester port books. Unfortunately, however, it was not possible to use the Chester accounts to gauge the relative importance of Irish imports because, as the century progressed, increasing quantities of goods were grouped and recorded under headings such as 'and other goods valued at …'. Woodward estimated that in the 1583/4 account, up to 80 per cent of goods were recorded in this manner.[27] Duncan Taylor's recent study of changes in the maritime trade of the smaller ports in the Bristol Channel in the sixteenth century, based on overseas customs accounts and coastal customs records, although not a study of consumption patterns, has also shed some light on changing trends in Anglo-Irish trade in this period.[28]

In addition to sixteenth-century studies, use has also been made of customs data to plot changes in the importation of specific consumer goods in early seventeenth-century Ireland. Raymond Gillespie and R. J. Hunter, for example, both used customs data to examine changes in the book trade in early modern Ireland.[29] Louis Cullen's general analysis of Anglo-Irish trade between 1660 and 1800 also demonstrated the value of the exchequer customs accounts.[30] It must be noted, however, that from as early as 1608, customs officials in Bristol began to adopt similar recording methods to those noted by Woodward in the Chester accounts in the sixteenth century. As the seventeenth century progressed, the aggregation of large volumes of goods under the heading 'wares' became increasingly common and, as such, the seventeenth-century accounts are of much less value than those for the sixteenth century in the analysis of changing consumption patterns in Ireland.[31]

The statistical framework of this study is drawn from a series of 11 annual Bristol customs accounts and port books, which cover the entire years: 1503/4, 1516/17, 1525/6, 1541/2, 1542/3, 1545/6, 1550/1, 1563/4, 1575/6, 1594/5 and 1600/1. In addition, gross values of Ireland's import trade were obtained from three further accounts, covering the years: 1576/7, 1591/2 and 1598/9. It may appear unusual that such emphasis is placed on the use of the Bristol accounts for the study of Irish social and economic history but there are a number of valid reasons for this. First, no comparable set of customs accounts have survived from Ireland, any continental

[26]Childs, 'Ireland's trade with England', pp. 5–33; W. Childs and T. O' Neill, 'Overseas trade' in A. Cosgrove (ed.), *A New History of Ireland, II, Medieval Ireland* (Oxford, 1993), pp. 492–524.

[27]Woodward, *Trade*, p. 12.

[28]D. Taylor, 'The maritime trade of the smaller Bristol Channel ports in the sixteenth century' (University of Bristol Ph.D. thesis, 2009).

[29]R. J. Hunter, 'Chester and the Irish book trade, 1681' in *Irish Economic and Social History*, 15 (1988), pp. 89–93; R. Gillespie, 'The book trade in southern Ireland, 1590–1640', in *Books Beyond the Pale: Aspects of the Provincial Book Trade in Ireland before 1850* (Dublin, 1996), pp. 1–17.

[30]L. Cullen, *Anglo-Irish Trade, 1600/1800* (Manchester, 1968).

[31]My thanks to Dr Richard Stone, a former Ph.D. student at the University of Bristol, for sharing his seventeenth-century data with me.

port or any other English port. No national accounts exist for Chester, for example, before 1565, and the fragmentary Palatinate accounts that do survive rarely give any detailed information, omitting in many cases the type of cargo, values and even port of origin of the ship, thus making even a basic study of trade impossible for this route in Ireland's trade.[32] After 1565, the Chester port books are of more use but, as noted above, these cannot be used for the detailed study of imported consumables imported to Ireland from Chester.

Second, it is generally agreed that trade between Bristol and Ireland had long been the most important branch of Ireland's overseas trade and that England remained Ireland's principal trading partner during the Tudor period.[33] The Bristol accounts can therefore be used to develop a very detailed picture of Ireland's import trade in the period. Specifically, they facilitate the chronological identification of major changes in the consumption of goods intended for everyday use; goods that were relatively inexpensive, had a short lifespan or were produced for fairly immediate consumption, and which therefore do not figure often in inventories, wills or indeed the archaeological evidence; items such as children's bibs and bottles, lightweight fabrics, and various herbal remedies and cooking ingredients. They therefore permit a thorough examination of the evolving use of a broad range of commodities that relate very directly to the activities of daily living and present a picture of changing patterns in the consumption of goods that were not necessarily the preserve of people of a particular age or income scale. In addition, after 1565, the accounts record the exact port at which these commodities were arriving in Ireland, along with the domicile and occupation of each merchant. These are very important details, since they throw light on the probable diffusion of goods after their arrival, allowing an exploration of the commercial relationships between entry ports and their hinterlands in a way that would not be possible using surviving Irish sources.

Bristol's main trade in this period was with south-east Ireland. The data considered here relates predominantly to one region of what was a very fragmented society and economy. This region appears to have been the most economically developed part of Ireland, distinguished by a high degree of urbanisation, established agricultural practices and Anglicisation. The merchants and consumers represented in the data therefore are primarily the Anglo-Irish or 'Old English' communities of the south-eastern towns, outside of the 'Pale' (the most English part of Ireland), and their extensive hinterlands. These, of course, represent a particularly interesting group in terms of a consideration of changing material culture, due to the complex and highly contested nature of their identity in sixteenth-century Ireland.[34]

[32]Childs, 'Ireland's trade with England', p. 23.

[33]Ibid., pp. 8–10; Carus-Wilson, 'Overseas trade', pp. 183–246 (p. 192).

[34]N. Canny, 'Identity formation in Ireland: the emergence of the Anglo-Irish,' in N. Canny and A. Pagden (eds) *Colonial Identity in the Atlantic World, 1500-1800* (New Jersey, 1987), pp. 159–212; B. Bradshaw, *The Irish Constitutional Revolution of the Sixteenth Century* (Cambridge, 1979); B. Bradshaw, 'Revising Irish history' in D.Ó Cellaigh (ed.), *Reconsiderations of Irish History and Culture* (Dublin, 1994), pp. 27–41; S. G. Ellis, 'More Irish than the Irish themselves? – the 'Anglo-Irish'

An obvious consideration is the extent to which this data can be compared with other studies and whether comparisons can be made with other regions in early modern Ireland and England. Certainly, wherever possible, the data from the Bristol accounts is correlated with Woodward's findings for Dublin's trade with Chester, to examine comparable change between the 'Pale' and the south-east of Ireland. Also, the 1503/4 account, which formed the basis of Longfield's earlier analyses, has been integrated into the data considered here. Beyond these measures, however, direct quantitative comparisons are impossible. As already noted, data does not exist to extend comparisons to any other region of Ireland. Nor is it possible to compare Irish consumption with any region in England. This is because analysis of consumption in England to date has been based almost entirely on probate inventory analysis, which, owing to the failure of source survival, is not possible for Ireland. Probate inventories, in any case, record an entirely different level of consumption to customs accounts and, with the exception of a small range of goods, there is little correspondence between the two sources. Inventories record the sorts of durable goods that had a second-hand value and generally omit items that were semi-durable or perishable in nature, or things that were too small and of too little value to be appraised in any detail, including goods such as buttons, lighter types of clothing, paper goods, and food and drink. This included many of the newer goods appearing on the market in the early modern period.

## III. Methods and approaches

While the Bristol customs accounts are an outstandingly detailed quantitative source for examining changes in consumption, a number of specific technical issues must be borne in mind if they are to be used in this way. It is important to remember that while there is a strong precedent for using customs accounts as a tool for studying trade and shipping, they were not created with this purpose in mind, but rather as a means of preventing customs evasion and, more importantly, fraud and embezzlement by customs officers. As fiscal rather than trade records, there are implications regarding how they can be used and interpreted, and their scope and reliability as a source.[35]

in Tudor Ireland', *History Ireland*, i (1999), pp. 22–6; S. G. Ellis, *Ireland in the Age of the Tudors 1447–1603: English Expansion and the End of Gaelic Rule* (London, 1998).

[35] See for example: N. J. Williams, 'Francis Shaxton and the Elizabethan Port Books', *English Historical Review*, lxvi (1950), pp. 387–95; J. H. Andrews, 'Two problems in the interpretation of the Port Books', *Economic History Review* (ser. 2) ix (1956), pp. 119–22 ; R. Hinton, *The Port Books of Boston* (Lincoln Record Society, 1956), G. D. Ramsay, 'The smugglers' trade: a neglected aspect of English commercial development', *Transactions of the Royal Historical Society*, ii (1952), pp. 131–57; G. D. Ramsay, *English Overseas Trade During the Centuries of Emergence* (London, 1957); E. T. Jones, 'Illicit business: accounting for smuggling in mid-sixteenth-century Bristol', *Economic History Review*, liv (2001), pp. 17–38.

First, when considering the gross value of trade in the accounts it is important to note that, as fiscal records, the accounts record nominal rather than market values for goods. In the sixteenth century most goods found in the accounts paid the subsidy of 'poundage', a one shilling in the pound (i.e. 5 per cent) *ad valorem* tax. To determine the duty, the customer would write down the nominal value of the goods, based on the 'book of rates'. The accounts, then, do not provide a record of the 'real' value of trade in any given year. This is advantageous to some extent, since the values in the accounts present a consistent basis on which comparisons can be made across different years and between different ports. There are two potential difficulties with this, however. First, wine and certain cloth types paid specific rather than *ad valorem* duties and were therefore not valued in the accounts. Second, the rates drawn up by the exchequer were subject to periodic revaluation, and therefore direct meaningful comparisons can only be made within periods subject to the same rating.

The method of valuing goods in this book has been to apply a reconstructed value to goods that paid specific duties. With regards to Irish imports, this relates predominantly to wine and English woollen cloth. In order to allow meaningful comparative analysis of such data across the period, woollen cloth and wine have been allocated values of £4 per tun for wine and £2 per cloth of assize.[36] These values are the same as those adopted originally by Wendy Childs in her study of Anglo-Irish trade in the later Middle Ages. Childs suggested that the values are in line with customs valuations, which rated goods at about half their market value.[37] This method of valuation was also adopted by Evan Jones in his examination of the Bristol shipping industry in the sixteenth century and has been used in the compilation of the database for the 'Ireland–Bristol' project.[38] These values have been raised to £8 per tun for wine and £4 per cloth of assize for the period after 1558, when there was a revision of the rates book, which approximately doubled the value of most goods paying

[36] For taxation purposes officials recorded the export of the traditional English woollen cloth in terms of nominal 'cloths of assize' rather than 'real' cloths. A nominal cloth was 24yd x 2yd. While a cloth of this size rarely existed in reality, 'broadcloth' was assessed for customs purposes in terms of how many cloths it would make up. For example, a 'Dozen Strait' was half the width and half the length of a standard cloth and was therefore taxed as a quarter of a cloth, a kersey was taxed at one-third the standard rate, and Bridgwaters at one-half. Throughout this study, derivatives of cloth of assize have been valued pro rata depending on the amount of custom they paid relative to a nominal cloth.

[37] Childs, 'Ireland's trade with England', p. 18.

[38] Jones, 'Bristol shipping industry', p. 34; Comparing the customs data with *Smyth's Ledger*, Jones noted that while imported iron was valued at £2 10s per ton, Smyth was selling it in Bristol for around £6 per ton, while olive oil, valued at £5 per ton, was being sold for £12–15 per ton: *Smyth's Ledger*, fos. 53, 84, 127, 178. Exports were also generally more expensive – for instance, calf-skins, valued at 3s 4d per dozen, cost Smyth around 6s per dozen in the early 1540s: ibid., fos. 6, 31. Further evidence to support the notion that £2 per cloth is a reasonable valuation comes from the 1503/4 account, where on a number of occasions, cloth of assize is listed as paying the poundage subsidy as is valued by the customs officers at £2 per cloth: TNA, E122/199/1 f. 23v; 29r; 74v; 27v. For a full explanation see: http://www.bris.ac.uk/Depts/History/Ireland/datasets.htm.

the *ad valorum* tax.[39] Also, to provide an approximate comparative value for trade in the accounts after 1558, the gross values have been deflated by half to bring them in line with the earlier accounts. This has been clearly noted on the relevant tables and charts. Because of the difficulties in using customs valuations over extended periods, this study, for the most part, uses volume rather than value measurements for comparative purposes. There is no problem, for example, in comparing yards of taffeta cloth, dozens of thimbles, pounds of saffron, and so on, over the course of the century. Likewise, it is also possible to compare the percentage share of the import trade between the various commodities across the period.

In addition to addressing the specific technical issues arising from the use of customs data as a source for consumption studies, it is also necessary to consider the wider and more general historiographical implications of approaching consumption and material culture from a quantitative perspective. Sara Pennell has recently identified an almost complete split in the current field of consumption historiography, between purely economic, quantitative-based projects on the one hand and 'semiotic, attitudinal and even literary' projects on the other.[40] Certainly of late, studies of the latter type have come to dominate this field. The publication of *The Birth of a Consumer Society* by McKendrick, *et al.*, in 1982, which proclaimed the advent of a 'consumer revolution' in eighteenth-century Britain, and sought to highlight the 'shameful' neglect by economic historians of the so-called 'revolution', has been particularly influential in shaping current historiograpical trends, 'liberating' the material world of production and consumption from the 'dead posivitist hand of the economic historian' and placing it within the realm of the cultural historian who invites us to 'frolic in the pleasure garden of consumption'.[41]

While *The Birth of a Consumer Society* has inevitably attracted criticism, its impact on the methodological approaches taken and the questions pursued by historians continues to be of major significance.[42] This includes the increasing tendency to represent consumption primarily as a cultural activity rather than as an economic or social one. For while McKendrick's original approach, with its emphasis on

[39] Although the re-valuation of goods was not by any uniform rate of increase, Willan found that valuations roughly doubled in 1558 and this also appears to be true of the main commodities traded between Bristol and Ireland. Aniseed, for example, rose in value from 13s 4d to 26s 8d per C (112lb), cloves from 2s 6d to 5s and salt from 10s to 20s per ton. While many goods double in value, however, some did not change at all. Irish frieze is found at 40s per piece before and after the rates increase and ginger is valued at 18d per pound throughout the century. On the other hand, some commodities rose by differing percentages; mantles from 3s 4d to 5s and barrels of salmon from 13s 4d to 30s, for example. See S. Willan, *A Tudor Book of Rates* (Manchester, 1962), p. xxviii.

[40] Pennell, 'Consumption and consumerism' pp. 549–64.

[41] de Vries, 'Purchasing power', p. 85.

[42] See, for example, J. C. D. Clark, *English Society, 1688-1832: Ideology, Social Structure and Political Practise During the Ancien Regime* (Cambridge, 1985); D. Spadafora, *The Idea of Progress in Eighteenth-Century Britain* (New Haven, 1990); N. Rowling, *Commodities: How The World was Taken to Market* (London, 1987), E. Yeo and S. Yeo (eds), *Popular Culture and Class Conflict* (Brighton, 1981); M. Golby and A. W. Purdue, *The Civilisation of the Crowd: Popular Culture in England, 1750–1900* (London, 1984).

consumer demand, did not entirely separate the quantitative from the qualitative, approaches that stress the former have become increasingly pronounced in later studies. Indeed, of the 25 essays in *Consumption and the World of Goods* (1993), the majority of data tables are found in just three of the essays, all of which were based on probate inventories.[43] Yet, even in that volume, T. H. Breen, exploring the 'meaning of things' in eighteenth-century America, expressed a 'certain uneasiness' about the use of quantitative evidence to 'map the world of goods', which he argued showed 'decontextualised things that have lost their meanings and that no longer tell us stories about the creative possibilities of possessions'.[44] Likewise, the aim of Berg and Clifford's *Consumers and Luxury* (1999) was to move beyond the enumeration of goods in inventory collections to further explore 'the language of desire and the meaning attached by groups and individuals to particular objects and practices'.[45]

The antipathy towards quantitative approaches to consumption is also a notable feature of some recent Irish studies. Martyn Powell, whose study of the politics of consumption in eighteenth-century Ireland did 'not stretch to an assessment of the penetration of consumer items into Ireland', wrote that 'there is a danger that when historians of consumption get to work, their research becomes little more than counting bonnets, and exclaiming with wonder at the fact that such items either have or have not been diffused from the metropolis to the further reaches of the provinces'.[46] He further remarked that the kinds of quantitative evidence used by many historians of consumption, including wills and shop-order books, do not lend themselves to sophisticated analyses.[47]

While it is obvious that the enumeration of goods alone does not generate complex analysis, such rigid dichotomies in approach are entirely unhelpful to developing sophisticated analyses of the political, social, cultural and economic significance of changing consumption patterns. However interesting a discussion of the 'semiotic significance' of any particular consumer good might be, the importance of this, as a means of understanding broader social change and values, can only be fully appreciated if the historian knows how widely diffused that item was, or when it was adopted into a society. In Irish historiography, in particular, the eschewal of any source base or approach is a worrying trend, since the severe lack of documentary source material and the limited amount of research undertaken in this field to date means that it very often remains necessary, as Barnard has pointed out, 'to establish the fundamentals' of consumption.[48] In the case of diet, for example, the basics of 'what was grown, imported and eaten, and how the staples changed' still need to be fully established before it is possible to develop sophisticated studies of hospi-

[43] Shammas, 'Changes', de Vries, 'Purchasing Power', and Weatherill, 'Meaning', pp. 206–27.

[44] T. H. Breen, 'The meanings of things: interpreting the consumer economy in the eighteenth-century', in Brewer and Porter (eds), *Consumption*, p. 251.

[45] Berg, *Consumers and Luxury*, p. 65.

[46] Powell, *Politics*, p. 2.

[47] Ibid.

[48] Barnard, *Guide*, p. 17.

tality and of the preparation and presentation of food.[49] As such, one of the major methodological concerns of this book is the development of an approach to the customs data that establishes the chronology, pace and extent of changes in Irish consumption patterns within a contextualised and meaningful framework of analysis.

With this in mind, the analysis is organised in three main parts. Part 1 considers the pace and extent of general changes in the nature of Irish consumption in the sixteenth century, based predominantly on the quantitative analysis of the Bristol customs accounts. It provides an overview of the main findings and discusses in broad terms the chronological, economic and geographical significance of changing trends in Irish consumption during this period. Parts 2 and 3 build on this to explore the importance of changes in Irish consumption at a microeconomic level. In particular, they integrate the quantitative data with qualitative sources – including wills, archaeological evidence, pictorial evidence, contemporary literature and legislation – to construct a detailed account of the changing ways in which Irish people, of various types, consumed goods over the course of the century.

The approach taken with regards to the structuring and organisation of analysis within parts 2 and 3 is quite different to that undertaken by previous historians examining the Irish import trade. Longfield and Woodward, for example, organised their analyses by grouping commodities together for discussion. Longfield's study considered diverse import commodities in decontextualised chapters such as 'Dyes, Drugs, Spices, Miscellanea, Etc.', while Woodward's commodity groupings left him with a large 'heterogeneous group of commodities', which he could only categorise under the general heading 're-exports'.[50] In contrast, this study does not examine groups of commodities, but rather explores the consumption of goods relating to two major activities of daily living: dress and diet. These specific activities were chosen for a number of reasons. First, items relating to the processes and rituals of dressing, eating and drinking show the most significant diversification of commodity types and growth in range of new products and materials. Second, changes in the nature of these areas of Irish consumption were also of considerable economic importance. Third, from a social and cultural perspective, dress and diet represent the most visible forms of material consumption. As such, these activities are central to any consideration of the nature of Irish self-representation during this period, particularly given the apparent significance attached to them in the process of conquest and colonisation.

Part 2, then, begins by exploring relevant dress historiography and considers how certain emergent themes can be applied to Irish studies. It then systematically approaches the consumption of commodities relating to Irish dress in the sixteenth century. It examines the significance of continental trade on the growing demand for consumer goods, and explores how changes in consumption in England and Europe stimulated Irish domestic production. It explores how changes in Irish consumption

[49] Ibid.

[50] Longfield, *Anglo-Irish Trade*, p. 178; Woodward, *Trade*, p. 11.

in this period can shed light on the factors that encouraged early modern people to consume. In particular, it considers the role of social emulation, religious affiliation, practicality and regionalism on consumption. It also extends the scope of analysis and the range of source materials used in part 1, to explore the social, political and cultural significance of changing consumption and material culture in Ireland. It looks beyond the geographical diffusion of goods to consider in detail the social distribution of dress-related commodities and, most importantly, it examines the significance of the evolving material culture of dress in a semi-colonised and regionalised society and economy where political, religious, social and cultural identities were highly contested.

Part 3 explores the extent to which Ireland was integrated into the 'widening world' of sixteenth-century food. It further develops the themes emerging in part 2, and considers the role of emulation in the changing material culture of diet. It adopts a comparative approach to British and Irish consumption and considers similarities and differences in diets in this period. In particular, it questions the impact of colonisation on the acquisition and interpretation of everyday items and examines the extent to which changing Irish patterns of consumption indicate the social and cultural assimilation of 'English' dietary habits in the sixteenth century. As in part 2, a major theme is the role of material culture in the construction of social, religious, cultural and political identities in Ireland. This topic is approached by a consideration of the comparative rituals of food and drink consumption in Britain and Ireland, with particular emphasis on the rituals of public drinking and the use of ceremonial vessels and utensils in Irish society.

Unless otherwise stated, the data presented in the tables and figures throughout this book are compiled from the Bristol customs and accounts and port books joint-edited by the author and Dr Evan Jones and published in the volume entitled *Bristol's Trade with Ireland and the Continent 1503–1601: The Evidence of the Exchequer Customs Accounts* (Dublin, 2009), pp. 1–942. Some of the tables in part 1 of this book are incorporated from an article entitled 'Consumption and material culture in sixteenth-century Ireland', published by the author in *Economic History Review* (2011). Electronic versions of the customs data is available at: http://rose.bris.ac.uk/dspace/handle/1983/594/browse-title.

# 1

# *The Expanding Trade*

At the beginning of the sixteenth century, the composition of the Irish import trade was fairly unexciting. Imports remained largely unchanged from the fifteenth century and earlier, and consisted of a range of around 60 items, including rather prosaic foodstuffs such as peas and beans, a narrow range of spices and a minor selection of haberdashery and dyestuff, along with large quantities of plain English woollen cloth.[1] Over the course of the century, however, the nature of the trade underwent an immense transformation and, by the 1590s, almost 400 different commodities were imported from Bristol, suggesting significant developments in many areas of Irish material culture and consumption.[2]

The boat called the *Peter* of Kinsale, under John Roche, master, departed for Ireland on the same day as the entry shown in Plate 1 (14 February 1504) and had on board:

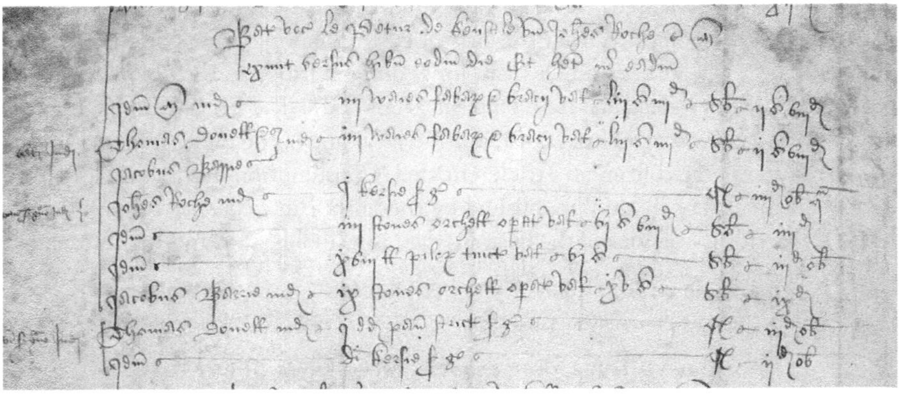

Plate 1 Entry from the 1503–04 'particular account', showing a typical import shipment.

[1] For a discussion of the late medieval trade see E. M. Carus-Wilson (ed.), *The Overseas Trade of Bristol in the Later Middle Ages* (Bristol Record Society publications, 7, 1937); E. M. Carus-Wilson, 'The Overseas trade of Bristol' in E. E. Power and M. M. Postan (eds), *Studies in English Trade in the Fifteenth Century* (London, 1933); W. R. Childs, 'Ireland's trade with England in the later Middle Ages', *Irish Economic & Social History*, ix (1982).

[2] See Appendix 1 for a comparative list of imports.

| | |
|---|---|
| Master indigenous | 4 weys beans and malt valued at 53s 4d |
| Thomas Donell and James Barrie, indigenous: | 4 weys beans and malt valued at 53s 4d |
| John Roche, indigenous: | 1 piece kersey without graynes<br>4st of worked orchil valued at 15s<br>18lb *pilus tinctus* |
| James Barrie, indigenous: | 9st worked orchil valued at 6s 8d |
| Thomas Donell, indigenous: | 1 piece of broadcloth, dozen strait, without graynes<br>half a piece of kersey |

Plate 2 Entry from the 1600–01 'port book', showing a typical import shipment.

The *Elizabeth* aforesaid,[3] 29 August 1601, had on board (as shown in Plate 2):

Robert Lewis of Limerick,
merchant indigenous:

12 yards of cotton cloth – 6d
10 yards of bay cloth – 8d
half a piece of fustian cloth – 4d
quarter clb of prunes – 1d ob
14lb currants – 2d quarter
4 dozen wool cards – 2s
half a gross of penny knives – 3d
1 dozen knives – 1d
2 gross of silk buttons – ob
half a piece of kersey – 1s 1d ob
2clb of hops – 1s
1 barrel of onions – 3d
2 butts of black thread – 2d ob
2lb piecing thread – 2d
2 gross of trenchers – 2d
2 dozen wooden cups – 1d
6lb packet thread – 1d quarter
8lb glue – ob
1 dozen bibs – quarter
half clb of black soap – 3d
1 dozen shoe horns – quarter
3 pairs of bellows – 1d ob
2 brushes – ob
4 dyed frieze mantles – 1s
1 ream of brown paper – ob
1 ream of white paper – 2d
1 burden of steel – 4d
1c taps and cannells – quarter
6M pins – 1d
2 clouts needles – 1d
2c Spanish needles – 1d
1 dozen drinking glasses – ob
1 dozen spurs – 2d
1lb mail – quarter
1 dozen leather girdles – 1d

[3]Unlike the 'particular' accounts, the port books record the actual day on which each merchant made his individual entry. This means that merchandise on outbound ships was often declared over a period of days or weeks, as is the case with the *Elizabeth*, shown in Plate 2. See Flavin and Jones, *Bristols' Trade with Ireland and the Continent 1503–1601: The Evidence of the Exchequer Customs Accounts* (Dublin, 2009), pp. xix–xxii for a discussion of the source.

24 pieces of inkle – 1d
2 gross thread points – 1d
1 gross leather points – quarter
6lb copperas – quarter
2lb galls – quarter
2 dozen wooden combs – ob
6 hats – 6d
1 gross statute lace – 4d
Value in total £11 7s 11d

The expansion of Irish imports occurred in two main areas. First, there was a growing diversification of product types, with items such as buttons, looking glasses, combs and girdles evolving from a single category to a range of subtypes. This occurred both in the variety and grade of such items. In addition to the emergence of a range of types of girdle – crewel, leather, silk, and so on – there was also further diversification in terms of the grade of the item, with the appearance of halfpenny, penny and twopenny girdles.

Second, there was a great increase in entirely new items in the trade, including, for example, various types of luxury cloths such as sarcenet, taffeta and fustian, along with numerous types of new haberdashery items; dyestuffs, including indigo; domestic utensils such as drinking glasses; new types of apparel for children and adults such as bibs and stockings; personal items, including spectacles and tobacco pipes; and luxury foodstuffs, including rice, comfits and sugar.

The reliability of the customs accounts as a source for the Irish import trade has been discussed in detail elsewhere, and a range of possible alternate explanations for the increased range of recorded imports have been considered.[4] It is possible, for example, that customs officers might have been instructed to differentiate into more detailed subcategories even if there had been no change in the nature of the merchandise. On the other hand, this could only account for a portion of the increase, given that many of the goods listed were new types of ware that had never been mentioned in the earlier period. In any case, in so far as more detailed records were required, this was most likely a response to the growing diversification of product ranges.

It may also be significant that new rates books were issued in 1545 and 1558, which contained far more subcategories of goods than the earlier known books. Yet, as Figure 1.1 demonstrates, such changes do not correspond to major changes in the apparent diversification of commodities. There is no difference in the range of goods imported into Ireland between 1541 and 1545 or between 1550 and 1563. If the increase in product types was simply the result of the officials being more discriminating, a sudden growth in the range of goods in the 1545 or 1563 accounts would be expected, rather than in 1575. Apart from the introduction of the new

[4] For a detailed discussion see Flavin, 'Consumption and material culture', pp. 1148–54.

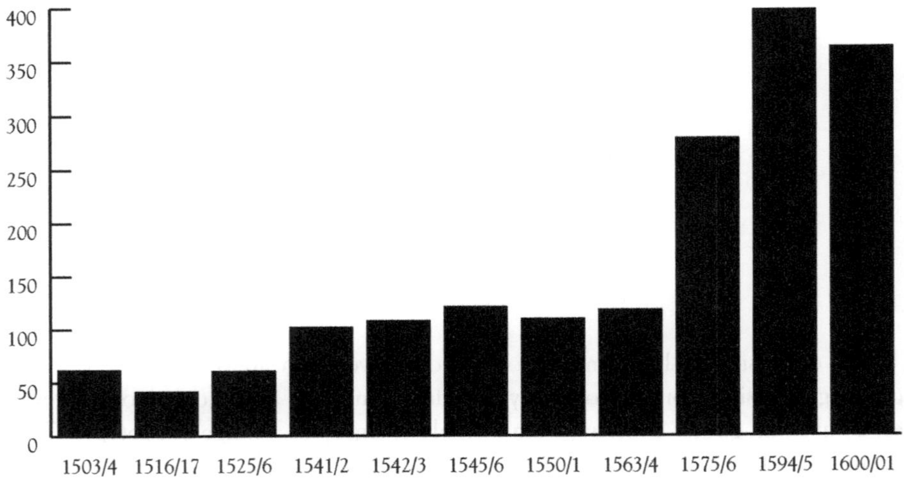


Figure 1.1 Range of individual commodities

rates books, there were no other major procedural changes that can account for the sorts of broad changes noted here. The customs receipts of Bristol were 'farmed' by Sir Francis Walsingham for the years 1585–90, but that had no impact on the accounts considered in this analysis. Obviously, given the wide time frame under consideration, it is not possible to consider in any detail the impact of changing customs personnel on the level of detail recorded in the accounts. However, it may be noted that the same collector, William Goodwyn, compiled the 1525/6, 1541/2 and 1545/6 accounts. Over the course of these accounts there was a 67 per cent increase in the range of commodities listed. Since the same officer compiled all three accounts, it is at least possible to say that this apparent period of growth was not a result of changing personnel.

Overall, then, it appears that the apparent growth in the range of commodities seen over the course of the century was for the most part real and not a statistical illusion caused by more detailed accounting practices. Still, even if we can be confident in the reliability of the accounts in this context, to what extent is it safe to equate these sorts of changes with *actual* consumption patterns in Ireland? In this regard, a couple of questions arise. Assuming, for example, that the goods laded in Bristol made it to their designated port-of-call in Ireland, what actually happened to them once they arrived? Were they always purchased and used by a consumer? This, of course, is impossible to assess and certainly, as is equally true today, a portion of any merchandise shipped to Ireland would have remained unsold. In the sixteenth century this was even more of a problem than it is today, with factors such as piracy, sinking or leaking ships, and adverse weather conditions affecting the survival rate of any cargo. Also, as is equally true today, certain items may have remained unsold because they deteriorated – or were perhaps sold but at a heavy loss to the merchant. Again, as in any period, fashionable items that were imported to test the market may not have generated consumer interest. It would therefore be unwise to place too much significance on a limited number of shipments of a new or exotic good, or to obvious irregularities of specific years. Nonetheless, it seems reasonable to assume that if an item appears in the import accounts on a frequent basis over a period of time, imported by different merchants, then there was indeed a market in Ireland for such goods. Ultimately, it must be remembered that what we are looking at here is long-term, broad trends in Anglo-Irish trade and consumption.

## I. Chronology of change

Examining the range of commodities imported into Ireland over the course of the century suggests that there were two significant and distinct periods of growth (as shown in Figure 1.1). An initial increase occurred between 1526 and 1541, and a second and more significant one between 1563 and 1575, when there was a dramatic increase of 140 per cent in the range of imported goods. This peaked in 1594, with a further 43 per cent increase. These two marked periods of growth occurred under distinctly different political, social and economic conditions, and will be considered in turn.

The first half of the sixteenth century was a relatively stable and prosperous period in south-east Ireland. Evidence from the *Liber Antiquissimus* or *The Great Parchment Book of Waterford* and Smith's *Ancient and Present State of Waterford* (1746) show that the power structure of that city remained stable, with most of the families that dominated around the middle of the sixteenth century also having figured prominently in the fifteenth-century lists.[5] During this time the region also witnessed an impressive period of building projects in stone throughout the country as townsmen and nobles invested their wealth. In Kilkenny, for example, the four gates were rebuilt in 1500, a tholsel completed in 1507, and a new gate constructed in 1517. There was also the flourishing of a new style of architecture, late Irish Gothic, and throughout the country belfry towers and arcades were added to abbeys, and 40 new friaries were founded in the south and west.

The stability was not restricted to the south-east. Analysis of surnames on the Kildare Manor in Maynooth, for example, shows that most of the tenants who were there in 1518 were still present in 1540.[6] More strikingly, recent analysis of the assessments undertaken with regards to payment of the Irish parliamentary subsidy, a tax assessed on acres of cultivated land per barony, shows that throughout the English Pale, tillage increased substantially in the first half of the century (1479–1533), particularly in the Dublin region, but also in Louth, Meath and Kildare.

[5] J. Walton, 'The merchant community of Waterford in the sixteenth and seventeenth centuries', in P. Butel and L. M. Cullen (eds), *Cities and Merchants: French and Irish Perspectives on Urban Development, 1500–1900* (Dublin, 1986), p. 185.

[6] Ellis, *Ireland*, p. 33.

This suggests not only stable and peaceful living conditions but also, perhaps, an increasing population.[7]

Returning to the south-east, a number of factors contributed to growing prosperity in the early sixteenth century. Perhaps the most significant was the liberties and privileges accumulated by the towns as a result of the Crown's desire to nurture the 'traditional harmonious relations with the towns in Ireland'.[8] Indeed, even by 1592, when the Munster Commissioners inspected the charters of Waterford, Limerick, Kinsale, Cork and Clonmel, they found that their liberties were greater than those of most cities in England.[9] This was also a period when Anglo-Irish merchants faced few restrictions in engaging in commerce with the resurgent Gaelic Irish.[10] From the late fifteenth century, the pattern of legalised exemptions to trade with the Irish began to increase and, in 1463, Waterford corporation, Cork, Limerick and Youghal were all empowered to trade with the Irish, followed closely by Galway and Ross.[11] It was stated in the act that the profit of every market, city and town in Ireland depended on the resort of Irish people with their merchandise.[12] The supply of many of the commodities of Irish trade, particularly hides, depended on this co-operation between the Anglo-Irish and Gaelic communities.

This was a dynamic period in Irish economic development, and a close examination of the customs material shows some dramatic changes and suggests that the economy of south-east Ireland underwent a major transformation between the late fifteenth century and the mid-sixteenth century.[13] Analysis of the 1503/4, 1516/17 and 1540s accounts, for example, show that the gross value of trade between Ireland and Bristol rose from an average of £3,202 per annum in the late fifteenth century to an average of £5,361 per annum in the sixteenth century accounts – an increase of 67 per cent. Also, the percentage of Irish trade conducted on Irish ships rose over time, from 50 per cent of total trade in 1503/4 to 75 per cent by the 1540s. In addition, the nature of Irish exports during this period shows very dramatic change. Ireland's export of cloth and clothing increased from about one-tenth of total exports in the late fifteenth century to half of exports by the 1540s. In addition the nature of Irish exports during this period shows considerable change. Ireland's export of cloth and clothing increased from about one-tenth of its total exports in the late fifteenth

[7] For Meath see: S. Ellis 'Region and frontier in the English state: Co. Meath and the English pale, 1460–1542' in Helge Vidar Holm, Sissel Lægreid and Torgeir Skorgen (eds.), *The Borders of Europe: Hegemony, Aesthetics, and Border Poetics* (Aarhus, 2012), p. 49–70. For the English Pale more generally, see: Ellis, 'Ireland's "lost" English region: the English pale in early Tudor times' in Raingard Esser and S. G. Ellis (eds), *Frontier and Border Regions in Early Modern Europe* (Hannover, 2013).

[8] S. Ellis, 'Historical revision xix: the Irish customs administration under the early Tudors', *Irish Historical Studies*, 22 (1980–81), p. 271.

[9] W. O'Sullivan, *The Economic History of Cork City to 1800* (Cork, 1937), p. 60.

[10] C. Lennon, *Sixteenth-century Ireland, The Incomplete Conquest* (Dublin, 1994), p. 40.

[11] Ibid., p. 39.

[12] O' Sullivan, *Economic History*, p. 54.

[13] *See* Jones, 'Bristol shipping industry'; Flavin, 'Development of Anglo-Irish trade'.

Table 1.1
Gross value of Ireland–Bristol trade (deflated)*

| Year | Gross Value |
|---|---|
| 1479/80 | £4,624 |
| 1485/6 | £2,771 |
| 1486/7 | £2,619 |
| 1492/3 | £1,818 |
| 1503/4 | £5,249 |
| 1516/17 | £5,788 |
| 1525/6 | £5,748 |
| 1541/2 | £6,387 |
| 1542/3 | £4,324 |
| 1545/6 | £5,055 |
| 1550/1 | £4,998 |
| 1563/4 | £1,276 |
| 1575/6 | £453 |
| 1594/5 | £2,640 |
| 1600/1 | £1,429 |

* For a discussion of methodology see the Introduction.

Table 1.2
Gross value Irish imports (deflated)

| Year | Gross Value |
|---|---|
| 1479/80 | £1,535 |
| 1485/6 | £980 |
| 1486/7 | £1,191 |
| 1492/3 | £1,358 |
| 1503/4 | £1,880 |
| 1516/17 | £2,098 |
| 1525/6 | £2,094 |
| 1541/2 | £2,053 |
| 1542/3 | £1,583 |
| 1545/6 | £2,186 |
| 1550/1 | £2,377 |
| 1563/4 | £473 |
| 1575/6 | £419 |
| 1576/7 | £251 |
| 1591/2 | £1,395 |
| 1594/5 | £929 |
| 1598/9 | £302 |
| 1600/1 | £873 |

Table 1.3
Gross value Irish exports (deflated)

| Year | Gross Value |
|---|---|
| 1479/80 | £3,089 |
| 1485/6 | £1,791 |
| 1486/7 | £1,428 |
| 1492/3 | £1,460 |
| 1503/4 | £3,369 |
| 1516/17 | £3,960 |
| 1525/6 | £3,654 |
| 1541/2 | £4,334 |
| 1542/3 | £2,741 |
| 1545/6 | £2,869 |
| 1550/1 | £2,621 |
| 1563/4 | £803 |
| 1575/6 | £202 |
| 1594/5 | £1,711 |
| 1600/1 | £556 |

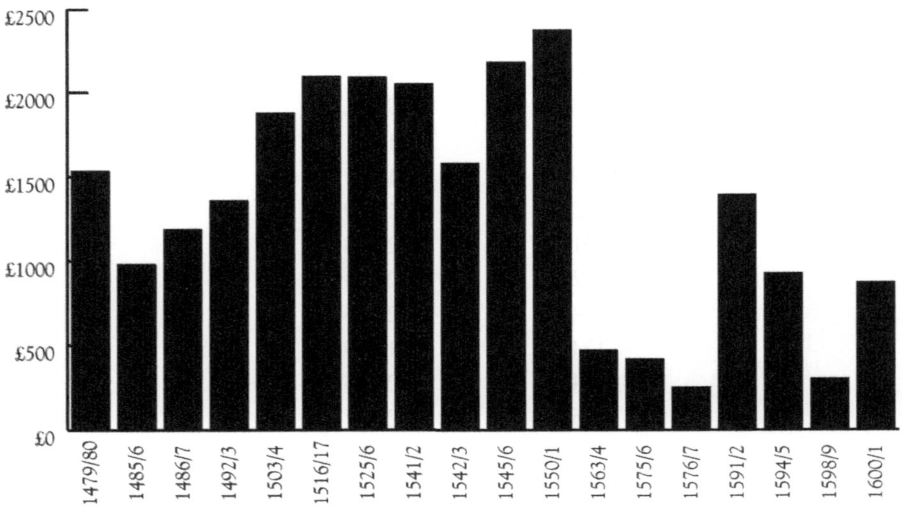


Figure 1.2 Gross value of Irish imports (deflated)

Source: Childs (1982), pp.17–20; Flavin and Jones, *Bristol's Trade*, pp. 1–942. Table 1.2 and Figure 1.2 include the addition of gross import values for three additional fiscal years: 1576/7, 1591/2 and 1598/9–TNA, Exchequer: King's Remembrancer port books E190/1129/23, E190/1131/4, E190/1131/8, E190/1132/8.

Table 1.4
Percentage of Irish exports comprised of manufactured goods

| Year | % of Exports |
|---|---|
| 1503/4 | 12 |
| 1516/17 | 13 |
| 1525/6 | 15 |
| 1541/2 | 56 |
| 1542/3 | 52 |
| 1545/6 | 42 |
| 1550/1 | 48 |
| 1563/4 | 18 |
| 1575/6 | 53 |
| 1594/5 | 46 |
| 1600/1 | 45 |

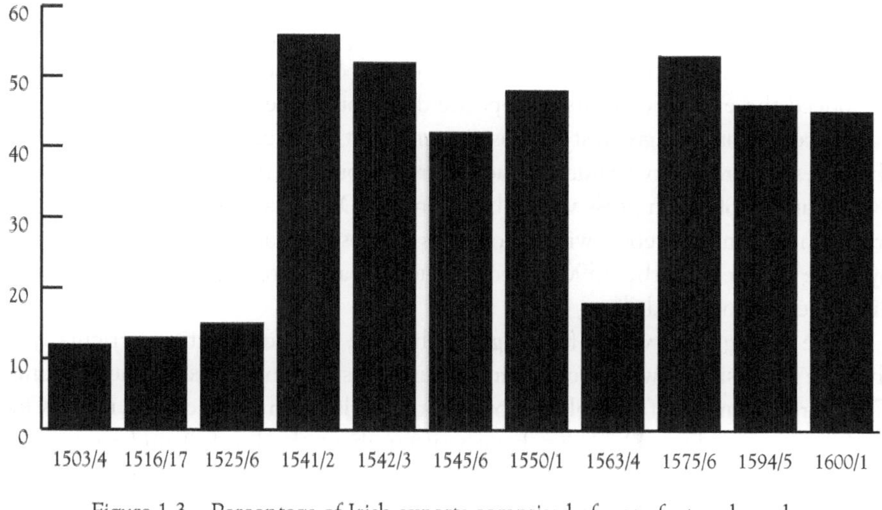


Figure 1.3 Percentage of Irish exports comprised of manufactured goods

century to half by the 1540s. The significance of this cannot be understated. By the 1540s, the majority of Ireland's export trade to England consisted not of fish and hides, as is generally assumed, but of manufactured goods. This was a state of affairs that Ireland would not enjoy again until modern times.

While work on the general development of the Irish economy in this period is ongoing, two important points can be made relating broad trends in Anglo-Irish trade to changing Irish import and consumption patterns. While the figures for Ireland's trade with Bristol (Tables 1.1, 1.2 and 1.3, and Figure 1.2) show that the value of this trade rose considerably between the end of the fifteenth century and the middle of the sixteenth, there was no clear correlation between the increasing value of the trade and the growing range of Irish consumer goods. Trade with England was growing in volume from the end of the fifteenth century, but there was little significant shift in the nature of imports until between 1526 and 1541.

On the other hand, there appears to be a strong correlation between the growth in Irish exports of manufactured goods (as shown in Table 1.4 and Figure 1.3) and the increasing importation of new consumer goods. In 1526, check cloth still accounted for only 1 per cent of exports to Bristol. The dramatic growth in cloth exports occurred between 1526 and 1541, in line with the first period of significant growth in Irish consumption. This suggests that there was a dynamic link between increasing domestic production and increasing consumption in sixteenth-century Ireland.

## II. The end of the century: paradoxical trends

In striking contrast to the first period of growth, what is particularly interesting about the increasing range of consumer goods in the last quarter of the century is that it was not related to the rising value of this branch of Ireland's trade. Indeed the reverse is true. While the range of commodities imported rose very significantly, the value of the recorded trade with England, both imports and exports, fell dramatically. Indeed the evidence points in opposite directions. The 1575 account paradoxically records both the greatest increase in terms of the range of goods imported, and the lowest recorded gross value for trade over the course of the century. Interestingly, a comparison of rough gross values between the Dublin and south-eastern import trades shows similar trends, with an obvious collapse in trade in the 1560s followed by some recovery in the 1590s, accompanied by an increasing range of new and diversified import goods.[14]

These falling gross values for Anglo-Irish trade are problematic, particularly as they are inconsistent with the growing luxury consumption noted in the accounts. There are a number of possible reasons for the collapse in the recorded trade. One of these is smuggling. Much has been written about the level of under-recording in the customs accounts, but perhaps the most relevant study is that of E. T. Jones, whose examination of the private commercial ledgers of Bristol merchants of the 1530s and 1540s found that the city's merchants only resorted to smuggling when there were strong economic incentives to do so.[15] In practice, this meant that they did not bother to smuggle goods that were only subject to 'poundage', a 5 per cent duty levied on the value of goods listed in the book of rates. Since this was true of

[14] Woodward, *Trade*, p. 5.

[15] E. T. Jones, 'Illicit business: accounting for smuggling in mid-sixteenth century Bristol', *Economic History Review*, liii (2001), p. 18; E. T. Jones, *Inside the Illicit Economy, Reconstructing the Smugglers' Trade of Sixteenth Century Bristol* (Farnham, 2012), p. 21.

almost all the trade between Bristol and Ireland, there is little reason to suspect that smuggling was widespread on this route.[16]

In contrast to the relative stability noted during the first half of the century, the second apparent period of growth in Irish consumption occurred during a period of major political and social upheaval. In Munster, the Desmond risings (1569–73, 1579–83) led to widespread disruption in the region. In 1579, during the second rebellion, two of the south-eastern port towns, Youghal and Kinsale, were sacked by the earl of Desmond. The scorched-earth warfare of the rebellions led to widespread famine, the effects of which were documented by both Gaelic and English observers. According to a well-known entry in the *Annals of the Four Masters*:

> The whole tract of country from Waterford to Lothra, and from Cnamhchoill to the county of Kilkenny, was suffered to remain one surface of weeds and waste ... At this period it was commonly said, that the lowing of a cow, or the whistle of the ploughboy, could scarcely be heard from Dun-Caoin to Cashel in Munster.[17]

Ada Longfield, in her study of sixteenth-century Anglo-Irish trade, referred to 'the general economic depression of Munster' after the rebellions but cited no specific evidence of this phenomenon.[18] Whatever the economic impact of the Munster rebellions, it is certainly not possible to blame this for the apparent decrease in Anglo-Irish trade noted in the customs accounts, as very similar figures are noted for trade in both 1563, before the outbreak of war, and in 1575. Indeed, it may well be that the falling gross values for Anglo-Irish trade in the second half of the century are not indicative of a weakened Irish economy. Analysis of the exportation of manufactured goods from Ireland shows that, as in the 1540s, cloth and clothing continued to account for around half of the value of Irish exports to Bristol in the last quarter of the century. The second half of the sixteenth century also marked a growing diversity in the types of Irish textile produced for the export market. Compared to the first half of the century, when exported cloth was mostly in the form of mantles, with the addition of a tiny amount of frieze and check, the accounts from the last decade of the century show a much greater variety of textiles, including cadows, coverlets, check cloth, Irish linen, Irish fustian, Irish frieze, canvas and rugg. This is corroborated by other sources. In 1592, for example, the examinations of the High Court of Admiralty show that a merchant living in Caen, Normandy, was dealing in 'fine blue frieze', just one of the types of Irish-made cloth that was seemingly taken

[16]The only exception to the general lack of incentive to smuggle goods to Ireland concerns grain, the exportation of which was normally prohibited, and which could therefore only be sent abroad if the merchant first obtained a costly licence from the Crown. Since grain was certainly sent to Ireland during years in which prices were higher in Ireland than in England, and there were certainly numerous allegations of grain being sent there illicitly, it is likely that the true level of grain exports to Ireland was much higher than is recorded in the books. And, as such, it must be borne in mind that the accounts probably underestimate the gross value of Irish imports from Bristol.

[17]AFM, p. 1785.

[18]Longfield, *Anglo-Irish Trade*, p. 36.

as wrongful prize from Irish merchants travelling on the *Peter* of Waterford en route to Lisbon.[19] As even basic cloth production was a complex and labour-intensive exercise, this evidence of diversity and the relative stability in the scale of the output suggests a significant amount of organisation and skill specialisation and perhaps a sustained attempt to develop Irish industry.

There is other evidence to indicate the overall health of the Irish economy in this period. Gillespie noted the evidence from coin hoards, which suggests a large influx of English coin with a high silver content in the 1570s and 1580s, along with the relative stability of the Irish pound's exchange rate with British sterling between 1561 and 1600, despite the growing range of luxury imports. He suggested that Irish prosperity was related to the remarkable price stability, which seems to have prevailed in later sixteenth-century Ireland, in contrast to the inflation occurring in England.[20] Evidence for price movements in Ireland is scant but analysis of prices in the corporation book of the town of Kilkenny shows little movement in local Irish prices during the late sixteenth century.[21] Although Gillespie's analysis must remain speculative, in view of the paucity of the evidence, he noted that inflation in England occurred due to the inflow of precious metals that were turned into coin, and due to population growth, which put pressure on existing resources. In contrast, lower inflation in Ireland was due to the fact that the population remained low in relation to available land, and because Ireland did not have a mint and therefore could not increase its money supply. The result, he suggested, was that a low inflationary economy beside a high inflationary one gave Anglo-Irish merchants a considerable advantage over their English counterparts.[22] Certainly, it is likely that the relatively low population in Ireland would have restricted inflation. The lack of a mint was probably a less significant factor, however, since there was little to stop Irish people from using foreign coin, as indeed often happened in England.

The observation that the population in Ireland remained low in relation to available land is worthy of consideration in establishing further reasons for rising consumption during this period. Historians in England have noted that growing consumer demand in the sixteenth century was in part because the affluent were multiplying more rapidly than the population as a whole, with the economic consequences of a rising population bringing about a redistribution of wealth in their favour.[23] Archer has noted that 'although rising population without commensurate

[19] J. Appleby (ed.), *A Calendar of Material Relating to Ireland from the High Court of Admiralty Examinations 1536–1641* (Dublin, 1992), pp. 68–70.

[20] Gillespie, *Transformation*, p. 9; Cullen, *et al.*, 'Wages', pp. 105–16.

[21] Gillespie, *Transformation*, p. 9. This was not across the board, however. Ainsworth has remarked that in the two decades from 1582, beef rose in price from 2s 6d to 6s 8d per quarter; pork from 12d to 2s 4d, and mutton from 6d to 12d. See J. Ainsworth, 'Corporation book of the Irishtown of Kilkenny, 1537–1628', *Analecta Hibernica*, xxviii (1978), p. 4.

[22] Gillespie, *Transformation*, p. 10.

[23] C. G. A. Clay, *Economic Expansion and Social Change: England 1500–1700: Volume 2, Industry, Trade and Government: Industry, Trade and Government* (Cambridge, 1984), p. 123.

increases in output resulted in poverty for the labouring class, it increased the income of the middling groups in society who were able to benefit from rising property values' and who, as a result, enjoyed rising standards of domestic comfort.[24]

The link between population growth and the growing luxury consumption of the middle classes is difficult to establish in the Irish case. Evidence for population trends in sixteenth-century Ireland is scant, as the first figures of any value only become available in the 1670s. Rough estimates suggest that the sixteenth-century growth rate was within the 'normal' European pre-industrial pattern, and there is little doubt that urban populations rose in Ireland in this period, but the scale, timing and, importantly, the location of such changes is unknown.[25] There are of course two obvious differences between the factors influencing English and Irish population growth in the later century – plantation and war. Plantation added to the population, but this may well have been balanced by Irish emigration, especially to England and the Continent and by the effects of the Nine Years' War.[26] Also, we currently know nothing about the size of the native population or the level of its commercialisation. It is impossible, therefore, to establish clear links between population and consumption patterns.

It can, however, be noted that population in Ireland was not evenly spread across the country. Certainly there were areas that were very sparsely populated and where there was no competition for land. The southern parts of Munster, for example, seem to have a very low population density in the late sixteenth century.[27] On the other hand, there were also areas of dense settlement. Edwards noted that in the midland plain of County Kilkenny, the 'teeming populace faced intense competition for land'.[28] This, he suggested, greatly benefited local landlords, whose estates in this region were worth on average three times more than those situated in the northern and southern uplands and the lowlands of the shire.[29] Likewise, in the Pale, pressure on land was so great that Pale lords could treat tenants as they wished, 'suffering no tenant to have assurance underneath him but until another will give him more'.[30] It is likely that, in these areas, the growing sixteenth-century population increased the spending power of the gentry and middle classes at the expense of the poor, and gave rise to a similar situation as that observed by historians in England.

However, the land market in Ireland was very different to that of England. In the absence of strong central government, power was focused on lordships, which were a key component of social, political and economic life.[31] Edwards has discussed in

[24] Ibid., p. 29.

[25] Gillespie, *Transformation*, p. 13.

[26] Ibid., p. 14.

[27] Ibid.

[28] D. Edwards, *Ormond Lordship in County Kilkenny, 1515–1642: The Rise and Fall of Butler Feudal Power* (Dublin, 2002), p. 36.

[29] Ibid.

[30] TNA, SP63/32/61, cited in Gillespie, *Transformation*, p. 14.

[31] Edwards, *Ormond Lordship*, p. 1.

detail the impact of the monopolistic landholding patterns of the Ormond lordship in County Kilkenny in this period. The Butler estate grew massively over the period, from 45,000 acres in 1515 to 90,000 in 1614, which amounted to one out of every three acres available in the county. This growth was greatly enhanced by the fact that the Butlers were given 75 per cent of all monastic land in the county after the dissolution, as a bribe to support Henry VIII's breach with Rome. In contrast to England, ex-monastic land in the region was not sold off to the gentry, but remained in Butler hands, a factor that 'greatly stifled' the progression of the Irish gentry and increased Ormond dominance of them. Such massive monopolisation of land meant that the economic rewards of a rising population were, in some areas, enjoyed predominantly by the nobility and not, as in England and Wales, by the gentry and merchant classes.

The foregoing discussion has considered general economic factors that may help to reconcile the paradox of growing luxury consumption in a period of political and social turmoil, and collapsing gross values for trade. It has argued that the falling gross values in the trade do not necessarily indicate the weakness of the Irish economy, which evidence suggests was actually prospering. Although the source of this prosperity in the later century is not clear, it had an impact on the ability and desire of Irish consumers to participate in the wider changing consumer trends of the later sixteenth century. In addition to the apparent general prosperity, however, the chronology of these developments suggest specific social and political driving forces that must be considered.

## III. Colonisation and consumption

What is particularly notable about the findings from the Bristol accounts is that the most significant period of change in consumption seems to have occurred between 1568 and 1575. There was, of course, one major contemporary social upheaval that might explain changes of this sort. This was the plantation of Munster, during which the Crown attempted to stabilise and Anglicise the country by planting an estimated 606 households of loyal 'New English' settlers, amounting to around 3,000–4,000 people.[32] It is natural to assume that these new arrivals would have wanted to retain access to the sorts of goods used at home and that their differing tastes would have had an impact on the range of consumer goods imported into Munster. This settlement, however, did not begin until 1586–87. The data considered here indicates that major changes were under way well before this. While there was a small colony established at Kerricurihy, near Cork, as early as the 1560s, only 11 per cent of the total value of imports was shipped to Cork and Kinsale in 1575, and only 9.5 per cent was imported by merchants from the Cork area, so it is unlikely that this had more than a minimal impact on the upward trend.

[32] M. MacCarthy Morrogh, *The Munster Plantation: English Migration to Southern Ireland, 1583–1641* (Oxford, 1986), p. 115.

Table 1.5 Volume of re-exported continental foods 1542–1601 (lb)

| | Currants | Sugar | Rice | Raisins |
|---|---|---|---|---|
| *1542/3* | 0 | 0 | 0 | 372 |
| *1545/6* | 0 | 0 | 0 | 0 |
| *1550/1* | 0 | 0 | 0 | 24,826 |
| *1563/4* | 0 | 54 | 0 | 93 |
| *1575/6* | 7 | 89 | 56 | 0 |
| *1594/5* | 528 | 871 | 826 | 2,623 |
| *1600/1* | 1,314 | 461 | 348 | 3,098 |

It is certainly likely that the further growth seen in 1594 was related to this influx of 'New English' settlers. The volume of certain luxury items increased significantly in 1594, notably luxury re-exported foods such as currants, sugar and rice (Table 1.5). However, while the Munster plantation was destroyed in 1598, and not re-established until after 1601, there was no significant difference in the range or volume of goods, or in the gross value of the trade between the 1594/5 and 1600/1 accounts. In 1600/1, for example, while sugar and rice imports fell, the import of currants more than doubled. Overall, it is difficult to find any clear correlation between the settlement by the 'New English' and the changes in consumption patterns.

Thirsk has suggested another possible cause of the growing importation of luxury goods into Ireland in this period. She asserted that the luxury goods found as imports to Ireland from Chester in the 1570s were for the commanding officers of the English army, which was in Ireland in considerable numbers at this time to deal with with the Desmond rebellion. Less luxurious items, such as woollen stockings, she suggested, were purchased by the lower ranks of soldier. English soldiers and civil servants spread fashions to the Irish, causing the filtration of demand for consumer goods into the lower classes in Ireland. Thirsk based this argument on the writings of Barnabe Rich, an English propagandist, who came to Ireland in 1573 as a member of the Ulster expedition of the 1st earl of Essex.[33] Rich, writing in 1610, seems to state that Dublin merchants found their customers for luxury goods among the English, not the Irish:

> It is the nicitie of the English (that are every day innovating and devising of new fashions) that helpeth them away with their sattins, their silkes, their fine cloath, both woollen and linnen, their new striped stuffes, their lace of gold, of silver, of silke, and a number of other gaudy devices, that the English do use to buy at unreasonable rates, that would never be vented amongst the Irish themselves.[34]

[33]Thirsk, *Economic Policy*, p. 125, n.47.
[34]Rich, *Description of Ireland*, quoted in Longfield, *Anglo-Irish Trade*, p. 149.

Barnabe Rich, who also suggested the gelding of Irish males as a means of achieving control of Ireland, was not the most objective observer of Irish habits.[35] Indeed he found it necessary to write a defence of his book two years later in respect of his apparent claim, in particular, that the Irish were cannibals.[36] It is instructive to compare his statement to that of another English observer, Luke Gernon, who, in 1620, wrote of the Irish that: 'the better sorte are apparelled at all poynts like the English onely they retayne theyr mantle which is a garment not indecent'.[37]

While it is possible that the military, who, according to the State Papers, numbered around 1,700 troops in total in 1576, had an indirect impact on changing tastes, the significant upward trend in the 1540s accounts indicates that the Irish consumers of these goods were already receptive to changing tastes and fashions and to the increasing availability of luxury goods well before the military incursions of the 1570s. Indeed, if the military had an impact on changing fashions, it was not a rapid one. In 1591/2, 220 pairs of stockings were exported to Ireland, in 1594/5 this had increased to 382 pairs of various types, dropping again in 1600/1 to just 76 pairs. It is indeed not clear if these were for male or female consumption. Overall, then, the chronology of changing consumption patterns suggests that the causes for these developments were rooted in Irish society and economy, rather than in external factors such as colonisation or military incursions.

## IV. The widening world of goods

Closer analysis of the nature of Ireland's import commodities towards the end of the sixteenth century shows some fundamental changes in the nature of Anglo-Irish trade overall that may help to reconcile the paradoxical plummeting gross values of this branch of Ireland's import trade with the increasing diversity and volume of luxury goods. Table 1.6 shows that while the variety, and in many cases the volume, of certain items was increasing – luxury European cloth, foodstuffs, spices, items of clothing, domestic utensils and other small manufactured goods, for example – there was a significant corresponding fall in the traditional staple bulk Irish imports, specifically English woollen cloth, saffron and worked silk, which together comprised about 70 per cent of the gross value of Ireland's import trade in the first half of the century. The importation of traditional English 'cloth of assize' or broadcloth, and also 'worked silk', fell steadily towards the end of the century, in line with the increasing availability of new ranges of lighter cloths, silks and silk mixes, a significant proportion of which, in common with the vast majority of haberdashery and luxury foodstuffs, were still of continental rather than English origin.[38] Table 1.7 shows a

[35]Rich, *Description of Ireland*, p. 136.

[36]Rich, A *True and Kinde Excuse written in Defence of that Booke* (1612), pp. 8–9.

[37]L. Gernon, *Discourse of Ireland Anno 1620* (Cork, 2007), p. 356. CELT edition. Available from: http://www.ucc.ie/celt/published/E620001/index.html [accessed 17 January 2013].

[38]Thirsk, *Economic Policy*, p. 121; Strictly speaking, many of the cloths in this category had their own customary sizes but the term 'cloth of assize' has been used throughout this book to distinguish

Table 1.6
Percentage of gross value of imports comprised by 'cloth of assize', saffron and silk

| Year | Cloth of Assize | Saffron | Silk |
|---|---|---|---|
| 1503/4 | 50 | 11 | 8.52 |
| 1516/17 | 42 | 11 | 9.50 |
| 1525/6 | 20 | 12 | 9.47 |
| 1541/2 | 33 | 13 | 16.56 |
| 1542/3 | 30 | 17 | 15.21 |
| 1545/6 | 22 | 19 | 13.80 |
| 1550/1 | 16 | 16 | 15.52 |
| 1563/4 | 33 | 9 | 5.49* |
| 1575/6 | 10 | 1 | 4.84† |
| 1594/5 | 8.5 | 0 | 1.41‡ |
| 1600/1 | 5.6 | 0.07 | 0.50§ |

*This is raw silk as opposed to the 'worked silk' that occurs in every account prior to 1563/4.
†Paris silk makes up 4.52 per cent of this figure. Small quantities of Flanders and raw silk account for the remaining.
‡Comprised of small quantities of Paris, coloured, nobs, raw and slewe silk.
§Spanish, Bruge, slewed and black silks.

detailed breakdown of the range of cloth imported at the beginning and end of the period. The quantities of these new items imported to Ireland via Bristol, it appears, was never significant enough to maintain the gross value of the trade at the levels noted in the earlier accounts, and it might therefore be that Irish merchants were sourcing a greater proportion of commodities elsewhere, either via another English port or directly from the Continent.

The economic significance of Ireland's direct continental trade, and the impact of continental trade links on Irish consumption patterns in this period, awaits detailed study. Unless new evidence comes to light, however, this is not an area of economic development that can ever be quantified. Ada Longfield noted that Waterford merchants obtained many trading licenses when embargoes were imposed on foreign trade but that their 'addiction to continental traffic' was frowned upon, even though

those cloths of English production that are generally found to be customed pro rata in relation to the standard woollen broadcloth and therefore paid specific rather than 'poundage' duties. These cloths usually did not have nominal values ascribed to them in the accounts. They were taxed in this manner because of the difficulties associated with the many different types, sizes and weights of cloth produced in England. It is clear from the often inconsistent methods of estimating cloth duties used by the customs officers, that a certain amount of rough estimation was used to value such cloths. Due to this and various other methodological issues, any analysis of the relative importance of woollen cloth over the course of the century can only produce broad trends.

Table 1.7 Comparative cloth imports, 1503/4; 1594/5

| 1503/4 | Vol. | Unit[*] | % Imports | 1594/5 | Vol. | Unit | % Imports |
|---|---|---|---|---|---|---|---|
| fustian | 1 | piece | 0.01 | bay | 865 | yd | 3.33 |
| silk, worked[†] | 240 | lb | 8.52 | buckram | 3 5/.5 | roll/ yd | 0.02 |
| woollen, broad cloth | 10,663 | yd | 49.84 | buffin | 1 | piece | 0.03 |
| | | | | bumbazin | 82 | lb | |
| woollen, kersey | 9 | piece | 0.33 | calico | 4 | piece | 0.07 |
| woollen, Welsh | 2.5 | piece | 0.5 | canvas, striped | 8.5 | piece | 0.08 |
| | | | | cotton | 1,400 | yd | 0.92 |
| | | | | cyprus, coarse | 20 | roll | 0.04 |
| | | | | cyprus, white | 2 | piece | 0 |
| | | | | crest | 36 | yd | 0 |
| | | | | dornick | 74.5 | yd | 0.13 |
| | | | | flannel | 18 | yd | 0.02 |
| | | | | frieze, Bristol | Mar-60 | piece/ yd | 0.28 |
| | | | | frieze, Welsh | 2 | piece | 0.1 |
| | | | | fustian | 3.5 | yd | 0.01 |
| | | | | fustian, holmes | 435 | yd | 0.41 |
| | | | | fustian, Genoa | 630 | yd | 0.64 |
| | | | | fustian, Milan | 9 | piece | 0.48 |
| | | | | fustian, Osborne | 20 | piece | 0.59 |
| | | | | Ghentish carpet cloth | 3 | yd | 0.02 |
| | | | | hair cloth | 12 | yd | 0 |
| | | | | Holland cloth | 49.65 | yd | 0.16 |
| | | | | Holland, coarse | 12.75 | yd | 0.03 |
| | | | | new cloth | 5. 00 | yd | 0.07 |

| | | | | | |
|---|---|---|---|---|---|
| | | sack cloth | 3 | piece | 0.14 |
| | | sarcenet | 4.5 | yd | 0.1 |
| | | sarcenet, Bologna | 16 | yd | 0.14 |
| | | saye | 12 | piece | 0.64 |
| | | silk, Cyprus | 24 | yd | 0.05 |
| | | silk, black | 3 | oz. | 0.01 |
| | | silk, coloured | 8 | oz | 0.02 |
| | | silk, ferret | 3 | lb | 0.06 |
| | | silk, nobs | 10 | lb | 0.02 |
| | | silk, Paris | 62.5 | lb | 1.12 |
| | | silk, raw | 3.5 | lb | 0.06 |
| | | silk, slewe | 10 | lb | 0.1 |
| | | taffeta | 12 | yd | 0.23 |
| | | taffeta, broad | 11.55 | yd | 0.23 |
| | | taffeta, Levant | 514.5 | yd | 0.93 |
| | | woollen broad cloth | 622.15 | yd | 5.84 |
| | | woollen, green kersey | 12 | yd | 0.07 |
| | | woollen, kersey | 7.5 /80 | piece/ yd | 1.01 |
| | | woollen, northern | 1.5 /9 | piece/ yd | 0.61 |
| | | woollen, penistone | 6 | yd | 0.02 |
| Total | 59.2 | | | | 18.83 |

* Given in yards where possible but measurements vary. A piece can be anything from 15 to 30 yards, depending on the cloth.

† It could be suggested that 'worked' silk encompasses some of the types appearing later, however based on its value, which is constant throughout the accounts at 13s 4d per lb, it seems that this is in fact one variety. The various silks appearing later are found at widely varying values.

it was a source of information about Spanish intrigues.[39] Cork merchants also had license to engage in continental trade in time of war. In 1576, Elizabeth I granted to the municipality the power to appoint its own gauger and searcher and a license to trade during wartime with 'foreigners and enemies, excepting pirates, in any goods, excepting arms and munitions of war, foreigners and enemies trading not to be molested in the city and port'.[40]

Pauline Croft has also noted that Hiberno-Spanish trade flourished during wartime.[41] While the Irish had always been distinguished from English merchants in Spain and Portugal, and before the war had enjoyed separate and often greater privileges, their Catholicism and hostility towards the English ensured that they continued to be allowed to freely enter Spanish ports after 1585. Indeed, such was the freedom of Irish merchants in Spain that large numbers of English ships tried to pass themselves off as Irish in order to gain access to Spanish trade.[42]

The State Papers provide ample evidence of the extensive continental trade networks of Irish merchants, and indicate that these were exploited to their own political and, no doubt, economic advantage. In 1586, the lord deputy wrote to Walsingham that a Galway merchant, named Kyst:

> this day arrived here out of Lisbon, saith that at his first coming thither, he meant to pretend himself and his goods to be French, as some few Englishmen there do, but perceiving straight all Irishmen had free traffic and safe access thither, he showed himself to be as he was, and so was freely communicated of all things that his countrymen knew, of whom divers are residents there.[43]

Likewise, examinations taken before the lord chancellor of Ireland, on 14 January 1590, note that James Synnot, a Wexford merchant:

> arriving then in the harbour of Dublin, being come from St. Mary Port in Andalusia … saith that he lately received a letter from Sir Patrick Synnot, his brother, being a priest at the Court of Spain, that the King's fleet would not be in readiness to make any invasion the next spring. And saith that his said brother likewise wrote unto him, that in case the fleet should sooner be ready, he would signify the same to this examinate by something in writing which should be delivered to this examinate's son, dwelling in Lisbon.[44]

Another 'examinate', Edward Madden, a Waterford merchant:

> saith that at his being at Madryle seven days before St. Andrew's last, Sir William Stanley was not then come thither, but he heard by common report, that the King [Philip] daily expected, his coming. And further saith that there is at Ferrol, within the river of the Groin, 70 or 80 sail of ships whereof two are galliasses. The King's soldiers are cessed near

[39] Longfield, *Anglo-Irish Trade*, p. 34.

[40] *Reports of the Deputy Keeper of the Public Records, Ireland* (Dublin, 1869), Fiants, Report 12, Appendix V, pp. 179–80, cited in Longfield, *Anglo-Irish Trade*, p. 35.

[41] P. Croft, 'Trading with the enemy', *Historical Journal* xxxii, ii (June, 1989), pp. 281–302.

[42] Ibid., p. 287.

[43] C.S.P. Ire., 1586–1588, p. 25.

[44] C.S.P. Ire., 1588–1592, p. 292.

> to them in the country, and Baltinglass, Cahil O'Conor, Maurice Fitzjohn, and all the rest of the Irishmen that are in pay, or with the King, are there.[45]

It seems, however, that Irish merchants suffered from divided loyalties. The examinates claimed that 'all Waterford men, as well they which reside in Spain as the rest that do use traffic thither are traitors, and do not stick to say when they are in Spain that they acknowledge no other prince but the Pope and the King of Spain'.[46]

Perhaps it was accusations such as this that prompted Richard Ailward, the mayor of Waterford, to write to the lord deputy in 1593 regarding information received from Edward Leonard, a Waterford merchant, who arrived back from Lisbon in 'a Frenchman laden with salt to Cork', bringing news that his ship, the *Sunday*, had allegedly been taken by four Spanish ships off Cape Finisterre, 'who spoiled, rifled, and stript them of their clothes with such inhumanity and cruelty as they could not be used more miserably among Turks'. After a lengthy description of apparent Spanish preparations for 'war and shipping', he noted that 'there is none of our ships yet come home nor none of our merchants but this deponent … My very good lord, the proud Spaniards hath so maliciously spoiled and dealt with our merchants this voyage, as all the Spaniards are grown into great hate to the merchants of this city'.[47]

However useful Irish mercantile contacts in Spain might have been to the English war effort, it is clear that the extent of Ireland's trade with Spain was of concern to the English administration. A letter from the Privy Council to the lord deputy in 1602, for example, noted the need to select and limit the Irish merchants trading with Spain, which was 'exceedingly hurtful and dangerous'.[48] While in 1611, in a letter from Edward Hayes to Lord Carew, it was noted that:

> From England the importation is greater than the exportation of Ireland, because Ireland hath not commodity of many sorts to fit England, as England hath to serve Ireland … The case stands otherwise between Ireland and Spain, for Ireland yields and may increase a multitude of commodities whereof Spain and its dominions stand in great need, namely, corn, fish, bacon, hides, tallow, fells, wax, pipe staves, &c., for which money will be returned out of Spain.[49]

Although it is impossible to assess exhaustively the direct commercial networks of Irish merchants and mercantile groups in this period, and the commodities in which they traded, they may be illuminated by evidence to be found in a range of other sources. The last will of Patrick Myagh, a Cork merchant, written in 1569, suggests that his brother traded in both Spain and Flanders. He noted: 'I do owe to my brother John £3 2*s*. with a head and some rest in his last bill from Flanders, to the

45 Ibid., p. 293.

46 Ibid.

47 C.S.P. Ire., 1592–1596, p. 73.

48 J. S. Brewer and W. Bullen (eds) *Calendar of the Carew Manuscripts Preserved in the Archiepiscopal Library at Lambeth*, (6 vols., 1867–73), iv, p. 388.

49 Cal. Carew. MSS., vi, p. 138.

which I left with him certain Spanish iron …'[50] Likewise, in 1582, James Fitzandrew Brown, another Cork merchant, made his last will, being 'now bound for Bordeaux'. The same merchant owned a shop in Cork, under his house, where he presumably displayed and sold the merchandise he procured in France.[51]

Cork merchants had well-established networks in the Low Countries. In the High Court of Admiralty examinations, a deposition of Stephen Skiddye, taken in 1596, details the activities of the city's merchants in Middelburg in November that year. Skiddye, who was working in partnership with two other Cork merchants, freighted the *James* of Kinsale with hides, Irish cloth and other commodities and sailed directly to Middelburg. On selling part of their goods, they teamed up with one Thomas Moroughe, whom they found in the town, and together they bought a wide range of luxury goods including brass pans, orchil, Holland cloth, damask, tablecloths, fruit plates and cushions, to the value of a significant £600–700. This was put on the account of the merchants and their 'friends'. Unfortunately, the *James* was taken by pirates, near Mount's Bay, en route back to Cork. Only two of the crew survived and all that remained of the cargo was the captain's chest and some Holland cloth, which was salvaged by a gentlewoman who found it on the shore.[52]

Drogheda, Waterford and Limerick merchants are also prominent in the examinations, and can be found carrying frieze, linen, blankets, mantles and leather to the Continent in exchange for a wide range of luxury goods. In 1591, the *Michael* of Le Croisic was laded at El Puerto de Santa María with 40 tuns of sack, grocery wares, suckets, calico and 'other goods' consigned to Drogheda.[53] In 1592, the *Mary* of Waterford was laded at Lisbon with a range of luxury items, including suckets and marmalade, calico, sugar, silver cups, green ginger, Spanish silk, conserved rose flowers, silk lace and gold jewels, Spanish taffeta, and spices to the value of about £800.[54] In 1598, Thomas Burghe, a Limerick merchant, laded the *Nicholas Bonadventure* of Wexford at Limerick with goods including tallow, and leather consigned to Lisbon. This ship, like the others, was taken as prize, 'for she was going to the enemy with prohibited wares'.[55] It was alleged that when taken, the crew cast overboard 'writings', including a popish book called 'an *Officium*'.

The customs data further illustrates the extent and significance of Ireland's commercial integration in this period. In 1594, for example, Dominic Copinger, a Kinsale merchant, exported a significant quantity of expensive Spanish hat wool to Bristol.[56] This amounted to four times the total value of Irish wool exports to Bristol that year, and again indicates well-developed Irish mercantile contacts with Spain for commercial raw materials and suggests that Irish merchants were capitalising on

[50] Cork City and County Archives, Caulfield Will Transcripts, U226, p. 2.
[51] Ibid., p. 9.
[52] Appleby, *Calendar of Material*, p. 84.
[53] Ibid., p. 67.
[54] Ibid., pp. 68–9.
[55] Ibid., p. 91.
[56] Flavin and Jones, *Bristol's Trade*, p. 773.

new fashions, in this case, the late sixteenth-century fashion in England for felt hats. Also found among Irish exports in 1594 were marmalade and wine, which comprised almost one-quarter of the total value of Irish exports. Likewise, in 1600, Seville oil comprised 11 per cent of Irish exports to Bristol.

It is probable, then, that Irish merchants were being increasingly drawn towards European markets towards the end of the century. This would certainly help to reconcile the paradoxical falling values for Anglo-Irish trade and apparently increasing luxury consumption in Ireland. Most importantly, if this was indeed the case, it has major implications for our understanding of changes in the nature of Irish consumption patterns. Certainly, what we are seeing in the Bristol accounts represents only a fraction of the new European consumer goods arriving into Ireland by the end of the century, and it may be that certain new tastes and fashions entered Ireland via continental trade before they ever appeared as Irish imports from England. The fiants of Henry VIII provide some interesting incidental information in this regard. A fiant from 1541, an order of the lord chancellor and council (upon a petition to Parliament by Powyll Fayof of little Egypt and Company, Egyptians sojourning in Dublin), discharging Powyll from an indictment in the king's bench, alleged that he had stolen 'newe color sarsenet, blacksatten, and blacke damaske at Swerdes', the goods of Richard Russell, a Drogheda merchant. This suggests that these particular luxury cloths were being sold in Ireland a decade or so before they appeared as imports from England.[57]

That imports via England sometimes came slightly later than from the Continent is further suggested by comparing evidence from the customs accounts with inventory evidence for Cork. An inventory of the goods of Richard Tyrry Fitzadam, taken in 1582, the last year of the devastating second Desmond rebellion, included, among a range of luxury cloth, a 'pounde and a quarter of Spanishe silks', valued at 40s. Spanish silk did not occur as an import to Ireland from Bristol in any of the accounts examined prior to 1601, when 1lb was imported by a Cork merchant, Edmund Mowrough, and a 'paper' was imported by a Kilkenny merchant, John Rothe.[58] Fitzadam's inventory also included 13.5yd of silk grogram valued at £3 8s., 6.5yd of silk grogram valued at 32s 6d and a piece of 'Turky grogram' valued at £3 16s. Grogram was a coarse silk fabric, which could be mixed with mohair or wool and was often stiffened with gum.[59] It did not occur as an import before 1601, when two pieces were exported to Ireland by a London merchant, Josiah King, and even then, this was of a 'coarse' variety, in contrast to the luxury silk and Turkish types appearing in the Cork inventory almost two decades earlier. That Richard Tyrry Fitzadam acquired these items directly from Spain is suggested in the same

[57] *Deputy Keeper of Public Records in Ireland* (Dublin, 1869), Report 7, App. 10. p. 58, no. 264, cited in Longfield, *Anglo-Irish Trade*, p. 155.

[58] A paper of Spanish silk is possibly 2lb, based on customs valuations.

[59] A coarse fabric of silk, of mohair and wool, or of these mixed with silk; often stiffened with gum (OED).

inventory which notes that a quantity of 'new hides' belonging to him were 'with David Carrvill in Spaine'.[60]

Perhaps the best example of Ireland's direct access to exotic luxury goods in this period is the shipment of 1,400lb of sucket and marmalade to Waterford on the *Mary* of Waterford in 1592. Suckets, or candied fruit, were a very fashionable foodstuff among the middling sort and the upper classes in the late sixteenth and seventeenth centuries, but were are not found among Irish imports from Bristol in any of the accounts examined before or after 1594, when just 4lb was imported. Based on the customs accounts alone, it would appear that there was little market for such luxuries in Ireland. In reality, it appears that Irish merchants were catering to the sweet tooth of their customers via direct trade with Portugal, and such exotic treats were available well before they turned up among imports from England.[61]

[60] Cork City and County Archives, Caulfield Will Transcripts, U226, p. 21.
[61] Appleby, *Calendar of Material*, pp. 67, 68.

# 2

# *The Dynamics of the Trade*

Very little is known about the conduct of Irish trade in the sixteenth century and pre-existing analyses are based primarily on the 'particular' accounts, which, while very useful in many respects, are quite limited in detail. The 'particular' accounts (to 1565) record the port of registration of a ship and whether the ship was entering or exiting the port, but they have little to say in terms of the performance of specific Irish ports or the activities of merchants. This chapter is based on the analysis of the 'port books' (1565 onwards), which include additional information including the exact port from which ships were arriving from or departing to, the approximate tonnage, and the name, domicile and occupation of each merchant. This additional information is utilised here to establish the geography of changing consumption patterns in Ireland in the latter half of the century. In particular, the inclusion of merchant domicile combined with the specific port of arrival of ships in Ireland opens up an entirely new line of investigation, indicating the probable diffusion of goods after their arrival on the Irish coast, shedding light on the commercial relationship of the Irish coast and its hinterland and on Anglo-Irish mercantile connections and networks.

## I. Goods and ports

Examining the relative importance of Irish ports in the sixteenth century presents a challenge. Pre-existing work on the activity of specific ports has been based solely on the information in the 'particular accounts', which, as already noted, record only the port of registration and not the port of arrival or departure of vessels. Given that there was always a tendency for merchants to use ships of their own locality, analysis of the port of registration does provide some indication of the relative activity of the Irish ports servicing the import trade. Nevertheless, using the port of registration as a means of examining the performance of ports can produce misleading results. For example, in the case of Cork, it has been noted that Cork's involvement in the trade with Bristol had dropped significantly by the 1540s, when ships registered there carried only 3 per cent of the trade.[1] The port books present a much clearer picture of

[1] Jones, 'Bristol shipping industry', p. 164.

Cork's role in the import trade. For example, although there are no ships registered in Cork found in the 1595 account, 9.5 per cent of the total value of Irish imports arrived there in that year. Indeed, throughout the 1590s it appears that Cork ranked second to Waterford in its importance as a centre for the distribution of import commodities. In 1598/9, for example, it received a very significant 28 per cent of the gross value of imports (See Appendix 2).

All of the previous analyses of Irish trade agree that the port of Waterford was the pre-eminent port in south-east Ireland during the sixteenth century. Indeed, Jones noted a dramatic rise in the relative importance of the port during the 1540s, when ships registered at Waterford carried 58 per cent of the total value of Ireland–Bristol trade.[2] Analysis of the port of arrival of imports in Ireland in the port books supports these findings with regards to the importance of Waterford as an entrepôt for southern Irish trade. At its peak, in 1591/2, Waterford received just over three-quarters of the value of Irish imports from Bristol and an average of 57 per cent of the value of imports between 1575 and 1601.

In addition to Waterford and Cork, the smaller ports on the south-east coast also played a role in the import trade and ships regularly departed Bristol for Dungarvan, Fethard-on-Sea, Kinsale, New Ross, Wexford and Youghal. What is significant, however, is that trade between Bristol and Ireland was not exclusively with the south-eastern ports of Ireland. In 1575/6, 9 per cent of imports were shipped to Drogheda and 3 per cent to Galway.[3] In 1576/7, Drogheda received 8 per cent of the value of imports, Dublin 4 per cent and Galway 5 per cent. In 1594/5, commodities were shipped directly from Bristol to Dundalk in the north-east of the country and to Sligo on the west coast. And in 1600/1, commodities were shipped from Bristol directly to Limerick. The volume of goods shipped into these ports, particularly on the west coast, was small, but it is very significant that shipments into Limerick, Galway, Drogheda and Dublin recorded very similar ranges of goods to those arriving into the south-east.

### *Ia. Merchant domicile and the diffusion of goods*

Examining the domicile of the merchants importing these goods helps to develop this picture more clearly and also sheds light on a number of important issues such as the size of the hinterland supplied with the commodities that arrived into these ports, the internal dynamics of commodity distribution, the extent of Irish control of the import trade and the activities of English merchants in the Irish trade.

First, assuming that goods imported by merchants living in inland towns were mainly intended for transport overland to those towns and their commercial hinterlands, this data gives a sense of inland trade connexions in Ireland, entirely unavailable from other sources. Indeed it seems that goods arriving into the south-eastern ports could penetrate far inland. Map 1, for example, plots the port of arrival of

[2] Ibid.

[3] Refers to percentage of the gross value of imports.

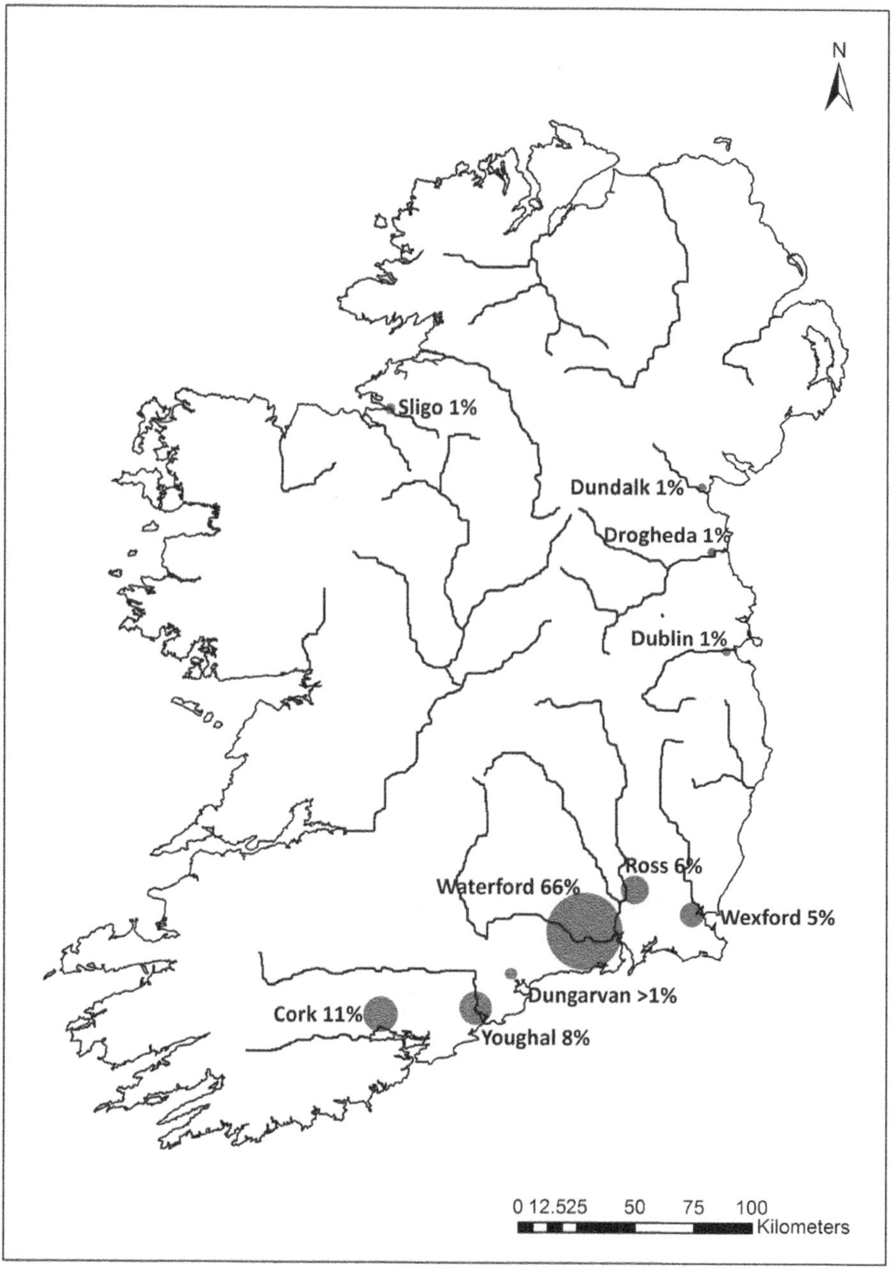


Map 1 Imports to Ireland from Bristol, 1594/5.

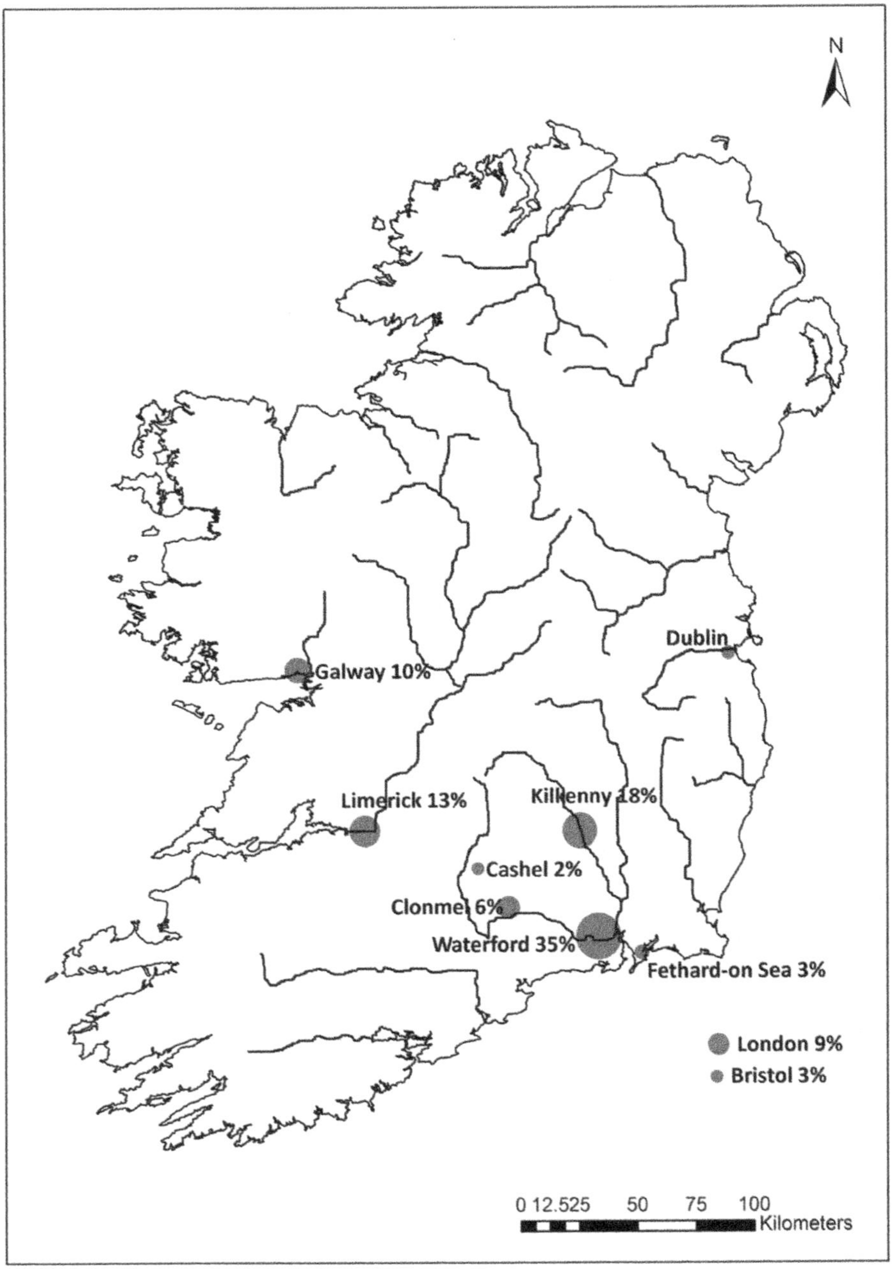


Map 2 Imports to Waterford by merchant domicile, 1594/5.

imports in 1594. Map 2 plots the domicile of merchants who shipped goods into Waterford in 1594/5. Waterford received two-thirds of the value of the import trade in that year. Of the 73 per cent of trade shipped by Irish merchants, 28 per cent was by merchants from Waterford itself. The remainder of the trade belonged to what appears to be a well-established nexus of merchants supplying not only the other towns in the south-east, in County Tipperary and County Kilkenny, but a hinterland that stretched as far west as Limerick some 80 miles away, and Galway some 137 miles away. These smaller ports also had significant hinterlands. In 1591, for example, merchants from Limerick shipped goods into Dungarvan, while in 1594, Robert Ashfield, described as 'armiger' (esquire), domiciled in Kerry, shipped goods into Youghal. Overall, however, the largest proportion of the trade in the small ports was generally shipped by local merchants. A detailed breakdown of the percentage of trade owned by merchants from each town for six individual years between 1575 and 1601 is provided in Appendix 2.

It is clear, then, that the much diversified range of consumer wares imported from Bristol entered Ireland not only through the south-eastern ports but also through ports in the west and north-east of the country. These wares were distributed across a wide area, with goods travelling well beyond the primary areas of English control. It is notable that the shipments into the western ports and into the south-east by western merchants contain a similar range of import commodities as those being imported by merchants in the north and east of the country. This is of particular importance since it suggests a comparable level of demand for new consumer goods within the Pale and in the areas of Anglo-Irish control most geographically removed from the centre of government in Ireland. The Anglo-Irish consumers of these commodities, to some extent, shared a material culture, despite the fragmented nature of their society and economy and the geographical isolation of their more western communities.

A breakdown of the relative volumes of the trade owned by merchants from each recorded town, or domicile, shows that levels of participation in the import trade varied considerably. Table 2.1 shows a breakdown of the percentages of the gross value of trade imported by merchants from the most frequently represented towns between 1575 and 1601. Unsurprisingly, merchants from Waterford imported the largest percentage of the trade in every year, peaking at 50 per cent in 1591/2. Of the other towns, Kilkenny is the best represented overall. Excluding Waterford's interests, Kilkenny merchants owned the largest percentage of the gross value of imports from Bristol in 1576/7, 1594/5, 1598/9 and 1600/1, at 20 per cent, 14 per cent, 20 per cent and 11 per cent respectively.

The 'dogged pursuit' of overseas trade by Kilkenny merchants in this period has been discussed by David Edwards, whose comments on the commercial organisation of the city's merchants sheds further light on the extent of the geographical diffusion of goods arriving from Bristol.[4] Edwards notes that for an inland town, Kilkenny

[4]Edwards, *Ormond Lordship*, p. 44.

Table 2.1 Percentage of gross value of imports by Irish merchant domicile

| | 1575 | 1576 | 1591 | 1594 | 1598 | 1600 |
|---|---|---|---|---|---|---|
| Cork | 6.76 | 6.19 | 9.5 | 9.5 | 20.29 | 11.19 |
| Dublin | 13.5 | 2.97 | 0 | 0 | 0 | 3.91 |
| Galway | 3.29 | 5.36 | 0.79 | 6.39 | 0 | 0 |
| Kilkenny | 11.27 | 20.04 | 8.79 | 14.57 | 20.88 | 11.23 |
| Limerick | 5.54 | 4.93 | 7.97 | 9.96 | 3.16 | 7.66 |
| New Ross | 6.08 | 1.23 | 0.92 | 4.32 | 9.15 | 4.13 |
| Waterford | 21.52 | 31.1 | 50.57 | 19.29 | 29.15 | 22.34 |
| Wexford | 13.75 | 5.12 | 1.36 | 3.77 | 7.29 | 1.02 |

developed 'an unusual commercial empire during the sixteenth century, distributing foreign goods to neighbouring areas to the north, east and west'.[5] Import commodities were sold to individuals in Tipperary and Queen's County, but more distant markets were also within the reach of Kilkenny merchants. In 1560, for example, James Cantwell set himself up as a fruit-and-spice merchant in Baltinglass, County Wicklow, selling marmalade, sugar, ginger and nutmeg, while at the same time Kilkenny vintners were selling high-quality white wine to the residents of Kilkee Castle in County Kildare.[6] In 1584, trade with Kildare had 'advanced to Naas', where special arrangements were made to ensure that all such 'wares and merchandises' that Kilkenny merchants sold there would be exempt from the usual tolls.[7]

Given the acknowledged role of Kilkenny as 'the major entrepôt for the mid-south', the level of involvement by Kilkenny merchants in the import trade from Bristol is not surprising. What is surprising is that Cork merchants matched the volumes of trade imported by Kilkenny merchants in 1598/9 and 1600/1 and indeed outperformed them in 1591/2. According to O'Sullivan, 'despite evidence of greater trading connections between Cork and the southern English ports during this period ... it cannot be said that trade and commerce flourished in Cork from 1500 to the end of the Elizabethan wars'.[8] He suggested that political upheavals, and the fact the Irish trade was in large part controlled by the native Irish, prevented Cork citizens from engaging in 'the trade which was developing as a result of the greater knowledge acquired in ocean transport'. The port books indicate that this was not the case and that Cork merchants were highly active participants in the supply of new consumer goods in southern Ireland.

[5] Ibid., p. 44.
[6] Ibid.
[7] Ibid.
[8] O'Sullivan, *Economic History*, p. 84.

## II. Control of the trade

In broader terms, the merchant domicile data also sheds light on the nationality of the merchants driving the import trade. The shipping details in the 'particular' accounts have shown that Irish shipping generally carried the larger portion of the Ireland–Bristol trade in the sixteenth century. Jones, for example, noted that in the 1540s, the volume of Anglo-Irish trade carried on Irish ships had risen to an impressive 75 per cent of total trade.[9] Without specific information regarding the domicile of merchants, however, it has hitherto been difficult to assess the exact significance of these developments for the Irish economy and the extent to which the trade was in the hands of Irish merchants. The predominance of Irish names in the accounts

Table 2.2 Percentage of gross value of imports by merchant domicile

| Year | Ireland | Bristol | London | Other |
|---|---|---|---|---|
| 1575/6 | 95.28 | 0.71 | 2.36 | 1.65 |
| 1576/7 | 97.28 | 0.79 | 0.74 | 1.19 |
| 1591/2 | 85.98 | 4.34 | 8.47 | 1.21 |
| 1594/5 | 79.42 | 4.91 | 14.91 | 0.76 |
| 1598/9 | 96.12 | 3.88 | 0.00 | 0.00 |
| 1600/1 | 76.61 | 18.21 | 3.91 | 1.28 |

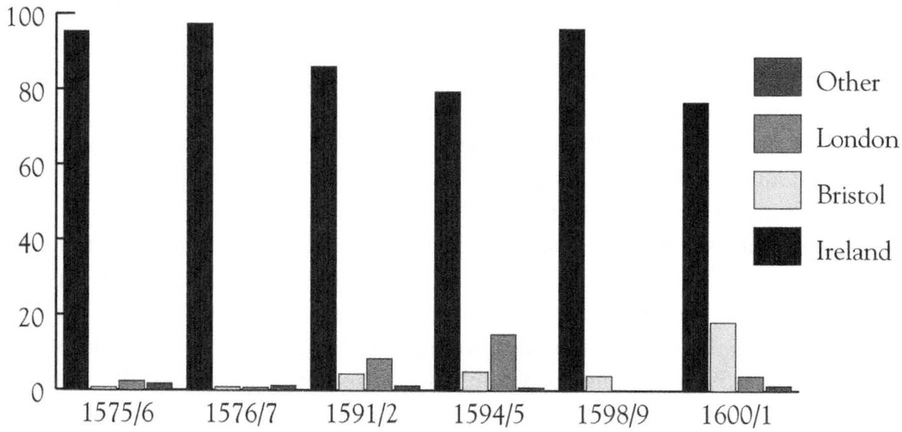


Figure 2.1 Percentage of gross value of imports by merchant domicile

Source: Flavin and Jones, Bristol's Trade, pp. 672–942; with the addition of gross import values for: 1576/7, 1591/2 and 1598/9–TNA, E190/1129/23, E190/1131/4, E190/1131/8, E190/1132/8.

[9] Jones, 'Bristol shipping industry', p. 39.

and the fact that Irish ships carried such a significant percentage of the trade, however, has been taken as an indication that a significant proportion of trade in the first half of the century remained in the hands of Irish merchants.[10] On the other hand, it is not possible to put hard figures on this.

Examining the domicile of merchants importing goods shows that the vast proportion of Ireland–Bristol trade was in the hands of Irish merchants (Table 2.2; Figure 2.1). In 1576/7, Irish merchants controlled a massive 97 per cent of the value of imported commodities from Bristol, and in the six fiscal years examined this never fell below three-quarters of the value of the trade. It is instructive to note that even in 1600/1, when the amount of trade carried on Irish ships fell significantly – Irish ships carrying only 16 per cent of imports in that year – Irish merchants still very much dominated the trade, controlling 76 per cent of the value of imports. It is clear, then, that Irish, rather than English or foreign merchants, were reaping the profits from the increasing luxury consumption in Ireland. Still, the decreasing involvement of Irish merchants on this route in the late century is worth keeping in mind, especially when considered in light of both the falling value of the Anglo-Irish trade overall, and the evidence for the increasing integration of Irish merchants in continental markets. The decrease of approximately 22 per cent in their activity on this route further supports the argument that the interests of Irish merchants were moving elsewhere towards the end of the century.

Although Irish merchants clearly dominated this trade, some important points can be made about the relative participation of non-Irish merchants. In particular, it is interesting to note that London merchants in general controlled a much larger portion of the trade than Bristol merchants. This is very significant, since before these findings evidence did not exist to indicate the level of involvement of London merchants on this route in Anglo-Irish trade.

The accounts suggest that merchant strangers domiciled in London were engaged in specialised and bulk trade to Ireland. In 1592, Roger Vancolege, a merchant stranger domiciled in London, exported 220 pairs of woollen stockings to Youghal on *The Three Kings* of Amsterdam. In 1595, the same merchant exported 170 tablecloths and diapers, valued at £34, along with Bay and Saye cloth, again to Youghal, on the *White Falcon* of Danzig. This is particularly unusual since tablecloths are not usually found amongst Irish imports in this period. The activities of London merchants, and particularly merchant strangers in Youghal, may be part of a wider enterprise. In 1599, for example, Veron Martyns of London freighted the *Angel* of Hoorn to sail from London to Youghal to lade pipestaves and to ship these from Youghal to the Canary Islands. Youghal, it appears, was prominent in the pipestave industry and it may be that the shipping of luxury goods into the port by London merchants was the first part of a triangular trade route between London, Ireland and the Canary Islands: London merchants shipping luxury goods into Youghal in

[10] Flavin, 'Development of Anglo-Irish trade', p. 31.

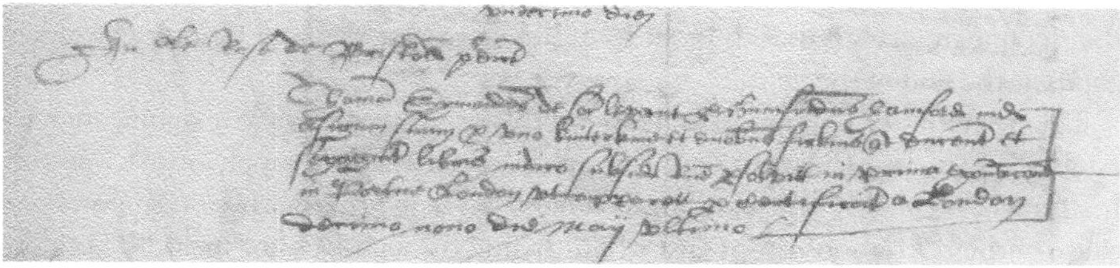

Plate 3 Image from the 1594–95 'port book' showing activity of the Levant Company in Irish trade.

exchange for pipestaves that they shipped to Spain to supply the needs of the wine barrel industry, and then returning to London with wine.[11]

There is other tantalising evidence to suggest the wider integration of Irish trade and markets with London's interests in this period. Of particular significance is a bulk shipment of 260lb of indigo that left Bristol for Waterford on 11 June 1595, as shown in Plate 3. This was shipped by Thomas Symondes of the Levant Company, a factor for Humphrey Hamford. Symondes appears to have become consul for Zante, in the dominions of Venice, in April 1638, but in 1594/5 was probably based at Aleppo.[12] A Chancery pleading from 1599 records a case between various merchants of London and Thomas Symonds, for payment of life insurance for Symondes' servant, who died at Aleppo when the ship was insured only as far as Greece.[13]

Aleppo was amongst the principal trading centres in Asia in the sixteenth century and, along with Damascus, was the 'terminus for the great caravan routes from Persia and Mesopotania' and, as such, an entrepôt for Eastern trade.[14] The Levant Company, which was formed in 1592, from a merger between the Turkey Company and the Venice Company, sent out cloth and tin to Chios, Istanbul, Syria and Egypt and returned with raw silk, mohair, cotton wool, carpets, currants, drugs, spices and indigo. Currants and indigo, according to Balfour-Paul, were the most profitable of the commodities imported to England and were imported in bulk in the first 30 years of the company's life, before the rival Cape route was fully established.[15]

The occupations of London traders on this route are also of importance. In 1594, Christopher Comen, a fruiterer, exported a range of goods to Ireland, including Ghentish carpet cloth, falling bands, knives and stockings, and excluding any fruit. In the same year, a skinner, John Hiron, exported large quantities of aniseed, battery and hops to Ireland, while in 1601 Richard Birchely, a girdler, exported a range of dressmaking haberdashery items along with onion seed. This suggests that those London merchants previously involved in specialised areas of trade were broadening

[11] In 1604, for example, the *Peter* of Irvine was freighted by George Foster to carry pipestaves from Youghal to Tenerife. See H. C. A. 13/37 printed in Appleby, *Calendar of Material*, p. 107.

[12] A. C. Wood, *History of the Levant Company* (London, 1964), p. 67.

[13] TNA, C 2/Eliz/A5/22.

[14] J. Balfour-Paul, *Indigo in the Arab World* (London, 1997), p. 35.

[15] Ibid., p. 35.

their commercial activities to profit from the increasing demand for new consumer goods at the end of the century.

The activities of London merchants on this route may be of key significance to establishing wider mercantile connections in Ireland and the supply of goods in the Irish trade. It is likely that London merchants favoured the south-eastern ports because of the restrictions they faced when trading through Dublin. In 1538, London merchants complained that 'the mayor and citizens of Dublin will not suffer them to buy and sell without intolerable restrictions' and that they had no more privileges 'than if they were foreigners or pagans'.[16]

The significance of mercantile connections between London and Ireland becomes more apparent when Bristol's continental imports are compared with its exports to Ireland, as it is clear that significant discrepancies exist. In the first half of the century, silk and saffron were two of Bristol's major exports to Ireland, yet they are never found among the city's continental imports. In terms of luxury spices: cinnamon, cloves and nutmeg are rarely found as imports to Bristol and never in quantities as large as Bristol's exports to Ireland. Frequently, more unusual luxuries such as beads and incense are found as exports to Ireland, along with luxury cloths such as damask and calico, without ever turning up in Bristol's import accounts. These, of course, are things we know were not produced in England, so we have to suppose that they were coming from another English port – probably London – and sent overland to Bristol for export to Ireland. This is not the case in general; many regular Irish import items such as expensive dyestuffs, other spices such as aniseed and ginger, and luxury foodstuffs such as raisins and figs are usually found as regular Bristol imports and exports. By the end of the century, the discrepancy does become more pronounced, with very long lists of Irish imports, in particular luxury cloths such as Levant taffeta, French crewel, Paris silk and Bologna sarcenet not appearing as imports to Bristol at all. It appears, then, that in the case of many commodities, Irish merchants were using Bristol mainly as a point of embarkation, a gateway to the south-east of Ireland and its extensive hinterland and, as well as maintaining direct trading networks with the Continent, were also closely connected to the wider mercantile community operating out of London.

It would be instructive to compare the range of goods coming into London with the goods exported to Ireland. This might give some sense of the extent to which the material culture of the more affluent and integrated parts of Ireland kept pace with or diverged from changes at the centre of English consumption. Unfortunately, it is impossible to do this with any consistency. This is because only two accounts survive for London's Elizabethan import trade, covering the fiscal years 1567/8 and 1587/8. Neither recorded the imports of alien merchants and, to date, only the 1567/8 account has been published.[17] In addition, fragmented government surveys of Lon-

[16] *Calendar of Letters and Papers, Henry VIII*, xiii, i 1538, pp. 540–1; cited in Woodward, *Trade*, p. 28.

[17] Dietz, *Port and Trade of Early Elizabethan London* (1972).

don's imports survive for 1558 and 1565. Excluding items that were produced in Ireland, approximately 53 per cent of the items recorded in the more detailed 1558 survey of London's imports are also listed amongst Ireland's imports from Bristol in 1575. Moreover, this rises to approximately 63 per cent in 1594/5. Comparing the more detailed data in the 1567/8 London import account with Irish imports also shows considerable similarities. In particular, the range of goods imported into London from Antwerp in 1567/8 compares well with the range of Irish imports from 1575 onwards. The vast majority of continental cloth types and haberdashery items imported into London, for example, are found amongst Irish imports.

### III. Seasons and trade

A key feature of Anglo-Irish trade in this period was its seasonality.[18] The volume of trade conducted and the movement of ships between Bristol and Ireland was not even throughout any given year (See Appendix 4). A major reason was the concentration of commercial activity around the time of Bristol's major fairs. These were St James' fair and Candlemas fair. Of these, St James' fair, held on 20 July and for nine days afterwards, was by far the more important event in a merchant's schedule. In eight out of the eleven years examined (Tables 2.3 and 2.4), the value of Irish imports peaked in July or August.[19] The fair continued to dominate Irish trade schedules to the end of the century. In 1575, in the 10 days leading up to the St James' fair and during the fair, 12 ships arrived in Bristol from Ireland, carrying 71 per cent of the annual value of Ireland's recorded exports. Between 28 July and 15 August, 16 ships left Bristol for Ireland, including all of the Irish ships that had entered before and during the fair. Almost half of the gross value of Irish imports was shipped to Ireland between 28 July and the end of August in that year. A very similar trend is noted in 1594/5 when, between 7 and 26 July, 21 ships entered Bristol from Ireland, carrying 72 per cent of the annual gross value of Irish exports to the city, while 42 per cent of gross value Irish imports was shipped to Ireland between 30 July and the end of August.

Candlemas fair was held 2–9 February between 1529 and 1543.[20] Although banned in 1543, it was replaced less than six years later with a January fair. This was held for eight days beginning on the conversion of St Paul, 25 January.[21] The Candlemas fair was stopped after a petition to Star Chamber, from the mayor, aldermen, council and masters of the more influential Bristol guilds, who complained that before 1529, men from Ireland, Wales, Cornwall and Devon would come regularly to

[18] For a discussion of the problems of using the port books to measure seasonal variations in trade, see Flavin, 'Consumption and material culture', p. 52.

[19] The exceptional years being 1503, 1525 and 1550.

[20] J. Vanes, *The Port of Bristol in the Sixteenth Century* (Bristol, 1977), p. 19.

[21] Ibid., p. 20.

Table 2.3 Monthly breakdown of gross value of imports (deflated)

| | 1503/4 | 1516/17 | 1525/6 | 1541/2 | 1542/3 | 1545/6 | 1550/1 | 1563/4 | 1575/6 | 1594/5 | 1600/1 |
|---|---|---|---|---|---|---|---|---|---|---|---|
| Oct | 219.61 | 56.01 | 46.72 | 0.00 | 201.54 | 34.30 | 62.10 | 101.27 | 0.00 | 3.04 | 30.79 |
| Nov | 132.50 | 217.58 | 99.09 | 337.83 | 157.15 | 380.50 | 734.72 | 210.43 | 0.00 | 4.14 | 18.30 |
| Dec | 50.00 | 48.43 | 12.00 | 10.98 | 5.00 | 23.07 | 130.02 | 0.00 | 0.00 | 26.99 | 11.75 |
| Jan | 110.69 | 134.60 | 0.00 | 20.19 | 11.20 | 109.27 | 13.99 | 4.33 | 3.76 | 19.49 | 7.43 |
| Feb | 397.03 | 55.57 | 535.58 | 288.87 | 312.52 | 0.00 | 160.59 | 39.43 | 0.00 | 23.42 | 12.18 |
| Mar | 293.33 | 343.12 | 38.35 | 335.30 | 166.54 | 600.02 | 410.92 | 11.58 | 62.93 | 57.35 | 88.78 |
| Apr | 16.80 | 193.94 | 98.94 | 113.27 | 7.67 | 172.41 | 278.10 | 100.48 | 92.20 | 61.57 | 5.75 |
| May | 99.49 | 205.57 | 190.78 | 2.00 | 151.42 | 125.08 | 27.37 | 29.41 | 25.41 | 111.49 | 41.30 |
| Jun | 32.20 | 139.51 | 331.71 | 168.19 | 75.29 | 52.33 | 73.53 | 57.96 | 28.09 | 154.66 | 47.69 |
| Jul | 140.30 | 143.22 | 418.67 | 674.22 | 164.99 | 74.16 | 69.08 | 79.85 | 27.95 | 63.32 | 118.30 |
| Aug | 326.85 | 560.63 | 163.93 | 71.35 | 317.60 | 615.15 | 403.24 | 253.71 | 178.70 | 360.44 | 352.91 |
| Sept | 61.31 | 0.00 | 16.25 | 30.50 | 14.00 | 0.00 | 13.44 | 57.29 | 0.00 | 43.61 | 128.72 |
| Totals | 1,880.11 | 2,098.18 | 1,952.02 | 2,052.7 | 1,584.92 | 2,186.29 | 2,377.10 | 945.74 | 419.04 | 929.52 | 863.90 |

Table 2.4 Monthly breakdown of gross value of exports (deflated)

| | 1503/4 | 1516/17 | 1525/6 | 1541/2 | 1542/3 | 1545/6 | 1550/1 | 1563/4 | 1575/6 | 1594/5 | 1600/1 |
|---|---|---|---|---|---|---|---|---|---|---|---|
| Sept | 0 | 10 | 0 | 0 | 0 | 0 | 0 | 0 | 0 | 2.66 | 0 |
| Oct | 449.56 | 28.79 | 50.39 | 683.3 | 598.46 | 602.29 | 210.13 | 115.38 | 0 | 3 | 12 |
| Nov | 298.33 | 597.34 | 22.58 | 188.01 | 22.29 | 153.6 | 678.55 | 169.2 | 0 | 6.79 | 70.41 |
| Dec | 379.93 | 201.3 | 575.31 | 54.81 | 8.63 | 58.1 | 67.76 | 99.67 | 0 | 14.83 | 0 |
| Jan | 605.45 | 93.38 | 1346.3 | 631.37 | 490.44 | 10.75 | 0 | 124 | 0 | 49.04 | 2.66 |
| Feb | 380.41 | 334.86 | 531.8 | 350.32 | 412.97 | 73.54 | 247.8 | 253.2 | 0 | 103.3 | 18.87 |
| Mar | 549.79 | 1,440.84 | 9 | 111.44 | 52.19 | 930.74 | 268.18 | 206.56 | 0 | 25.19 | 8.62 |
| Apr | 118.29 | 36.06 | 199.89 | 113.14 | 92.04 | 127.43 | 3.17 | 4.92 | 6.87 | 30.41 | 12.75 |
| May | 9.38 | 452.17 | 99.65 | 189.12 | 137.1 | 45.2 | 110.58 | 328.75 | 36.75 | 138.16 | 0 |
| Jun | 174.85 | 146.04 | 158.23 | 31.01 | 158.7 | 95.85 | 80.67 | 14.57 | 0 | 97.08 | 30.49 |
| Jul | 251.15 | 579.98 | 399.69 | 1512.85 | 693.06 | 770.27 | 837.04 | 280.7 | 144.31 | 1,235.16 | 386.79 |
| Aug | 44.1 | 41.87 | 261.41 | 259.59 | 30.3 | 1.75 | 44.5 | 0 | 14.33 | 5.5 | 13.73 |
| Sept | 108.2 | 7.5 | 0 | 108.8 | 45.18 | 0 | 72.38 | 10.58 | 0 | 0 | 0 |
| Totals | 3,369.44 | 3,970.13 | 3,654.25 | 4,233.76 | 2,741.36 | 2,869.52 | 2,620.76 | 1,607.53 | 202.26 | 1,711.12 | 556.32 |

Bristol from Michaelmas to the middle of Lent with boatloads of fish, and that since 1529 they only came to the fair, to avoid the payment of tolls.[22]

The importance of the fair in Irish trade is suggested by the 1541/2 account. In February 1542, 12 ships arrived from Ireland in the 10 days prior to the fair, and 11 left for Ireland within 10 days of its completion.[23] On the other hand, however, in 1503 and 1525, before the inception of the fair, Irish exports peaked in January and imports in February. Therefore, the activity in the 1541/2 account might not necessarily testify to the popularity of the fair. Certainly, the January fair that replaced the Candlemas fair does not appear to have featured significantly in the schedules of Irish merchants. The 1550/1 account shows no concentration of trade around the time of the fair and, in 1575, no ships entered Bristol from Ireland in January or left for Ireland after the fair in February.

The St James' fair, then, was the principal fair at which Irish merchants accessed new consumer goods on this route in Anglo-Irish trade. It provided ready access not only to local produce but to Bristol's continental re-exports and also to new consumer items arriving into England via other Anglo-Continental trade routes, particularly London trade, as discussed above. Archer, in his discussion of the London Haberdashers' Company, noted the growing involvement of company members in overseas trade and in the distributive trades to the provinces from the late fifteenth century, in particular their tendency to 'haunt provincial fairs' siphoning off trade that would otherwise have come to the London mercers and grocers.[24]

The activity of London merchants at the Bristol fairs in particular has been discussed by Latimer, who noted that a large number of London tradesmen regularly attended the fair, bringing vast amounts of stock with them.[25] An entry in the Privy Council minutes for January 1597 indicates the extent of the business transacted by Londoners at the fair in Bristol. In that year a mercer sought the help of the Privy Council alleging that his servants, on the way home from the Bristol fair, were robbed of £1,700, along with bills and notes.[26]

That Bristol merchants resented the involvement of Londoners in the trade is clear. A plea from Bristol corporation to the Privy Council in response to Elizabeth's revival of the impost of ship money in 1596 noted that Londoners had monopolised internal trade to within 10 miles of Bristol, along with the southern European trade. It was argued that ships entering the River Avon mostly belonged to merchant strangers who would not export Bristol goods, 'whereby manufactures are towards an utter overthrow'.[27] Their pleas were ignored, perhaps being considered an exaggeration. The activities of London merchants in the Bristol–Ireland trade noted earlier, however, may suggest that there was indeed some merit to their case.

[22] Ibid.
[23] Jones, 'Bristol shipping industry', p. 76.
[24] Archer, *Haberdashers' Company*, p. 31.
[25] J. Latimer, *Sixteenth-Century Bristol* (Bristol, 1908), p. 113.
[26] Ibid.
[27] Ibid.

Apart from the concentration in trade around the summer fair, certain years show an intense concentration of trade in March. This is very unlikely to relate to the January fair, which ended on 2 February, since it relates both to imports and exports and since it occurs not only in 1550 but also in 1516 and 1545, years where no fair took place. Most likely such peaks in imports and exports were driven predominantly by the seasonality of Irish exports, which dictated the trading patterns of Irish merchants. Irish exports were highly seasonal in character. For example, in 1516/17, over 90 per cent of hake was shipped between January and March. Likewise, salmon had two distinct seasons, with exports peaking mainly from November to March and again in July.[28] Jones has also noted that in the 1540s, 69 per cent of the herring was imported into Bristol between October and November and 84 per cent of hake was imported between January and March.[29]

Irish imports, in contrast to exports, show no apparent seasonal variation (Appendix 3 gives a monthly breakdown of import commodities by value from two sample years). Although the volume of trade was seasonal, the range of goods imported remained fairly constant over the course of the year. This is unsurprising given that manufactured consumer items, spices, medicines and so on are all quite durable in nature. It is notable, however, that even perishables that should show seasonal variation were in demand and obtained by Irish merchants out of season. In 1601, for example, three individual Cork merchants each imported a barrel of apples into Ireland in March. Thirsk noted that, in 1703, Nicholas Blundell in Lancashire also enjoyed eating apples in March – by storing them in barrels of dry sand. He noted in his diary that on opening the barrel on 22 March that year, his apples were found to be firm and sound.[30]

[28] Flavin, 'Development of Anglo-Irish trade', p. 36.
[29] Jones, 'Bristol shipping industry', p. 76.
[30] Thirsk, *Economic Policy*, p. 300.

# *Part I – Summary*

Although the evidence is patchy, and the picture far from clear, it is becoming apparent that this was by no means a static period in Irish social and economic development. Indeed it seems that in the sixteenth century, south-east Ireland witnessed significant changes in consumption, which mirrored, in many ways, the sorts of changes occurring in the Pale, in England and across Europe during the period. While not vast in terms of value, the progressively complex range of goods imported demonstrates that, whether or not Ireland was as 'backward' as many contemporaries felt, it was gaining access to the increasingly sophisticated and diversified range of consumer goods being produced and traded in England and mainland Europe at this time. Ireland was able to participate in an evolving European consumer culture during this period, even if it was not at the forefront. Although the relative importance of the factors driving these changes remains unclear, the evidence explored here suggests that the growing participation of Irish merchants in European markets and increasing Irish commercial production were of fundamental importance, creating economic prosperity in the port towns and their hinterlands, and stimulating the desire for new tastes and fashions.

An examination of macroeconomic trends in the sixteenth-century Irish import trade, based on the data in the Bristol 'particular' customs accounts and port books, indicates a dramatic increase in the range of goods imported by Irish merchants over the course of the century, both in terms of the growing diversification of pre-existing product types and in the appearance of entirely new products in the trade. These trends cannot be explained by procedural changes, and appear, for the most part, to represent real changes in the nature of Irish consumption in this period.

Exploring the pace of these changes, it has been found that there were two main periods of growth, one in the 1540s and a second, and more significant, in the last quarter of the century. These changes were not highly localised and import commodities were diffused throughout the south-east of the country and into parts of the south-west; in other words, well outside the areas of centralised English control. It has also been shown that these changes mirrored those occurring in the Pale during the same period. These findings are of particular significance since they suggest a comparable level of demand for new consumer goods within the Pale and in the areas of Anglo-Irish control most geographically removed from the centre of government in Ireland, such as Galway, Sligo and Limerick. The Anglo-Irish consumers of these commodities, to some extent, shared a material culture, despite the fragmented nature of their society and economy and the geographical isolation of their more western communities. Although the relative importance of the factors driving these changes remains unclear, the evidence suggests that the growing participation of Irish merchants in European markets, and increasing Irish commercial production, were of fundamental importance to the trends noted here, creating economic prosperity in the port towns and their hinterlands, and stimulating the desire for new tastes and fashions. It is also of great importance that it was Irish, rather than English, merchants who dominated this trade and who, therefore, reaped the larger share of the profit of Ireland's growing luxury consumption. Overall, these findings suggest the buoyancy of the Anglo-Irish economy in this period, a picture that marries very well with David Edwards' study of the Ormond Lordship of County Kilkenny, which also portrayed a far more dynamic and integrated economy than that suggested by the standard narrative of Irish economic development.

# Part II

# *Dress*

It is written by Aristotle that when Cyrus had overcome the Lydians, that were a warlike nation, and devised to bring them to a more peaceable life, he changed their apparel and music, and instead of their short warlike coat, clothed them in long garments like women, and instead of their warlike music, appointed to them certain lascivious lays and loose gigs, by which in short space their minds were so mollified and abated that they forgot their former fierceness and became most tender and effeminate, whereby it appeareth that there is not a little in the garment to the fashioning of the mind and conditions.

Edmund Spenser
*View of the Present State of Ireland* (1596)

# 3

# *Consuming Fashion*

The history of clothing has seen a 'recent explosion of methods and approaches', and a growing interest in the consumption of fashion in English historiography has shed much light both on patterns of ownership and use of clothing and textiles in early modern England, and on the cultural significance of dress.[1] The division of labour amongst historians in the field of general consumption is not quite as pronounced in the area of clothing consumption.[2] While some studies do tend to focus on either the functional and economic importance of dress, or on its cultural meaning, new histories of dress are emerging that are 'sensitive to the disparities between representation and experience and which immerse clothing fully in its context of ideological, social and economic change'.[3] Richardson has noted, for example, that historians investigating 'the social reception of religious ideas, gender, identity or social status', have now also begun to make use of the evidence of clothing consumption.[4]

Furthermore, in contrast to general consumption studies, recent work on dress has done much to broaden the chronological scope of analysis to include the later Middle Ages and the sixteenth century.[5] The sixteenth century has indeed been acknowledged as a period of very significant change in the consumption of dress across Europe. Developing markets and production methods made available new types of fabrics and dress to societies. Traditional heavyweight woollen cloths were replaced by lighter weight 'new draperies' that became available in an increasing range of colours and textures. In addition, the Reformation changed the material culture of religion and added a significant moral dimension to the accepted modes

[1] Richardson, *Clothing Culture*, p. 5; A. Buck, 'Clothing and textiles in Bedfordshire inventories, 1617–1620', *Costume*, xxxiv (2000), pp. 25–38; B. Lemire, *Fashions Favourite: The Cotton Trade and the Consumer in Britain, 1660-1800* (Oxford, 1991); B. Lemire, *Dress, Culture and Commerce: The English Clothing Trade Before the Factory, 1660–1800* (Basingstoke, 1997); Vincent, *Dressing*; L. Weatherill, 'Consumer behaviour, textiles, dress in the late seventeenth and early eighteenth centuries', *Textile History*, xxii (1991), pp. 297–310.

[2] Pennell, 'Consumption and consumerism', p. 551.

[3] Richardson, *Clothing Culture*, p. 6.

[4] Ibid.

[5] See for example, Jones and Stallybrass, *Renaissance Clothing*; Vincent, *Dressing*.

of dress. According to Stallybrass and Jones, 'it was in the sixteenth century that the word "fashion" first took on the sense of restless change'. They noted that the first reference in the *Oxford English Dictionary* to the term 'the fashion' as referring to the 'mode of dress ... adopted in society for the time being' occurred in 1568.[6]

The study of dress has, in recent years, become central to a number of academic debates. Roze Hentschell, for example, examined the contemporary critiques of sixteenth- and seventeenth-century English citizens who dressed in continental fabrics and were accused of 'disturbing the notion of what it meant to be English'. She noted that the English cloth industry, throughout most of the sixteenth century, was 'a source of pride and a locus for organising fantasies of national solidarity', and that consumers turning away from the domestic industry was a 'blow to the unified vision of the nation based upon domestic cloth'.[7] Similar themes were examined by Oksana Sekatcheva, who discussed the role of clothing in the consolidation of Russian national identity in the sixteenth and seventeenth centuries.[8]

The evolving role of clothing in marking social distinctions and in the display and dissemination of political power in an increasingly mobile early modern society has also generated discussion.[9] Maria Hayward considered the political use of clothing by Henry VIII through gift giving, and noted that power was disseminated at court through items of apparel.[10] Much attention has also been given to the economic, social and moral regulation by law of clothing consumption, which increased markedly over the course of the sixteenth century in England in response to increasing social mobility, mercantilism and evolving ideas about the morality of excess, instituted by religious change.[11]

Historians have also considered changes in clothing in order to further understand the impact of religious change on social and cultural behaviour and on the display of spiritual and moral identity. Richardson noted that the very different aesthetics of Protestantism and Catholicism 'have consequences for clothing because they suggest different moralisations of display, of luxury, and of the connections of

[6] Jones and Stallybrass, *Renaissance Clothing*, p. 1.

[7] R. Hentschell, 'A question of nation: foreign clothes on the English subject', in Richardson (ed.), *Clothing Culture*, pp. 49–62. R. Hentschell 'Treasonous textiles: foreign cloth and the construction of Englishness', *Journal of Medieval and Early Modern Studies* xxxii, iii, pp. 543–70.

[8] O. Sekatcheva, 'The formation of Russian women's costume at the time before the reforms of Peter the Great', in Richardson (ed.), *Clothing Culture*, pp. 77–94.

[9] See for example, P. Raffield, 'Reformation, regulation and the image: sumptuary legislation and the subject of law', *Law and Critique* xiii, ii (2002) pp. 127–50.

[10] M. Hayward, 'Fashion, finance, foreign politics and the wardrobe of Henry VIII', in Richardson (ed.), *Clothing Culture*, pp. 165–77.

[11] N. B Harte, 'State control of dress and social change in pre-industrial England' in D. C. Coleman and A. H. John (eds) *Trade, Government and Economy in Pre-Industrial England, Essays Presented to F. J. Fisher* (London, 1976); F. E. Baldwin, 'Sumptuary legislation and personal legislation in England', in *Johns Hopkins University Studies in Historical and Political Science*, xxxxiv, i (Baltimore, 1923); M. Hayward, *Rich Apparel: Clothing and the Law in Henry VIII's England* (Aldershot, 2009); W. Hooper, 'The Tudor sumptuary laws', in *English Historical Review*, 30, 119, pp. 433–49; C. Breward, *The Culture of Fashion* (Manchester, 1995) pp. 41–105.

both to the representation of status'.[12] The exact significance of the religious Reformation and the emerging 'Protestant Ethic' on changing fashions, however, remains uncertain.[13] Claire Bartram, analysing the text of a 1560s pamphlet debate between a pair of cloth and velvet breeches has indeed noted a paradox of Protestant gentry identity: the perceived need to 'display worthiness of status' while simultaneously 'eschewing conspicuous consumption'.[14] Similar ideas have been explored by Susan Vincent, who noted the often luxurious nature of Puritan dress, despite the use of clothing as 'a metaphor for virtuous spirituality'.[15]

In addition to work on the significance of clothing in the formation and display of personal and public identity, clothing has also been studied as a tool of dissent and opposition to political and social control. Elizabeth Wilson examined this phenomenon with specific reference to the nineteenth and twentieth centuries.[16] More recently, Steeve O. Buckridge has discussed the impact of colonisation on dress customs in Jamaica and in particular has argued how dress 'functioned as a symbol of both resistance to slavery and accommodation to white culture in pre- and post-emancipation Jamaican society, 1760–1890'.[17] Other historians, too, have noted the importance of clothing in the delineation of power in colonised societies. Karen Ordahl Kupperman, examining the complexities of Indian and English social interaction in sixteenth-century America has painted a vivid and nuanced picture of the role of dress in the construction and negotiation of identity in early America. According to Kupperman, 'English and Indians both considered clothing a fundamental demarcator as well as the most immediate emblem of the difference between the two peoples'.[18]

The increasing interest in the material culture of dress, and particularly sixteenth-century dress, has had little impact in Ireland. In a volume of papers presented at the 1st Annual Conference of the Irish Post-Medieval Archaeology Group, published in 2007, Elizabeth Wincott Heckett noted the dearth of work in the field and the pertinence of studying the available archaeological and historical evidence to see whether 'any viable assessment can be made of the pace or extent of the changes in dress taking place in Ireland' in the sixteenth century, when the 'habits and customs of medieval Ireland were changed beyond recourse'.[19] As part of her proposed 'framework for the study of post-medieval dress', she suggested the benefit of comparing extant garments and contemporary figure sculptures and also suggested

[12] Richardson (ed.), *Clothing Culture*, p. 15.

[13] E. Wilson, *Adorned in Dreams* (London, 1985), p. 54.

[14] Richardson (ed.), *Clothing Culture*, p. 22.; C. Bartram, 'Social fabric in Thynnes debate between pride and lowliness', in Richardson (ed.), *Clothing Culture*, pp. 137–52.

[15] Vincent, *Dressing*, p. 86.

[16] Wilson, *Adorned*, pp. 179–206.

[17] S. O. Buckridge, *The Language of Dress, Resistance and Accommodation in Jamaica, 1790–1890* (Jamaica, 2004).

[18] K. Kupperman, *Indians and English, Facing off in Early America* (New York, 2000), p. 53.

[19] Heckett, 'Town and country: an overview of Irish archaeological cloth and clothing, 1550/1850', in Horning *et al.* (eds), *Post-Medieval Archaeology*, p. 464.

comparing Scottish, English and Welsh evidence, to establish regional differences in the sixteenth and seventeenth centuries.[20] As yet, however, there has been little development in this field of study. Since Major Henry Foster McClintock's survey (1959) of Irish historical dress in the 1540s, the only other major work has been that of Mairead Dunlevy, a curator at the National Museum of Ireland.[21] Dunlevy's work, while important, is 'traditional' in its approach, surveying changes in the materiality of Irish garments by examining the construction, cut and cloth of Irish dress from the Bronze Age to the early twentieth century.

Exploring changes in the consumption and culture of clothing in sixteenth-century Ireland can contribute significantly to wider historiographical debates, providing a unique opportunity to examine the significance of dress in a semi-colonised and regionalised society and economy where political, religious, social and cultural identities were highly contested. As Kupperman has noted, because attire played such a key role in maintaining categories in England, colonists assumed that native dress and hairstyles were society's most important markers. With regards to Indians, this meant that even brief accounts sometimes contained elaborate descriptions of the various different hair and clothing fashions encountered. In Ireland such differences were used as ammunition in the process of conquest and colonisation. This is evident from both the contemporary writings of English observers on the subject of Irish dress and from legislative efforts to regulate it.

The legal regulation of apparel was not unique to Ireland. Late medieval and Tudor monarchs, recognising the 'innovative force of fashion' and the importance of clothing in conferring status, identity and social class, legislated repeatedly with regards to the attire of their citizens during this period.[22] In Ireland, however, such legislation had additional political and cultural significance. Tudor legislation specifically targeted the wearing of Irish dress styles and was designed not only to integrate Ireland into 'modern' English society, but also to suppress any sense of a distinctive Irish identity, evidence of which was viewed as resistance to English rule.[23] Irish resistance to English modes of dress was constantly lamented by the 'New English' elite, who particularly condemned the defection to Irish customs and tastes by the 'Old English' communities, which they interpreted as an indication of degeneracy and disloyalty. In 1596, Edmund Spenser claimed of the 'Old English' that 'the most part of them are degenerated and grown almost mere Irish, yea, and more malicious

[20] Ibid.

[21] H. F McClintock, *Old Irish and Highland Dress* (1950), M. Dunlevy, *Dress in Ireland* (London, 1989).

[22] Jones and Stallybrass, *Renaissance Clothing*, p. 1; Vincent, *Dressing*, p. 118; F. Baldwin, *Sumptuary Legislation and Personal Regulation in England* (Baltimore, 1926). Elizabeth I alone issued a total of 12 proclamations on apparel. Such legislation was designed to limit the personal expenditure of citizens, protect home industries by outlawing the wearing of foreign fashions, prevent the moral evils of the display of pride and vanity, and maintain the appearance of social distinction expressed through dress.

[23] Heckett, 'Town and country', p. 464.

to the English than the very Irish themselves'.[24] While in *An Itinerary*, published in 1617, Fynes Moryson claimed that the 'English-Irish' had:

> been infected with the barbarous customs of the mere Irish and with the Roman religion, so as they grew not only as adverse to the reformation of civil policy and religion as the mere Irish but even combined with them and showed such malice to the English nation, as if they were ashamed to have community with it, of country, blood, religion, apparel or any such general bond of amity.[25]

Furthermore, he suggested that 'such of the English-Irish as are become of that nature must be content to be joined with them, till they return to their English manners and affections' and that commands to counter such degenerate behaviour should be proclaimed 'at the point of a sword'.[26]

John Davies made even more explicit the perceived link between Irish dress and subjugation to English rule, proclaiming that the Irish did not rise 'from barbarisme to civilitie' under earlier sovereigns because these rulers did not abolish the Irish customs.[27] He noted that 'the execution of the Law doth make the Irish grow civil, and become English' but to impose English law on the Irish, the English must make 'them to cut off their glibs and long haire, to convert their mantles into cloaks'.[28]

Tudor monarchs certainly pursued a legislative offensive against Irish dress. In 1536, Henry VIII decreed that all the inhabitants of Galway should:

> shave their over lips, called crompeaulis, and suffer the hair of their heads to grow till it cover their ears; and that every of them wear English caps. That no man or man child do wear mantles in the streets, but cloaks or gowns, coats, doublets and hose, shapen after the English fashion. That no man, woman, or child do wear saffron in their shirts, smocks, or any other garments, or have more cloth in the same than five standard ells of that country cloth.[29]

In 1537, the Act for the English Order, Habit and Language prohibited any person in Ireland to dress their hair in the Irish fashion, or to:

> wear any shirt, smock, kerchor, bendel, neckerchour, mocket, or linen cappe coloured, or dyed with saffron, ne yet to use, or weare in any their shirts or smockes above seven yerdes of cloth … and that also no woman use or weare any kyrtell … imbroydered or garnished with silke, or courched ne layd with usker, after the Irish fashion, and that no person or persons, of what estate, condition or degree they be, shall use, or weare any mantles, cote, or hood, made after the Irish fashion.[30]

[24] Spenser, 'View', in Myers (ed.), *Elizabethan Ireland*, p. 78.

[25] Moryson, 'An Itinerary' (c.1617), in Myers (ed.), *Elizabethan Ireland*, p. 205.

[26] Ibid., p. 236.

[27] J. Davies, 'A discovery of the true causes why Ireland was never entirely subdued …', in Myers (ed.), *Elizabethan Ireland*, p. 147.

[28] Ibid., p. 207.

[29] Cal. Carew MSS., i, p. 91.

[30] 28 Hen. VIII, Cap. XV. An Act for the English Order, Habit and Language, in *A Collection of all the Statutes now in use in the Kingdom of Ireland* (Dublin, 1678) p. 92.

In 1541 an Act of Parliament at Dublin limited the amount of linen cloth to be worn in the shirts of various classes of inhabitants.[31] While in 1571, ordinances proclaimed at Limerick by Sir John Perrot, the lord president of Munster, declared that:

> no maid or single woman shall wear or put on any great roll or kercher of linen cloth upon their heads, neither any great smock with great sleeves, but to put on hats, French hoods, tippets, or some civil attire upon their heads.[32]

Whether or not the repetition of such legislation indicates a 'tacit admission of failure', as is sometimes assumed, comments from contemporaries suggest that such legislation had limited effect. For example, Spenser commented on the perceived inefficacy of such statutes and ordinances in Ireland when he wrote:

> What do statutes avail without penalties, or laws without charge of execution? For so there is another law enacted against the wearing of Irish apparel, but neverthemore it is observed by any or executed by them that have the charge, for they in their private discretions think it not fit to be forced upon the poor wretches of that country, which are not worth the price of English apparel, nor expedient to be practiced against the abler sort, by reason that the bare country doth yield no better.[33]

Given, then, the significance attached to dress in the process of colonisation and conquest, and also the wider changes occurring in the nature of European clothing fashions during this period, a re-evaluation of developments in this area of Irish material culture is overdue. From a social and cultural perspective, dress – as the most visible form of material consumption – is central to any consideration of the nature of Irish self-representation during this period, and understanding developments in Irish dress can uncover not only its role in colonisation, but also its oppositional use as a tool of protest and dissent, and its use in political mediation and conciliation.

The study of clothing consumption in the sixteenth century can also contribute in a vital way to our understanding of the relative development of the Irish economy and society. A cursory examination of the make-up of Irish shipments indicates that, by the later sixteenth century, significant changes had taken place in the nature of dress-related consumption. Indeed, many of the developments noted by Toby Barnard in his study of sartorial consumption in Ascendancy Ireland – the importation of ranges of light luxury cloths, the development of cheaper types of goods, the manufacture of home-produced copies, and the diversification of clothing types – were already becoming established in the sixteenth century. In fact, items that can be considered in this category show the most significant diversification of commodity types and growth in range of new products and materials. It has been reckoned that in 1750 one-quarter of Irish people used imported commodities, of which, after tobacco, cloth and clothing were the most valuable.[34] Although it is impossible to

[31] Cal. Carew MSS., i, pp. 180–3.
[32] Ibid., pp. 409–11.
[33] Spenser, *View*, in Myers (ed.), *Elizabethan Ireland*, p. 98.
[34] Barnard, *Making the Grand Figure*, p. 256.

establish the proportion of the population engaged in the consumption of imported clothing in the sixteenth century, there are indications that, in relative terms, this was already one of the most important areas of consumption. Throughout the century, commodities that relate to this particular activity of daily living were the most highly represented among imports from Bristol. In 1503/4, 42 per cent of individual entries for imports from Bristol relate in some way to dress, while in 1575, 1594 and 1600, the figures are 46 per cent, 53 per cent and 50 per cent respectively. Furthermore, changes in the nature of this particular area of Irish consumption were of considerable economic importance – the decline in the importation of saffron dyestuff, which will be examined in chapter 6, for example, had a major impact on the gross value of Anglo-Irish trade.

The following three chapters use the evidence from the exchequer customs accounts to provide a framework on which to examine the pace and extent of changes in Irish dress during the sixteenth century. The customs accounts are the only source available to facilitate both the accurate dating of developments in this area of Irish material consumption and the analysis of the geographical diffusion of new types of clothing and dress-related commodities. Social historians define dress in broad terms: as 'an assemblage of modifications of the body and/or suppleants to the body'.[35] As such, dress includes many forms of adornment: hairstyles, skin make-up, accessories, jewellery, as well as garments, and 'other modifications of and items added to the body'.[36] Taking dress in its widest context, then, these chapters will consider who was consuming the new ranges of apparel, dressmaking haberdashery, *passementerie*, accessories and dyestuff that appeared amongst Irish imports, and what specific changes in this area of Irish consumption might signify about the nature of Ireland's economy, society and culture during this period.

[35] Buckridge, *The Language of Dress*, p. 3.
[36] Ibid.

# 4

# *From Head to Toe*

## I. Headwear

According to Fynes Moryson, the 'English-Irish for the most part have for many ages had the same attire and apparel with the mere Irish, namely the nourishing of long hair which hangs down to the shoulders ... and this hair being exceedingly long, they have no use of cap or hat'.[1] Edmund Spenser noted that this glib hairstyle was 'a long curled bush of hair, hanging down over the eye, and monstrously disguising them, which are both very bad and hurtful'.[2] He further complained that:

> besides their 'savage brutishness and loathly filthyness ... they [glibs] are fit masks as a mantle is to a thief, for whensoever he hath run himself into that peril of the law that he will not be known, he either cutteth off his glib quite, by which he becometh nothing like himself, or pulleth it so low down over his eyes that it is very hard to discern his thievish countenance ...[3]

English attempts to ban the wearing of the Irish glib hairstyle in favour of the shorter hair and 'civil' hats or caps sported by Englishmen were closely tied to efforts to enforce English law in Ireland. Spenser makes it clear that Irish hairstyles were seen as a method of disguise and law evasion. As Christian Huck has pointed out, in order to be subject to the law inhabitants had to be identifiable, which was impossible as long as they were 'monstrously disguised' in the Irish fashion.[4]

Moryson's comments are likely to apply predominantly to the Irish kern, usually depicted bareheaded with long hair, as in the image drawn by an unknown English artist, shown in Plate 4. It is clear, however, that even within one of the most Anglicised of Irish towns, persuasion was required to ensure conformity to English styles. In 1592, in Waterford, for example, it was enacted that 'every of the rate shall wear his gowne of English broode cloth and a round cap the next Christemas day uppon paine of vi s viii d sterling'. [5]

[1] Moryson, 'An Itinerary', in Myers (ed.), *Elizabethan Ireland*, p. 206.

[2] Spenser, 'View', in Myers (ed.), *Elizabethan Ireland*, p. 80.

[3] Ibid., p. 84.

[4] C. Huck, 'Clothes make the Irish: Irish dressing and the question of identity', *Irish Studies Review*, 11, 3 (2003), p. 275.

[5] N. J. Byrne, *The Great Parchment Book of Waterford: Liber Antiquissimus Civitatis Waterfordiae* (Dublin, 2007) p. 178.

Plate 4 *Draun after the Quicke*, English print c.1550 by an unknown artist, apparently drawn from life. The drawing depicts six Irish chieftains of the second half of the sixteenth century, armed with ring-pommelled swords.

It is also evident that in some parts of Ireland, hats remained a means of distinguishing and identifying political allegiance. A declaration by Darby Newman of speeches used by the earl of Tyrone in 1593 stated, for example, that 'Maguire is very strong and will not suffer a man to pass that wears a hat on his head or a cloak on his back'.[6] But headwear was of even more complex political and social significance than merely distinguishing allegiance. In England, a code of painstakingly complex etiquette existed around the wearing and handling of headwear. Vincent notes that at a basic level, this code dictated that men would remove their headwear for superiors while their head would remain covered in the presence of those of lesser status.[7] Between these actions, however, 'lay a range of possible responses through which the hat wearer could articulate his attitudes to authority, his relationship with others, his assessment of his own status. "Aggression, defiance, salutation, respect, submission, entreaty, and emotion, were all readily conveyed by adroit handling."'[8] It is clear that this code of behaviour was both understood and practised in Ireland:

> Tyrone came where Ormonde was, and used most reverend and humble speeches of Her Majesty. Then he came to a moor side, a good way distant from me, where, with his hat in his hand, he with a loud voice saluted me, and such noblemen and captains as were with

[6]C.S.P. Ire., 1592–1596, p. 215.

[7]Vincent, *Dressing*, p. 88.

[8]Ibid., p. 89; P. Corfield, 'Dress for deference and dissent: hats and the decline of hat honour', *Costume*, 23 (1989), pp. 64–79.

Plate 5 The submission of Turlough Luineach O'Neill, John Derricke, *The Image of Irelande*, (London, 1581).

me, saying he was glad it pleased Her Majesty to appoint me her Lieutenant, hoping I would deal better with him ... than others did before.[9]

Notable also, when the earl of Ormond was taken by Irish rebels in 1600, he 'received no hurt, but his hat, George, sword, and dagger, were taken from him'.[10] Taking the earl's hat was perceived to be as disempowering as taking his weapons.

English propagandists, while constantly bemoaning the lack of Irish conformity to English styles, were careful to portray compliance with English practices, when it suited their own purposes. In John Derricke's image of the submission of Turlough Luineach O'Neill (Plate 5) O'Neill is pointedly depicted kneeling before Sidney, holding his English-style hat in his hand in a deferential manner.

Despite English comments suggesting otherwise, it is clear that both the Anglo- and Gaelic Irish did wear hats and caps. Archaeological, pictorial and literary evidence for Irish headgear in the sixteenth century suggests the very diverse nature of Irish tastes in this period. There is significant evidence to suggest that some medieval Irish hat styles persisted into the late seventeenth century.[11] The Phrygian cap, as seen for example on the chieftain in Derricke's image of the chieftain, kern and houseboy, c.1581 (Plate 6) went out of fashion in England in the thirteenth century, but was still commonly worn in Ireland as late as 1650.[12] Obviously, Derricke's illustrations must be used with caution. His work was, after all, dedicated to the

[9]C.S.P. Ire., 1596–1597, p. 468.
[10]C.S.P. Ire., 1600, pp. 66–137.
[11]Dunlevy, *Dress*, p. 61.
[12]Ibid., p. 61.

Plate 6 A soldier holding a battle-axe hands a spear to an Irish chieftain in full dress, with a page holding the chieftain's horse, John Derricke, *The Image of Irelande* (London, 1581).

lord deputy, Sir Henry Sidney, whose task was to subdue the Irish.[13] Nonetheless, the accuracy of his depictions of Irish dress have been considered in detail by both McClintock and Dunlevy, who agree that where points of detail can be corroborated by other pictures, contemporary sources or archaeological evidence, they appear to be correct. Dunlevy noted, for example, that descriptions of clothing by Andrew Trollope and William Camden, in 1581 and 1589 respectively, confirm the accuracy of Derricke's illustrations. She also noted that a suit of clothes found in Kilcommon bog, in County Tipperary, closely relates to the garments depicted by Derricke. This is particularly significant, since Derricke's images were made in Ulster, and suggests similar clothing styles in the north and south of the country.[14]

Likewise, the very distinctive linen headdress of Irish women, which intrigued numerous travellers in Ireland and involved the wearing of long rolls of linen in what Fynes Moryson described as a 'Turkish manner' on top of their heads was noted by Luke Gernon as typically Irish as late as 1620.[15] This style of headdress may have been influenced by regional trends. In 1581, an unknown traveller in Ireland, probably Spanish, described these as 'large linen wide-spreading bonnets'.[16] In 1588, Don Francisco de Cuellar, a Spanish captain wrecked in one of the ships of the Spanish

[13] Ibid., p. 56. For a discussion of Derricke's *Image* as a source see: Vincent P Carey, 'John Derricke's Image of Irelande, Sir Henry Sidney, and the Massacre at Mullaghmast, 1578' in *Irish Historical Studies*, 31, 123 (May 1999), pp. 305–27.

[14] Dunlevy, *Dress*, p. 57; McClintock, *Old Irish Dress*, p. 31.

[15] F. Moryson, *The Manners and Customs of Ireland*, p. 321. Available from: http://www.ucc.ie/celt/online/T100073.html [acessed 16 January 2011]; Gernon, *Discourse*, p. 358.

[16] An Unknown Traveller's Account of Ireland (1579) tr. and pr. in Rev. P. F. Moran, *History of the Catholic Archbishops of Dublin* (1864), pp. 91–3. Reprinted in Maxwell, *Irish History*, p. 320.

Armada, noted that the women in the mountains of Sligo and Donegal wore a 'linen cloth, much doubled, over the head, and tied in front', while in 1596, Edmund Spenser described them simply as 'great linen rolls'.[17] Spenser claimed that these rolls were worn by women 'to keep their heads warm after cutting their hair' and in 'any sickness'.[18] Dunlevy has commented that this style was worn by women after the birth of their first child, but unfortunately cites no evidence for this.[19] If this were true, it suggests that Irish women were being influenced by the social and marital symbolism that developed around headwear in early modern Europe. Certainly, an act by the corporation of Kilkenny in 1579 indicates the social and economic significance of such items of headwear. The act, which prohibited feasting at christenings and the churching of women after childbirth, on grounds of cost, declared that it was lawful for anyone who 'spieth' men or women coming from such a celebration 'to take away theire hatts or rolls or mantles, and the same to forfeytie, and to take away the midwife's roll and mantle that goeth to warne the people, other than those which by this statute are allowed ...'[20] It is difficult to imagine how such corporation-endorsed spying would have operated in practice but the prescribed punishment implies not only the financial value of hats, rolls and mantles but suggests that the removal of these items served a social function of public humiliation and shame.

The survival of this distinctive Irish headdress after the process of conquest and colonisation is interesting. Buckridge has discussed in detail the survival of traditional headdresses amongst African slave women in Jamaica in the late eighteenth and nineteenth centuries, whose head-wraps, he suggested, 'represented the continuity of African heritage and served as a symbol of resistance'.[21] Head-wraps served as a 'uniform of communal identity' but also as a 'uniform of rebellion', signifying absolute resistance to the loss of self-definition and de-culturation'.[22] In Jamaica, the head-wrap was an emblem and tool in armed resistance movements. Women sometimes wrapped their heads in a specific way to signal an act or state of war when fighting the English.[23] Buckridge further noted that in Jamaica, the Caribbean and the West Indies, head-wraps were diverse and ornate and reflected the stylists' creativity and individuality, as appears to have been the case in Ireland. They were also sometimes coded and had specific meanings and names, and – as also appears to have been the case in Ireland – styles varied between regions.

[17] Don Francisco Cuellar was a Spanish captain who was wrecked off the coast of Sligo after the defeat of the Spanish Armada. His narrative was written in the form of a letter dated 1589 and was first published by Duro in his *La uArmada Invencible* (1885). Translations are also found in *The Proceedings of the Royal Irish Academy* (1893), iii. pp. 175–217 and in Maxwell, *Irish History*, p. 318–19, Spenser, 'View', in Myers (ed.), *Elizabethan Ireland*, p. 98.

[18] Spenser, 'View', in Myers (ed.), *Elizabethan Ireland*, p. 98.

[19] Dunlevy, *Dress*, p. 62.

[20] Ainsworth, 'Corporation book', p. 40.

[21] Buckridge, *Language*, p. 86.

[22] Ibid., p. 88.

[23] Ibid., p. 95.

It is very likely that the survival of specifically Irish forms of female headwear in Ireland also indicates, to some extent, resistance to 'the loss of self-definition'.[24] Heckett has discussed the headdress depicted on the effigy of Margaret Fitzgerald, the wife of the earl of Ormond, which she states was no longer current in upper-class European circles and had 'some developments specific to Ireland'. The headdress was similar to the early fourteenth-century styles worn in Europe, but had developed differently, with the cloth between the horns being quite distinctive from other examples. Likewise, the Honoria Grace tomb sculpture (1596) in Kilkenny also suggests the survival of archaic dress until at least the end of the century. This trend, Heckett suggests, may represent the conservatism often displayed by aristocrats, an independent decision related to sense of identity and an affirmation of status in society.[25] Similarly, for non-elite Irish women, the wearing of the various styles of linen headdress was perhaps, during a period of upheaval and dispossession, a means of displaying not only their social position within their own communities but simultaneously their creativity and personal identity.

Evidence also suggests that some of the more traditional styles of Irish headwear evolved under the influence of European fashion. Dunlevy has noted the influence of the 'Burgundian sugar-loaf hat' in the phrygian styles worn by the gallowglass on the charter of Queen Elizabeth I to the city of Dublin in 1582, as well as by an Irish soldier illustrated by Caspar Rutz in 1588.[26] Likewise, three hats made of thick felt,

Plate 7 The MacSweynes seated at dinner, John Derricke, *The Image of Irelande* (London, 1581).

[24] Buckridge, *Language*, p 86.

[25] Heckett, 'Tomb effigies', p. 72; Heckett, 'Town and Country: an overview of Irish archaeological cloth and clothing, 1550/1850, in Horning *et al.* (eds), *Post-Medieval Archaeology*, p. 464.

[26] Dunlevy, *Dress*, p. 62.

Plate 8 Noblewoman, townswoman and 'wild Irish', Lucas de Heere c.1575 in *Corte Beschryuinghe van Enghekanssd, Schotland, ende Irland*, 1570s watercolour.

found in Boolabaun, County Tipperary, were found to be very similar in style to those in fifteenth- and sixteenth-century illustrations of German and French peasants.[27]

Despite evidence of continuity in styles, many of the newer-style European and English hats appearing in the sixteenth century were also embraced by some of the Irish, whether imported from abroad or produced and adapted at home. A bonnet with a halo trim, which was fashionable in England from the 1520s to around 1550, was seemingly worn by both Gaelic and Anglo-Irish women, as depicted in Derricke's woodcuts, showing the MacSweynes seated at dinner (Plate 7).[28] In addition, fashionable 'high-crowned' or 'chimney-pot-shaped' hats, which had Spanish and Italian origins, were worn by women such as the townswoman painted by Lucas de Heere around 1575 (Plate 8). De Heere's paintings must also be used with caution, since there is no evidence that he ever visited Ireland. It has been suggested by D. B. Quinn that he copied illustrations made by another artist who visited Ireland before 1547, and that some of his fashions should be dated to this time. Quinn makes a possible exception for the image shown in Plate 8, however, which he suggests, based on the style of their clothing, may possibly date from the 1570s.[29]

Bog finds have also shed light on the types of hats imported and also the influence of foreign styles on Irish productions. Adapted versions of popular types of felt hats have been found in bogs in Donegal, Mayo and Sligo.[30] Derricke's image of the submission of Turlough Luineach O'Neill, clearly shows him holding a 'Copotain'-style felt hat, a style that was very popular and fashionable in England from around 1560–1610, while a hat found in a bog in County Sligo shows a newer style of this type of hat, fashionable around 30 years later, which has a dramatically wide brim and high crown.[31]

It appears, then, that while some Irish people may have clung to traditional styles of headwear, some were very receptive to changing tastes and fashions and to the increasing availability of new varieties. The customs data supports these findings and shows the economic and social significance of headwear throughout the sixteenth century. Table 4.1 shows the volume and range of various types of headwear imported from Bristol over the course of the century. Table 4.2 and Figure 4.1 show the percentage of the gross value of the import trade comprised of various types of headwear, and Table 4.3 and Figure 4.2 show the volume of hats imported.

[27] Ibid.

[28] This style of hat is also shown in Derricke's image 'An armed company of the kerne, carrying halberds and pikes and led by a piper, attack and burn a farmhouse and drive off the horses and cattle', John Derricke, *The Image of Irelande* (London, 1581), Edinburgh University Library.

[29] D. B. Quinn, *The Elizabethans and the Irish* (New York, 1966), p. 94.

[30] Heckett, 'Town and country', pp. 454–55.

[31] See: http://www.fashionencyclopedia.com/fashion_costume_culture/European-Culture-16th-Century/Sixteenth-Century-Headwear.html [accessed 9 January 2010]; Dunlevy, *Dress*, p. 64.

Table 4.1 Volume of headwear imports, 1503–1601 (piece)

| | 1503 | 1516 | 1525 | 1541 | 1542 | 1545 | 1550 | 1563 | 1575 | 1594 | 1600 |
|---|---|---|---|---|---|---|---|---|---|---|---|
| caps | 414 | 99 | 671 | 742 | 344 | 132 | 335 | 192 | 45 | - | - |
| caps, Monmouth | - | - | - | - | - | - | - | - | - | - | 32 |
| caps, velvet | - | - | - | - | - | - | - | - | 2 | - | - |
| cauls, children | - | - | - | - | - | - | - | - | - | 6 | - |
| coif, velvet | - | - | - | - | 8 | - | 12 | - | - | - | - |
| hats | - | - | - | 111 | - | 90 | 33 | 18 | 276 | 1,145 | 346 |
| hats, black | | | | | | | | | | 24 | 12 |
| hats, children | - | - | - | - | - | - | - | - | 110 | 348 | 212 |
| hats, coarse | - | - | - | - | - | - | - | - | - | 95 | 60 |
| hats, felt | - | - | - | - | - | 28 | - | 9 | 42 | 24 | - |
| hats, women's | | | | | | | | | | 6 | 7 |
| nightcaps | - | - | - | 102 | 54 | 12 | 36 | - | - | - | - |
| nightcaps, velvet | - | - | - | 9 | - | 40 | - | 10 | - | - | - |
| nightcaps, satin | - | - | - | 9 | - | 21 | - | - | - | - | - |
| nightcaps, woollen | - | - | - | 12 | - | 36 | - | - | - | - | - |

Table 4.2
Headwear as a percentage of total import value

| Year | % Import value |
|---|---|
| 1503/4 | 0.61 |
| 1516/17 | 0.26 |
| 1525/6 | 1.33 |
| 1541/2 | 1.84 |
| 1542/3 | 1.02 |
| 1545/6 | 1.59 |
| 1550/1 | 0.7 |
| 1563/4 | 1.67 |
| 1575/6 | 3.14 |
| 1594/5 | 10.13 |
| 1600/1 | 3.15 |

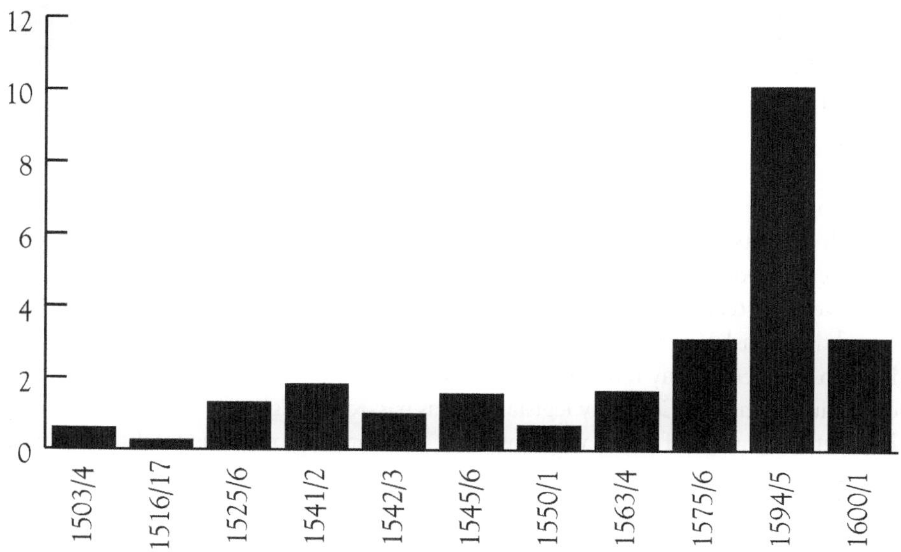


Figure 4.1 Headwear as a percentage of total import value

Table 4.3
Volume of hats imported, 1541–1601

| Year | Volume (piece) |
|---|---|
| 1541/2 | 111 |
| 1542/3 | 0 |
| 1545/6 | 118 |
| 1550/1 | 33 |
| 1563/4 | 27 |
| 1575/6 | 372 |
| 1594/5 | 1,529 |
| 1600/1 | 571 |

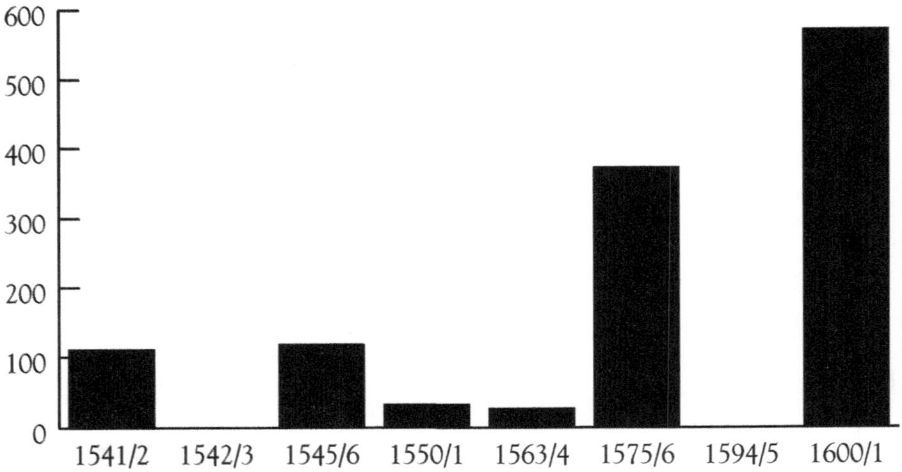


Figure 4.2 Volume of hats imported, 1541–1601

Throughout the century, headwear of various types comprised a small proportion of Irish imports from Bristol. Until the last quarter of the century, the main type of headwear imported was knitted woollen caps, with small quantities of luxury satin or velvet nightcaps appearing in accounts between the 1540s and 1563/4. Dunlevy noted that legislation passed in Galway in 1536, which demanded that citizens wear English-style caps, may have partly been an attempt to protect the woollen cap industry in England.[32] Certainly legislation was passed in England for this purpose. An Elizabethan statute of 1571, which was an 'Act for the continuance of the making of caps', decreed that every male over the age of six must, on Sundays and holy days, wear 'one cap of wool knit, thicked and dressed in England', upon forfeiture of 3s 4d

[32] Ibid., p. 63.

and that all citizens wives must wear 'white knit caps of woollen yarn', unless their husbands were of good value in the Queens book, or could prove themselves gentlemen by descent.[33] Though gentlemen's wives were exempt from Elizabeth I's cap act, which was repealed in 1597, woollen caps were seemingly also worn by the upper classes. It has been noted, for example, that the earliest mention of a Monmouth cap by name is in 1576, in a letter from Lord Gilbert Talbot of Goodrich Castle to his father, the 9th earl of Shrewsbury, accompanying a gift to the earl of 'a Monmouth Cappe'.[34]

If the legislative pressure to conform to the wearing of English-style headwear, or indeed the popularity of woollen caps in England had any impact on the wearing of English caps in Ireland, the most likely source of evidence would be the Bristol customs accounts. The Welsh town of Monmouth was one of the main producers of knitted caps worn in England in this period and, on account of the river trade, had close ties with the port of Bristol. There was also a cap-making industry in Bristol itself as, in 1529, Bristol's cappers were complaining to the court of Star Chamber that cappers from London were threatening the livelihood of hundreds of carders, spinners and knitters in Bristol.[35]According to Buckland, Bristol was 'the main outlet for the finished article, explaining its surprisingly worldwide distribution'.[36] There is no evidence whatsoever in the Bristol overseas customs accounts to support this view, however; not a single cap was exported from Bristol to any destination other than Ireland throughout the sixteenth century.

As Table 4.1 indicates, the accounts certainly show an increase in the importation of caps by Irish merchants in 1541, but overall, in the first three-quarters of the century, the importation of caps or hats from Bristol never constituted more than 2 per cent of the total value of Irish imports, and the trade in caps seems to have collapsed after 1575/6. Recent research by Chris Heal, a research student at the University of Bristol, has suggested that this may be because the cappers were 'ousted' by new felt-maker technology – probably the bow – which arrived from Europe via the early London Huguenots. The bow made felt-hat-making possible as a cottage occupation, whereas previously felt was mill-or feet-fulled.[37]

Certainly, while the volumes are relatively low, the 1575 account shows the importation of an increasing volume and range of hats, including the appearance of hats for children. The types of hats are not detailed in the accounts, but comparing their varying customs values to those recorded for hats in the 1582 rates book, which includes the nominal value for all goods paying duty, these appear to have included

[33] K. Buckland, 'The Monmouth cap', *Costume*, XIII (1979), p. 4; *Statutes of the Realm*, 13 Eliz. C. 19.

[34] J. Carlson, 'A short history of the Monmouth cap'. Available from: http://www.personal.utulsa.edu/~Marc-Carlson/jennifer/Monmouth.htm [accessed 16 July 2013].

[35] Buckland, 'The Monmouth cap', p. 3.

[36] Ibid.

[37] My thanks to Chris Heal for this suggestion, and for sharing his research on the hat industry with me.

felt hats, satin hats and 'hats of wul or worsted being thrommed', along with others that cannot be identified.[38] There were also at least three different varieties of children's hats. It will be noted in Table 4.3 that there was a very significant increase in the volume of hats imported in 1594/5, when hats accounted for a very significant 10 per cent of the gross value of the import trade from Bristol.

Tables 4.4 and 4.5 show the probable inland distribution of these hats in 1594/5, based on the domicile of the merchants importing them. Hats were apparently widely distributed throughout the south-eastern towns, with the largest volumes going to Waterford and Kilkenny. Both adult's and children's hats were imported by Galway merchants also, suggesting similar fashions in both the eastern and western Anglo-Irish towns. Again, apart from felt hats and children's hats, the variety of hat is not specified. All adult hats listed in 1594/5, however, paid 1s 6d per dozen in duty, giving them a nominal value of 30s. The most expensive type of hat found in the 1582 rates book are 'hats of silk French making for men or women', which are the only hats listed at this value. Likewise, the 1600/1 account records what appears to be, based on their values, worsted hats from Bruges and French silk hats.[39] Clearly, then, these were high-end luxury hats and possibly of continental rather than English origin.[40] On the other hand, it may well be that Bristol manufacturers were copying continental styles by this period and that the customs officers valued the hats based on their similarity to those found in the rates book. Interestingly, as with

Table 4.4
Distribution of adult's hats in 1594/5,
based on merchant domicile

| Merchant Domicile | Volume (piece) |
|---|---|
| Cashel | 12 |
| Clonmel | 44 |
| Cork | 162 |
| Fethard-on-Sea | 63 |
| Galway | 120 |
| Kilkenny | 300 |
| Limerick | 255 |
| London | 24 |
| New Ross | 66 |
| Waterford | 790 |
| Youghal | 24 |

[38] Willan, *Tudor Book*, p. 32.
[39] Thrummed means fringed.
[40] Willan, *Tudor Book*, p. 32.

Table 4.5
Distribution of children's hats in 1594/5, based on merchant domicile

| Merchant Domicile | Volume (piece) |
|---|---|
| Clonmel | 24 |
| Cork | 72 |
| Galway | 24 |
| Kilkenny | 36 |
| Limerick | 144 |
| Waterford | 35 |
| Wexford | 39 |

many other continental goods, these hats are not found amongst Bristol's continental imports and might therefore have been sourced by Irish merchants from another port, such as London, and transported overland to Bristol for export.

As well as benefiting directly from the importation and sale of luxury continental headwear, certain Irish merchants also capitalised on the hat-making industry in indirect ways. In 1594 Dominic Copinger, a Kinsale merchant, exported Spanish hat wool valued at £125 to Bristol. This was four times the value of all the Irish wool exported to Bristol in that year, and indicates the well-developed Irish mercantile contacts with Spain for the commercial raw materials necessary for the production of felt hats, something that English merchants may indeed have relied on during periods of Anglo-Spanish hostility in order to supply the English hat-making industry.

It is difficult to say with any certainty who was consuming the luxurious and fashionable headwear appearing in the accounts towards the end of the century. Although the sharpest rise in the volume of hats imported does correspond well with the influx of new settlers who arrived as part of the Munster plantation, the qualitative evidence examined above shows that some Irish people were interested in and able to access and acquire luxury European hats well before this date. Testamentary and inventory evidence also shows this to be the case. An inventory of the goods of a Cork citizen, Richard Tyrry Fitzadam, taken in 1582, which appears to record the contents of a shop, including, for example, a box of 36 combs, shows that he owned five taffeta hats, while an inventory of the goods of Andrew Galway of Cork, taken in 1580, shows that he too had both hats and caps for sale in his shop in Cork.[41] Nevertheless, the very specific timing of this significant increase in what appears to be predominantly one particular style of hat does suggest that the 'New English' settlers influenced the demand for this particular item in Ireland.

The appearance of significant numbers of children's hats towards the end of the century is particularly interesting since there is no pictorial evidence and very little

[41] Cork City and County Archives, Caulfield Will Transcripts, U226, p. 20, 41.

archaeological evidence to indicate what Irish children wore during this period. According to Buck:

> The dress of children shares the complex and changing pattern of adult dress but, provided by the parents, it is edited by them for each stage of childhood. This gives the dress of children a movement and pattern of its own within the changes of adult dress, a pattern based on the process of growing up and parental ideas of upbringing.[42]

It has been suggested that by the end of the sixteenth century, even children in Ireland conformed to new fashions. In 1599, Hugh O'Neill's sons were seen in 'good towardly spirit-in English clothes like a nobleman's sons; with velvet jerkins and gold lace'.[43] Certainly the customs data indicates that children were indeed partaking in new clothing fashions, and that developments in their headdress mirrored that of adults. This was obviously very variable, however. Archaeological evidence from a child's burial at Emlagh, County Kerry included a distinctly medieval-style children's gown, dated to the seventeenth century.[44] Clearly, in some areas, and at lower social levels, children's fashion, like adult's, evolved slowly during this period.

## II. Neckwear

The garment that most conspicuously displayed wealth, grandeur and style in the second half of the sixteenth century was beyond any doubt the ruff. It originated as a small frill drawn up at the neck of a shirt but by the 1570s had grown in size and complexity so that it had to be detachable.[45] The ruff was a distinctly elite form of dress, having no apparent practical function whatsoever and being very restrictive on both movement and vision. Wearing a ruff was a means of displaying the 'possession of leisure' or the 'dissociation from manual occupation'.[46]

The fashion of ruffs in England began in the 1560s, under the influence of Dutch style, and this led to a corresponding demand for starch, for which there had been little requirement before. Rather than being of a permanent nature, ruffs were remade at every wash, and the highly skilled process of starching, ironing and pinning of linen required to create one ruff could take up to five hours at every laundering.[47] In 1564, Flemish refugee Dinghen ven der Plasse set up a starching business in London, and charged women £4–£5 to teach them the skill of starching, and another 20s to teach them how to prepare starch.[48]

[42] A. Buck, *Clothes and the Child* (Bedford, 1996) p. 13.

[43] Sir John Harrington, 'Report of a journey into the north of Ireland written to Justice Carey' (1599). Pr. *Nugae Antiquae* (1792), i. pp. 247–51, reprinted in Maxwell, *Contemporary Sources*, p. 338.

[44] Heckett, 'Town and country', p. 455.

[45] Vincent, *Dressing*, p. 32.

[46] Ibid., p. 33.

[47] Ibid., p. 32.

[48] Jones and Stallybrass, *Renaissance Clothing*, p. 68.

Table 4.6
Volume of starch imported (lb)

| Year | Vol. ( lb) |
|---|---|
| 1550/1 | 2 |
| 1563/4 | 2 |
| 1575/6 | 2 |
| 1576/7 | 6 |
| 1591/2 | 73 |
| 1594/5 | 79 |
| 1600/1 | 34 |

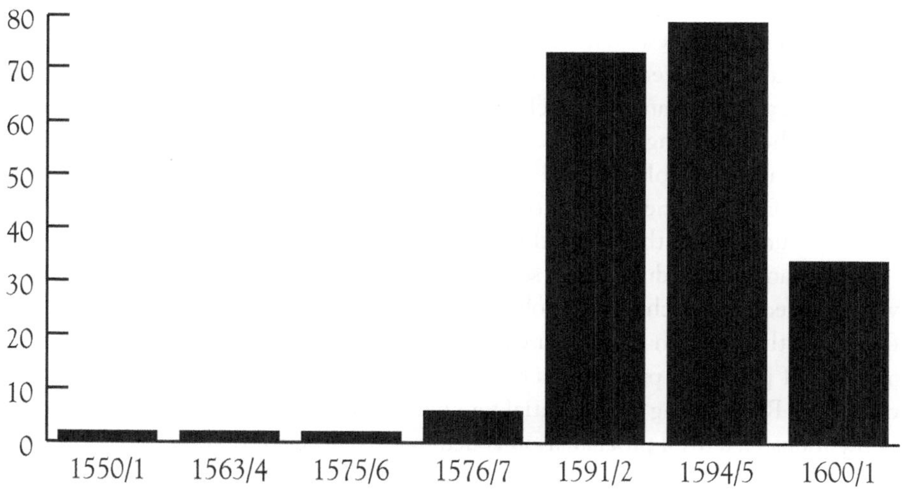


Figure 4.3 Volume of starch imported (lb)

There was probably quite a time lag before this fashion gained a significant number of followers in Ireland. Certainly, there is no evidence that starch was manufactured in Ireland before 1610, when a licence was issued to Hugh Pollard to 'make, vend and sell' starch for 21 years. Another such licence was issued to John Pollard on 4 February 1611, to make starch in Leinster, Connacht and Munster for 21 years and, on 1 April 1613, Francis Pollard received a licence to make starch for six years.[49] Tiny quantities of starch are found in the customs accounts from 1550, and in 1576 only 6lb of starch was imported from Bristol (see Table 4.6, Figure 4.3). This may have been due to a lack of skilled laundresses or starchers in the south-east region. The volume of imported starch rose significantly in 1591, however, with the

[49] TNA, HO 42/218.

importation of 73lb, rising again in 1594 to 76lb. It is clear that this starch was used to make ruffs, as the 1591 account also records an entry for 'poking sticks', which were rods used for stiffening the pleats on the ruffs.[50] While 76lb may not seem like a very significant quantity, it was potentially enough to starch a very large number of ruffs. Melanie Schuessler has noted that it takes approximately one cup of laundry starch to create 12 medium-sized ruffs. There are around three cups of starch in a pound, therefore 76lb could have starched up to 2,736 medium-sized ruffs. The amount required would have varied depending on the size of the ruff and, after 1580 some of the ruffs in question would probably have been very large ones, although some of the middle classes continued to wear smaller ruffs through to the end of the century.[51] This imported starch was widely distributed in 1591/2 and 1594/5, being distributed by merchants from Cashel, Clonmel, Kilkenny, Limerick, Galway, Waterford and Cork. Clearly, by this date the skills required to create such extravagant frills had been imported by the Irish elite also.

There is indeed evidence that, in Dublin at least, some less affluent citizens were also embracing this new trend. In 1573, the apprentices of Dublin were limited to wearing a ruff no greater than 1yd in length.[52] It is possible, given the specific timing of the increasing demand for starch in south-east Ireland, that this trend was influenced by the 'New English' elite. It is notable also that the volume dropped again in 1600/1, after the collapse of the Munster plantation, although this may also be due to the fact that the fashion for ruffs declined in Ireland, as it did elsewhere in Western Europe from the end of the sixteenth century.

In England, the industry that supplied starch was rife with controversy. Starch was attacked for enriching the nobility at the expense of the poor, as it was made from corn that could have been used to make bread. In 1595, in Cheapside, during a period of particular privation, a crowd made a carman unload the starch he was carrying.[53] Recognising the potential for civil unrest, and to capitalise on the profits of the industry, a royal proclamation issued in 1576 declared that:

> Her majesty, being informed of an abuse greatly tending to make scarcity of corn meet to make bread by making starch within the realm, doth straightly command that no manner of person shall make any starch of any corn or bran of corn grown within the realm, or that is or shall be brought into the realm, not wittingly sell or utter any such starch except such as hath been made by virtue of her majesty's letters patent.[54]

It is unclear what the poor in Ireland made of such excessive and conspicuous waste of food. A comment by Moryson, which must of course be treated with caution,

[50] TNA, E190/1131/8 f19r.

[51] My thanks to Melanie Schuessler, associate professor of costume design at the Eastern Michigan University for this information.

[52] L. M. Cullen, *Life in Ireland* (Dublin, 1968), p. 48.

[53] Jones and Stallybrass, *Renaissance Clothing*, p. 69.

[54] P. L. Hughes and J. F. Larkin, *Tudor Royal Proclamations* (New Haven, 1969), iii, pp. 166, 188.

suggests that the 'wilde Irishe' at least, were entirely unfamiliar with the product, while also reflecting indirectly the ongoing controversy in England:

> It is strange and ridiculous but most true, that some of our carriage horses, falling into their hands, when they found soap and starch carried for the use of our laundresses, they thinking them to be some dainty meats did eat them greedily, and when they stuck in their teeth cursed bitterly the gluttony of us English churls, for so they term us.[55]

Starch was also attacked in England by militant Protestants who saw its use simultaneously as 'foreign, effeminating and demonic', as well as being responsible for food shortages.[56] In 1608, a monopoly on starch was granted to the earl of Northampton – a 'life-long Catholic' and the 'recipient of money from Spain' and, from the perspective of Protestant critics, the 'least English of James's English councillors' – which further increased its political volatility and caused it to become associated not just with the foreign, but also with the 'Catholic'.[57] Pressure from the Protestant faction eventually led to the absolute prohibition of starch-making in 1610, but it of course continued to be manufactured in large quantities.[58]

Certainly, the Catholic and foreign, rather than purely English, association of the ruff make it less surprising that Domhnall O'Sullivan Beare, in the oldest surviving portrait of an Irish chieftain (1613), is depicted wearing a rather spectacular example of a 'cartwheel'-style ruff.[59] O'Sullivan Beare is noted for his close economic and political continental ties, carrying on extensive trade with Spain and being exiled there after the Nine Years' War. In 1605 he wrote to Philip II and noted that each year at least 500 Spanish fishing boats came to his ports. Archaeological evidence further suggests these links. Pottery evidence from O'Sullivan's stronghold in Berehaven includes sixteenth-century pottery from France, Spain, the Netherlands and even some China Ming. O'Sullivan's choice of apparel in this portrait, which is typical of elite Spanish attire during this period, made a statement not only about his wealth but also his cultural and political affiliations.

Apart from evidence for the wearing of ruffs in Ireland, the accounts show the appearance of other forms of neckwear towards the end of the century (Table 4.7). Falling bands, which succeeded the ruff in England and became popular from around 1615 onwards, are found as Irish imports in small quantities as early as 1594. Also of note is the appearance of further items for children. Bibs were a common import after 1575 and were listed simply as 'bibs' or were described as 'sucking bibs' or 'children's bibs' and all paid the same duty – one farthing per piece. A bib is 'a

[55] Moryson, 'An Itinerary', in Myers (ed.), *Elizabethan Ireland*, p. 189.

[56] Jones and Stallybrass, *Renaissance Clothing*, p. 68.

[57] Ibid., p. 69.

[58] Ibid.

[59] The portrait of Domhnall O'Sullivan Beare came from the Irish College in Salamanca and is now in St Patrick's College, Maynooth. Reference: *Portrait of Donal O'Sullivan Beare, 1613, aged* 53, with the inscription: 'O'Sullevanus Bearrus Bearrae et Beantriae Comes Actatis suae LIII Christi Vero Domini MDCXIII anno'. Oil painting 190cm x 98cm. Maynooth College.

Table 4.7 Volume of neckwear imported (piece)

| Year | 1575/6 | 1594/5 | 1600/1 |
|---|---|---|---|
| Bands, falling | - | 30 | 12 |
| Bands, plain | - | 12 | - |
| Bibs | 48 | 444 | 504 |
| Bibs, children's | - | - | 60 |
| Bibs, sucking | - | - | 96 |

cloth placed under a child's or infant's chin to keep the front of the dress clean at meals'.[60] Buck has noted, however, that from the sixteenth century, while they were still used for their original protective purposes, they had also acquired a decorative function, and were 'essential for the well-dressed child', often being lace-edged or embroidered.[61] She further suggested that bibs and aprons were worn by wealthier children, while poorer children commonly wore the 'pincloth', which was 'a simpler and more practical alternative'. It is likely, then, that bibs imported into Ireland fulfilled a decorative purpose also, since any scrap of material would have sufficed for the simple protection of clothing. This suggests that parents in Ireland were being influenced by children's fashions from elsewhere and that changes in the nature of adult dress were being mirrored in that of children's. It also indicates an awareness of evolving practices in child-rearing in the wider world. This is further suggested by the importation of copies of conduct books for children, such as Francis Seager's *The School of Virtue* along with other 'small books for children' from the last quarter of the century. Seager's manual, a didactic work for children on morals and social behaviour, was first published in England in the 1550s. It was illustrated by woodcuts and included detailed instructions on how to behave at the table. The importation of such educational literature was rare in the first three-quarters of the century, but the variety and number of children's books increased towards the end of the century, suggesting perhaps the concern of newly arrived 'New English' parents to promote and maintain the 'civility' of their offspring in a 'barbaric' country.[62]

[60] OED.

[61] Buck, *Clothes and the Child*, p. 71.

[62] In the first half of the century, the only books found in the accounts are 'primers'. The 1575/6 account contains two entries for books, one for primers and one for 'books for children' (pro pueris). It is not until 1594/5 and 1600/1 that a greater variety is seen, with the appearance of fable books, 'books of the School of Virtue', small books, small books for children, grammar books, horn books and also 'Catoes and Pueriles'. *Catoes* refers to the classical works of Cato, which were used in schools, and *Pueriles* is Evaldus Gallus' *Pueriles Confabulatiunculae*, which Gillespie suggests was probably in translation by Leonhard Culmann and was used to teach Latin to those too young for longer colloquies. Horn books were a leaf of paper containing the alphabet (often with the addition of the 10 digits, some elements of spelling, and the Lord's Prayer) protected by a thin plate of translucent horn, and mounted on a tablet of wood with a projecting piece for a handle. For a detailed examination of the book trade see: R. Gillespie, 'The book trade in southern Ireland, 1590–1640'

### III. Legwear

The growth of the English stocking-knitting industry is first traceable in the 1560s.[63] Before the availability and fashion for knitted stockings, fabric hose was worn by both men and women in England. Hose comprised two sections: the upper and nether. The upper hose, or breeches, were worn to the knee and the nether hose or stockings covered the lower portion of the leg and were gartered either over or underneath the breeches.[64]

The better-off Irish townspeople seem to have worn similar styles. As expected, those associated with administration, even outside the Pale, wore very luxurious versions. Nicholas Pett, the provost marshal of Munster, in his will dated 1572, bequeathed to his brother a violet cloak laid with gold lace, a pair of breeches of the same colour, laid with gold lace, and a pair of 'shamois' hose, laid with black lace. Chamois was a soft leather made from a capriform antelope – an antelope that lived in the mountain ranges of Europe and Asia. To his godson, waiting on Sir Henry Sidney, Pett left a blue velvet doublet, laid with gold lace, and 'breeches suitable to the same'.[65]

Hose seem to have been commonly worn by Cork citizens also. James Fitzandrew Brown, in 1582, bequeathed 'his best pair of hose' to his cousin, John Gold, along with a clock and his 'best ring of gold', and another pair of hose to George Gold Fitzedmond. Likewise, Nicholas Faggan, a Cork merchant, in 1578 bequeathed two pairs of hose, one of which was valued at the substantial sum of 18s.[66] Henry Verdon bequeathed a 'white hosen briche' to his cousin and another pair of hose to Richard Mathowe.[67] Hose begin to appear in the customs accounts from 1550, and occur in small quantities until the end of the century. The fact that large quantities of garters were also imported in 1575, and the raw materials to make garters thereafter, suggests that the use of hose or similar legwear was much more widespread than the accounts reveal. Garters were often made of costly materials, and they could be highly decorated with embroidery or fringe or made of ribbon. Because they were so small, they were one means by which the less affluent could make a statement of wealth without actually having to spend too much money.[68]

As with other types of apparel, legwear fashions evolved significantly over the course of the century. Padded doublets became very fashionable and trunk hose,

in Gerard Long (ed.), *Books Beyond the Pale: Aspects of the Provincial Book Trade in Ireland Before 1850* (Dublin, 1996).

[63] Thirsk, *Economic Policy*, p. 45.

[64] Vincent, *Dressing*, pp. 16–17.

[65] Cork City and County Archives, Caulfield Will Transcripts, U226, p. 6.

[66] Ibid., p. 33.

[67] Ibid., p. 36.

[68] Melanie Schuessler's research page is available from: http://www.faucet.net/costume/research/hose.html. [accessed 5 January 2014].

'to bear out their fullness', were 'padded and stuffed to glorious proportions'.[69] Also fashionable was the codpiece, which was originally a flap in the hose that improved its fit and was 'the equivalent of the modern fly'.[70] This underwent an 'exaggeration of form' in the later sixteenth century, however, as the fashion for doublets became shorter and the codpiece became padded to emphasise the male genitals.[71] Vincent notes that the 'sexual significance' of the codpiece, while undeniable, should not be overstated. Certainly it became an item of humour and derision. François Rabelais, for example, refers to a book titled *On the Dignity of the Codpiece* in the Foreword to his book *The Histories of Gargantua and Pantagruel*, while Michel de Montaigne called the codpiece a 'laughter-moving, the maids looke-drawing peece'.[72]

Dunlevy suggested that this style was worn by some of the 'Old English' and the Irish, noting that 'legs displayed in trunk-hose or breeches and hose sometimes required the extra shaping which bombast could provide while a fashionable emphasis on the codpiece continued for the confident male throughout much of the century'.[73] There does not appear to be any pictorial evidence to prove this theory, although it seems that apprentices in Dublin were indeed following the trend in 1573, when regulations were introduced to forbid them from wearing bombast in either the breeches or upper stocks.[74] Bombast was a cotton wool used as padding or stuffing for clothes. Philip Stubbes noted that one doublet might be filled with 'foure, five or six pound of bombas at least'.[75] It does not occur as an import from Bristol in any of the years examined except 1594/5, when 82lb of bombast was imported by Limerick and Cork merchants. It may be that in the south-east other materials were used to pad hose, such as wool or hair, or it may also be that this fashion was not embraced much outside the Pale. The relatively small amount imported in 1594/5 may well have been for the 'New English' elite who arrived with the Munster plantation and who continued to follow English fashions.

Joan Thirsk has noted that the first English-produced knitted stockings to be exported abroad went to Ireland from Chester in the later 1570s, based on evidence from an account from 1577.[76] The stocking industry was of very great economic importance in England from the end of the sixteenth century and developed as a result of improved knitting techniques, connected to the development of finer wools, under the influence of continental fashions.[77] As early as the 1590s it was an

[69] Vincent, *Dressing*, p. 30.

[70] Ibid., p. 31.

[71] Ibid.

[72] J. I. M. Stewart (ed.) *Montaignes Essays: John Florio's Translation* (London, 1931), ii, p. 254; *The Works of Rabelais*, trans. Sir Thomas Urquhart (London, 1933), i, 8, pp. 29–30, cited in Vincent, *Dressing*, p. 32.

[73] Dunlevy, *Dress*, p. 45.

[74] Ibid.

[75] P. Stubbes, *The Anatomie of Abuses* (London, 1583; repr. Amsterdam, 1972), sig. E2 v, cited in Vincent, *Dressing*, p. 30.

[76] Thirsk, *Economic Policy*, p. 125.

[77] Ibid., p. 45.

Table 4.8 Volume of legwear imported (piece)

| | 1550/1 | 1563/4 | 1575/6 | 1594/5 | 1600/1 |
|---|---|---|---|---|---|
| buskins | 80 | - | - | - | - |
| garters, check | - | - | 96 | - | - |
| garters, crewel | - | - | 1,260 | - | - |
| garters, coloured | - | - | 72 | - | - |
| garters, coarse | - | - | - | 12 | 12 |
| garters, broad | - | - | - | 6 | - |
| garters, ribbon | - | - | 288 | - | - |
| garters, Manchester | - | | - | - | 12 |
| hose, men's | 21 | - | 149 | - | 6 |
| hose, short | - | - | - | - | 10 |
| hose, short children | - | - | - | - | 8 |
| hose, women's | 12 | 36 | 153 | 12 | - |
| hose, woollen | - | - | - | - | 6 |
| hose, worsted | - | - | - | - | 22 |
| stockings | - | - | - | 12 | - |
| stockings, coarse (pairs) | - | - | 30 | - | - |
| stockings, short | - | - | - | 210 | 18 |
| stockings, short knit | - | - | - | 12 | - |
| stockings, short women's | - | - | - | 6 | - |
| stockings, short woollen | - | - | - | 36 | 4 |
| stockings, short worsted | - | - | - | 16 | - |
| stockings, woollen | - | - | - | 72 | 30 |
| stockings, worsted | - | - | - | 18 | - |
| stockings, cloth | - | - | - | - | 12 |
| stockings, kersey | - | - | - | - | 12 |

'immense' industry, employing both men and women. Jersey, worsted and woollen stockings were being exported from London to France, Holland and Germany in consignments of 600 and 750 pairs at a time.[78]

The first instance of Irish importation of knitted stockings found in the Bristol accounts examined occurred in 1576 (see Table 4.8 for a detailed breakdown of legwear imports). These 'coarse' stockings were imported by a merchant from Drogheda rather than from the south-east of the country. It is certainly likely, however, that despite the lack of imports on this route, stockings were indeed entering the

[78] Ibid., p. 44.

south-east region at this time, although probably in very small numbers. While a number of Cork wills and inventories examined contain references to hose, as noted above, only one recorded knitted stockings – that of Richard Tyrry Fitzandrew, which lists three pairs of 'Jarnesey stockings', valued at 6s per pair, among what appears to be a shop inventory.[79]

Knitted stockings became a more frequent import later in the century. In 1591/2, 220 pairs were exported to Ireland by Roger Vancolege, a merchant stranger, on a ship registered in Amsterdam.[80] In 1594/5, 382 pairs of various types were imported. This nonetheless seems to be a relatively small number, given that Thirsk noted that 'the demand for English stockings built up on the Continent of Europe, revealing itself conspicuously in the port books by the 1590s'.[81] The volume of imported stockings in fact dropped again in 1600/1 to just 76 pairs. It is also notable, however, that despite Thirsk's point that by the beginning of the seventeenth century stockings were being manufactured in Wales, Gloucestershire, Cornwall and Devon, not a single pair of stockings was exported from Bristol or from any of the smaller Bristol Channel ports to any continental port in 1594/5 or 1600/1. The export industry in the south-west of England was perhaps not that well developed by the turn of the century and any demand in Ireland was most likely met by supplies from another route in Anglo-Irish trade or by continental imports.

Archaeological evidence sheds some light on the distribution of knitted stockings but without chronological specificity. A knitted wool stocking dating from the late sixteenth or early seventeenth century was found in a bog in Derrindafferg in County Mayo, so clearly stockings were infiltrating the country by this time. Also, in Waterford, excavations have revealed fragments of good-quality knitting, which, based on the shape, appear to be part of a stocking leg, probably made of linen, which may have been either from hand or frame knitting, dating to the late sixteenth or early seventeenth century.[82] This again suggests that new fashions stimulated a certain level of domestic production and that the Irish were importing new knitting techniques as well as the stockings themselves.

Thirsk has noted that woollen stockings were 'clearly not rich men's wares, but the clothing of the common people' and that 'the market was lodged mainly at the lower end of the social scale'.[83] The seemingly low level of interest in this commodity suggested by the Bristol accounts may be real in this case. Spenser observed in his *View of the Present State of Ireland* that 'men's apparel is commonly made according to their conditions, and their conditions are oftentimes governed by their garments'.[84] It seems that in this regard the less well-off Irish favoured a traditional type of legwear known as 'trews', a style of clothing of 'great antiquity', predating hose and

[79] Cork City and County Archives, Caulfield Will Transcripts, U226, p. 21.
[80] TNA, E190/1131/8 f16v.
[81] Thirsk, *Economic Policy*, p. 126.
[82] Heckett, 'Town and country' p. 460.
[83] Thirsk, *Economic Policy*, p. 127.
[84] Spenser, 'View', in Myers (ed.), *Elizabethan Ireland*, p. 99.

probably dating from 'pre-Gaelic days', the shorter version of which, McClintock suggests, were 'probably frequently worn to the last for economy and for greater freedom running etc.'.[85] Certainly, according to Barnabe Rich, 'the uncivil sort so disfigure themselves with their glibs, their *trowse* and their misshapen attire'.[86]

A suit of clothing found in a bog in Kilcommon, County Tipperary included a pair of trews, which were reinforced on the seat, inner legs, knees and fork, suggesting that the owner rode a horse. These trews were made in the traditional manner: a 'single piece of fabric was wound around the body, joined in a seam down one side and shaped to the waist'.[87] They were tailored to a very high quality and the fabric was 'cut on the bias' in order to give greater flexibility in the legs.[88] The longevity of this style is suggested by Gernon, who as late as 1620 noted that the 'churl' wore 'trowse' which:

> is along stocke of frise, close to his thighes, and drawne on almost to his waste, but very scant, and the pryde of it is, to weare it so in suspence, that the beholder may still suspecte it to be falling from his arse. It is cutt with a pouche before, which is drawne together with a string. He that will be counted a spruce ladd, tyes it up with a twisted band of two colours like the string of a clokebagge.[89]

It is likely, then, that for economic as well as practical reasons the lower-class Irish continued to wear tried and trusted traditional forms of legwear and that the demand for stockings increased slowly. In 1620 Gernon noted that the Irish in Thomond only 'beginne to weare knitt stockins coloured, but they have not disdayned to weare stockins of raw whyte frise, and broges'.[90]

This is significant as it contradicts the claims of Quentin Bell, who, when discussing the 'theories of fashion' noted that trade and the availability of new fashions stimulates change, even if the new items are far less suited to the climatic and other practical needs of consumers. He noted, for example, the evolution of the clothing of Eskimos, who had 'evolved a type of clothing which is severely practical and highly efficient'.[91] The clothes brought in by traders have been adopted although much less suited to the needs of the Arctic than traditional dress: 'shivering and disconsolate, but happy to think that they are chilly with the best people, the Eskimos are losing their old dressmaking skills and accepting the inadequate weeds of the foreigner'.[92] From the Irish evidence, it would appear that this is not always the case, or at least that the process sometimes takes a considerable amount of time.

Aside from continuing to wear seemingly archaic forms of legwear, because they were more practical to Irish conditions, it may be that the Irish also persisted in the

[85] McClintock, *Old Irish Dress*, p. 85.
[86] Rich, *A New Description of Ireland* (1610), p. 15.
[87] Dunlevy, *Dress*, p. 57.
[88] Ibid., p. 58.
[89] Gernon, *Discourse*, p. 359.
[90] Ibid.
[91] Q. Bell, *On Human Finery* (London, 1976), p. 95.
[92] Ibid., p. 97.

Plate 9 Detail from the *Effigy of Piers Butler* at St Canice's Cathedral, Kilkenny, c.1538.

use of 'old-fashioned' armour. The suit of armour worn by Piers Butler on his effigy at St Canice's Cathedral in Kilkenny (Plate 9), for example, is typical of the style worn at least 150 years earlier. John Hunt, in discussing medieval Irish armour has suggested that these individual pieces survived in Ireland because, although not the current fashion, they were better suited to the nature of military conflict in Ireland and were worn because more effective.[93] This is certainly possible, but it is very risky to assume that a tomb effigy reflects actual contemporary fashion. Evidence rarely exists regarding the commissioning of tombs or monuments and there are many reasons why a patron might be depicted in archaic armour: conscious conservatism; a desire to visually reference medieval constructs of the knight and chivalric ideals; an effort to show the continuity of ancestry. Likewise, an apparently archaic style or design may simply reflect the fact that metropolitan work and the skilled artisans that created it travelled slowly to outlying places and that trends in provincial sculpture were slow to evolve. Effigies were also sometimes pre-commissioned and occasionally made many years after death and historicised.[94] Taking all this into account, however, there is other evidence to support the idea that Irish armour, even by the late sixteenth century, was very different to that worn by the English. An entry in the annals in 1596 notes: 'some say that no army like this had for a long time before been mustered in that part of Ireland possessed by the Sovereign *of England*, in the numbers of the muster, the exotic and strange character of their equipment and appearance'.[95]

[93]Heckett, 'Tomb effigies', p. 71; J. Hunt, *Irish Medieval Figure Sculpture 1200–1600* (Dublin and London, 1974), pp. 61–7.

[94]Very kind thanks to Dr Christine Faunch for her comments on archaic styles in effigies.

[95]AFM, 1596.

# 5

# *Wearing, Making and Embellishing*

## I. Clothing in context

Notably absent amongst Irish imports are ready-made outerwear garments such as gowns, doublets, cloaks and breeches. Throughout the accounts examined, there are in fact only four occurrences of such items; in 1550, John Fleatt imported 100 petticoats; in 1575, a Kilkenny merchant, Martin Archer, imported 4 leather jerkins, and in the same year, George Purkell, a London merchant, imported 12 sack cloth and 12 canvas doublets.[1] It may be the case that these imported items were banned in this region, as they had been in Dublin in 1555 when the tailors, shoemakers and other tradesmen in the city felt so threatened by foreign imports that they banned the importation of ready-made hose, doublets, trews, jerkins, boots and shoes.[2] As yet, there is no evidence to suggest this, however. The near absence of such items may indicate a fundamental difference in tastes between Irish and English consumers, and a preference for domestically produced apparel, but it must of course be noted that very little clothing was sold 'off the peg' in any country in the sixteenth century, with most households purchasing cloth and either making up clothing themselves or getting a tailor to do so.

Analysis of costumes recovered from bogs shows that there were at least three different gown styles worn in sixteenth-century Ireland. These have been considered in detail by Dunlevy, who noted distinct differences between English and Irish styles and argued that Irish fashion as a separate and distinctive entity continued to evolve in the sixteenth century; the Irish incorporated and adapted selected aspects of foreign styles into their costume as the century progressed.[3] A particular style of gown worn by Irish women had 'a distinctively Irish strip of fabric which covers the top of the arm from each shoulder and which is anchored at the waist with a cuff or tie band'.[4] These, visible on the picture by de Heere (Plate 8), were described by Spenser as 'hanging' sleeves and appear to be unique to Irish dress.[5] Also notable is a gown found in a bog in County Tipperary, which shows similarities to the Spanish

[1] TNA, E122/22/4 f20r; TNA, E190/1129/12 f10r., f19r.

[2] J. T. Gilbert, *Calendar of Ancient Records of Dublin*, i, p. 450.

[3] Dunlevy, *Dress*, p. 47.

[4] Ibid., p. 48.

[5] Spenser, 'View', in Myers (ed.), *Elizabethan Ireland*, p. 90.

*Ropa* or to the Dutch *Vlieger* and indicates the awareness of continental dress changes in Ireland.[6] Furthermore, while there appears to have been some similarities between the 'figure-hugging' styles used in both England and Ireland in the earlier part of the century, Irish women continued to favour v-shaped rather than the English square neck-line style.[7] These findings again contradict those of Quentin Bell, who, when discussing the impact of trade and foreign influences on the development of fashion, wrote that 'wherever a more sumptuous style is encountered it tends to be imitated'.[8] Rather, it appears that, to a large extent, outside fashions were followed discriminately and interpreted independently, and this is perhaps one of the reasons why they were produced at home rather than imported from England.

The merging of certain aspects of foreign and native fashion is a feature in the development of dress of colonial societies. Commenting on an illustration by Agostino Brunias (c.1775–79) from the British Caribbean, Buckridge suggested that it may reflect what occurred in Jamaica and he identified the merging of African and European dress styles. In the image, mulatto women wear long skirts, popular amongst British women, but most of the outfits are accessorised with the retained African-style headwrap. This hybrid fashion also evolved in Ireland. Genett Creagh, for example, whose last will was proved in 1582, bequeathed to both her daughters a combination of Irish- and English-styled clothing. Catherine received her best head roll or 'breyd' and her English broad cloth coat, while Ellyn received her 'other roll and her pinked coat 'with new sleeves'. Genett was clearly up to date with the latest styles, having modified her coat to keep up with the latest sartorial fashions.[9] Yet she chose to retain her Irish head roll, and to bequeath her eclectic wardrobe to her daughters.

While people might own both English and traditional Irish dress styles, it is clear that they sometimes chose to wear one style specifically, depending on the image they wished to portray. Dunlevy suggested that outside the Pale 'where people fought to retain their family lands' it is possible that few, 'even of the wealthy wished to encumber themselves with foreign fashions which signified defeat in the eyes of their neighbours'.[10] She wondered whether noblemen, outside the Pale, followed the sorts of styles displayed by those involved in the Dublin administration.[11] Inventory evidence suggests that, in Cork, members of the merchant class wore clothing just as opulent in material as that worn by the lord deputy, Sir Henry Sidney, in Dublin, and that Sidney was indeed 'considered something of a dandy at court'.[12] An inventory of the goods of Nicholas Faggan, a Cork merchant, taken in

[6] Dunlevy, *Dress*, p. 48.
[7] Ibid., p. 50.
[8] Bell, *Human Finery*, p. 96.
[9] R. Caulfield (ed.), 'Wills and inventories, Cork, temp, Elizabeth', in *Gentemen's Magazine* (July, 1861), p. 35.
[10] Dunlevy, *Dress*, p. 44.
[11] Ibid.
[12] Thirsk, *Economic Policy*, p.120.

1578, records exactly those items that Dunlevy suggested would have been worn by a male conforming to English standards, including a black satin doublet and a red taffeta doublet, along with men's hose. The inventory also contains a very luxurious black pinked gown faced with budge, valued at £4, another pinked gown faced with damask, valued at £2 13s 4d, and a black gown valued at 30s.[13] Pinking (slashing) refers to the cutting of the outside layer of the fabric of a garment in order to display the contrasting lining underneath. It was very fashionable in the sixteenth century and was a technique reserved for high-quality cloth. A bill for fur for the lord deputy in 1572 lists items made of similar fabrics, including damask and fur.[14] The last will of Henry Verdon, another Cork citizen, also records English-style clothing including cassocks, gowns, a velvet cap, a 'pinked' coat, white hose and leather jerkins.[15]

Other citizens possessed both English- and Irish-style clothes and presumably wore both types for different reasons and at different times. The earl of Desmond, Garrett Fitzgerald, was apparently wearing English clothes when detained in London between 1567 and 1573. After escaping and returning to his lands in Munster, he and his wife called a hosting of their retainers and clansmen at Lough Gur, County Limerick. The earl 'put on Irish rayment and made proclamation that no deputie nor constable nor sherrife should practice their office in his countreye'.[16] Heckett suggested from this that clothes could be an 'investiture that validated the person' and that the earl was 'claiming back his palatinate rights while wearing the clothes that incorporated his authority'.[17]

Less illustrious citizens also owned both styles of clothing. In the last will of Ellyne Ny Connyly, dated 1581, she bequeathed a coat and smock and also a new white Irish mantle.[18] Likewise, the effigy of Johanna Purcell in St John's Augustinian Priory, Kilkenny, uses a mixture of Irish and English styles. Johanna is depicted wearing an Irish gown but with a characteristically English neck covering, or barbe, to denote widowhood.[19] It appears that a clear distinction continued to exist in Ireland between different styles of dress. Dunlevy noted that in Kilkenny, in the 1560s, tailors still distinguished between clothes made in the 'Irish' style and those made in the 'English' style.[20]

While it is clear that wealthy Anglo-Irish citizens in the south-east of the country were just as easily able to access and acquire the latest English and European fashions when they chose to do so, it is difficult to establish the extent to which

[13] Cork City and County Archives, Caulfield Will Transcripts, U226, p. 33.

[14] *Report on the Manuscripts of Lord de L'Isle and Dudley Preserved at Penhurst Place*, Vol. 1. Historical Manuscripts Commission, HMSO, (1925), pp. 263–4, reprinted in Dunlevy, *Dress*, p. 44.

[15] Cork City and County Archives, Caulfield Will Transcripts, U226, p. 35.

[16] S.P., 63/43/6 i, Justice Walsh to Lord Deputie, 24 November 1573, cited in A. Chambers, *Eleanor Countess of Desmond* (Dublin, 1979), p. 89.

[17] Heckett, 'Tomb effigies', p. 70.

[18] Cork City and County Archives, Caulfield Will Transcripts, U226, p. 15.

[19] Dunlevy, *Dress*, p. 52.

[20] Ibid., p. 59.

the changing fashions indicated by the customs accounts were embraced by the less affluent citizens in Ireland. Clearly, even for the 'New English' settlers, keeping up with English fashions was not always possible, due to economic constraints. In 1593, it was noted that the 'Munster undertakers grow daily poorer for Irish rents will not maintain English diet and apparel'.[21] This further suggests, of course, that English 'apparel' was more expensive than Irish, which may be a reason why many of the 'Old English' chose to wear native rather than English styles.

It is likely, however, that some of these new consumer goods were accessed by the lower classes of Anglo-Irish society. As already noted, the diversification of goods in the accounts shows a growing variety of less expensive versions of many imports, such as halfpenny combs, girdles, looking glasses and lace, along with 'coarse' hats and gloves, which were probably purchased by less affluent citizens. Qualitative evidence also indicates that new fashions were permeating the lower social classes. An entry in *The Great Parchment Book of Waterford* in 1599, for example, shows that even servants were wearing imported luxury cloth, to the alleged detriment of the local economy:

> How greatly the city is impoverished and dayly like to decay that not onely the ablest and wealthiest persons do weare in their attire no part or parcel of any thinge wrought within this Citie or Realme, but also their man servants and nurses in like manner do wear [?] … it is enacted … that from henceforth (10th October 1599) no nurse man servant or maydservannt shall weare in their attire or garment any furr frandge, lace, silcke or any woollen or lynnen, save such as shalbe wrought within this citie or Balive upon payne of forfeiture of all such garments, and their boddyes to be imprisoned, there to remayne until they pay six shillings eight pence as a fine towards the reparacion of the walls of this Citie as often as they or any of them shall offend in that case.[22]

Similarly, in Dublin in 1573 it was found necessary to introduce regulations to forbid the less wealthy from dressing above their status and means. The apprentices of Dublin were limited to a coat of cloth, decently made without cutting, or silk; a doublet of the same material; a shirt of Irish cloth with a decent band or plain falling collar; a ruff 1yd long and hose of no more than 2yd of fabric.[23]

Testamentary evidence shows how luxury clothing and new fashions might be acquired by less affluent citizens. Nicholas Pett, the provost marshal of Munster, who made his last will in 1572, bequeathed to his maid Anastas two cows and a calf, two goats, four sheep and £4 sterling along with 'a black pinke coat clothe, now in her custodie'.[24] An idea of the value of such an item is suggested by the last will of Henry Verdon, another Cork citizen, who in 1579 left a 'pinked cott' to Sir John Carbalhy, a much-higher-status recipient.[25] Elizabeth Wilson has also noted

[21] C.S.P. Ire., 1592–1596, p. 145.
[22] GPB, pp. 189-90.
[23] Dunlevy, *Dress*, p. 45.
[24] Cork City and County Archives, Caulfield Will Transcripts, U226, p. 5.
[25] Ibid., p. 36.

that domestic servants in England, particularly female upper servants, 'followed the fashions' although in less luxurious materials than their employers. She noted that domestic retainers might be given 'cast-off' fashionable garments, still in good condition, by their employers, and 'thus it was that they were able to parade the city streets in finery that appalled the moralists of the day'.[26]

As already noted, contemporary propaganda regularly lamented what the 'New English' saw as the degeneracy and 'Gaelicisation' of the Anglo-Irish, which was interpreted and feared as a sign of independence and disloyalty to the Crown. Little, then or now, has been written about the reverse side of the coin – the impact of English influences on Gaelic culture and tastes. Cultural exchange, however, could be a two-way process of acculturation, yet the extent to which the native population were involved in the changing clothing fashions noted here is very uncertain.

T. H. Breen, when considering consumer behaviour in eighteenth-century America, observed that even Native Americans were caught up in 'a sudden swirl of fashion'. According to Dr Alexander Hamilton, a Scottish physician travelling in America, the Mohawk sachems in Boston 'had all laced hats, and some of them laced matchcoats and ruffled shirts' and that they appeared 'à la mode Francois'.[27] This was perhaps the case, but care needs to be taken not to oversimplify native responses to imported colonial fashions, and it is very instructive to compare Breen's comments with the work of Kupperman and Buckridge, both of whom acknowledge the complexity of the use and significance of dress in colonised societies.

Certainly in early America, both natives and English were aware of the potentially transformative and 'role-enforcing power' of clothes.[28] Extravagant gifts of clothing were made to Indian chiefs, in the hope that by transforming their appearance their identity too would become English, civil and Christian.[29] Kupperman notes, for example, that when the Chickahominies became allies of the English, both sides 'honoured the power of self-definition through clothing'.[30] The elders donned red coats adorned with copper engravings of King James, which signified their change of identity. On the other hand, more reluctant chiefs were less willing to accept the clothes of the English. Powhatan, for example, was very reluctant to put on the scarlet cloak and clothing sent to him by the English until his adviser Namontacke, who had been to England, persuaded him that 'they would doe him no hurt'.[31]

Clothes were also used as a ruse to encourage Irish chieftains to conform to English modes and manners, acceptance of gifts taken to accept acknowledgement of English rule in Ireland. Turlough Luineach O' Neill refused a taffeta hat with a band set with bugle beads in 1568, while in 1578, when negotiations were under way to create him earl of Clonconnel, his wife was happy to accept one of Queen Elizabeth

[26] Wilson, *Adorned*, p. 23.
[27] Breen, 'Meanings of things' p. 252.
[28] Kupperman, *Indians and English*, p. 71.
[29] Ibid.
[30] Ibid, p. 72.
[31] Ibid.

I's gowns.[32] Similarly, another of the queen's gowns, made of cloth-of-gold, was given to the countess of Desmond. When the lord deputy discovered that the fronts of the two gowns were 'slobbered', he ordered new foreparts from London. Dunlevy remarked that 'more reliable donees may have been pleased to receive food stains with their finery'.[33]

There is certainly good evidence that the Gaelic elite wore English apparel when they felt it to be appropriate. Manus O'Donnell, when he met St Leger in 1541, wore a coat of crimson velvet with ties that had gold and silver tags, a great double cloak of crimson satin trimmed with black velvet, and a bonnet with a feather and gold aiglets or ties.[34] Evidence in the State Papers suggests, however, that there was sometimes an element of coercion behind such displays of English finery. In 1588, in 'a brief declaration of part of the services done to your Majesty by Sir John Perrot, knight, during the time of his deputation in the realm of Ireland', Perrot claimed that he had 'caused Feagh M'Hugh O'Byrne to come divers times in English apparel to me to Dublin without protection'.[35] The wearing of English clothes, however, did not indicate genuine or lasting transformation of identity or allegiance. Gernon noted Irish ambivalence, claiming that:

> Because they are commmanded at publicke assemblyes to come in English habit, they have a tricke agaynst those times, to take off the fringe, and to putt on a cape, and after the assembly past, they resume it agayne. If you aske an Irishman for his cloke, he will tell you it is in his pocket and show you his cape.[36]

Interestingly, this was also a feature of the native Indian response to the imposition of English attire. According to Williams, the Narragansetts also adopted a flexible approach to clothing. He noted that: 'While they are amongst the Englishe, they keep on the Englishe apparel but pull off all as soone as they come againe into their owne houses and company.'[37]

Gaelic sources, such as the *Annals of the Four Masters*, cast a little light on the clothes worn by the native Irish, but generally record evidence of Gaelic material culture only incidentally, when the use of an item relates to an extraordinary event, such as the loss of two toes by Hugh O'Donnell owing to the inadequacy of his shoes during his second escape from prison – his shoes having caused him problems during his first escape also.[38] The annals do suggest, however, that even at the end of the century there still existed in Ireland two distinctive material cultures. In 1596 it was recorded that 'some say that no army like this had for a long time before

[32] Dunlevy, *Dress*, p. 45.
[33] Ibid.
[34] C.S.P. Henry VIII, iii, iii, 1538–46 (1834), p. 320.
[35] C.S.P. Ire.,1588–1592, p. 83.
[36] Gernon, *Discourse*, p. 356.
[37] R. Williams, *A Key into the Language of America* (London, 1643), p. 113.
[38] AFM, 1592.

been mustered in that part of Ireland possessed by the Sovereign *of England*, in the numbers of the muster, the exotic and strange character of their equipment and appearance'.[39]

Perhaps one of the most telling pieces of evidence of Gaelic Irish attitudes to English-style clothing is a Bardic poem by Laoiseach Mac an Bhaird, dating probably to the sixteenth century. The poem was apparently intended as a reproach to someone who has adopted the dress and manners of a Tudor courtier and he is contrasted with Eóghan Bán, a native rebel, who has remained faithful to Gaelic customs:

> O man who follow English ways, who cut your thick-clustering hair, graceful hand of my choice, you are not Donnchadh's good son!
> If you were, you would not give up your hair for an artificial English mode – the fairest ornament of Fódla! –
> And your head would not be tonsured.
> You think the yellow head of hair unfashionable, he detests both locks and going bald after the English style; your characters are different indeed.
> A man who never loved English ways is Eóghan Bán, beloved of noble ladies. To English ways he never gave his heart: a savage life he chose.
> Your mind is nothing to Eóghan Bán, a man who would give breeches for a trifle, who asked no cloak but a rag, who had no wish for coat or legging.
> He would hate to carry at his ankle a jewelled spur on a boot, or stockings in the English style; he will have no locks upon him…
> Little he cares for a mantle gold-embroidered, or a high ornamental collar, or a gold ring that would only be irksome, or a satin scarf down to the heels…
> How unlike are you to Eóghan Bán – they laugh at your foot on the stepping stone. Pity that you have not seen your fault,
> O man who follow English ways.[40]

The poem is significant for a number of reasons. The writer is careful to point out the masculinity of Eóghan Bán, who is 'beloved by noble ladies' despite, or because of, the fact that he does not follow English styles. English fashion here is viewed as restrictive and impeding freedom. Jewellery, for example, is merely 'irksome' while the writer seems preoccupied with items that potentially impede movement: a satin scarf down to the heels, locks, a jewelled spur and stockings. The tone of the poem is condescending and gives a distinct sense of the writer's belief in the superiority of the rugged and 'savage' Irish appearance over the effeminate English style.

Despite such evidence, however, other sources suggest that by 1620, at least, many of the Irish were following English fashions. Gernon noted that the 'better sort' of Gaelic Irish were 'apparelled at all poynts like the English onely they retayne theyr mantle which is a garment not indecent' and of the women that: 'In the country even among theyr Irish habitts they have sundry fashions.'[41] Of course, Gernon was

[39] AFM, 1596.

[40] Poem by Laoiseach Mac an Bhaird. tr. by Osborn Bergin, in C. Maxwell, *Irish History from Contemporary Sources 1509-1610* (Dublin, 1923), p. 351.

[41] Gernon, *Discourse*, p. 358.

writing after 20 years of relative peace in Ireland, and Gaelic clothing presumably varied considerably depending on geographical location, wealth, political allegiance and the fluctuating stability of Anglo-Irish relations. A Spanish captain wrecked in one of the ships of the Armada, wrote in 1588 that the women he encountered in the mountains of Sligo and Donegal were 'very beautiful, but badly dressed. They do not wear more than a chemise, and a blanket, with which they cover themselves, and a linen cloth, much doubled, over the head, and tied in front.'[42]

It is likely, overall, that new fashions were mainly embraced by Anglo-Irish townspeople. In Ireland, as elsewhere, towns played a major role in the spread of fashions. According to Richardson:

> Towns provide a unique context for clothing because the density of daily living within them brings individuals from all social groups into close proximity with one another. Visual familiarity with other people's often vastly different dress compels citizens to make sense of their own clothing choices in relation to a comprehensive range of possible cloths and cuts. This is not about full economic participation in the markets of opportunity so much as the precise ability to place each choice on an all embracing scale.[43]

Other historians have observed a 'provincial fashionability' in England that rivalled London in terms of both trends and prices. Thirsk, for example, quoted a draper's inventory from 1578, from Kirkby Lonsdale, Westmorland, which stocked an outstanding array of luxury clothing items despite its distance from the metropolis.[44] Likewise, Breward has noted the research of Alice Friedman on the lifestyle of the Willoughby family, Northamptonshire magnates, which he suggests shows by its luxurious nature that 'the divergence of old country and new town attitudes' was 'not so explicit' in sixteenth-century England.[45]

The situation was, of course, very different in less urbanised parts of Ireland and particularly in places close to Gaelic frontiers, where conditions were very unsettled during this period. While it is likely that Anglo-Irish gentry living in rural parts of the country would have had access to luxury clothing, it is unlikely that this was widespread. In 1589, for example, Sir Edward Denny wrote to Walsingham:

> Now is the best time to plant Kerry with English, and to reduce it to civility, while the people are under hand … Sir William Herbert hath used matters' in Kerry for his glory's sake. He hath given it out in England that all here go in English apparel, but untrue for the most part, and those that are as he terms them in English apparel are 'most' thus clad, as for example I send you a cloak; for the rest of their garments they be all Irish, or the men naked with only such a cloak.[46]

[42] *Account of the Irish* (1589), tr. R. Crawford in H. Allingham, *Captain Cuellers's Adventures in Connacht and Ulster*, pp. 61–2, reprinted in Maxwell, *Contemporary Sources*, p. 319.

[43] Richardson, *Clothing Culture*, p. 12.

[44] Thirsk, *Economic Policy*, p. 121.

[45] Breward, *Culture*, p. 59.

[46] C.S.P. Ire., 1588–1592, pp. 221–2.

## II. Haberdashery and *passementerie*

Regardless of what styles people chose to wear and why, it appears that most of what was worn was manufactured in Ireland, and that the raw materials for its production and embellishment evolved significantly over the course of the century. Wares used to make, embellish and decorate clothing are found very frequently among Irish imports and include a wide range of items such as needles, pins, buttons, threads, beads, fringe, ribbons and crewel. This particular area of Irish consumption clearly illustrates the growing diversification of Irish material culture in the sixteenth century and also tells us something about the domestic manufacture of clothing in Ireland.

Heckett has discussed evidence from excavations at Upper Bridge Street in Dublin, which contained deposits from what appears to be a sixteenth-century 'tailor's workshop catering to the gentry'.[47] Along with various pieces of luxury cloth, including continental velvets and silks, a significant number of which had been reused from other garments, the excavation also revealed woven cords, silk braids, bands and laces, or the types of 'ornamental trimmings or *passementerie* so loved by people at this time and used lavishly on their clothes'.[48] Table 5.1 shows that this sort of ornamentation was not unique to Dublin and the Pale, and gives a sense of the chronological pace of change regarding the demand for such items in the south-east of the country.

First, the accounts contain items that had no apparent function besides the embellishment of garments. Such trimmings began to appear and diversify in the accounts from 1574/5. These included fringe, which was an 'ornamental bordering, consisting of a narrow band to which were attached threads of silk, or cotton, etc., either loose or formed into tassels'; crewel, both of French and Spanish origin, which was a 'thin worsted yarn of two threads, used for tapestry and embroidery and for making fringes'; various types of lace, including chain lace, which, according to the *Oxford English Dictionary*, was lace made of chain-stitch and also green and black silk lace. Also found among imports in this category are bugle beads: tube-shaped glass beads, usually black, of which over 11,000 were imported in 1594/5 and 12,000 in 1600; and ribbons, made of caddis, saye, silk and check.

Along with these embellishments, more functional haberdashery items evolved to become decorative and fashionable. A small quantity of buttons first occurs amongst Irish imports in 1545 and by the end of the century there were at least 12 different varieties in use, including some made of unusual materials, such as shell. The volumes imported also increased considerably, and while the most frequently imported were the more prosaic varieties such as thread buttons, almost 11,000 glass buttons

[47] Heckett, 'Town and country', p. 457.
[48] Ibid., p. 459.

were imported in 1594. A similar trend can be noted in the importation of points, which also diversified significantly towards the end of the century.[49]

Also in this category are the functional dressmaking items such as needles, thread, pins and thimbles. A number of points may be made about these seemingly prosaic items. Most obviously, the importation of items such as pins and needles reinforces the fact that Ireland remained entirely dependent on imports for everyday manufactured goods. However, although most Irish clothing was seemingly manufactured at home rather than imported ready-made from England, the volume of pins imported remained very low. Pins, as Joan Thirsk noted, were one of life's necessities, essential to tailors, dressmakers, hat makers, and lace makers, and 'not a soul in the kingdom could dispense entirely with pins'.[50] While needles are recorded throughout the century, in seemingly small quantities, pins do not occur at all amongst Irish imports from Bristol before 1594/5.

In the *Discourse of the Commonweal* in 1549, Sir Thomas Smith named pins as one of the commodities that ought to be manufactured in England, yet as late as 1597 £40,000 worth of pins and needles was said to have been imported into England, the vast majority of these from Holland, which, for reasons discussed in detail by Thirsk, was able to produce them much more cheaply, and in some cases for half as much as their English equivalent.[51] The 'wrangling' about whether or not to restrict the import of foreign pins in England indicates the economic importance of this industry.[52] Imported pins were banned in 1563, allowed by proclamation in 1564 and by a statute of 1565, and then banned again in 1571, for the rest of Elizabeth I's reign. Despite this legislation, pins were continuously imported from Holland throughout the century.[53]

The absence of this essential commodity amongst Irish imports from Bristol before 1594/5 suggests that Irish merchants also had direct access to Dutch exports, without needing to obtain them via the English market. Given the relatively low volumes imported from England in 1594/5 and 1600/1, it is likely that they continued to favour the Dutch product even after English production increased. The pins imported from Bristol may have been 'medium-quality' pins, which, Thirsk argues, were the sort that English manufacturers were more competitive in, whereas the Dutch specialised in low-priced pins and were also far better at making pins for use

[49] These were originally the 'metal tags on thongs of leather. By the fifteenth century the metal tags were called 'aiguillettes' and the thongs 'points'. They were used on clothing by 'placing a corresponding row of eyelet holes in the garment and the garment to which it was to be attached, threading the points through the holes and tying the ends together'. A useful tailoring glossary is available from: the 'Renaissance Tailor' website: http://www.renaissancetailor.com/research_vocabulary.htm#p [accessed 9 March 2014].

[50] Thirsk, *Economic Policy*, p. 78.

[51] E. Lamond and W. Cunningham (eds), *A Discourse of the Common Weal of this Realm of England: First Printed in 1581 and Commonly Attributed to W. S.* (Cambridge, 1893), p. 16; Thirsk, *Economic Policy*, p. 78.

[52] Thirsk, *Economic Policy*, p. 81.

[53] Ibid., p. 79.

Table 5.1 Volume of dress/cloth-making haberdashery and passementerie

| | 1503 | 1516 | 1525 | 1541 | 1542 | 1545 | 1550 | 1563 | 1575 | 1594 | 1600 |
|---|---|---|---|---|---|---|---|---|---|---|---|
| beads, bugle | - | - | - | - | - | - | - | - | - | 11,144 | 12,000 |
| beads, unspecified | - | - | - | - | 3,168 | 36 | - | - | - | - | - |
| buttons, brass | - | - | - | - | - | - | - | - | 720 | - | - |
| buttons, copper | - | - | - | - | - | - | - | - | - | 1,076 | - |
| buttons, crewel & silk | - | - | - | - | - | - | - | - | - | 2,880 | - |
| buttons, glass | - | - | - | - | - | - | - | | 36 | 10,944 | 1,152 |
| buttons, hair | - | - | - | - | - | - | - | - | - | 2,808 | 1,008 |
| buttons, pewter | - | - | - | - | - | - | - | - | 144 | - | - |
| buttons, Scottish | - | - | - | - | - | - | - | - | 288 | - | - |
| buttons, shell | - | - | - | - | - | - | - | - | 144 | - | - |
| buttons, silk | - | - | - | - | - | - | - | 432 | 3,456 | 4,176 | 10,368 |
| buttons, steel | - | - | - | - | - | - | - | - | 8,640 | - | - |
| buttons, thread | - | - | - | - | - | - | - | 600 | 56,160 | 40,320 | 16,416 |
| buttons, thread and hair | - | - | - | - | - | - | - | - | 2,736 | - | - |
| buttons, tin | - | - | - | - | - | - | - | - | 288 | - | - |
| buttons, unspecified | - | - | - | - | - | 72 | 288 | - | - | 288 | 144 |
| buttons, gold | - | - | - | - | - | - | - | - | - | - | 144 |
| crewel (lb) | - | - | - | - | - | - | - | - | 4 | - | 3 |
| crewel, Cadiz | - | - | - | - | - | - | - | - | - | - | 36 |
| crewel, French (lb) | - | - | - | - | - | - | - | - | 7 | - | - |
| fringe, coarse crewel (lb) | - | - | - | - | - | - | - | - | - | - | 2 |
| fringe, crewel (lb) | - | - | - | - | - | - | - | - | 13 | 1.25 | 12 |
| fringe, unspecified (lb) | - | - | - | - | - | - | - | - | 3 | - | 3 |
| gartering (piece/lb?) | - | - | - | - | - | - | - | - | - | 468 | 1,518 |

| | | | | | | | | | | |
|---|---|---|---|---|---|---|---|---|---|---|
| gartering (roll) | - | - | - | - | - | - | - | - | - | 2 | - |
| gartering , crewel (lb) | - | - | - | - | - | - | - | - | - | 288 | - |
| gartering, caddis (lb) | - | - | - | - | - | - | 2 | - | - | - | - |
| gartering, crewel (roll) | - | - | - | - | - | - | - | - | 1 | 2 | - |
| gartering, inkle | - | - | - | - | - | - | - | - | - | - | 2 |
| gartering, Manchester (piece /lb?) | - | - | - | - | - | - | - | - | - | - | 468 |
| gartering, Norwich (piece /lb?) | - | - | - | - | - | - | - | - | - | 4,032 | 720 |
| gartering, worsted (roll) | - | - | - | - | - | - | - | - | 1 | - | - |
| girdling (lb) | - | - | - | - | - | - | - | - | 3 | - | - |
| inkle (lb) | - | - | - | - | - | - | - | - | - | - | 9 |
| inkle (piece) | - | - | - | - | - | - | - | - | - | 6 | 71 |
| inkle, coarse (lb) | - | - | - | - | - | - | - | - | - | - | 6 |
| inkle, coarse (piece) | - | - | - | - | - | - | - | - | - | - | 8 |
| inkle, coloured (lb) | - | - | - | - | - | - | - | - | - | - | 1 |
| inkle, narrow (piece) | - | - | - | - | - | - | - | - | - | - | 10 |
| inkle, white (lb) | - | - | - | - | - | - | - | - | - | - | 1 |
| knives, shoemaker | - | - | - | - | - | - | - | - | 6 | - | 12 |
| lace, 2d (lb) | - | - | - | - | - | - | - | - | 0.5 | - | - |
| lace, black silk | - | - | - | - | - | - | - | - | 2 oz | - | - |
| lace, chain (lb) | - | - | - | - | - | - | - | - | 4 oz | - | 0.5 |
| lace, cox (lb) | - | - | - | - | - | - | - | - | 2.5 | - | - |
| lace, green silk (lb) | - | - | - | - | - | - | - | - | 1 | - | - |
| lace, statute (gross) | - | - | - | - | - | - | - | - | 7 | 31.83 | 51.75 |
| needles (clout) | 1.5 | - | - | 19.5 | 7 | 39 | 6 | 4 | 41.5 | 78 | 69 |
| needles, jhus (?) | - | - | - | - | - | - | - | - | - | - | 24,620 |
| needles, Spanish | - | - | - | - | - | - | - | - | - | - | 2128 |
| needles, yellow band | - | - | - | - | - | - | - | - | - | - | 6,720 |
| pins (M) | - | - | - | - | - | - | - | - | - | 61 | 123 |

| | | | | | | | | | | | |
|---|---|---|---|---|---|---|---|---|---|---|---|
| points, bugle | - | - | - | - | - | - | - | - | - | 24 | - |
| points, copper | - | - | - | - | - | - | - | - | 48 | - | - |
| points, copper (oz) | - | - | - | - | - | - | - | - | - | - | 4 |
| points, crewel | - | - | - | - | - | - | - | - | 1.5 gross, 15lb | 1,224 | - |
| points, green (lb) | - | - | - | - | - | - | - | - | 1 | - | - |
| points, inkle | - | - | - | - | - | - | - | - | - | - | 648 |
| points, leather | - | - | - | - | - | - | - | 5328 | 1,008 | 3,420 | 864 |
| points, Paris red | - | - | - | - | - | - | - | - | 432 | - | - |
| points, red | - | - | - | - | - | - | - | 144 | 6,336 | 5,544 | - |
| points, saye | - | - | - | - | - | - | - | - | 180 | - | - |
| points, silk | - | - | - | 24 | 60 | 864 | - | - | 384 | 144 | 144 |
| points, thread | - | - | - | - | - | - | - | - | 648 | 18,576 | 13,104 |
| points, thread & leather | - | - | - | - | - | - | - | - | 6,912 | - | - |
| points, white & red | - | - | - | - | - | - | - | - | 1,440 | - | - |
| points, white leather | - | - | - | - | - | - | - | - | 576 | - | 144 |
| points, unspecified | 38,376 | 72,000 | 119,592 | 23,7456 | 174,456 | 233,136 | 165,744 | 97,632 | 49,752 | 4,608 | 144 |
| ribbon, broad 1d (lb) | - | - | - | - | - | - | - | - | - | 1.5 | - |
| ribbons, caddis | - | - | - | - | 12 | - | - | - | - | - | - |
| ribbons, check | - | - | - | - | - | - | - | - | - | - | 36 |
| ribbons, saye | - | - | - | - | - | 24 | - | - | - | - | - |
| ribbons, silk | - | - | - | - | - | - | - | - | - | 36 | - |
| ribbons, unspecified | - | - | - | 792 | 288 | - | - | - | 36 | 84 | - |
| ribbons, unspecified (yd) | - | - | - | - | 24 | | - | | - | - | - |
| scissors | - | - | - | - | - | - | - | - | 12 | - | - |
| stock-cards (pair) | 12 | 12 | - | 74 | 42 | 110 | 116 | 94 | 230 | 774 | 155 |
| teazles (M) | - | - | - | - | - | 3 | - | 34.5 | 28 | - | 3.16 |
| thimbles | 72 | - | 28 | 288 | 480 | - | - | 224? | 56 | 108 | 288 |

| | | | | | | | | | | |
|---|---|---|---|---|---|---|---|---|---|---|
| thread, unspecified (lb) | 9 | 20 | 37 | 93 | 12.5 | 80 | 12 | 25.5 | 17.5 | 21 | 1 |
| thread, unspecified (butt) | - | - | - | - | - | - | - | - | - | 2 | 8 |
| thread, black (bolt/butt) | - | - | - | - | - | - | - | - | - | 8 bolt / 18 butt | 51 butt |
| thread, black (lb) | - | - | - | - | - | - | - | - | 5 | 16 | 4 |
| thread, black and brown (lb) | - | - | - | - | - | - | - | - | - | - | 18 |
| thread, blue (lb) | - | - | - | - | - | 4 | - | | - | 1 | - |
| thread, brown (lb) | - | - | - | - | - | - | - | - | - | 24 | 66 |
| thread, coloured (lb) | - | - | - | - | - | - | - | - | - | 4 | 20 |
| thread, coventry (lb) | - | - | - | - | - | - | - | - | - | - | 3 |
| thread, coventry (lb) | - | - | - | - | - | - | - | - | - | - | 3 |
| thread, fine brown (lb) | - | - | - | - | - | - | - | - | - | - | 36 |
| thread, inkle (lb) | - | - | - | - | - | - | - | - | 3 | 1 gross / 1 qtr | - |
| thread, Outnal | - | - | - | - | - | - | - | - | - | - | 6 |
| thread, Paris (bolt) | - | - | - | - | - | - | - | - | 1 | - | - |
| thread, piecing (lb) | - | - | - | - | - | - | - | - | - | 10 | 18 |
| thread, shoemakers | - | - | - | - | - | - | - | - | - | - | 4 |
| thread, sisters (lb) | - | - | - | - | - | - | - | - | - | 0.5 | 2.5 |
| thread, unspecified (bolt) | - | - | - | 49 | 23 | 63 | 92 | 29 | 38 | - | - |
| thread, white (lb) | - | - | - | - | - | - | - | - | 1 | - | 1 |
| wool-cards | - | - | 24 | 264 | 246 | 942 | 42 | 168 | 84 | 2,376 | 1,416 |
| wool-cards, old (pair) | - | - | - | - | - | - | - | - | - | 636 | 780 |
| wool-cards, Paris | - | - | - | - | - | - | - | - | 39 | - | - |

with very fine cloth, such as lawn and cambric.[54] It is indeed likely that numerous other small wares were imported directly from the Continent. Scissors, for example, occur only in one account, that of 1575/6, and then only 12 pairs. Likewise the volume of items such as thimbles imported from Bristol was insufficient to meet domestic needs.

Despite the fact that Ireland remained dependent on imports for most everyday manufactured goods, imports within this category again suggest that increasing demand for new fashions stimulated some level of specialised domestic production. In 1600, a London girdler, Richard Birchely, exported a very large quantity of specialised needles, including yellow band and Spanish needles, along with high-quality fine threads to Ireland, indicating the manufacture, decoration or embellishment of girdles in Ireland.[55] Girdle makers certainly resided in Waterford. The *Great Parchment Book of Waterford*, in 1594, lists girdle makers, along with other makers of apparel such as shoemakers, cordwainers, lacers, fullers, cobblers and glovers among other tradesmen being incorporated into a single guild.[56] Further evidence for the production as well as the importation of girdles is the presence of 'girdling', the material used for making girdles, amongst the imports of a Wexford merchant, Gareth Sinnot, in 1576.[57] Likewise, the appearance of at least six different varieties of 'gartering', distributed throughout the south-east region in increasing quantities from 1594/5, indicates that garters were also manufactured in Ireland as well as being imported.

Also of significance in terms of Irish production is the importation of Flemish thread by a Kilkenny merchant in 1600, which might have been used for making specialist cloth or for embroidering or decorating other items, and indicates the continuing influence of Flemish style in Kilkenny, which was first introduced with the importation of cloth makers by Piers Butler, earl of Ormond, in around 1525.[58] Other evidence suggests that Irish tailors were keeping up to date with the latest European fashions and dressmaking techniques. Heckett noted amongst the surviving pieces of cloth in the Upper Bridge Street excavation, a piece of taffeta silk that was 'pinked', which was a then current fashion for slitting fabrics to produce a decorative effect.[59] Clothing made with this technique was evidently popular in Cork also. As noted above, Nicholas Pett, the provost marshal of Munster, the Cork merchant Nicholas Faggan, and the Cork citizen Henry Verdon, all owned and bequeathed coats or gowns that had been embellished with this technique.

Significant also in relation to Irish production was the importation of teazles, which began to occur around the same time as the increase in luxury cloth imports. Teazles, which were used to draw out the ends of wool to make a fine, high-quality

[54] Ibid., p. 81.
[55] TNA, E190/1132/11 f22v.
[56] GPB, p. 61.
[57] TNA, E190/1129/12.
[58] Longfield, *Anglo-Irish Trade*, p. 81.
[59] Heckett, 'Town and country', p. 458.

cloth, occur in both the 1575 and 1600 accounts and their importation was highly localised. In 1575, all teazles were imported by Drogheda merchants and in 1600 all were imported by Cork merchants. It is likely that some of this high-quality cloth was in fact for export, as the later accounts show exports of Irish fustians to Bristol, along with the usual coarser woollen products.

### III. Accessories

In Gernon's discussion of Irish women's apparel, he noted:

> They weare no bands, but the ornament of theyr neckes is a carkanett of goldsmyths worke besett with precious stones, some of them very ritch, but most of them gawdy and made of paynted glasse and at the end of them a crucifixe. They weare also braceletts, and many rings.[60]

As Table 5.2 illustrates, the customs accounts say very little about the use of jewellery in sixteenth-century Ireland. Bracelets, as were recorded in 1595, were imported by merchants from Clonmel, Waterford, Galway and Fethard-on-Sea. They are not listed in the 1582 rates book and so there is no way to identify the type of bracelet that was imported. The customs duty paid varied very significantly, however, between each of the shipments, suggesting the importation of four different varieties in that year. These were clearly not expensive items and were probably made from beads of some sort. Edward Hackett, for example, paid 2s duty for 4 dickers or 40 bracelets in 1595, giving them a nominal customs value of 10s per dicker or 1s per bracelet, and these were the most expensive sort imported that year. The 1594/5 account also records small amounts of neckbracelets, neckbands and necklaces, but again without descriptions. It is probable, however, that these necklaces were made of bugle beads, as two dozen of these occur in the 1600/1 account, paying the same duty.

Other qualitative evidence supports Gernon's description of Irish jewellery during this period. The Dutch watercolour by de Heere (Plate 8) depicts both noblewoman and townswoman wearing large ornate crucifixes around their necks. It has been suggested that men also wore crosses as an item of personal adornment, by tucking them into their belts.[61] This choice of ornamentation is particularly significant since it suggests the use of dress to 'reflect and advertise religious identity' in sixteenth-century Ireland, which may have been intended as an expression of religious and social independence.[62] While the use of crucifixes for personal adornment was not actually banned in post-Reformation England, they were not worn openly as depicted by de Heere. Protestant reformers viewed the crucifix as 'the ultimate symbol of Catholic

[60] Gernon, *Discourse*, p. 358.

[61] *Self-Representation in the Middle-Ages* Project- Department of Medieval Studies at Central European University, Budapest. Available from: http://web.ceu.hu/mtud/manual/SRM/types.htm [accessed 6 June 2009].

[62] *Clothing, Culture and Identity in Early Modern England* Project: http://www.shakespeare2.bham.ac.uk/clothing/home.html. [accessed 4 June 2009].

Table 5.2 Volume of clothing accessories imported (piece)

| | 1503 | 1516 | 1525 | 1541 | 1542 | 1545 | 1550 | 1563 | 1575 | 1594 | 1600 |
|---|---|---|---|---|---|---|---|---|---|---|---|
| belts | - | - | - | - | - | - | - | - | - | 24 | 108 |
| bracelets | - | - | - | - | - | - | - | - | - | 312 | 140 |
| buckles | - | - | - | - | - | - | - | - | 144 | - | 72 |
| buckles, boot | - | - | - | - | - | - | - | - | 144 | - | - |
| girdles, 1d | - | - | - | - | - | - | - | - | 2,604 | 2,340 | 1,080 |
| girdles, 2d | - | - | - | - | - | - | - | - | 36 | 48 | - |
| girdles, caddis | - | - | - | - | 180 | 96 | 192 | - | - | - | |
| girdles, caddis (lb) | - | - | - | - | - | - | 37 | - | - | - | - |
| girdles, check (lb) | - | - | - | - | - | - | 4 | - | - | - | - |
| girdles, crewel | - | - | - | - | - | - | - | - | - | 72 | - |
| girdles, for penners | - | - | - | 18 | - | - | - | - | - | - | - |
| girdles, leather | - | - | - | - | 12 | 48 | 168 | - | 180 | 252 | 132 |
| girdles, leather 1d | - | - | - | - | - | - | - | 1,176 | 300 | 180 | 228 |
| girdles, leather 2d | - | - | - | - | - | - | - | 396 | - | - | - |
| girdles, leather (ob.) | - | - | - | - | - | - | - | - | - | 24 | - |
| girdles, nobs silk (lb) | - | - | - | - | - | - | - | - | - | 87 | 141 |
| girdles, ob. | - | - | - | - | - | - | - | 36 | 576 | 84 | - |
| girdles, ribbon | - | - | - | - | 12 | 24 | - | 288 | 48 | - | - |
| girdles, round silk | - | - | - | - | - | - | - | - | - | - | 36 |
| (lb) | - | - | - | - | - | - | - | - | - | 4 | - |
| girdles, seal | - | - | - | - | - | - | 40 | - | - | - | - |
| girdles, silk | - | - | - | 24 | 12 | 6 | - | - | 4 lb | 24 | - |
| girdles, sword | - | - | - | - | - | - | 12 | 24 | - | - | - |
| girdles, unspecified | 48 | - | 126 | 2,244 | 936 | 2,508 | 942 | - | 276 | 972 | 108 |

| | | | | | | | | | | | |
|---|---|---|---|---|---|---|---|---|---|---|---|
| girdles, waist | - | - | - | - | - | - | - | - | 168 | 120 | 12 |
| girdles, wool | - | - | - | - | - | - | 144 | - | - | - | - |
| girdles, yellow | - | - | - | - | - | - | - | - | - | - | 24 |
| gloves, coarse (pair) | - | - | - | - | - | - | - | - | 36 | 102 | 12 |
| gloves, unspecified | - | - | - | - | - | - | - | - | - | - | 2 |
| (pair) | - | - | - | 12 | - | - | - | - | - | - | 60 |
| gloves, Venice | - | - | - | - | - | - | - | 6 | - | - | - |
| neckbands | - | - | - | - | - | - | - | - | - | 6 | - |
| neck bracelets | - | - | - | - | - | - | - | - | - | 6 | - |
| necklaces | - | - | - | - | - | - | - | - | - | 12 | - |
| necklaces, bugle | - | - | - | - | - | - | - | - | - | - | 24 |
| purses | - | - | - | 468 | 2,160 | 432 | 96 | - | - | - | - |
| purses, belt | - | - | - | - | - | 72 | - | - | - | - | - |
| purses, children's | - | - | - | - | - | - | - | - | 6 | - | - |
| purses, cord | - | - | - | - | 36 | - | - | - | - | - | - |
| purses, taffeta | - | - | - | - | - | - | - | - | - | 4 | - |
| purses, women's | - | - | - | - | - | - | - | 12 | - | - | - |
| spectacles | - | - | - | - | 252 | 1,668 | - | - | 96 | 60 | - |
| spectacles, pocket | - | - | - | - | - | 144 | - | - | - | - | - |

idolatry' but it has been suggested that in England they nonetheless 'continued to function as important anchors of private devotion' and 'served as markers of family unity, passed down from generation to generation among those who still adhered to the traditional religion'.[63]

Irish testamentary evidence shows this to have also been the case in Ireland. James Fitzandrew Brown, a Cork merchant, bequeathed to his son in 1578 his two best gold crosses and a gold ring. To his cousin John Gold Fitz Edmond he bequeathed his best gold ring, to Andrew Skyddy his second best ring. To Morris Roche, his third best ring, to Walter Fitzandrew Galwey, a 'little cross of gold' and a gold ring, to James Clowse another gold cross. Rather unsurprisingly, he seems to have been on familiar terms with the goldsmith Richard Roche, too, and bequeathed to him and his wife, Ellice Walsh, the sum of 10s. Similarly, Christopher Galway, a Cork citizen who made his last will in 1582, bequeathed to his daughter 'all the jewels within a small bladder in my smale chest and the two gold crosses in a little white bladder and my mother's bigg coife'.[64]

Gernon also described another clothing accessory worn in Ireland:

> they girde theyr gowne with a silke girdle, the tassell whereof must hang downe poynt blanke before to the fringe of theyr peticotes, but I will not descend to theyr petycotes, least you should thinke that I have bene under them.[65]

Girdles were a regular Irish import from the 1540s and the types in demand diversified significantly towards the end of the century, in terms of both variety and grade. For example, in addition to the appearance of new types of girdle – such as ribbon and nobs or embroidered silk girdles – there was also further diversification in terms of the grade of the item, with the appearance of halfpenny, penny and twopenny girdles. Girdles had utilitarian functions and were used to carry purses, daggers, keys, penners, inkhorns, seals and swords. They were also, however, a means of displaying wealth and social status, and towards the end of the century were frequently made of precious metals and could be set lavishly with jewels. The vast majority of girdles appearing as imports from Bristol appear to have been more functional than decorative in nature; leather and penny girdles occurred in the greatest numbers towards the end of the century. It is likely, however, that some of the silk and ribbon styles may have been further embellished by their owners after purchase and were worn for purely decorative purposes.

A final 'accessory' worth noting amongst Irish imports during this period was spectacles. These were first recorded in 1542/3 and, by the middle of the century, large volumes of what appear to be pocket spectacles were imported (Table 5.3; Figure 5.1).

[63] E. Williamson, 'The domestication of religious objects in The White Devil', *SEL Studies in English Literature 1500–1900*, xlvii (2007) p. 475.

[64] Cork City and County Archives, Caulfield Will Transcripts, U226, p. 25.

[65] Gernon, *Discourse*, p. 359.

Table 5.3
Volume of spectacles imported, 1503–1601 (piece)

| Year | Vol. (piece) |
|---|---|
| 1503/4 | 0 |
| 1516/17 | 0 |
| 1525/6 | 0 |
| 1541/2 | 0 |
| 1542/3 | 252 |
| 1545/6 | 1,812 |
| 1550/1 | 0 |
| 1563/4 | 0 |
| 1575/6 | 0 |
| 1594/5 | 96 |
| 1600/1 | 60 |

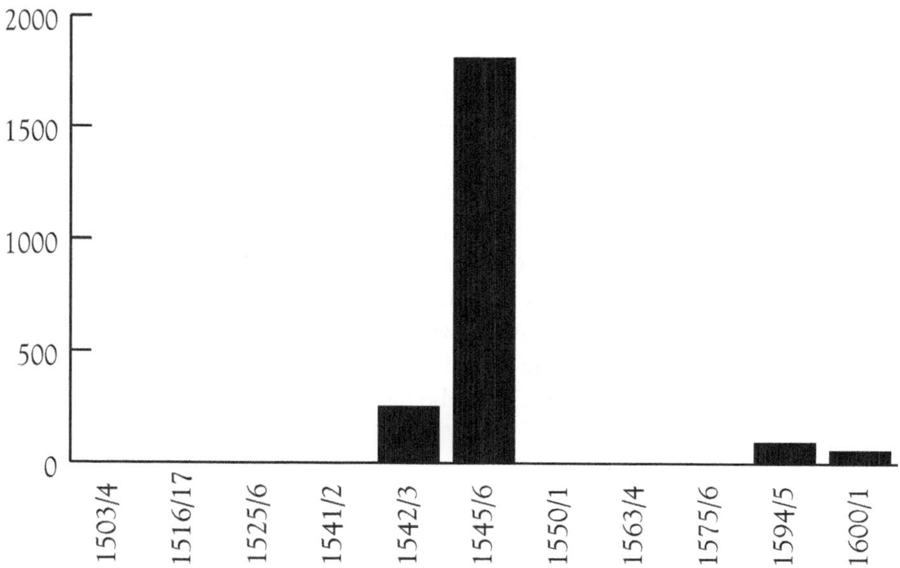


Figure 5.1 Volume of spectacles imported, 1503–1601

Vincent Ilardi has recently examined evidence for the early diffusion of spectacles, following their invention in Italy in about 1280, and has argued that, by the fourteenth century, ordinary as opposed to luxury spectacles were 'neither scarce nor expensive' in Europe and that their use as a vision aid was widely diffused through all levels of society.[66] Early customs records show surprisingly large quantities of spectacles arriving in England in this period. In 1384, for example, 1,152 pairs of eyeglasses were imported into London in the three-month period between 1 July and 29 September in non-English ships.[67] In May–June 1390, 764 pairs were imported, while in April–May 1381 this rose to 4,104 pairs, with the May shipment alone amounting to 3,744 pairs.[68] This, according to Ilardi, was a record for fourteenth-century Europe. Indeed in the fifteenth century, England appears to have been second only to Italy in the volume of spectacle imports discovered to date. Between 8 November 1480 and 21 July 1481, customs records of the port of London recorded the importation, predominantly by Dutch merchants, of 4,320 spectacle cases and 6,072 pairs of spectacles, while in 1509, 1,872 pairs were imported over a two-month period.[69]

Given the early and continuing demand for spectacles in England, the complete absence of this commodity among Irish imports until the middle of the sixteenth century is surprising. It is very likely that spectacles were imported to Ireland directly from the Continent from an earlier date. Certainly, it appears that the large volume of spectacles imported in 1545/6 was destined for an established market, since it is unlikely that 23 individual merchants would import such a significant volume of spectacles in order to test the market with a novelty commodity.

Whatever the reasons for the apparently delayed and erratic importation of this commodity, spectacles were clearly in demand in Ireland from the middle of the sixteenth century. To what use might they have been put in Irish society? There is evidence to suggest that in Europe, at least, spectacles had a general role in the correction of short-sightedness during this period. An exhibition held in Amsterdam in 1926, which displayed several hundred paintings and drawings depicting the early modern use of spectacles, showed them being worn by shoemakers, clockmakers, tailors, hermits, doctors, alchemists, usurers and school masters, among others.[70] The most common use of spectacles in this period was as an aid to reading.[71] It is worth considering, therefore, whether the sudden increase in the importation of spectacles noted in the Bristol accounts correlates with what we currently understand about the diffusion of the skill of reading in early modern Ireland. This does not seem to have been the case. Raymond Gillespie, who has examined changes in the southern

[66] V. Ilardi, *Renaissance Vision from Spectacles to Telescopes* (Philadelphia, 2007), p. 53.

[67] Ilardi, *Renaissance Vision*, p. 72; M. Rhodes, 'A pair of fifteenth-century spectacle frames from the city of London', *Antiquaries Journal*, 62 (1982) p. 64.

[68] Ilardi, *Renaissance Vision*, p. 72.

[69] Ilardi, *Renaissance Vision*, p. 130; H. Cobb, *The Overseas Trade of London: Exchequer Customs Accounts 1480–1* (London, 1990); Rhodes, 'A pair of fifteenth-century spectacle frames', p. 66, based on data published by N. S. B Gras, *The Early English Customs System* (Cambridge, 1918), pp. 560, 562–3, 570, 575, 580.

[70] R. von Greef, *Katalog Einer Bilderausstellung Zur Geschichte der Brille: XIII Internationalen Ophthamologischen Kongresses* (Amsterdam, 1929), cited in G. Walsh, 'Spectacles through the ages and period inaccuracies', OT (December, 2001): www.optometry.co.uk/articles/docs/d39361fd0467fb5f5b732f88449c00d4_walsh20011214 [accessed 19 October 2010].

[71] Walsh, 'Spectacles', p. 32.

Irish book trade during this period, noted 'dramatic' changes in the expansion of the trade, particularly including the importation of cheap books intended for mass circulation, from the last decade of the sixteenth century into the early seventeenth century. Books were a rare Irish import before the end of the century.[72]

Spectacles were of significance, however, beyond their practical functions, and they developed important cultural and social associations in the medieval and early modern world. In Renaissance artistic representations, while they were initially associated with elderly, scholarly and saintly figures, spectacles came to convey not only old age but also 'gravitas, wisdom, intellectuality, and scholarship' and as such developed a considerable 'prestige factor'.[73] Paradoxically they were not a luxury item. The market value of spectacles seems to have been relatively low. In 1545, for example, Henry VIII purchased 10 pairs of spectacles at just 4d each.[74] To put this in perspective in an English context, the daily wage for a carpenter working outside London was 5.25d in 1500.[75] Certainly, in Europe, their symbolic associations seem to have been appreciated beyond elite culture. An Italian carnival song from the early sixteenth century stated that 'they make men wise when they use these spectacles'.[76]

Although there is no pictorial or documentary evidence to elucidate Irish attitudes to spectacles in the sixteenth century, they perhaps had symbolic as well as functional significance, as in England and Europe, and as such served a role in the fashioning of Anglo-Irish identity. Spectacles portrayed the literacy, gravitas and wisdom of the wearer. They also represented the engagement of Anglo-Irish consumers with the growing material culture of science and technology in early modern Europe.

[72] Gillespie, 'Book trade', p. 6.

[73] Ilardi, *Renaissance Vision*, pp. 263–4.

[74] C. B Fryer, 'Ophthalmics in the Reign of Henry VIII', *Ophthalmic Antiques*, xlvii (1994), p. 7.

[75] Ilardi, *Renaissance Vision*, p. 130; D. L Farmer, 'Prices and wages 1300–1500', in E. Miller, (ed.), *The Agrarian History of England and Wales*, iii (Cambridge, 1991), p. 471.

[76] C. S. Singleton (ed.), *Canti Carnascialeschi del Rinascimento* (Bari, 1936) trans. by Ilardi in *Renaissance Vision*, p. 160.

# 6

# *Colour and Cleanliness*

### I. Dyestuff

Comparing de Heere's sixteenth-century illustrations of Irishwomen and Englishwomen, Dunlevy noted distinct differences in their styles of headwear, ruffs, sleeve shapes and also, significantly, in the colour of their clothing. The English, she remarked, were depicted in patterned fabrics with muted, dark tones in contrast with the brighter colours worn by the Irish.[1] This was a fact also acknowledged by contemporary literary commentators on Irish habits. Spenser remarked, for example, that Irishwomen 'will devise some colour, for either of necessity, or of antiquity or of comeliness'.[2] Likewise, Gernon noted that the mantles worn by Irishwomen were 'commonly of a browne blew colour with fringe alike, but those that love to be gallant were them of greene, redd, yellow, and other light colours, with fringes diversifyed'.[3] The apparent differences in Irish and English colour preferences during this period may perhaps be further understood in light of recent discussion on the evolving significance of colour and on the ideological factors that influenced its use during this period.

Paul Raffield has argued that the expansion of sumptuary legislation in England, which included the regulation of clothing colour, was driven predominantly by the Protestant Reformation and Renaissance Humanism. He has suggested that the regulation of dress became an important means of expressing the authority and 'indivisibility of divine and common law'.[4] In contrast to the sumptuary laws enacted prior to the Act of Supremacy (1534), the purpose of which was to enforce respect for a feudal hierarchy and restrict the import of foreign goods, legislation enacted after the Henrician Reformation 'reflected an emergent, modern constitution which embodied a particular, English form of Protestantism based upon moderation, repression of excessive individualism and a belief in the divinity of law and its institutions'.[5]

The regulation of colour was central to this so-called 'reformation of the image'.[6] Legislation enacted by the Crown in 1533, in an attempt to depict the monarch as

[1] Dunlevy, *Dress*, p. 52.
[2] Spenser, 'View', in Myers (ed.), *Elizabethan Ireland*, p. 98.
[3] Gernon, *Discourse*, p. 359.
[4] Raffield, 'Sumptuary legislation', p. 128.
[5] Ibid., p. 132.
[6] Ibid., p. 127.

the 'unique embodiment of divine law' stated that no person should 'use or weare in any maner their apparel, or upon their horse, mule, or other beast, any silke of the colour of purpure, ne any cloth of Gold tissue, but onely the King' and certain specified close relatives.[7] Based on Legh's explanation of the significance of the colour purple, which 'sheweth jurisdiction, a ruler of laws, and in justice, to be equal with a prince', Raffield suggested that the appropriation of the colour by the king was intended to represent 'authority, legitimacy and justice' in the person of the monarch.[8]

Raffield also noted further evidence of the influence of ideological change on the regulation of colour during this period. In 1584, regulations of the Middle Temple forbade members of the legal profession from wearing great ruffs, white colour in doublets or hose, and any gowns 'but suche as were of a sad colour'.[9] This, Raffield argued, showed the influence of Renaissance Humanism on the concept of 'governmentality within the emergent English constitution'.[10] The insistence on 'sad' or dull colours illustrated the engagement of the legal profession with Stoic philosophy, which regarded a 'melancholic predisposition' as a means of self-discovery.[11] The wearing of 'flamboyant foreign styles and coloured fabrics offended against the ordered principles of propriety, reason and authority' as defined by Renaissance Humanist ideology. This standardisation of dress of the members of the Inns of Court, Raffield argued, reflected a movement towards the overall standardisation of common law in the sixteenth century and an acknowledgement of the classical principle that 'the repression of individual desire in the greater interest of community is a prerequisite for civic cohesion'.[12]

The entrenchment and evolution of these ideas surrounding the significance of colour is suggested by the furore that arose in early seventeenth-century England following the short-lived adoption of the foreign fashion for yellow bands and ruffs in English society.[13] If wearing sad colours was perceived as symbolising civic cohesion, reason and authority in the emerging Protestant state, the colour yellow seems to have developed quite the opposite connotations. Between c.1610 and the mid-1620s English satirists, including Joseph Martin, John Heath, Richard Niccols and Richard Braithwaite raged against the use of yellow starch, which was perceived as foreign, papist, demonic and effeminating, and a traitorous 'disfigurement of the nation'.[14] According to Robert Anton, in 1616, saffron turned 'Gentilitie' into some 'painted whoore'. Anton questioned:

[7] Ibid., p. 138; W. Rastall, *Collection in English of the Statutes Now in Force* (London, 1594), f.14 [24 Hen. VIII, ch. 13 (1532)].

[8] Raffield, 'Sumptuary legislation', p. 138; G. Legh, *The Accedens of Armorie* (London, 1576), f.10b.

[9] W. Dugdale, *Origines Juridiciales or Historical Memorials of the English Laws* (1666), f.191, cited in Raffield, 'Sumptuary legislation', p. 144.

[10] Raffield, 'Sumptuary legislation' p. 145.

[11] Ibid.

[12] Ibid., p. 147.

[13] Jones and Stallybrass, *Renaissance Clothing*, pp. 59–86.

[14] Ibid., p. 73.

> Where are those
> That had more honour in their mindes than clothes;
> Great Caesers court did shine with warlick hands;
> Icer Atlas. Icer, and laugh at yellow bands,
> That now do staine the times.[15]

The foreign and papist associations with the colour yellow, which made it so abhorrent to English commentators, were motivated to a large extent by its traditional connection with Ireland, where saffron had been in use as a dyestuff probably from the late tenth century.[16] Saffron was a very expensive commodity and its use in Ireland was seen by the administration as an unnecessary indulgence. In an effort to curtail native extravagance, legislation was first enacted against the use of the dye in Ireland in 1466, when women in Dublin were forbidden to wear saffron-coloured smocks and kerchiefs.[17] Then, in 1536, Henry VIII forbade the citizens of Galway from wearing any saffron in their clothing and the following year extended the prohibition to the rest of the country.[18]

In addition to being seen as wasteful indulgence, the use of saffron was paradoxically viewed as a sign of poverty, of the 'uncouth roughness of a people who owned too few clothes and harboured vermin as a result'.[19] Spenser and Moryson both suggested that the Irish dyed their linen with saffron to prevent lice.[20] This was also remarked upon in a report by the Venetian ambassador Ludovico Falier to his senate in 1531.[21] English commentators also remarked on the fact that the Irish used urine to intensify the saffron dye. In William Camden's history of Britain he quotes William Good, a priest and school master in Limerick, who, in 1566, commented on the technique noting that their way was not to boil the garment for long but to let it soak for some days in urine so that the colour would be deeper and more durable.[22] This was probably correct, since urine was commonly used by dyers as a detergent and as a mordant to make colours more durable. Camden, however, was either unaware of this or chose to ignore it since he went on to use the fact to illustrate the 'debasement' of the Irish, noting that when Shane O'Neill visited Queen Elizabeth I, his bodyguards were dressed in shirts dyed with saffron and 'vel humana urina infectis'.[23]

[15] Ibid.

[16] Dunlevy, *Dress*, p. 54.

[17] Ibid; J. C. Walker, *An Historical Essay on the Dress of the Irish* (1788), p. 42.

[18] Cal. Carew MSS., i, p. 91.

[19] Jones and Stallybrass, *Renaissance Clothing*, p. 67.

[20] Moryson, 'An Itinerary', Vol. 4, (1907), p. 236; Spenser, 'View', in Myers (ed.) *Elizabethan Ireland*, p. 90.

[21] McClintock, *Old Irish Dress*, p. 54; C.S.P. Venetian, iv, no. 694.

[22] McClintock, Old Irish Dress, p. 53; W. Camden, Britannia (1607): http://www.visionofbritain.org.uk/text/chap_page.jsp?t_id=Camden&c_id=34 [accessed 18 January 2011].

[23] McClintock, *Old Irish Dress*, p. 54.

Saffron yellow, then, was 'a culturally freighted colour', one that in English minds linked luxury and contaminating waste.[24] It was perceived as a product of 'the common school of all vanitie' that originated with England's traditional enemies, in particular Ireland and Spain. As such, it was symbolically antithetic to the political and social values of the emerging sixteenth-century Protestant nation state. Yet despite legislation banning its use in Ireland, it is clear that the use of saffron continued, at least throughout the first half of the sixteenth century. Dunlevy suggested that its survival was due to the impoverishment of Irish chieftains, which, in turn, resulted in their ownership of less changes of clothing and so encouraged them to place reliance on a well tried and trusted dye; a dye that, it was traditionally believed, would protect the body from ill health while ensuring that the fabric would stay clean longer.[25] This seems an unlikely explanation. First, the volume of saffron imported from Bristol to the south-east of Ireland in the sixteenth century shows that the affluent Anglo-Irish were just as partial to the colour as the native Irish during this period. Second, as McClintock has argued, there is no evidence to suggest that dyeing a fabric with saffron would cause it to stay clean for longer or provide it with immunity from lice. Had this been the case, the Irish would also have dyed woollen garments in the same way, rather than just linen.[26] It seems more likely that the survival of the fashion for saffron-dyed clothes in Ireland was a function of cultural preference and tradition. There may also have been an element of ideological resistance in the persistence of its popularity. If the adoption of sad or dull colours did represent, to some extent, the repression of excessive individualism in early modern English society, then the wearing of bright vibrant colours such as saffron yellow was perhaps embraced as an expression of cultural independence. It might be noted that yellow dye was not only used to colour clothing during this period; it was also a favoured colour for the decoration and adornment of both public and private domestic spaces in Anglo-Irish homes. An inventory of the contents of Maynooth Castle, owned by Gerald, the 11th earl of Kildare, which was taken in 1575, lists 'chaires of velvet yelow', among the furnishings of the great chamber. The rooms inventoried included a 'yelow chamber' and a 'little yelow chamber' and the contents of 'my ladies wardrobe' included 'a canapie of yellow sarsenet'.[27] Likewise, the last will of Thomas Butler, 10th earl of Ormonde, records the bequest of 'a bed with the twelve apostles' and 'a quilt of yellow taffety', to his daughter.[28]

The chronology of the decline in use of this important commodity in Ireland is uncertain. Archaeological evidence is of no help in shedding light on the use of dyestuff, and the documentary evidence presents conflicting opinions. In 1571 Edmund Campion remarked that the Irish had forsaken their saffron and 'learnt to

[24] Jones and Stallybrass, *Renaissance Clothing*, p. 67.

[25] Dunlevy, *Dress*, p. 55.

[26] McClintock, *Old Irish Dress*, p. 55.

[27] J. Fenlon, *Goods and Chattels: A Survey of Early Household Inventories in Ireland* (Kilkenny, 2003), pp. 11–12.

[28] Fenlon, *Goods*, p. 16.

Table 6.1
Volume of saffron imported, 1503–1601 (lb)

| Year | Vol. (lb) |
|---|---|
| 1503/4 | 635 |
| 1516/17 | 485 |
| 1525/6 | 502 |
| 1541/2 | 543 |
| 1542/3 | 538 |
| 1545/6 | 832 |
| 1550/1 | 734 |
| 1563/4 | 131 |
| 1575/6 | 20 |
| 1594/5 | 0.25 |
| 1600/1 | 2 |

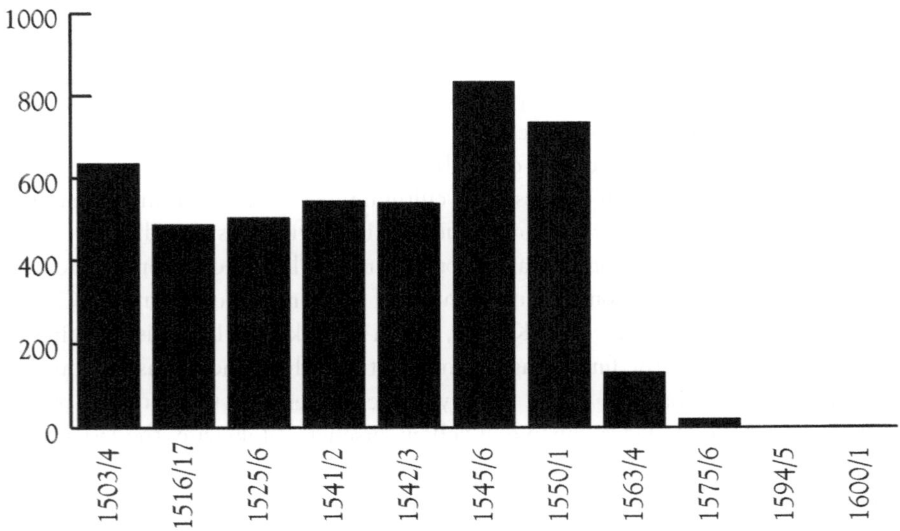


Figure 6.1 Volume of saffron imported, 1503–1601 (lb)

wash their shirts four or five times a year'.[29] In 1577, however, enough saffron was sold in Galway to warrant charging a toll on it of twopence per pound to help pay for enclosing the town and, in 1578, Chancellor Gerrarde complained that even the English in Dublin used Irish colours.[30]

[29] E. Campion, *History of Ireland*, in Myers (ed.), *Elizabethan Ireland*, p. 28.
[30] Dunlevy, *Dress*, p. 55.

Table 6.2 Saffron as a percentage of the gross value of Irish imports from Bristol 1503–1601

| Year | % |
|---|---|
| 1503/4 | 11 |
| 1516/17 | 11 |
| 1525/6 | 12 |
| 1541/2 | 13 |
| 1542/3 | 17 |
| 1545/6 | 19 |
| 1550/1 | 16 |
| 1563/4 | 9 |
| 1575/6 | 1 |
| 1594/5 | 0 |
| 1600/1 | 0.07 |

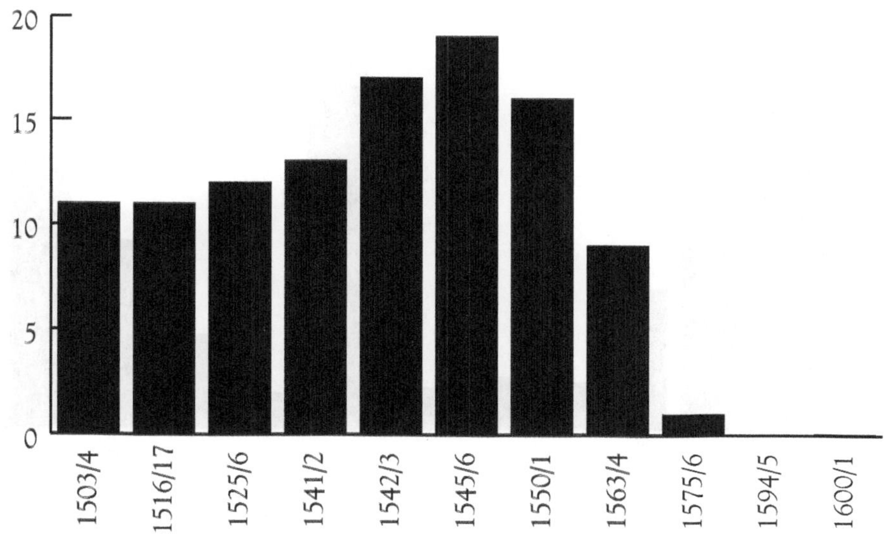


Figure 6.2 Saffron as a percentage of the gross value of Irish imports from Bristol 1503–1601

It is most likely that the fashion died out at different times in different regions of the country. Certainly, in the south-east the importation of saffron declined greatly in the second half of the century. Between 1551 and 1563 the volume imported fell by a massive 82 per cent. This had a major effect on the overall composition of the Irish import trade, since in the first half of the century saffron had been a staple import, which at its peak comprised 19 per cent of the value of Irish annual imports from Bristol. By 1575, this figure was just 1 per cent, and at the end of the century

Table 6.3
Volume of orchil imported, 1503–1601 (lb)

| Year | Vol. (lb) |
|---|---|
| 1503/4 | 5,411 |
| 1516/17 | 2,660 |
| 1525/6 | 2,030 |
| 1541/2 | 686 |
| 1542/3 | 756 |
| 1545/6 | 595 |
| 1550/1 | 5,872 |
| 1563/4 | 518 |
| 1575/6 | 1,358 |
| 1594/5 | 2,716 |
| 1600/1 | 3,976 |

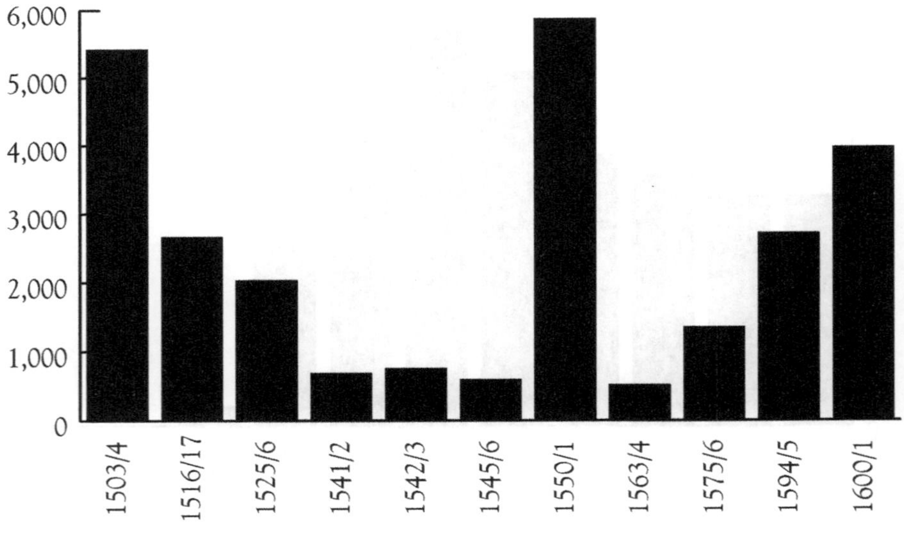


Figure 6.3 Volume of orchil imported, 1503–1601 (lb)

the volumes imported from Bristol were inconsequential and may well represent use of the commodity as a food-flavouring rather than as a dyestuff (see Table 6.1, Figure 6.1, Table 6.2, Figure 6.2).

It is not clear why the use of saffron declined in Ireland. Longfield suggested that the greater attractiveness in the variety of new goods that became available in the later part of the century may have played a role in its decline.[31] This may partly explain the trend. There may, however, have been other factors behind the sharp fall in saffron imports. The importation of 227lb of yellow ochre by Thomas Archer, a Kilkenny merchant in 1575, suggests that there was still a demand for yellow dye in the south-east of Ireland at this point. Yellow ochre produced a pale brownish yellow colour and was relatively inexpensive, being valued in the account at only 10s per cwt (112lb) in contrast to saffron, which was valued at 13s 4d per single pound. It may be that ochre was imported in 1575, a year when the gross value of Anglo-Irish trade collapsed, as a less expensive substitute for saffron – and economic factors should therefore not be ruled out as a cause in the decline of the trade.

In addition to the decline in saffron imports, Longfield also remarked upon a similar fall later in the century in the importation of orchil, a purple dye obtained from the moss *orchellus linnatus*.[32] This dual decline in the use of yellow and purple, she suggested, was because there was less intercourse between the Anglo- and Gaelic Irish during the second half of the sixteenth century, since these two colours are well known to have been favoured by the native Irish.[33] Longfield did not provide any evidence to support these remarks and her assumption was incorrect. The importation of orchil did not decline over the course of the century (see Table 6.3, Figure 6.3). On the contrary, in the 1540s, a period during which Anglo-Irish and native co-operation was at its peak, an average of only 679lb of orchil was imported from Bristol annually.[34] In contrast, in the last quarter of the century, an average volume of 2,683lb of orchil was imported. That the Anglo-Irish were partial to the colour is evident from an inventory of the goods of Richard Tyrry Fitzadam of Cork, which lists two pieces of purple buffin: 8.25yd of which was valued at 20s, while 13.5yd was valued at 5 nobles, or £1 13s 4d. Buffin was a coarse 'cotton' fabric worn by the lower classes and tradespeople, and it therefore appears that purple was not restricted to elite consumption in Ireland during this period.

The description of orchil as a purple dye, however, needs further clarification. Purple was regarded as a royal colour in England and its use was restricted by Sumptuary Law. In 1574, the Statutes of Apparel reinforced the regulation of the colour, proclaiming that:

> None shall wear in his apparel:
> Any silk of the color of purple, cloth of gold tissued, nor fur of sables, but only the King, Queen, King's mother, children, brethren, and sisters, uncles and aunts; and except dukes, marquises, and earls, who may wear the same in doublets, jerkins, linings of cloaks, gowns, and hose; and those of the Garter, purple in mantles only.[35]

[31] Longfield, *Anglo-Irish Trade*, p. 180.

[32] Ibid., p. 181.

[33] Ibid.

[34] C. Lennon, *Sixteenth-Century Ireland, The Incomplete Conquest* (Dublin, 1994), p. 40; Flavin, 'Development of Anglo-Irish trade', p. 45; Longfield, *Anglo-Irish Trade*, p. 27.

[35] *Enforcing Statutes of Apparel: Greenwich, 15 June 1574, 16 Elizabeth I*; TNA, SP/12/23, fol. 19v.

Table 6.4 Volume of dyestuff imported, 1503–1601 (lb)

| Year | 1503 | 1516 | 1525 | 1541 | 1542 | 1545 | 1550 | 1563 | 1575 | 1594 | 1600 |
|---|---|---|---|---|---|---|---|---|---|---|---|
| alum | 814 | 1,290 | 1,680 | 1,018 | 1,096* | 570 | 1140 | 90 | 700 | 714 | 140 |
| brazilwood | 10 | - | 25 | 528 | 90 | 318 | - | - | - | 336 | 952 |
| kermes | 2 | - | 1 | 3 | 1 | 34.5 | - | - | - | .5 | - |
| orchil | 5,411 | 2,660 | 2,030 | 686 | 756 | 595 | 5,872 | 518 | 1,358 | 2,716 | 3,976 |
| saffron | 635 | 485 | 502 | 543 | 538 | 832 | 734 | 131 | 20 | .25 | 2 |
| verdigris | 11 | 4 | 19 | 93 | 77 | 78 | 18.5 | 30 | - | 12 | .5 |
| wood ashes (seam) | - | - | 20 | 2 | 1 | 18 | 2 | - | - | - | - |
| woad, Azores | - | - | - | - | - | - | 112 | - | - | - | - |
| madder | - | - | - | 560 | | | 504 | | 140 | | |
| ochre, yellow | - | - | - | - | - | - | - | - | 227 | | |
| copperas | - | - | - | - | - | - | - | - | - | 33 | 22 |
| indigo | - | - | - | - | - | - | - | - | - | 288 | - |
| logwood | - | - | - | - | - | - | - | - | - | 1,414 | - |
| turnsole | - | - | - | - | - | - | - | - | - | 9 | 7 |

*There is 8lb of alum in a stone.

It would therefore be of considerable cultural and political significance if the general populace of Gaelic and Anglo-Ireland were indeed wearing 'purple'-coloured clothing. The colour achieved by dying fabric with orchil in fact bore little resemblance to 'royal or 'Tyrian' purple, which was closer in colour to crimson red than what is now defined as purple. Tyrian purple was obtained from murex molluscs found in the eastern Mediterranean and it has been estimated that some 'twelve thousand snails of Murex brandaris yield no more than 1.4 g of pure dye, enough to color only the trim of a single garment'.[36] This expense rendered purple-dyed textiles as status symbols, hence the restriction of the colour by law. In contrast, the 'purples' obtained from cheaper orchil lichens were bluish or violet shades, which unlike the brilliant mollusc colours were extremely fugitive, especially when exposed to bright sunlight.[37]

In addition to assuming a decline in the importation of orchil in the later sixteenth century, Longfield also remarked on a corresponding increase in the importation of madder and woad and suggested that it was highly likely that a mixture of these two dyes replaced orchil.[38] This was not the case. Madder, which produced red pigments, occurred as an irregular import from Bristol throughout the century, and did not appear at all in the accounts examined after 1575. Likewise, woad, which produced blue pigments, was found only in 1551, when 112lb of 'Azores' woad was imported. See Table 6.4.

Attempts were made in the later sixteenth century to develop both the madder and woad industries in Ireland.[39] While it has been assumed that these projects did not prosper, the absence of both these dyestuffs in the accounts at the end of the century may indicate that sufficient quantities were produced in Ireland to at least satisfy domestic demand. It is of course possible that Irish merchants obtained woad via direct trade with Portugal. However, the price of Azores woad rose substantially in the late 1570s, and the supply of woad was disrupted by disputes between Spain and the Netherlands.[40] As a result, woad cultivation surged in England, particularly in the 1580s. By 1585, it was growing in at least 12 English counties and occupying nearly 5,000 acres of land.[41] It seems likely, therefore, that if demand in Ireland was not being met by domestic production, supply would have been met by imports from England rather than from the Continent, and this was not the case.

Finally, it is worth considering a number of exotic new dyestuffs that entered the Irish import trade during the sixteenth century, namely brazilwood, indigo and logwood, none of which were noted by Longfield in her study of imported dyes.[42] In

[36] D. Jacoby, 'Silk economics and cross-cultural artistic interaction: Byzantium, the Muslim world, and the Christian West', *Dumbarton Oaks Papers*, 58 (2004) p. 210.

[37] A. Kok, 'A short history of the orchil dyes', *Lichenologist* (1966), pp. 248–72.

[38] Longfield, *Anglo-Irish Trade*, p. 181.

[39] Thirsk, *Economic Policy*, pp. 75–7; Longfield, *Anglo-Irish Trade*, pp. 181–4.

[40] Thirsk, *Economic Policy*, p. 29.

[41] Ibid.

[42] Longfield, *Anglo-Irish Trade*. pp. 178–85.

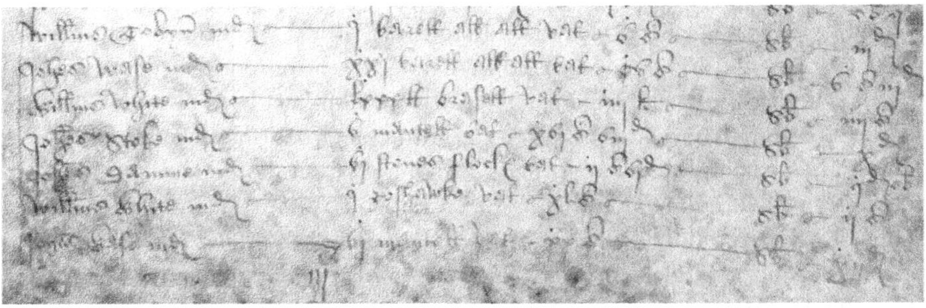

Plate 10 Image from the 1503–04 'particular account' showing Irish re-exports of brazilwood.

1500, when the Portuguese 'discovered' present-day Brazil, they found an abundant supply of dyewood trees, closely related to the Asian sappanwood tree. Sappanwood, which produced a bright crimson dye, was until then obtained from India, Malaya and Ceylon and was a rare and very highly valued dyestuff in Europe. In 1502 King Manuel of Portugal awarded a monopoly of the brazilwood trade to a consortium of Lisbon merchants, who immediately began felling trees and exporting the dyestuff to Europe. The immediacy of the Portuguese exploitation of this resource is evident from the customs accounts. In 1503 9,464lb of 'New World' brazilwood was exported to Bristol by two Portuguese merchants, Manuel Caldeira and Alerno Pymento.[43] Notably, however, there was no time lag between the 'discovery' and exploitation of brazilwood and its introduction to Ireland. In the same year, it appeared as a re-export to Ireland, when four merchants each imported 10lb of the dye, presumably to test the market. And indeed there appears to have been a growing market for the luxury dye. In the 1540s imports grew to an average of 312lb per annum and by 1600 this had multiplied threefold, to 952lb. Much more significant, however, is the fact that even at the earliest stage in the trade, Irish merchants were capitalising on the re-export of brazilwood. In the 1503 account (Plate 10) 80lb – worth £4 – was re-exported from Ireland to Bristol by William White.[44] This is further evidence of the dynamic participation of Irish merchants in emerging continental markets.

Logwood and indigo also appeared among Irish imports at the end of the century. Both of these dyestuffs were recorded in the 1594/5 account in large volumes. Since they were not imported before or after the Munster plantation, it is reasonable to assume that their consumption was linked to the arrival of 'New English' settlers. This is somewhat surprising since both of these dyes were banned in England during this period. An Act of Parliament in 1581 prohibited the use of logwood as a dye, claiming that it was 'false and deceitful' and 'only sold and uttered to the great deceit of the Queens loving Subjects, within this her Realm of England, but also beyond the Seas, to the great discredit and slander, as well of the Merchants, as the Dyers of

[43] Flavin and Jones, *Bristol's Trade*, pp. 12, 81.
[44] Flavin and Jones, *Bristol's Trade*, p. 5.

this Realm'.[45] A more pressing reason, however, was to protect the indigenous woad industry, and for the same reason a similar prohibition was issued against Indian indigo. The act was repealed in 1662, but in other European countries where there were similar restrictions, the prohibition remained in force for another century.

Logwood, which was discovered by the Spanish in America, was used to produce blues and purples on wool and violet on silk, but its chief interest was as a cost-effective source of black dye for cotton, wool and silk. Black was a difficult colour to achieve to a good, fast standard in dyeing, and the traditional way of producing it involved a complicated method of repeatedly immersing cloth in a vat with woad or indigo and overlaying it with madder. Logwood offered a more straightforward alternative but its use was not perfected until the late seventeenth century, when it was acknowledged that 'the ingenious Industry of these Times hath taught the Dyers of England the Art of fixing the Colours made of Logwood alias Blockwood, so as that by Experience they are found as lasting and serviceable as the Colours made with any other sort of Dying-wood whatsoever'.[46]

Black was a particularly important colour in early modern England and was widely used. It signified death and mourning and there was a large market for black funerary textiles and haberdashery. It also signified status and was the prescribed colour for professionals such as physicians, lawyers and clergymen who were expected to wear black fabrics of a type appropriate to their status.[47] Black also appears to have been a particularly fashionable colour choice for garments in England and Europe during this period.[48] An entry in the Irish State Papers with reference to William Cane, a Dublin merchant, who was arrested and tried as a spy in Spain, noted that 'William Stanley with five Englishmen, an Irish boy, and a Fleming came to the court at Madrid apparelled in black cloth with sleeves of black taffeta after the Spanish fashion'.[49]

It is certainly clear from the documentary evidence that black was commonly worn by the English administration and the 'New English' settlers in Ireland. The will of Nicholas Pett, the provost marshal of Munster, in 1572, records bequests of a 'nywe' black gown, black lace hose, a 'nywe' velvet cap with a black feather and an expensive black 'pinked' coat fabric.[50] Unsurprisingly, black was also associated with funerals and mourning. Brian Mac Cuarta has noted the copious quantities of expensive black cloth, lace, buttons and various other haberdashery bought for the

[45] 23 Eliz. c.9; *Jn. i*, pp. 130-1.

[46] 'Charles II, 1662: An Act for preventing Frauds and regulating Abuses in His Majesties Customes.'

[47] Dictionary of Traded Goods and Commodities, 1550/1820 (2007). Available from: http://www.british-history.ac.uk/report.aspx?compid=58700 [accessed 3 November 2013].

[48] J. H Munro, 'The anti-red shift – to the dark side: colour changes in Flemish luxury woollens, 1300–1550', in R. Netherton and G. R. Owen-Crocker (eds), *Medieval Clothing and Textiles*, vol. 3 (Woodbridge, 2007).

[49] C.S.P. Ire., 1588–1592, p. 307.

[50] Cork City and County Archives, Caulfield Will Transcripts, U226, p. 21.

funeral of Sir Mathew De Renzy, a middle-ranking administrator based in Dublin in 1634. After De Renzy's death, the tailor's bills amounted to the huge sum of £100, and included such fabrics as 'rich taffety' and 'best silk moughere', which were made up as mourning clothes for his extended family.[51]

Despite comments by contemporary observers on the Irish preference for bright colours, noted above, black fabrics and clothing did feature among the possessions of the Anglo-Irish during this period. An inventory of the goods of Richard Tyrry Fitzadam, taken in 1582, listed black buffins, fustians and bays. Likewise, an inventory of the goods of Nicholas Faggan, taken in 1578, listed luxurious black 'pinked' gowns, faced with 'budge' and damask along with a black satin doublet.[52] Unfortunately, it is impossible to say if such items were reserved for mourning or other specific formal occasions or were worn on a daily basis as a means of displaying status.

## II. Hygiene and grooming

W. A. Cohen recently commented that while anthropologists and psychoanalysts have long recognised that the 'designation and rejection of filthy objects serve crucial functions in social management, psychological formation and cultural identity', historians and literary scholars have only recently begun to interpret 'the representation and significance of filth within particular cultures'.[53] Significantly, a large portion of recent historiography on this topic has focused on how discourses on 'dirt' and 'filth' were constructed as social controls in various colonial contexts.[54]

Cleanliness, of course, exists in the eye of the beholder and every culture defines it differently. As such, lack of hygiene has always, and continues to be, a convenient

[51] *Moughere* is most likely mohair. B. Mac Cuarta, 'A planters funeral, legacies, and inventory: Sir Mathew De Renzy (1577–1634), *Journal of the Royal Society of Antiquaries of Ireland*, vol. 127 (1996), pp. 18–33; For further analysis of early modern Irish funerary procedures see R. Gillespie 'Funerals and society in early seventeenth-century Ireland', *JRSAI*, 115 (1985), pp. 86–91; C. Tait, 'Colonising memory: maanipulations of burial and commemoration in the career of the "great" earl of Cork', *Proceedings of the Royal Irish Academy* 101 (2001), pp.107–34; C. Tait, *Death, Burial and Commemoration in Ireland, 1550–1650* (Hampshire, 2002).

[52] Cork City and County Archives, Caulfield Will Transcripts, U226, pp. 21, 33.

[53] M. Douglas, *Purity and Danger: An Analysis of Concepts of Pollution and Taboo* (London, 1966); J. Kristeva, *Powers of Horror: An Essay on Abjection* (Columbia, 1984); W. A. Cohen and R. Johnson (eds), *Filth: Dirt, Disgust, and Modern Life* (Minnesota, 2004), p. viii; E. Cockayne, *Hubbub: Filth, Noise and Stench in England, 1600/1770* (Yale, 2008); K. Ashenburg, *Clean: An Unsanitised History of Washing* (London, 2009); V. Smith, *Clean: A History of Personal Hygiene and Purity* (Oxford, 2007).

[54] D. Spurr, *The Rhetoric of Empire: Colonial Discourse in Journalism, Travel Writing and Imperial Administration* (North Carolina, 1993), pp. 76–91, W. Anderson, 'Excremental colonialism: public health and the poetics of pollution', *Critical Inquiry*, xxi, iii (1995), pp. 640–69; Alexander Butchart, *The Anatomy of Power: European Constructions of the African Body*, (London and New York, 1998); J. and J. L. Comaroff, 'Home-made hegemony: modernity, domesticity and colonialism in South Africa', in K. Tranberg Hansen (ed.), *African Encounters with Domesticity* (New Jersey, 1992), pp. 37–74; A. McClintock, *Imperial Leather: Race, Gender and Sexuality in the Colonial Conquest*, (New York, 1995).

stick with which to beat other cultures, 'who usually err on the side of dirtiness'.[55] The antecedents of the modern 'racial worldview', which brands colonised races as filthy and debased in order to distinguish them as 'other', were clearly present in sixteenth-century English attitudes to the Irish.[56] The word 'filth' and its derivatives, however, had multiple meanings. 'Filth' as defined by the *Oxford English Dictionary* could refer to 'moral defilement, corruption and obscenity'. This sense of the word probably lay in part behind Spenser's description of the 'loathly filthyness' of the Irish glib, which, as discussed above, was seen as morally offensive and corrupt by English observers.[57] 'Filth' also had sexual associations, in particular with regards to female sexuality.[58] This understanding of the term is apparent in Moryson's discussion of the 'barbarous and most filthy' Irish diet. He wrote: 'At Cork, I have seen with these eyes young maides, stark naked, grinding of corn with certain stones to make cakes therof, and striking off into the tub of meal such reliques therof as stuck on their belly, thighs and more unseemly parts.'[59] Likewise, Barnabe Rich claimed to have seen in Dublin alehouses 'common housewives' who were in reality 'filthy' and 'beastly' alehouse keepers, capable of 'all manner of idleness, of whoredom and many other abominations'.[60]

Aside from its moral and sexual connotations, 'filth' also clearly defined the perceived uncleanliness of the Irish from the point of view of English observers. This was a particular concern with regard to Irish laundry. According to Barnabe Rich:

> In the manner of their washing, they are yet more filthy than in any other of their exercises wherein they are most uncleanly, and I do almost loath but to think of their scouring stuff which they do use instead of soap. But he that came in place when they were in their laundry, in their netting, as they call it, would never after stop his nose if he chanced to go by where they were scouring of a privy.[61]

The emphasis placed by English commentators on the techniques and tools used to wash clothing in Ireland illustrates the fundamental differences between modern and early modern attitudes to personal hygiene. The modern regimen locates hygiene 'in cleansing the skin of alien matter by the agency of water', whereas in the

[55] Ashenburg, *Clean*, p. 2.

[56] A. Smedley, 'Antecedents of the racial worldview', in T. D. Gupta (ed.) *Race and Racialization: Essential Readings* (Toronto, 2007), pp. 31–44.

[57] Spenser, 'View', in Myers (ed.), *Elizabethan Ireland*, p. 84.

[58] Kristeva, *Powers of Horror*. Also, Spring has noted that the term was used to describe the 'seemingly unrepressed sexuality' of Native Americans who were frequently described as 'filthy' by English colonists. See J. H. Spring, *The Cultural Transformation of a Native American Family and its Tribe, 1763–1995* (1996), p. 19; see also R. Takaki, 'The tempest in the wilderness: the racialization of savagery', *The Journal of American History*, lxxix, iii, *Discovering America: A Special Issue* (Dec., 1992), p. 895.

[59] F. Moryson, 'The Itinerary of Fynes Moryson', in C. L. Falkiner (ed.), *Illustrations of Irish History and Topography, Mainly of the Seventeenth Century* (London, 1904), pp. 225–30.

[60] Rich, *A New Description of Ireland*, p. 11.

[61] Idid., p. 26.

early modern period the emphasis was placed on 'removing impurities generated from within and excreted to the body's surface'.[62] This was achieved by wearing linen underwear next to the skin to absorb impurities, and washing and changing it as often as possible. The cleanliness attained by 'shifting' or changing linen undergarments measured civility and good manners in English society. Fresh – and, in particular, white – linen was a sign of a 'refined and disciplined body' and showed a high standard of personal grooming.[63] Outer garments were brushed and cleaned by other 'dry cleaning' techniques, but never laundered.

Divergent attitudes to hygiene were a clear delineator between the English and the native societies they encountered. William Wood, writing in 1634, noted that native Indians rejected imported English apparel partly because they refused to spend extra time dressing themselves and partly because 'their women cannot wash them when they bee soyled, and their meanes will not reach to buy new when they have done with the old … therefore they had rather goe naked than be lousie and bring their bodies out of their old tune, making them more tender by a new acquired habit, which poverty would constraine them to leave'.[64] As Kupperman notes, wearing the same outer clothes day after day did not bother the English unduly, and most were used to living with lice and fleas.[65] Wood is therefore implying that the simplicity of Indian apparel led to a better standard of hygiene than English apparel.

There were certainly also some fundamental differences in attitude to the meaning of hygiene in England and Ireland during this period. While the English insisted on the 'whiteness' of linen undergarments, both Gaelic and Anglo-Irish went to great expense to dye their linen yellow, a colour that, for reasons discussed earlier, was symbolically diametric to white. Nevertheless, the evidence indicates that there were definite similarities in the material culture of Irish and English cleaning practices during this period.

With regard to soap, it appears that by the early seventeenth century, when Barnabe Rich was writing, commercially manufactured soap was fairly widely used in parts of England. In 1565, imports of Castile soap into London were valued at £4,422, which according to Thirsk, put soap imports in the intermediate range of goods measured by value and on a par with many other consumer goods such as pins and Spanish leather.[66] Indeed such demand prompted projecting in England and, in 1561, a patent was granted to Stephen Groyett and Anthony le Lewyer to make hard white soap, equivalent in quality to the Spanish Castile soap that was

[62] Vincent, *Dressing*, p. 52.

[63] Ibid., p. 52.

[64] W. Wood, *New England's Prospect* (1634), pp. 63, 65, cited in Kupperman, *Indians and English*, p. 53.

[65] Kupperman, *Indians and English*, p. 53; See also Lois Green Carr *et al.*, *Robert Cole's World: Agriculture and Society in Early Maryland* (1991), p. 71, and Laurel Thatcher Ulrich, *Good Wives: Image and Reality in the Lives of Women in Northern New England, 1650–1750* (New York, 1982), p. 28.

[66] Thirsk, *Economic Policy*, p. 54. n.11.

made in Triana and Seville.[67] The best soap made in England prior to this was a soft, mottled Bristol soap, which was of a high quality but was considered unsuitable for laundering fine linen.[68]

For the less well-off, who did not wear delicate linens, the most commonly used soap in England was 'black soap'. This was a soft soap with a jelly-like consistency and was made from inferior materials such as train or fish oil, in comparison to hard Castile soap, which was made from olive oil. The retailer stored it in a barrel, but it was purchased by the pound, typically at around 3d per pound.[69] Black soap was used as an all-purpose soap by those who could not afford superior types. In 1693, a French visitor to England seemed surprised by the quantities of soap being used in the country, remarking that:

> At London, and in all other parts of the country where they do not burn wood, they do not make lye. All their linnen, coarse and fine, is wash'd with soap. When you are in a place where the linnen can be rinc'd in any large water, the stink of the black soap is almost all clear'd away.[70]

The customs accounts show regular imports of various types of soap to south-east Ireland throughout the sixteenth century. Even the earliest accounts examined, 1503/4 and 1516/17, record imports of 'smigmates', which according to Carus Wilson, based on an entry in *The Account Book of the Abbey of Durham*, were a type of soap.[71] Although it is sometimes difficult to establish the type or volume of soap in the accounts, it is clear that by 1550, at least, large quantities of hard soap were being imported. The 1550/1 account records various entries for a total of 1,100lb of an unspecified 'soap' along with one single entry for 26 serons of soap, which was valued at a significant £26 10s. A seron was a bale or package made up in an animal's hide, containing an unspecified volume. Based on the value of the soap, however, the 26 serons contained approximately 4,700lb. This was obviously re-exported continental soap, since the English-produced soaps were soft, and were shipped and stored in barrels.[72]

The accounts from the later century are more precise in distinguishing different types of soap. Considerable volumes of black soap were recorded in the later accounts, at a value of 6s 8d per c (112lb). Indeed in 1575/6, 6,552lb of black soap was imported from Bristol. As in England, this was probably used by those who could not

[67] Ibid., p. 55.

[68] Ibid.

[69] From: 'Black parchment – Black work', Dictionary of Traded Goods and Commodities, 1550/1820 (2007). Available from: http://www.british-history.ac.uk/report.aspx?compid=58702 [accessed 25 October 2010].

[70] M. Misson, *Memoirs and Observations in his Travels over England* (London, 1719), p. 303.

[71] Carus-Wilson, 'Overseas trade', p. 338. Also, Classical Latin has *smegma* or *smigma* (for which one form of the dative plural is *smegmatis*). The definition in Lewis and Short is 'cleansing medicine or detergent', as opposed to 'soap' for *sapo*. Url: http://www.perseus.tufts.edu/cgibin/ptext [accessed 15 October 2008].

[72] Thirsk, *Economic Policy*, p. 54; A Sim, *The Tudor Housewife* (2001), p. 53.

afford better quality soaps. Fine quality white Castile soap was also available to those who could afford it. This is first found in small quantities in 1563, when 35lb was imported. By 1575, the volume had risen to 587lb, an increase of 1,577 per cent. The timing of this increase is significant since it occurred before the Munster plantation and it is notable that the volumes imported actually fell in the 1594/5 and 1600/1 accounts, to 282lb and 203lb respectively.

Castile soap was not just used for laundering finer cloth but also for personal hygiene. A particular sixteenth-century trend was the use of castile soap to make wash-balls. Sir Hugh Platt gave a recipe for 'a delicate washing ball' in his *Delightes for Ladies*, which basically gives directions for scenting toilet soap. Sim noted that 'this is the sort of thing a lady would use for her daily wash', but wash-balls also had a function in the general washing of the hands and face and in shaving.[73] These wash-balls could, of course, have been made at home, but there is evidence that Irish consumers also demanded an imported variety. In 1576, for example, John Archer, a Kilkenny merchant, imported 72 'washing balls'.[74] Other imports, too, suggest that some in Ireland were concerned with smelling sweet. Bay oil, for example, which was made from laurel berries and used to make a perfumed oil, was imported in 1526, while sandalwood and aniseed, both of which were used to make perfumes, were regular imports.

Other imported items related to grooming were combs and looking glasses. It is not always possible to establish the exact volume of combs imported, since they were sometimes recorded by the box. Nevertheless, the volumes imported were large. The 1545/6 account, for example, recorded 4,320 combs, while in 1563/4 approximately 2,350 combs were imported. Later accounts show the types of combs available in Ireland, which included wooden, light wooden, bone, ivory, penny and halfpenny varieties. The function of these is unclear. They may, for example, have been used to comb the hair, to secure long hair in place creating fashionable up-styles; as a decoration; and to secure the heavy linen rolls to the head. On the other hand, combs may have had more practical functions in the maintenance of personal hygiene, namely the removal of lice and other vermin from the hair.

Looking glasses first appeared as an import to Ireland in 1526, when a dozen were imported by James Fox.[75] They did not occur again until 1550, when 396 were imported by seven different merchants. By 1594/5, the volume had increased to 738 glasses, falling again to 282 in 1600/1. This was a period of major change in the production of looking glasses in Europe.[76] From around 1500, Murano glassmakers began to make expensive glass mirrors, which used tin foil and mercury to produce a reflective surface on flat glass. Before this, 'glasses to look in' were not made of glass at all but of polished steel, and sometimes, according to William Harrison, of tin or

[73] Sim, *Tudor Housewife*, p. 44; OED.
[74] TNA, E190/1129/23 f07r.
[75] Flavin and Jones, *Bristol's Trade*, p. 224.
[76] For a detailed discussion see S. Melchoir-Bonnet, *The Mirror-A History* (New York, 2002).

silver.[77] There also existed glass mirrors that were 'silvered' with lead, tin, pewter or mercury. These, however, produced a very imperfect image, and while they became relatively popular throughout Europe they never replaced steel mirrors, which were used for everyday grooming.[78]

With the exception of one entry in 1594, for what appear to be 'christall' glasses, all of the other 'glasses' in the accounts were very inexpensive 'peny ware', valued at up to 4d per dozen.[79] These were most likely small metal pocket mirrors, which were intended for everyday use and could be worn attached to girdles, inserted into fans, or fastened to a chain and worn around the neck.[80]

Given that in the sixteenth century such looking glasses were 'an indispensable tool for grooming' in England and Europe and were available at 'almost any price and of any quality', the volumes imported into Ireland remained quite low.[81] Although the accounts record 'penny' and 'halfpenny' varieties, which were affordable beyond the elite consumer, the volume imported suggests that there was little demand for portable looking glasses in Ireland. Certainly, of the wills of affluent Cork citizens transcribed by Caulfield, looking glasses do not feature among bequests at all, nor do they feature in surviving Irish inventories from this period. The will of Thomas Butler, 10th earl of Ormond, however, shows the presence of elaborate looking glasses in elite Irish households. Butler left his wife a 'canopy of white network with tassels of gold with two little curtains for a looking glass'.[82] Fenlon has noted the European influences behind the use of such curtains, which were seen in Dutch paintings – by Vermeer, for example – and were also hung in front of paintings to protect them.[83]

The relatively low interest in looking glasses in sixteenth-century Ireland raises some intriguing questions about the extent to which affluent Irish townswomen partook in other contemporary grooming fashions and rituals. During the sixteenth and seventeenth centuries, a good complexion was considered highly important in England. This period saw a proliferation of recipe manuals instructing women how to dye their hair, colour their skin, and perfume and beautify their bodies. It also saw a proliferation of an anti-cosmetic literature, driven by current religious and social anxieties.[84] The religious argument against cosmetics was concerned with the 'blasphemous' adulteration of the body:

> This adulteration and changing of God's handiwork by painting women's hair to make it seem fair and yellow, or of their cheeks to make them look ruddy, or of their forehead to hide the wrinkles and to make them look smooth, is of the devil's invention and never of God's

[77] W. Harrison, *Description of England*, chapter xi, (1577) p. 9.

[78] Melchoir-Bonnet, *Mirror*, p. 16.

[79] Willan, *Tudor Book*, pp. 29, 39.

[80] Melchoir-Bonnet, *Mirror*, p. 23.

[81] Ibid; J. L. Singman, *Daily Life in Elizabethan England* (Conneticut, 1995), p. 108.

[82] Fenlon, *Goods*, p. 16.

[83] Ibid., p. 18.

[84] Farah Karim-Cooper, '"This alters not thy beauty": face-paint, gender and race in Richard Brome's The English Moor', in *Early Theatre*, 10, 2 (2007), pp. 140–9.

> teaching. Therefore I must exhort all women to beware of counterfeiting, adulterating, or changing the fashion and form of God's work, either by yellow colour, black or red powder, or by any other medicine corrupting or changing the natural lineaments of favour of man or woman.[85]

The social anxieties surrounding cosmetics were multifaceted and linked to mercantilism and developing ideas about nation and race. There was a sense, for example, that painting the face with foreign ingredients or using foreign recipes would somehow permeate the identities of English women, making them less English.[86] This was exemplified by John Bulwer, a seventeenth-century physician:

> Our English Ladies, who seeme to have borrowed some of their Cosmeticall conceits from Barbarous Nations, are seldome known to be contented with a Face of Gods making; for they are either adding, detracting, or altering continually, having many Fucusses in readiness of the same purpose.[87]

Still, despite concerns about the evils of make-up, by the mid-seventeenth century, as Karim-Cooper notes, recipe manuals and defences of cosmetics dominated the cosmetics discourse, suggesting that 'beautification had not only demonstrated its commercial viability, but also its aesthetic appeal'.[88]

One of the most desirable features of a good complexion in this period was pallor. This was a means of demonstrating status and gentility, since it indicated a sedentary indoor lifestyle, rather than one spent toiling in the fields. From the later sixteenth century, white lead was used as a way of attaining a pale complexion and for covering up various skin imperfections such as pockmarks, pimples and freckles. The best white lead, called ceruse, was imported from Venice. It was shipped as a paste and had to be mixed with water or egg white before application to the skin. Mixing it with egg white meant, of course, that the make-up cracked when the wearer smiled, but there were other, more serious negative effects too. After a few hours white lead would turn a very unflattering grey colour. It also caused hair loss and could cause eyebrows to fall off. Worst of all, it was poisonous and when absorbed by the skin over years led to lead poisoning, a very serious condition.

It is very difficult to assess the extent to which women in Ireland bought into the fashion for pasty white faces in the sixteenth century. Certainly, the ingredients for make-up were imported, but before the Munster plantation this was in small quantities. In 1575, for example, 3lb of ceruse was imported to Waterford, perhaps to test the market. By 1601, there may well have been a small but growing market for white make-up. In that year 84lb of a cheaper white lead was imported. Other items used to create cosmetics are also found in the accounts at the end of the century, including chalk and red lead, which was used to re-create the appearance of a reddened

[85] Roger Edgeworth, 'Sermon', in Paul A. Welsby (ed.), *Sermons and Society* (1970), p. 50.
[86] Ibid.
[87] John Bulwer, *Anthropometamorphosis: or Man Transform'd* (London, 1653), p. 260.
[88] Karim-Cooper, 'This alters not thy beauty', p. 140.

cheek. The difficulty is, of course, that these items had more than one function and there is no way to establish whether they were used by women to paint their faces or by painters on canvas. Certainly, although criticised in many ways, contemporary male writers could be complementary about the natural complexions of Irish women. Gernon, for example, noted that the 'weomen of Ireland are very comely creatures … of complexion very fayre & cleare-skinnd (but frecled), with tresses of bright yellow hayre'. Unfortunately, though, this natural beauty was fleeting. Due to 'theyr propensity to generation', he claimed that 'they are wemen at thirteene, and olde wives at thirty' and that he 'never saw fayrer wenches nor fowler calliots, so we call the old wemen'.[89]

[89]Gernon, *Discourse*.

# *Part II – Summary*

In the sixteenth century, south-east Ireland and its extensive hinterland witnessed significant changes in the consumption of dress, which in many important ways mirrored the sorts of changes occurring in England and across Europe during the period. The foregoing chapters have considered the pace and extent of such changes, the factors that influenced the growing consumption of new fashions in Ireland and how clothing might have been used and interpreted by Irish consumers. A number of key themes have emerged.

Toby Barnard has stated of Ireland, with specific reference to the seventeenth and eighteenth centuries, that 'the extent to which legal dependency produced cultural deference even subservience, or aggressive assertions of independence, has not been resolved'.[90] He noted that:

> Certain accessories to everyday living are thought to denote the embrace not only of civility but of English traits, and even of Protestant values. Thus the spread into Ireland of habits of consumption akin to those in England, Wales and Scotland has been read as evidence of assimilation of the island to the modes and manners of its immediate neighbours.

Certainly, one of the major issues addressed here has been the extent to which the increasing ranges and volume of dress-related imports from England indicate social and cultural assimilation of English habits in sixteenth-century Ireland. The answer appears to be very little. The evidence suggests that, despite ready access to English and indeed European fashions, and political pressure to conform to English tastes, Irish consumers were not slavish emulators of either, and on the contrary, their use and interpretation of this growing range of new goods was unique and distinctive. Mairead Dunlevy has shown that Irish fashion continued to evolve as a separate and distinctive entity over the course of the sixteenth century, with the Irish incorporating and adapting selected aspects of foreign styles into their costume as the century progressed – and there is no evidence in the customs accounts to refute this claim.[91] The evidence indeed suggests that the rapid social and cultural change brought about by the influx of 'New English' settlers during the Munster plantation,

[90] Barnard, *Guide*, p. 15.
[91] Dunlevy, *Dress*, p. 47.

while significant, did not play a fundamental role in the changing tastes of pre-existing Irish communities. Certainly, while some of the items that turn up amongst Irish imports may indeed have been worn by those who wanted, or were required to, emphasise their English identity (English style caps, ruffs and falling bands, for example), the vast majority of the new ranges of items found in the accounts could be worn or used in any number of ways. The new range of luxury continental cloths arriving in Ireland could have been used to create Irish, English, European or hybrid styles; girdles and garters could be decorated with Irish embroidery and items of clothing dyed in typically Irish colours such as saffron yellow. Overall, the nature of Irish dress-related imports on this route, particularly the increasing range and volume of various types of ornamentation and trimmings, and other types of clothing haberdashery, suggests that growing consumption in Ireland, in large part, served to further the expression of cultural individuality and independence.

The extent to which religious affiliation, and in particular competing Protestant values, influenced the choice of dress in Ireland, unfortunately remains unclear. Indeed, the evidence sheds very little light on the use of dress as an expression of spirituality in Ireland during this period. It may be, however, as Vincent has suggested, that the changing material culture of religion after the Reformation had little impact on personal clothing and adornment. In this case, differences between Irish and English clothing, based on religious affiliation, may simply not have existed.[92] On the other hand, it may be that the continued use of saffron yellow in Irish clothing – a colour perceived in England as foreign, papist and at odds with the social values of the emerging Protestant state – may have been influenced in part by religious factors, but there is at present not enough evidence to reach any decisive conclusions about the social significance of colour in Irish attire.

The distinctive evolution of Irish dress in the sixteenth century discussed here raises interesting questions about the validity of certain influential theories used to explain increasing consumption, not just of fashion but of consumer goods in general. One of the most persuasive of these theories is that of social emulation, which argues that the main motivation to consume was a desire to emulate those of higher social rank. Lorna Weatherhill has suggested that emulation could not have worked in such a simple way as historians imply, and that the processes by which people learned about consumer goods were much more complex.[93] The trends noted here certainly illustrate the complex factors that influenced whether individuals, often regardless of status or wealth, chose to emulate fashionable dress. In Ireland, the increasing demand for new fashions in the sixteenth century did not progress in a straightforward 'top-down' manner and people did not necessarily learn about new consumer goods by observing elite consumption. Owing partly to the complexity of the social and political situation, as well as to a possible innate aristocratic conservatism, the Irish gentry seem to have displayed a taste for traditional and sometimes

[92] Vincent, *Dressing*, p. 86.
[93] Weatherill, 'Meaning', p. 208.

even archaic fashions. This is suggested from the archaic clothing depicted in the Butler and Honoria Grace effigies. On the other hand, wills and inventory evidence, although sparse, suggest that there was a market for luxury imported goods among the middling sort in Ireland, including merchants, aldermen and shopkeepers. The last will of the Cork merchant, Nicholas Faggan, aptly illustrates the luxury to which the merchant class in south-east Ireland aspired by the late 1570s.

Practical factors also significantly influenced the ownership of new clothing items. It is likely, for example, that certain traditional native styles, such as trews and possibly types of armour, persisted in Ireland simply because they were seen to have been more appropriate to local environmental conditions. Another important practical consideration was varying levels of regional access to specialist skills, such as starching and stocking knitting, for example, lack of which caused a time lag in the adoption of certain new styles in Ireland.

Regional economies and trade also played a very significant role in influencing ownership of clothing. It seems that the Anglo-Irish coastal towns were at the forefront of changing fashions in Ireland, due predominantly to their overseas trade, which generated wealth and provided ready access to foreign wares. The qualitative evidence clearly shows that Irish clothing was influenced by developing markets and production techniques not only in England, but in France, Germany, Italy, Spain and the Low Countries. Indeed some of these techniques, including stocking knitting, starching and Flemish weaving were imported into Ireland and stimulated domestic clothing production.

Finally, in Ireland, as elsewhere, clothing performed a vital role in the construction of social, cultural and political identity. Indeed dress may have served an even more explicitly political function in Ireland than in England. Clothing was used to distinguish and identify political allegiance and to confirm loyalty to the crown. It was also used as a tool of symbolic disempowerment, dissent and political propaganda. Perhaps the most important factor, given the semi-colonised nature of Irish society, is that the acknowledgement of the power of dress as a visual marker of political and social status was universal. Natives, 'Old English' and newcomers shared an understanding of the complexity and significance of dress, and each group used clothing as a means of both displaying and contesting allegiance and authority.

# Part III

## *Eating, Drinking and Making Merry*

After the delivery of your Honour's 'scoule,' [scull], to O'Neill, he took it in his hand and kissed it at least half-a-score times, and then presently he sent for two hogsheads of wine and christened your scull, and after he had drunk his fill, and he put on his shirt of mail and his jack, and called for a bowl of wine, and drank it to your Honour's health, withal he put on his scull and drew out his sword with a great oath, and said that Sir John Perrot was the truest man of his word that ever he knew …

C. S. P. Ire, 1588–92, p. 234

# 7

# *Food, Drink and Society*

Food and drink are not only vital for human sustenance and reproduction, they are also intrinsic to social, cultural and economic development. Yet, apart from in the areas of production and agriculture, historians have traditionally had very little to say about this area of consumption and material culture. In recent years, however, both the social and cultural significance of food and drink have begun to receive significant historiographical attention. According to Edward Muir: 'No rituals are more widely practiced, more formative of social identity or more differentiating of social groups than the daily habits of dining. The distinction between eating merely to consume food and dining as a form of sociability inhabits the very core of what we call culture.'[1] Likewise, Andrew Sherratt has written:

> Food and drink are the most fundamental, if short lived, media of material culture. The serving and sharing of these essential elements make up one of the central daily activities of the human domestic group ... the consumption of food is a paradigm for understanding the consumption of other materials, goods and services. Its constant physical necessity, and the variety of experiences which it encompasses, make it an especially useful medium for apprehending the ways in which societies and cultures are constituted and the manner in which they change.[2]

The growing interest in the material culture of food and drink has begun to influence studies of early modern Europe and England. In common with the current historiography of dress, recent efforts in this area have begun to acknowledge the sixteenth century as a period of very important changes in consumer demand and taste. European voyages of discovery to the 'new worlds' in the Americas, Africa and Asia brought travellers, merchants and administrators into direct contact with new foods and culinary practices. At the same time, the growth of international trade and intercultural contact entailed by these new encounters made Europeans aware of many new foodstuffs and other consumables, while the desire to profit from expanding overseas trade encouraged the development of new markets.[3] Other developments also impacted on diet. Renaissance humanist writers opened up a range of debates regarding what – and indeed how – to eat; table manners became formalised

[1] E. Muir, *Ritual in Early Modern Europe* (Cambridge, 2005), p. 134.

[2] A. Sherratt, 'Alcohol and its alternatives', in J. Goodman *et al.* (eds), *Consuming Habits, Global and Historical Perspectives on How Cultures Define Drugs* (Oxford, 1995), p. 13.

[3] See: B. Cowan, 'New worlds, new tastes: food fashions after the Renaissance'. Available from:: http://www.academia.edu/453702/New_Worlds_New_Tastes_Food_Fashions_After_the_Renaissance [accessed 29 August 2013]

and more elaborate; and the printing press made both culinary and courtesy literature available to mass audiences.[4]

In England, historians have found evidence of these changes in many aspects of food consumption and culture. Perhaps the most significant work is Joan Thirsk's recent exhaustive study of early modern food in England between 1500 and 1750. This study was based on evidence from sources including cookery books; scholarly and popular tracts; published descriptions of provincial diets and tastes; probate records; and household accounts. It revealed the considerable and increasing diversity of foods in early modern England, considering regional and class variations in diet and noting the impact of the port towns on the diffusion of new foodstuffs to more rural inland areas. It also examined the complexities of evolving food consumption habits, pointing out in particular that in England, long-established provincial tastes and cooking practices were sometimes slow to give way to new fashions, and were only gradually altered by novelties.[5]

Food and drink have not yet become as central as dress to current academic debates. Nevertheless, a number of important themes have recently emerged in food historiography. James Nicholls, for example, recognised a link between diet and nationalism in early modern England, arguing that concerns regarding drinking were often overlaid with concerns over national identity.[6] Changes in diet have also been examined in order to shed light on the impact of religious change on social and cultural behaviour and on the display of spiritual and moral identity. Mark Dawson, for instance, considered the impact of the Reformation on the pattern of feasts and fasting in the Willoughby households from the mid-sixteenth century.[7] The evolving role of food and drink in marking social and political distinctions and in the construction of elite identity has also been examined, with particular attention being paid to the significance of the economic and social regulation by law of public drinking in England, which, in a similar manner to the regulation of dress, increased over the course of the sixteenth century in response to rising social

[4] Ibid.

[5] Thirsk, *Food*. Thirsk's findings were complemented by a recent study by Mark Dawson, which examined the provisioning and consumption of food and drink of the Willoughby family in Nottingham and Warwickshire during the sixteenth century and revealed significant developments in diet during this period, including new styles of cookery, foodstuffs and domestic utensils, which were appearing on the market as a result of growing overseas trade. See M. Dawson, *Plenti and Grase: Food and Drink in a Sixteenth-Century Household* (Totnes, 2009). Other studies include: F. Heal, *Hospitality in Early Modern England* (Oxford University Press, 1990); S. Pennell, '"Pots and pans history': the material culture of the kitchen in early modern England', *Journal of Design History*, xi (1998), pp. 201–16; S. Pennell, 'The material culture of food in early modern England', in Sarah Tarlow and Susie West (eds), *The Familiar Past? Archaeologies of Later Historical Britain* (Routledge, 1999), pp. 35–50.

[6] J. Nicholls, *The Politics of Alcohol: A History of the Drink Question in England* (Manchester, 2010), p. 12.

[7] Dawson, *Plenti*, p. 221.

mobility, mercantilism and changing ideas about the morality of excess, instituted by religious change.[8]

There is certainly a 'telling contrast' between explorations of this subject in Ireland and other places.[9] This, as Barnard has noted, relates in large part to the lack of appropriate source material for Ireland, which means that it still remains necessary to establish fully the fundamentals of food consumption – 'what was grown, imported and eaten and how the staples changed'– before engaging in more detailed studies of hospitality and of the preparation and presentation of food.[10] Barnard has also suggested that there may be an element of ideological resistance to such topics in Ireland, noting that in a society where many died of famine, the materials of life, often not sufficing for subsistence, are assumed to be unworthy or too sparse to warrant investigation.[11]

Certainly, the Irish diet has long attracted the attention of historians. However, work has traditionally focused predominantly on the Irish dependence on the potato from the eighteenth century and, in particular, on the Great Famine that occurred between 1845 and 1852 as a result of crop failure.[12] Significant studies of diet in Ireland include A. T. Lucas' survey of Irish food consumption in the pre-famine centuries, which was based primarily on literary sources but paid little attention to the chronological, social or economic context of changing patterns of consumption.[13] Also significant is an earlier work by Patrick W. Joyce, who discussed food and drink in early Ireland, although not in an analytical manner.[14] Apart from such studies, few historians of Ireland have paid much attention to the study of food and drink, or to widening the examination of Irish consumption patterns beyond mere subsistence.

[8]Nicholls, *Politics*.

[9]Barnard, *Guide*, p. 16.

[10]Ibid., p. 17.

[11]Ibid.

[12]For example: T. Hayden (ed.), *Irish Hunger: Personal Reflections on the Legacy of the Famine* (Dublin, 1995); C. Kinealy, *This Great Calamity: The Irish Famine 1845–52* (Dublin, 1995); F. S. L. Lyons, *Ireland since the Famine* (London, 1973); A. Bourke, J. R. Hill and C. Ó Gráda (eds) *The Visitation of God : The Potato and the Great Irish Famine* (Dublin, 1993); J. S. Donnelly, *Black '47 and Beyond: The Great Irish Famine in History, Economy, and Memory* (Princeton, 1999); R. Dudley Edwards, T. D. Williams and C. Ó Gráda, *The Great Famin : Studies in Irish History 1845–52* (Dublin, 1994); P. Gray, *Famine, Land, and Politics: British Government and Irish Society, 1843–1850* (Dublin, 1999); P. Gray, 'The triumph of dogma: the ideology of famine relief', *History Ireland*, 3 (2), 1995; L. Kennedy, *Mapping the Great Irish Famin : A Survey of the Famine Decades* (Dublin, 1999); D. M. MacRaild, *The Great Famine and Beyond: Irish Migrants in Britain in the Nineteenth and Twentieth Centuries* (Dublin, 1999); C. Woodham Smith, *The Great Hunger: Ireland 1845–1849* (San Francisco, 1962); J. Makyr, *Why Ireland Starved, A Quantitative and Analytical History of the Irish Economy 1800–1850* (London, 1983); C. Ó Gráda, *Ireland's Great Famine: Interdisciplinary Perspectives* (Dublin, 2002); J. R. O'Neill, *The Irish Potato Famine* (2009); C. Woodham-Smith, *The Great Hunger* (London, 1991).

[13]A. T. Lucas, 'Irish food before the potato', *Gwerin*, iii (1960), pp. 8–43.

[14]P. W. Joyce, *A Social History of Ancient Ireland* (London, 1903); See also K. H. Connell, *The Population of Ireland 1750–1845* (Oxford, 1950).

In more recent years, however, there has been a change of emphasis in Irish food and related historiography, and attempts have been made to explore the social and cultural significance of the Irish diet. For the medieval period, Catherine O'Sullivan, influenced by Felicity Heal's work on early modern English hospitality and Katherine Simms' study of Gaelic Irish feasting, has examined key aspects of the practice of hospitality in Gaelic society, including guesting, feasting and gift giving.[15] As with consumption studies in general, however, the seventeenth and eighteenth centuries have received the greatest attention. Louis Cullen, for example, considered the impact of colonisation on dietary changes in Ireland from the eighteenth century.[16] More recently, Barnard's study *Making the Grand Figure* while omitting the subject of diet, nevertheless dealt in some detail with the material culture of eating and drinking in early modern Ireland.[17] Also of note is Jane Fenlon's study of the changing use of rooms in early modern elite Irish houses, which places Irish domestic developments in the context of wider changes in attitudes to issues such as privacy, civility, individuality and political change.[18]

Unsurprisingly, there has been very little work as yet on the sixteenth century. One exception to this is the examination by Clarkson and Crawford of diet and nutrition in Ireland between 1500 and 1920, *Feast and Famine* (2001). They consider changes in patterns of consumption over time among different social classes; the impact of new agricultural techniques and cultural values on Irish diet; and the relationship between food, nutrition, health and demography. The book includes a chapter on changing patterns of consumption in the sixteenth and seventeenth centuries and utilises evidence from contemporary writings, army purveyancing records and two elite household accounts. The authors concluded that late sixteenth-century colonisation wrought 'fundamental changes' in Irish dietary patterns, reversing the process of acculturation and imposing on the native population the dietary values of the settlers'.[19] This process of adaptation, they noted, took a long time.[20]

The following chapters in part 3 complement and augment Clarkson and Crawford's analysis, which was not supported by any quantitative evidence other than accounts of the food purchased for the lord deputy in Dublin in 1577, and the household expenditure of the earl of Sussex in 1562 – and which did not consider the material culture of eating and drinking.[21] The chapters in part 3 establish a quantitative framework for the consumption of a range of drink, food and related

[15] C. M. O'Sullivan, *Hospitality in Medieval Ireland, 900–1500* (Dublin, 2004); K. Simms, 'Guesting and feasting in Gaelic Ireland', *JRSAI* 108 (1978), pp. 67–100.

[16] Cullen, *Emergence*.

[17] Barnard, *Making the Grand Figure*, pp. 122–50.

[18] J. Fenlon, 'Moving towards the formal house: room usage in early modern Ireland', in E. Fitzpatrick and J. Kelly (eds), *Domestic Life in Ireland* (Dublin, 2011). See also Powell, *Politics*, pp. 7–41 for a study of the politics of food and drink in eighteenth-century Ireland.

[19] Clarkson and Crawford, *Feast*, pp. 25, 27.

[20] Ibid., p. 27.

[21] Ibid. pp. 21-2.

domestic items in sixteenth-century Anglo-Irish towns and, as such, represents the first historiographical attempt to deal with the subject of sixteenth-century diet in a systematic and analytical manner. Contemporary literature shows that English observers regarded with distaste the backward, 'sluttish and uncleanly' food production and eating habits of the Irish. According to Moryson, with the exception of Dublin and some of the 'better sort' in Waterford, the 'filthy' dietary practices of the Irish had 'little and little' affected the 'English-Irish', even in the cities.[22] This part of the book therefore considers the pace at which Irish urban tastes changed in comparison to English and European trends, in order to establish the extent to which Irish consumers embraced the 'widening world' of sixteenth-century food.[23] It also considers the significance of colonisation and overseas trade on such changes. The aim here is not to produce an exhaustive account of changes to Irish diet and nutrition but to move the discussion of Irish food-related consumption beyond basic subsistence. The present discussion, therefore, is predominantly confined to the changing consumption of imported foodstuffs and manufactured domestic utensils, and excludes any detailed consideration of such staples of sixteenth-century Irish diet such as grains, meat and dairy products, the consumption of which was discussed by Clarkson and Crawford.[24]

Chapter 8 considers the changing importation of a large and eclectic selection of foodstuffs, including spices, aromatics, salt, sugar, honey and vinegar. Dawson, who categorised such goods as 'sundries', suggested that a more inclusive term might be 'luxury foods' but noted that items such as salt were far from luxurious, being more of a necessity when it came to food preservation. Certainly, what these various goods had in common was that their role was essentially supportive to the preparation and preservation of other food groups. As Dawson remarked, 'without these "sundry" foods all you have is ingredients; with them you have cookery and cuisine'. It must be noted too, however, that most of these items, in particular sugar and spices, had dual gastronomic and medicinal uses, being widely used in cordials, health drinks and other distillations. As such, they can tell us something about the link between diet and health in the sixteenth century. Chapter 9 examines the production, importation and consumption of alcoholic drinks in Ireland, while chapter 10 looks in detail at the material culture of cooking and dining in Irish homes and at evidence for evolving rituals of the table in this period. Finally, Chapter 11 moves the study outside the home to examine the significance of public drinking and other forms of consumption and entertainment in Ireland.

[22] Moryson, 'An Itinerary', in Myers (ed.), *Elizabethan Ireland*, p. 186.
[23] Thirsk, *Food*, pp. 27–57.
[24] Clarkson and Crawford, *Feast*, pp. 13–20.

# 8

# *Provisions*

## I. Spices

In February 1576, Giles Wiggers of Antwerp set out on a voyage from Lisbon to Calais with a cargo of sugar and spices. En route, while most of the crew was sleeping, eight of the company 'fell upon' the rest, killing six. The master surrendered and was forced to bring his ship into the bay of Rosscarbery, in West Cork. Coming into the bay, he was greeted by Bishop Cornelius Brenner, who agreed to bring the ship safely ashore to Glandore Haven, with the help of local fishermen, in return for 30 ducats. This was to be paid with 60lb of spices, in lieu of money. Trusting the kindly bishop, the master asked for help in dispossessing the murderous mariners and reclaiming his ship and cargo. The bishop in turn promised him 'great friendship' and 'took him to his house'. Once there, however, the bishop held him hostage for four days, releasing him only when he agreed to pay a ransom of 732lb of spices: 200lb each of nutmeg, cinnamon and pepper and 132lb of cloves.[1] How the bishop disposed of his extorted spices is unfortunately unknown, but it is clear from this and other evidence that there was a market for such luxury foodstuffs in sixteenth-century Ireland.

Paul Freedman has recently examined the complex significance of spices in medieval culture and society. Among the reasons fuelling the medieval 'infatuation' with exotic spices was a fashion for spicy food and heavy-perfumed sauces, along with a deeply ingrained perception of their medicinal properties. Above all, however, their high price and mysterious origins meant that they were prized by the affluent as symbols of 'material comfort and social prominence'.[2] Over the course of the early modern period, the demand for spices waned. Rich but blander food became fashionable; new exotic goods such as sugar, tea and chocolate became available and eclipsed spices in popularity; and ideas about health and food evolved. In the sixteenth century, even as new trade routes increased the supply of spices, the fierce demand of the earlier period had probably already passed, but spices remained popular in cooking and were still essential on the shopping lists of the affluent consumer.

A large range of exotic spices were imported into Ireland throughout this period (see Table 8.1 and Figure 8.1). Interestingly, and probably in line with wider European trends, a detailed examination of the customs accounts suggests that there was

[1] Appleby, *Calendar of Material*, p. 84.

[2] P. Freedman, *Out of the East, Spices and the Medieval Imagination* (London, 2008), p. 2.

actually very little development in the Irish spice trade in the second half of the century. In terms of the range imported, most of the spices in demand at the end of the century – aniseed, cinnamon, cloves, mace, cumin, ginger, nutmeg, pepper and saffron – were imported from the 1540s and many of these are found in small quantities from the fifteenth century. With regard to the volumes imported, the most significant increase was between 1526 and the 1540s, when the volume of all imported spices increased, some by a very significant amount. Aniseed, for example, increased from an average volume of 2,056lb per annum between 1503 and 1526 to an average of 8,855lb in the 1540s, representing a 331 per cent increase. Likewise, cumin imports increased by 1,000 per cent, and liquorice by 1,219 per cent, in the same period. In contrast, at the end of the century, the volumes of spices imported became much more erratic and, despite the influx of 'New English' settlers in the 1580s, imports of spices actually fell at the end of the century.

The increasing demand for luxury foodstuffs in the 1540s is compatible with Irish economic developments during this period, as considered in chapter 1. It is also probable that demand was affected by the same developments that influenced changing attitudes to food in England from around the middle of the sixteenth century. Thirsk has noted that there were deepening debates about the relationship between food, health and medicine in Europe during this period. In 1527, Hieronymus Braunschweig's German work on distilling was translated into English, and this along with other publications slowly began to stimulate experimentation with the medicinal uses of essential oils distilled from various spices and herbs, which came to be consumed for their medicinal values and then appreciated as food flavourings.[3] Also, increasing overseas trade stimulated a heightened interest in food in general. This was diffused first by the conversation of overseas travellers and then by the translation of European and, in particular, Italian cookery books into English.[4] The prosperous conditions of economic life and trade in the Irish port towns in the middle of the century no doubt facilitated Irish engagement with developments in the world of food and the spread of new tastes in luxury foodstuffs.

Unsurprisingly, not all of the exotic foodstuffs arriving in London during this period featured amongst Irish imports. Certain items that appeared in the London port book of 1567/8 such as fenugreek, cucumber seed and turmeric were not recorded among Irish imports, even at the end of the century, and it was probably quite some time before elite Irish consumption, and indeed consumption in many other parts of England, could keep up with changing trends at the epicentre of English food fashion. Nevertheless, it does appear that the range of luxury spices supplied to the south-eastern Irish port towns and their hinterland from the 1540s was comparable with some other major English port towns during this period. Thirsk compared the food consumption of different regions in England, based on the evidence in inventories and trade records, and painted a picture of the luxury consumption of

[3] Thirsk, *Food*, p. 29; H. Braunschweig, *The Vertouse Boke of Distyllacion* (London, 1527).
[4] Thirsk, *Food*, p. 31.

Table 8.1 Volume of spices, medicines and preservatives imported 1503–1601(lb)

| | 1503 | 1516 | 1525 | 1541 | 1542 | 1545 | 1550 | 1563 | 1575 | 1594 | 1600 |
|---|---|---|---|---|---|---|---|---|---|---|---|
| aniseed | 1,000 | 1,618 | 3,550 | 2,847 | 12,038 | 11,682 | 464 | 3,248 | 118 | 5,826 | 112 |
| arsenic | - | - | - | - | - | - | 2 | 1 | 28 | - | - |
| benedict's laxative | - | - | - | - | - | - | - | - | - | - | 1 |
| bole armeniac | - | - | - | - | - | - | - | - | 20 | - | |
| candy, brown | - | - | - | - | - | - | - | - | - | - | 2 |
| candy, white | - | - | - | - | - | - | - | - | - | - | 8 |
| cinnamon | 5 | 1 | 1.5 | 20.5 | 22.25 | 24.5 | 16 | 0.5 | 5.5 | - | 2 |
| cinnamon/cloves | - | - | - | 14 | 14 | 4 | 1 | - | - | - | - |
| cinnamon/cloves/mace | - | - | - | 9 | 2.5 | - | - | - | - | - | - |
| cinnamon/mace | - | - | | 3 | 1.5 | 2 | - | - | - | - | - |
| cloves | - | - | 1 | 9.5 | 35 | 34.75 | 13 | 36.5 | 21 | 5.5 | - |
| cloves/mace | - | - | - | 8.5 | 3.5 | 10 | - | - | - | - | - |
| comfits | - | - | - | - | - | - | - | - | 10 | 25 | 21 |
| comfits, spice | - | - | - | - | - | - | - | - | 2 | - | - |
| cumin | | 15 | 74 | 404 | 189 | 397 | 114 | 126 | 238 | 12 | 64 |
| ginger | 4 | 2 | 4 | 20.5 | 8.75 | 90 | 2 | 13 | 2 | 23 | 50 |
| honey (flasket) | - | - | - | - | - | - | - | - | - | - | 1 |
| honey (barrel) | 12 | 1 | 9 | 10.5 | - | 2.75 | 18.5 | 1 | 3 | 1 | - |
| indigo | - | - | - | - | - | - | - | - | - | 288 | - |
| isinglass | - | - | - | - | - | - | - | - | - | 6 | 8 |

| | | | | | | | | | | | |
|---|---|---|---|---|---|---|---|---|---|---|---|
| liquorice | 26 | 58 | 23 | 489 | 281 | 656 | 82 | 108 | 1386 | 48 | 500 |
| mace | 1.25 | 1 | - | 10.25 | | 9.25 | 0.5 | 1 | - | - | - |
| nutmeg | - | - | | 4 | 6.5 | 14.5 | 4 | 6 | 0 | 3 | 1 |
| pepper | 18 | 2 | 22.5 | 76 | 98.25 | 61 | 50.5 | 108.5 | 5 | 13 | 10 |
| saffron | 635 | 485 | 502 | 543 | 538 | 832.5 | 734.5 | 131.5 | 20 | .25 | 2 |
| salt | | 14,000 | | | 284,480 | 193,088 | 22,400 | 5,040 | 15,680 | - | - |
| senna (lb) | - | - | - | - | 2.5 | 3 | - | - | 10 | 14.5 | 13 |
| succado/ marmalade | - | - | - | - | - | - | - | - | - | 4 | - |
| sugar | - | - | - | - | 6 | 188 | - | 54 | 89 | 871 | 461 |
| sugar candy | - | - | - | - | 1 | 1 | 2 | | 4 | 3 | - |
| sugar of roses | - | - | 2 oz. | - | - | - | 0.5 | - | - | - | - |
| terra sigillata | - | - | - | - | - | - | - | 1 | - | - | - |
| turnsole | - | - | - | - | - | - | - | - | - | 9 | 7 |
| vinegar (gallon)* | | 27,783 | 2,961 | 14,112 | 3,843 | 7,938 | 9,198 | 810.61 | 2,047.5 | 126 | 63 |
| wormseed | - | - | - | - | - | - | - | - | 1 | - | - |

*Listed as 'corrupt wine' in the accounts.

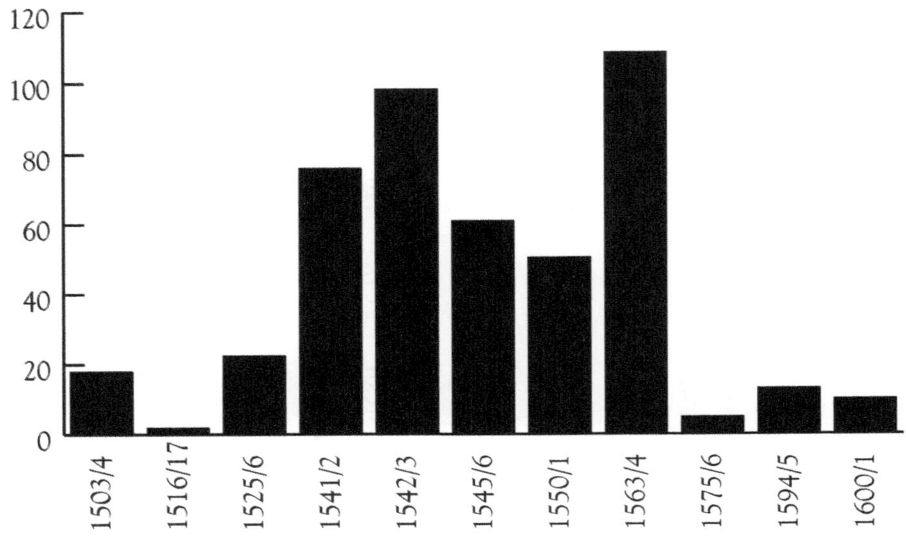


Figure 8.1 Volume of pepper imported, 1503–1601 (lb)

Southampton's citizens, which appears – in terms of the range of luxury foods – to compare well to that of the Irish port towns, at least by the end of the century.[5] An important point to note, however, is that there were significant regional variations in English diet during this period. Thirsk noted distinct differences in the diet of coastal areas, which was qualitatively different from those inland. The impact of overseas trade meant that foreign luxuries and food flavours became known and available to the citizens of port towns such as Southampton and Bristol, long before they reached inland.[6] It is very likely that this was also the case in Ireland, and while the accounts show that luxury foodstuffs were imported by merchants from all the main towns in the south-eastern hinterland, and indeed from Galway, the extent and pace at which they were diffused beyond the main towns remains uncertain.

If the range of exotic imported spices was comparable between southern port towns on both sides of the Celtic Sea, changes in the ranking of spices may also have shown some similarities. It has been noted that a change of taste may have lain behind the fact that cumin was noticeable in the cargoes arriving in Sandwich in 1302–03, but appeared only once in the London port book of 1567/8.[7] According to Alan Davidson, the use of cumin was replaced by caraway in the sixteenth century.[8] Irish imports also suggest a decline in the use of cumin at the end of the century. Whether or not this was replaced by caraway is uncertain, although it is notable that 4lb of caraway seed was imported by Michael Bray, a merchant from New Ross, in

[5] Ibid., p. 205.
[6] Ibid., p. 196.
[7] Ibid., p. 317.
[8] A. Davidson, *The Oxford Companion to Food* (Oxford, 1999), p. 233.

1576, perhaps indicating the introduction of the spice to Ireland. A similar decline has been noted in the use of saffron as a food colouring and seasoning in England during the sixteenth century.[9] This was despite the fact that it was produced in Essex during this period. Again, Irish imports, as discussed earlier, show a massive decline in the importation of saffron from 1575, and although the predominant use of saffron in Ireland seems to have been as a dyestuff, its decline may also relate, in part, to the similar changing food preferences of Irish consumers.

Although it is clear that that there was a demand for luxury imported spices in south-east Ireland during this period, closer consideration of the volumes of spices imported raises some important points. In general, while the volumes increased significantly in the 1540s, the overall amounts of many imported spices remained quite low. There were exceptions to this trend, however. Aniseed, in particular, was imported in very large quantities throughout most of the period, peaking in 1542 when over 12,000lb was imported. In contrast, the volume of imported pepper, which was one of the most widely consumed spices in England and Europe during this period, remained very low.[10] To put the volumes imported into Ireland into some perspective, the household accounts of the Willoughby family in Nottingham, analysed recently by Dawson, shows that in one year a single large English household could consume up to 37lb 8oz of pepper, whereas the largest amount imported into south-east Ireland in a single year was 108lb.[11]

A possible reason for this is that Irish merchants were meeting some of the demand for pepper throughout this period by direct continental trade, in particular with Portugal, which broke the Venetian monopoly on the pepper trade at the end of the fifteenth century.[12] There is certainly evidence that Irish merchants were re-exporting pepper to Bristol. Although untypical of general trends, in 1516/17 16 individual merchants exported a total of 2,624lb of pepper to Bristol. This accounted for 38 per cent of Bristol's pepper imports in that year.[13] Small quantities of expensive Moluccan spices including cinnamon, cloves and nutmeg were also exported to Bristol from Ireland in the same year.

It is also possible that the relatively low volumes of spices imported in general reflect fundamental differences in English and Irish food preferences. Certainly, contemporary writers remarked that the Irish favoured less seasoned foods than the English. Luke Gernon, for instance, claimed that Irish meat was 'ill cooked, and

[9] Dawson, *Plenti*, p. 165; Wilson, *Food*, p. 294.

[10] Dawson, *Plenti*, p. 167.

[11] Ibid., p. 168.

[12] For a detailed discussion see C. H. H. Wake, 'The changing patterns of Europe's pepper and spice imports, ca 1400–1700, *Journal of European Economic History*, viii (1979), p. 388; Wilson, *Food*, p. 292.

[13] Bristol would probably have obtained the vast majority of its pepper and spices via London, since spices were always of very high value relative to their weight and therefore overland transport costs were low.

without sauce'.[14] It may also be of social significance that pepper, in particular, was imported in low and decreasing volumes in this period. Pepper was an item in common use in England and Europe, and although its market value rose significantly over the century from 1½d per ounce in the 1520s to around 3d per ounce at the end of the century, it would still have been affordable to a substantial portion of the population.[15] Massive quantities of pepper were imported into England and, in 1565, the national total was officially valued at £27,000, the bulk of it coming into London from Antwerp.[16] Given the apparently widespread use of pepper in England and Europe, throughout the various social classes, the low and decreasing volumes imported into Ireland most likely indicate that the consumption of imported food flavourings and spices remained restricted to the upper classes.

As with other trends in Irish consumption, it does not seem that the influx of settlers during the Munster plantation had much immediate impact on the range or volume of luxury spices and other foodstuffs imported. Indeed, many of the new types of foodstuff imported at the end of the century had already appeared by 1575. Comfits, for example, which were a very fashionable luxury sweetmeat made of fruit and spices and preserved with sugar, certainly increased in volume in 1594, but were already in demand in 1575. This may well be due to Spanish rather than English influences on Irish tastes. Thirsk noted that while comfits were known by name in England from the 1480s, they became more widely consumed in the late sixteenth and early seventeenth centuries because 'Spanish confectioners had arrived to demonstrate the Moorish way with them'.[17]

On the other hand, a few of the new items arriving in Ireland after 1594 may well reflect the imported fashions and tastes of newcomers. Of note, for example, is the importation of isinglass in 1594 and 1600. Isinglass was a substance derived from sturgeon's sounds, or airbladders, which was introduced to Britain from Russia by Dutch merchants in the sixteenth century and was used to replace the airbladders of stockfish to set jelly.[18] Jellies were particularly popular in late sixteenth-century England, when they became part of the 'Tudor banquet', a third and final course to the formal dinner.[19] Whether they were made with fruit, fish or meat, however, jellies, like many other foods, were always very brightly coloured.[20] A jelly recipe from 1584 included, along with claret wine, spices and calves-foot liquour, 'isinglass being fair washed and laid in water a day before, turnsole being aired by the fire and dusted'.[21]

[14] Gernon, *Discourse*, p. 361.
[15] Dawson, *Plenti*, p. 167.
[16] Thirsk, *Food*, p. 321.
[17] Ibid., p. 56.
[18] Wilson, *Food*, p. 45.
[19] Ibid., p. 106.
[20] Ibid., p. 43.
[21] A. W., *A Book of Cookyre Very Necessary for all Such as Delight Therein, Gathered by* A. W. (1584), cited in Wilson, *Food*, p. 106,

This is significant since turnsole and indigo, both of which were used as a purple food colourant during this period, also appeared as imports to Ireland in 1594.[22]

### *Ia. Drugs and medicines*

In addition to the use of spices as food flavourings throughout this period, another major function was in the preparation of health drinks, cordial waters and various other distillations. In the last quarter of the century in particular, a number of books were published in England explaining the medicinal uses of distillations from spices, seeds, roots and flowers and offering advice on the extraction of alcohol from wines, the yield of essential oils, and how best to use distilling equipment.[23] Such works stimulated widespread experimentation with distillation. By the end of the century, while male apothecaries remained in charge of medicinal preparations for sale, a 'zest for this activity manifested itself on the domestic front and became a task firmly allotted to women'.[24] Indeed, by the 1590s, such was the vogue for medicinal waters that distilling equipment featured regularly in the accounts of the expenditure of the English gentry.[25] Platt's *Delightes for Ladies*, published in 1602, indicates how established the practice of distilling had become in England by that time. In this work he offered the 'secrets in distillation', which gave practical advice to ladies on the use of the still and showed how enthusiasm for distillation was spreading further and was yielding new flavours and fragrances in the making of flower waters and in the extraction of essential oils.[26]

The art of distillation was clearly known in Ireland in this period and the production of one type of 'cordial water' in particular appears to have been practised to perfection.[27] The Irish version of *aqua vitae*, called *usquebaugh* was 'world renowned' for its medicinal value and flavour. According to Moryson:

> The Irish aquavita, commonly called usquebaugh, is held the best in the world of that kind, which is made also in England, but nothing so good as that which is brought out of Ireland. And the usquebaugh is preferred before our aquavitae because the mingling of raisins, fennel-seed, and other things mitigating the heat and making the taste pleasant, makes it less inflame, and yet refresh the weak stomach with moderate heat and a good relish.[28]

Likewise, Gernon remarked that:

> The aquavitae or usquebath of Ireland is not such an extraction, as is made in England, but farre more holesome, and sweetened with licorissh. It is made potable, and is of the colour

[22] Wilson, *Food*, p. 287.

[23] J. Hester, *The True and Perfect Order to Distill Oyles …* (London, 1575); Hester, *A Joyfull Jewell …* (London, 1579); Hester, *A Compendium of the Rationall Secretes …* (London, 1582); J. Fitzherbert, *The Boke of Husbandrie* (London, 1598); H. Platt, *Sundrie New and Artificiall Remedies against Famine* (London, 1596); Platt, *Delightes for Ladies* (London, 1602). Wilson, *Food*, pp. 395–9.

[24] Thirsk, *Food*, p. 42.

[25] Ibid., p. 29.

[26] Ibid., p. 81.

[27] Wilson, *Food*, p. 396.

[28] Moryson, 'An Itinerary', in Myers (ed.) *Elizabethan Ireland*, p. 187.

> of Muscadine. It is a very holesome drinke, and naturall to digest the crudityes of the Irish feeding. You may drink a knaggin without offence, that is the fourth parte of a pynte.[29]

Gernon noted the use of liquorice in the distillation of usquebaugh, but it is most likely that the liquorice flavour was also achieved by the addition of aniseed, which would help to explain the massive quantities of that spice imported from Bristol, in relation to other imported spices. According to Wilson, English aqua vitae was made from four parts proof spirit to one of water and some aniseeds for flavouring, all rectified together and then sweetened with sugar, while a more strongly flavoured aniseed water was also available to 'strengthen the stomach'.[30]

Cordials such as aqua vitae were sold in England in drams by distillers and also by doctors and apothecaries 'whose recipes were often much more complex'.[31] The extent to which Irish practices evolved during this period to embrace the sort of complex experimentation that was in vogue in England is not clear, and it may be that the production and distribution of cordials remained predominantly in the hands of distillers. That skilled apothecaries were in short supply in south-east Ireland is suggested by the will of the provost marshal of Munster, Nicholas Pett, who retained close links with a Bristol apothecary during his time in Ireland. Pett left to 'Mr Hayson appothecarie dwelling upon the bridg of Bristowe in England two chife horses being collared none with all their furniture whearof one is in Kyerrycurrihy and thither at my house of Ballybeg with Patrick'.[32]

The first detailed evidence of the medicinal use of spices and distillations in Ireland is a 'note of what phisick was given to Sir Matheo de Rensi by his own and Mr Ferfex direction', in 1634.[33] De Renzy, an English planter and surveyor of the customs, was ministered by Thomas Fairfax and Robert Errgh, both physicians, and the medicines recommended to him were purchased from Jacob Ryckman, his apothecary. Ryckman was a native of the Low Countries and, as Mac Cuarta has noted, one of the many Dutch with technical skills who settled in Ireland in the early seventeenth century.[34] It is clear that by this date the 'cordial syrups', 'diet drinks' and flower distillations, popular in England and Europe, were available to purchase in Ireland. De Renzy paid £2 2s for 12 bottles of 'dyett drink', a herbal health drink, and up to 4s 6d per dose of cordial syrup. Among the other potions taken by the planter were exotic items including Barbary conserve, a sweet North African medicinal preparation and syrup of Althæa, presumably made from a distillation of the essential oils of flowers from the Althæa genus, such as marsh mallow and hollyhock.[35] Other 'medicines' included cinnamon, which was used by De Renzy as a 'laxative potion', nutmeg,

[29] Gernon, *Discourse*, p. 361.

[30] Wilson, *Food*, p. 398.

[31] Ibid.

[32] Cork City and County Archives, Caulfield Will Transcripts, U226, p. 4.

[33] B. Mac Cuarta, 'A planter's funeral, legacies, and inventory: Sir Matthew De Renzy (1577–1634)', *Journal of the Royal Society of Antiquaries of Ireland*, cxxvii (1996), p. 27.

[34] Ibid., p. 18.

[35] OED.

Plate 11 Old Bristol Bridge in English reader – *Quarto Anno*, 1912.

mace, sugar, prunes, almonds, isinglass, bole and rosewater. Of these items, most of the spices were regular imports to Ireland from the 1540s, while small quantities of bole Armeniac, an astringent earth used as an antidote and styptic, was imported in 1575, and 'sugar of roses' was imported in small quantities in 1526 and 1550. What is unclear, however, is the extent to which the use of these items changed after the Munster plantation and whether or not the skills required to interpret their medical uses existed in Ireland before the arrival of skilled settlers.

Certainly, the accounts show the pre-Munster plantation importation of a number of items that were undoubtedly intended for medicinal use. In 1550/1, for example, five merchants imported 492lb of 'spert' into Ireland. According to Cotgrave, 'spert' was an alternate name for the German herb hartwort.[36] Culpepper described hartwort as 'a warm martial plant, both heating and drying; it provokes urine and the menses, expels the birth and after-birth; and is good in disorders of the head and womb'.[37] Other medicines imported in very small quantities included arsenic, a poison for vermin that was also adapted for medicinal use, in particular to treat skin

[36] R. Cotgrave, *A Dictionarie of the French and English Tongues* (1611); OED.

[37] *Culpepper's Complete Herbal*, available from: http://www.complete-herbal.com/culpepper/sermountain.htm. [accessed 2 March 2009].

diseases; terra sigillata, an astringent bole, obtained from Lemnos, which was used as an antidote to treat infections and had a binding effect on the stomach or bowels; bole Armeniac, another astringent earth used as an antidote and styptic; senna, a cathartic and emetic; and wormseed, used to treat intestinal worms.[38] The irregularity with which these items appeared in the accounts, and the small volumes imported, however, suggests that there was not a ready demand for any of these medicines in Ireland during the sixteenth century.

## II. Sugar and preservatives

### *IIa. Sugar*

Developing skills in food preservation during this period had a major impact on nutrition and health, in particular by improving the quantity and variety of food that was available to all classes throughout the year.[39] This was of major economic significance, since emerging preservation techniques meant that when supply exceeded current needs, food that might otherwise have been wasted could be absorbed and this, in turn, encouraged greater food production. Thirsk noted the observations of Arthur Standish in this regard, who remarked that fruit in a plentiful year eased the price of victuals, or, in other words, that 'the greater diversity of foods in certain months noticeably eased the demand for cereals and wheat'.[40]

One of the most significant changes to take place in food preservation during the sixteenth century was the increasing use of sugar, the importance of which is evident in the proliferating recipe books of the period. Sugar was used extensively in medicine, distillation, fruit preservation and to create 'fanciful' decorations with sugar paste.[41] The preservation of fruit, in particular, was a major concern in late sixteenth-century cookbooks. A *Book of Cookerye*, written by an unknown author in 1588, devoted a substantial section to the preservation with sugar syrup of various fruits including cherries, gooseberries, damsons, pears, plums, barberries, quinces and oranges.[42] By the mid-seventeenth century, great detail was afforded in cookbooks to conserving and candying fruit and flowers, thus showing the further development of sugar preservation skills, which had been 'emerging experimentally' from the second half of the sixteenth century.[43]

While the qualitative evidence certainly suggests an increasing interest in and use of sugar in England, Thirsk has noted that no one has yet actually sought to measure

[38] *Dictionary of Traded Goods and Commodities, 1550/1820* (2007). Available from: http://www.britishhistory.ac.uk/report.aspx?compid=58689&strquery=arsenic [accessed 16 October 2008]; OED.

[39] Thirsk, *Food*, p. 94.

[40] A. Standish, *The Commons Complaint … Newly Corrected and Augmented* (1612), p. 36.

[41] Thirsk, *Food*, p. 50.

[42] Ibid., p. 51.

[43] Ibid., p. 106.

the trend and that it would be 'instructive if we had some measure of changing imports of sugar in the century 1550–1650', to support the idea of rising consumption.[44] The fragmented surviving customs accounts examined to date have shed some light on the growing importance of sugar in England in this period. The London port book of 1567/8 shows few cargoes of sugar arriving in London that year and these carrying modest quantities – 16.5C on one occasion and 397C on another.[45] From 1612, the Boston port books show a more regular trade in sugar, recording white sugar from 1612 onwards, refined sugar in 1616, and muscovado in 1617, but these were still in small quantities of one to two hundredweight.[46] In addition, studies of individual households have also shown an increase in sugar consumption over time. Mark Dawson, examining the accounts of the Willoughby family in Nottingham, found that between the 1520s and 1570s the annual amount of sugar purchased had roughly doubled from approximately 120lb to 230lb.[47]

The Bristol customs accounts allow a much more detailed examination of changing trends in sugar imports both in England and Ireland during the sixteenth century (Table 8.2 and Figure 8.2). Relatively low, but stable, quantities of sugar were imported into Bristol between 1503 and 1543. Between 1543 and 1546, however, sugar imports increased by a very significant 695 per cent, only to fall again until 1575. In 1594/5, sugar imports peaked at almost 376,000lb. In that year, sugar contributed to a massive 33 per cent of the total value of Bristol's imports. Other changes are notable also. Before 1594, all of the sugar listed (based on its value) was white sugar, whereas in 1594/5 imports diversified to include muscovado, which was a raw or unrefined sugar obtained from the juice of the sugar cane by evaporating it and draining off the molasses; panele, a brown unpurified sugar from the Caribbean and sugar powder, a refined sugar, crushed into powder.

The increasing volumes of unrefined brown sugar arriving into Bristol may indicate that sugar consumption was beginning to spread beyond the upper classes by this time, since unrefined brown sugar was valued at half the price of white sugar.[48] Of the sugar imported in 1595, 43 per cent was unrefined muscovado, 36 per cent unrefined panele and only 20 per cent refined white sugar. Ironically, of course, those who could not afford to purchase white sugar were much better off with the healthier brown substitute, which had not been whitened with lees of lime, which by the mid-seventeenth century was suspected of contributing to the high death rate in London.[49] Nevertheless, although New World sources caused the real price of sugar to drop by almost two-thirds in the sixteenth century, relatively high prices 'kept sugar out of the daily life of most people'. Shammas has noted that 1lb of sugar still

[44] Ibid., pp. 106–94.
[45] Thirsk, *Food*, p. 324.
[46] Ibid.
[47] Dawson, *Plenti*, p. 161.
[48] Flavin and Jones, *Bristol's Trade*, p. 961.
[49] Thirsk, *Food*, p. 80

Table 8.2
Volume of sugar imported to Bristol, 1503–1601 (lb)

| Year | Vol. (lb) |
|---|---|
| 1503/4 | 1,372 |
| 1516/17 | 2,460 |
| 1525/6 | 1,740 |
| 1541/2 | 990 |
| 1542/3 | 1,120 |
| 1545/6 | 8,903 |
| 1550/1 | 2,280 |
| 1563/4 | 1,232 |
| 1575/6 | 8,960 |
| 1594/5 | 375,984 |
| 1600/1 | 97,888 |

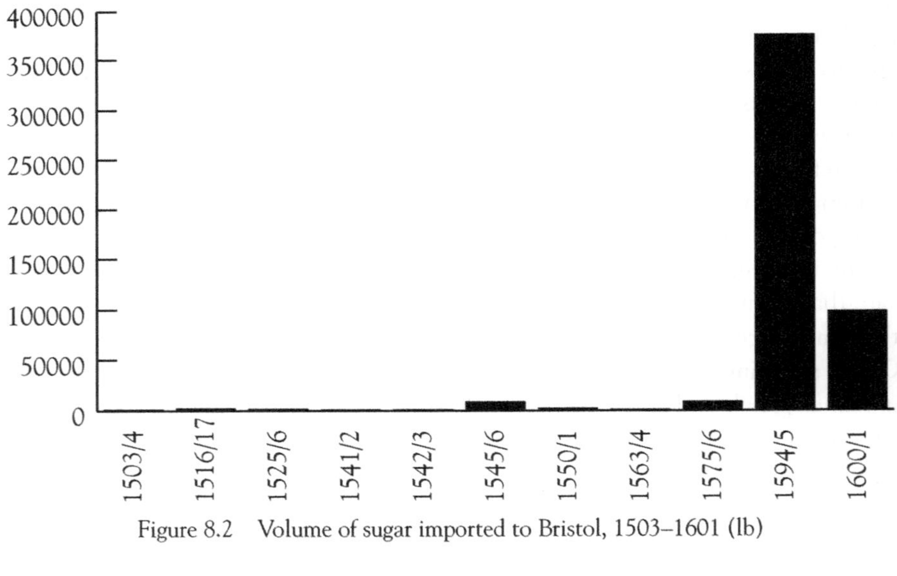


Figure 8.2 Volume of sugar imported to Bristol, 1503–1601 (lb)

cost over 1s in the sixteenth century, which was as much as a labourer's wage for two days' work.[50]

What is also noteworthy about Bristol's recorded sugar imports in 1595 is that it was all 'prize' sugar, taken 'from the sea' by privateers. Indeed, the State Papers indicate that even further quantities of 'prize sugar' arrived into Bristol that year. An entry on 9 February noted that John Hopkins and company had brought a prize of St

[50]Shammas, 'Changes', p. 182.

Table 8.3
Volume of sugar re-exported to Ireland from Bristol, 1503–1601 (lb)

| Year | Vol. (lb) |
|---|---|
| 1503/4 | 0 |
| 1516/17 | 0 |
| 1525/6 | 0 |
| 1541/2 | 0 |
| 1542/3 | 6 |
| 1545/6 | 188 |
| 1550/1 | 0 |
| 1563/4 | 54 |
| 1575/6 | 89 |
| 1594/5 | 871 |
| 1600/1 | 461 |

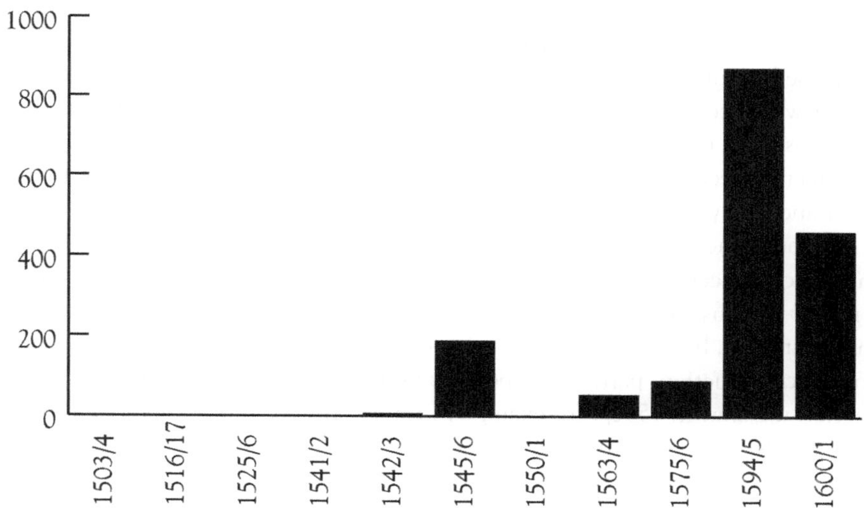


Figure 8.3 Volume of sugar re-exported to Ireland from Bristol, 1503–1601 (lb)

Thomas' sugar to Bristol and were overcharged custom.[51] Little is currently known about the genesis of the Bristol sugar refining industry before the early seventeenth century, but given the huge volumes of unrefined sugar taken by privateers in 1595 and the fact that, in contrast, all of the sugar exported to Ireland from Bristol in that year, as discussed below, was refined sugar, it may well be that small-scale sugar refining was under way in the city at this time (Table 8.3 and Figure 8.3). Since

[51] TNA, SP, 46/39 fol. 9.

Bristol went on to develop a major sugar refining industry in the seventeenth and eighteenth centuries, this is a line of investigation that warrants further attention.

Sugar was slow to gain ground in Ireland, even among the wealthy. Small quantities were imported after 1542, but the trade was irregular and there is no indication of steady growth in consumption. Even as late as 1575 the total volume of sugar imported was only 89lb. To put this in context, by 1524 a large English household such as the Willoughbys was using up to 110lb per annum some 50 years prior to this and, by 1572, this had almost doubled.[52] It is clear that by 1594/5, however, the demand for sugar was beginning to increase in Ireland, most likely due to the imported tastes of sweet-toothed 'New English' settlers. On the other hand, it is significant that the peak in Irish sugar imports correlates exactly with the peak in Bristol's imports. The massive quantities of sugar that arrived in Bristol in 1594, courtesy of privateers, perhaps caused the price to drop and thus stimulated demand in Ireland. In 1594 small volumes of sugar were imported by merchants from all of the main south-eastern towns, indicating widespread but elite consumption. It is also significant that all this sugar was white sugar, rather than the inferior brown muscovado or panele sugars, which were beginning to find a market in England. This again indicates that sugar remained firmly an item of elite consumption in south-east Ireland.

For more humble Irish citizens, it is likely that honey, the traditional sweetener, continued to suffice. Lucas, in his study of Irish food, noted rather unhelpfully that 'honey was of course the only sweetening agent and was so commonly used that it is unnecessary to refer to it in detail'.[53] Certainly, the corporation book of Irishtown, in Kilkenny, records among the rates for victuals in 1566 'honye' at 8d sterling per quart and 'honyed ale' at 4 harps per gallon, but there is no mention of sugar even at the end of the century.[54] Thirsk noted that in England 'humble country folk' were the principal beekeepers, supplying some of the market while keeping hives mainly for their own use and helping out their neighbours.[55] This was probably also the case in Ireland, but it also seems that imports were at times required to supplement domestic production, particularly perhaps during times of the year when hive production was low. In 1550/1 for example, 11 different merchants imported a total of 18.5 barrels of honey, all of which were shipped in November or December.

### *IIb. Salt*

Salt was one of the more prosaic of Irish imports but was of central importance to the Irish economy and diet in the sixteenth century. It had a pivotal role in food preparation and preservation, being vital to the fishing industry and also to the production of bacon, butter and cheese. The importation of salt from England was an erratic trade during this period. There are a number of reasons. First, as it was

[52] Dawson, *Plenti*, p. 162.
[53] Lucas, 'Irish food', p. 40.
[54] Ainsworth, 'Corporation book', p. 28.
[55] Thirsk, *Food*, p. 324.

Table 8.4
Volume of salt imported 1503–1601 (lb)

| Year | Vol. (lb) |
|---|---|
| 1503/4 | - |
| 1516/17 | 1,4000 |
| 1525/6 | - |
| 1541/2 | - |
| 1542/3 | 284,480 |
| 1545/6 | 193,088 |
| 1550/1 | 22,400 |
| 1563/4 | 5,040 |
| 1575/6 | 15,680 |
| 1594/5 | - |
| 1600/1 | - |

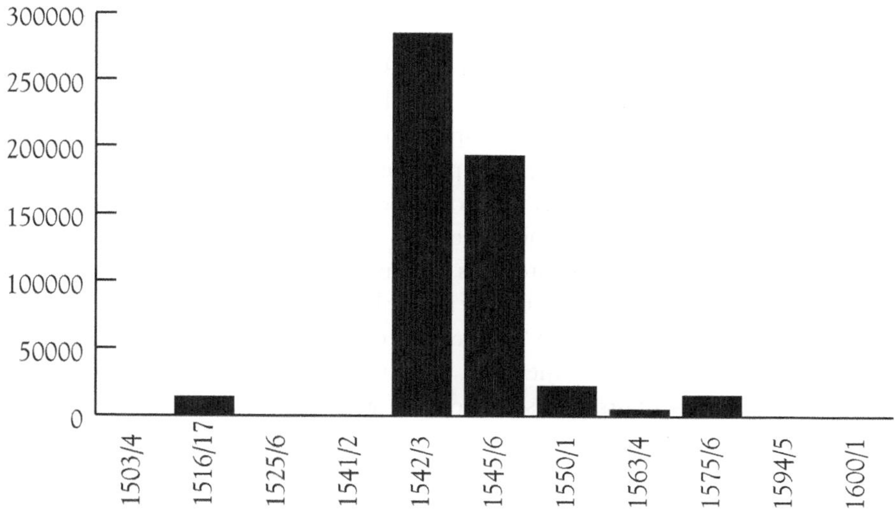


Figure 8.4 Volume of salt imported, 1503–1601 (lb)

durable, salt imported during one fiscal year was not necessarily expended within the same year.[56] Second, salt prices fluctuated significantly during this period, owing to competition between different European countries and the hazards of the trade when war disrupted trade routes.[57] Longfield noted that it is certain that the major portion of Ireland's salt supplies came from direct continental trade with France and

[56] Dawson, *Plenti*, p. 153.
[57] Thirsk, *Food*, p. 318.

Spain, the main salt-producing countries of Europe, and that trade via England, while important, formed a comparatively small proportion of the whole.[58]

Although the quantities of salt re-exported from England to Ireland fluctuated in a haphazard manner, one trend is clear. The salt trade was highly seasonable. In 1542/3, the year in which salt imports from England peaked, 79 per cent of the total annual volume was imported between 26 January and 26 February. Likewise, in 1545/6, 100 per cent of the annual volume of salt imported from England was shipped between 16 March and 10 April. As Easter fell in those years on 25 March and 25 April respectively, the massive concentration of salt imported during these months clearly relates to the preparation and preservation of fish, in particular herring, both for export and for domestic consumption during the Lenten fast. See Table 8.4 and Figure 8.4.

It is also clear from the accounts that this trade, although always haphazard, collapsed entirely at the end of the century. This, Longfield has suggested, was because Irish merchants succeeded in maintaining more frequent intercourse with France and Spain than the more law-abiding English traders.[59] While this is certainly the most likely explanation, other social and political changes may also have affected Irish demand for this commodity in the later sixteenth century. Most obviously, an English Act of Parliament in 1581, banning the importation of salt fish and herrings in an effort to protect English fishing, probably had a significant impact on the Irish industry and also on the demand for salt in Ireland.[60] It is unfortunately not possible to quantify the impact of this legislation on the Irish economy, since fish being imported into England was made exempt from duty at some point in the period October 1564–October 1575 and, therefore, does not appear in the customs records examined for the last quarter of the century.[61]

The protectionism that motivated this ban on imports also lay behind the official English policy of retaining the pattern of fasts inherited from the medieval Catholic Church, which was claimed to be 'for the good of the country's fishing industry and the preservation of livestock rather than for religious reasons'.[62] Despite the official sanction of traditional fasts, Dawson's detailed study of the household accounts of the Willoughbys revealed a parallel decrease in the consumption of preserved herring and salt during the later sixteenth century. Red and white herring, traditionally associated with fasting, were heavily salted and would have arrived at the table much more 'salty' than ling or dry-salted cod, which were generally soaked in several changes in water.[63] This decline, Dawson has suggested may be representative of a general shift in taste away from salty foods but also a decline in the observance of

[58]For documentary evidence of this trade see: Longfield, *Anglo-Irish Trade*, p. 164.

[59]Longfield, *Anglo-Irish Trade*, p. 164.

[60]23 Eliz. C7; H. Hall, *A History of the Custom Revenue of England from the Earliest Times to the year 1887* (London, 1892), p. 317.

[61]SP 12 46/35 fol. 120.

[62]Dawson, *Plenti*, p. 220.

[63]Ibid., p. 220.

religious fasts in the sixteenth century.[64] Overall, his investigation suggested that even in the final years of the sixteenth century, the Lenten fast was still observed in England and that household consumption continued to be shaped by the traditional pattern of fasting, with salted fish remaining an important part of the English diet.[65]

Source limitations make it impossible to compare the extent to which diet evolved in Anglo-Irish households as a result of the Reformation and whether salted foods, and in particular salted fish, remained a dietary staple in the late century. What is apparent, however, as will be discussed later, is that in English and Anglo-Irish households, salt continued to play a similar central role in the rituals of the dining table in the late sixteenth century.

## III. Fruit and vegetables

### *IIIa. Dried fruit*[66]

Wilson has noted that almonds were imported into England on an 'enormous scale' in the Middle Ages.[67] As early as 1286, the royal household consumed some 28,500lb of almonds, while Dame Alice de Bryene, who ran a relatively small household, bought 40lb in 1418–19.[68] Almonds were appreciated for their versatility as a foodstuff. They were eaten as a digestive after sour meats, and could be used in many different forms in cookery, being added to foods blanched, whole, fried, pounded or scattered over the top as decoration.[69] Their most important use, however, was as a substitute for proscribed foods on fasting days and especially during Lent.[70] Almond-milk was used to replace cow's milk and was also boiled with wine and vinegar to produce a butter substitute, which was eaten by those who could afford it, in fasting-day dishes.[71]

The importance of almonds was perhaps subject to regional variation in England in this period. While the London port book for 1567/8 showed almonds arriving from Malaga in significant quantities, Thirsk noted that between 1601 and 1640, the port books of Boston in Lincolnshire recorded only one shipment of 24lb of almonds, imported in 1617.[72] Based on this, she suggested that almonds 'were almost

[64] Ibid., p. 153.

[65] Ibid., p. 223.

[66] The term includes almonds.

[67] Wilson, *Food*, p. 336; T. Scully, *The Art of Cookery in the Middle Ages* (Woodbridge, 1997), p. 70.

[68] L. F. Salzman, *English Trade in the Middle Ages* (Oxford, 1931), p. 411; Dame Alice de Bryene, *The Household Book of Dame Alice de Bryene, of Acton Hall, Suffolk, Sept. 1412-Sept. 1413* (trans. M. K. Dale, ed. V. B. Redstone) (Ipswich, 1931), Appendix iii, p. 120, cited in Wilson, *Food*, p. 333.

[69] Wilson, *Food*, p. 336.

[70] Dawson, *Plenti*, p. 165; Wilson, *Food*, p. 336.

[71] Wilson, *Food*, p. 336.

[72] Ibid., p. 77.

certainly an unusual treat in fenland Lincolnshire'.[73] This may have been the case, but comparing trends from different ports across different time periods is very problematic and the low volumes of almonds found in Lincolnshire at this later date may well have been due to an overall decline in their consumption by the beginning of the seventeenth century. Dawson noted this trend in his analysis of the accounts of the Willoughby family during this period, which he suggested related to a decreasing adherence to the Lenten fast.[74]

Either way, it seems that the Irish, both rich and poor, adopted alternative approaches to fasting in the sixteenth century, perhaps relying on indigenous sources of protein, such as hazelnuts, during periods of fast.[75] Almonds were not recorded in the import accounts before 1575, when just 36lb were listed, and it is significant that these shipments showed no apparent seasonal pattern. The rates for the murage and ancient customs levied at Waterford, recorded in the *The Great Parchment Book* in 1572, also list almonds, which paid a duty of 4d per cwt, but there is no evidence, quantitative or qualitative, of their use prior to this.[76] The 1594/5 account shows a considerable increase in almond imports after the Munster plantation and their absence from the 1600/1 account may well reflect a demand driven by English settlers.

In addition to almonds, the consumption of dried fruit, in particular raisins, figs and dates, also seems to have been influenced by the liturgical year in England. These were eaten in vast quantities by the 'well-to-do', for their sweetness, while sugar was still rare and expensive.[77] The less affluent ate them principally in festive pies and pottages during the 12 days of Christmas, but the rich enjoyed them at other times also, especially on fasting days and during Lent.[78] Indeed, after Easter, the demand for dried fruit seems to decline until the following year. In 1473 a Bristol merchant, Nicholas Palmer, refused to accept a delivery of figs and raisins from Spain that had been delayed due to bad weather, because the ship did not reach the port until after Easter, 'when the season for such fruit was ended'.[79]

There is a strong indication that raisins, unlike almonds, did play a role in the Lenten fast in Ireland too. In 1550/1 and 1594/5, years when very large quantities of raisins were imported, shipments showed a distinct seasonal pattern. In 1551 a massive bulk import of 11 tons of raisins arrived in Ireland on 2 March, which was during the first half of the Lenten period. Likewise in 1594/5, 88 per cent of raisins arrived in Ireland before Lent and, again, there was a very large bulk import of 25 'pieces' or 2,325lb on 5 February, which was a couple of weeks before the beginning of Lent in that year. The accounts also record imports of unspecified 'fruit' in 1503/4,

[73] Ibid.

[74] Dawson, *Plenti*, p. 165.

[75] Hazelnut kernels are a very regular feature of Irish medieval urban archaeological excavations.

[76] GPB, p. 56.

[77] Wilson, *Food*, p. 333.

[78] Ibid., p. 333.

[79] TNA, C 1/48/114, published by Carus-Wilson, *Overseas Trade*, p. 147, cited in Wilson, *Food*, p. 333.

Table 8.5 Volume of dried fruit imported from Bristol, 1503–1601 (lb)

| | 1503/4 | 1516/17 | 1525/6 | 1541/2 | 1542/3 | 1545/6 | 1550/1 | 1563/4 | 1575/6 | 1594/5 | 1600/1 |
|---|---|---|---|---|---|---|---|---|---|---|---|
| almonds | - | - | - | - | - | - | - | - | 36 | 148 | - |
| currants | - | - | - | - | - | - | - | - | - | 528 | 1,342 |
| figs | - | - | - | - | - | - | 672 | - | - | 112 | - |
| Figs (barrel) | - | - | - | - | - | - | - | - | - | - | 2 |
| fruit (lb) | 420 | - | - | 560 | 1,306 | - | - | - | - | - | - |
| prunes | - | - | - | - | - | - | - | 12 | 98 | 210 | 4,172 |
| raisins, great | - | - | - | - | 373 | - | 24,826 | 93 | | 2,623 | 1,810 |
| raisins, Malaga | - | - | - | - | - | - | - | - | - | - | 224 |
| raisins, of the sun | - | - | - | - | - | - | - | - | - | - | 392 |
| raisins, rotta | - | - | - | - | - | - | - | - | - | - | 728 |

1541/2 and 1542/3. Based on its customs value, which was 24d per pound, this fruit also appears to have referred to raisins. Fresh fruit, such as oranges, paid six times less duty than dried, at only 4d per cwt. In each of those years, all of the 'fruit' was imported before or during Lent. See Table 8.5.

### *IIIb. Other fruit, vegetables and herbs*

As discussed earlier, the sixteenth century witnessed an upsurge of interest in fruit and vegetables in England, both in pre-existing English varieties and in newly introduced species.[80] Foreign influences had a major impact on stimulating interest in new varieties of produce and on elevating the status of gardening in general. Religious refugees from the Netherlands and France settled in English towns, bringing with them new types of vegetables and new market gardening and cultivation skills.[81] Gardening became fashionable and the English nobility and gentry took a lively interest in horticulture, exchanging seeds and employing gardeners to nurse new varieties of fruit and vegetables.[82] Foreign tastes also filtered in through 'opportunist merchants'.[83] In 1596, for example, Flemish traders brought 12,600 cabbages, 65 barrels of onions and 10,400 ropes of onions into the port of London.[84] This was not just a luxury enjoyed by Londoners only, however, since in 1593/4, onions, carrots and roots were also imported into Newcastle.[85] Thus, as Thirsk has noted, people throughout the country were made aware of new varieties of produce and of the higher quality of fruit and vegetables raised abroad.[86]

Outside influences were of fundamental importance to changing attitudes about the role of fruit and vegetables in the English diet. What might also be considered, however, are the possible psychological factors that contributed to the surge in popularity for ordered and fruitful gardens in early modern England. A productive garden symbolised many of the preoccupations and values of elite early modern society, representing a level of civility, learning, modernity and order. It is perhaps no coincidence, then, that gardening metaphors can be found seeping into English political discourse at the end of the century. Writing in 1598 to Sir Robert Cecil about the 'woeful' disorder and divided government in Ireland and of the growing threat of the earl of Tyrone, Sir Geoffrey Fenton remarked: 'I see no way to weed this garden, or prevent the overgrowing thereof with such pestilent weeds, as will not be plucked up but with more charges and trouble than the fruit of the garden will be worth.'[87]

There is certainly evidence to suggest that the better-off amongst the Irish engaged with the growing enthusiasm for gardening in the sixteenth century. Patrick

[80] Wilson, *Food*, p. 340.
[81] Ibid.
[82] Wilson, *Food*, p. 340; Dawson, *Plenti*, p. 144; Thirsk, *Food*, p. 286.
[83] Thirsk, *Food*, p. 286.
[84] Ibid., p. 286.
[85] Ibid.
[86] Ibid.
[87] C.S.P. Ire., 1598–1599, p. 229.

Myagh, a Cork citizen who made his last will in 1569, bequeathed to his son a 'dwelling house with a gardeyn in Shandon', while in 1581 William Galway bequeathed his wife the use of his house and orchard.[88] Likewise, William Skiddie bequeathed: 'a garden in Shandon which I purchased of one Richard McAlshe', along with a croft and a park, also in Shandon. Skiddie also bequeathed 'three bedds or plots of land' that he owned in a garden in Shandon, which he required be sold after his death 'to the most advantage'.[89] This is intriguing, as it suggests the existence of urban allotment gardens in sixteenth-century Cork. Other citizens, too, owned parts of gardens. Henry Verdon, for example, left to his daughter Susan his 'part of the Lords Garden' towards the maintenance of her children.[90] Verdon also bequeathed a 'small garden next the market house'; its proximity to the market perhaps indicating that this was a working garden, with a role in provisioning the market with fruit and vegetables.[91]

Perhaps the most significant evidence of Anglo-Irish engagement with gardening in the sixteenth century is a recent report on the garden archaeology of Rothe House in Kilkenny, owned by John Rothe, a merchant whose trade activities are recorded in the 1594/5 Bristol port book. The archaeology of the site and the available documentary evidence revealed that the garden of Rothe's townhouse contained two distinct walled compartments. The area closest to the kitchen was a kitchen garden where herbs and vegetables were grown, while the second compartment contained an orchard. This was planted with a variety of apple and other fruit trees and contained a dovecote and a summer house. The function of the dovecote was to supply the wealthy household with luxurious food: the tender meat of young pigeons. The tame dove, bred in a dovecote, was also believed to preserve against plague.[92] Surrounding the orchard were beds that were planted with climbers, flowering shrubs and fruit bushes. The garden also contained scented flowers and shrubs 'to add to the pleasure of strolling the garden paths'.[93] In general, the contents and layout of the garden fit very well with Thirsk's description of the gardens of the English gentry in this period, who created such elaborate spaces in order to make themselves as self-sufficient as possible, but also to make a strong impression on the local landscape.[94]

In terms of the specific types of produce grown in Rothe's town garden, the archaeology is imprecise. Cóilín Ó'Drisceoil noted that there is 'difficulty in extricating from the sites archaeobotanical records the evidence that relates directly to the plants that were growing within the garden at the time of the Rothes'. This is

[88] Cork City and County Archives, Caulfield Will Transcripts, U226, pp. 2; 17.

[89] Ibid., pp. 8–9.

[90] Ibid., p. 35.

[91] Ibid.

[92] Thirsk, *Food*, p. 28.

[93] Cóilín Ó'Drisceoil, 'The Rothe family garden rediscovered: an interim report on the 2007 archaeological excavation project', *Old Kilkenny Review*, lx (2008), p. 44.

[94] Thirsk, *Food*, p. 207.

because much of the material may have come from the house midden-heap or, in the case of pollen, may have been blown in from the surrounding area.[95] Analysis of pollen from the planting beds has so far resulted in the identification of a variety of species including oak, alder, birch, but in terms of edible plants, only cabbage, chicory and apiaceae flowers have been recorded.[96] Nevertheless, analysis of the charred seeds is still under way, and while preliminary results indicate large quantities of grain in the assemblage, which was probably waste from the brew-house, further analysis may yet shed light on what was grown in the garden and the extent to which this indicates engagement with current horticultural trends in England and Europe during this period.

William Harrison, writing in 1587, regarded in wonder the increasing range of fruits and vegetables entering the English market:

> It is a wonder also to see how many strange herbs plants and annual fruits are daily brought unto us from the Indies, the Americas, Taprobane (Ceylon), Canary Isles and all parts of the world ... I have seen in some one garden to the number of three or four hundred of them, if not more, the half of these names within forty years past we had no manner of knowledge.[97]

The purchase of seeds from abroad was one of the foreign influences that drove this sixteenth-century 'horticultural revolution'.[98] There is no evidence in the customs accounts to suggest that this so-called 'revolution' had any major impact on Irish production, and indeed there was little change in the range of seeds imported to Ireland over the course of the century (see Table 8.6). Very small quantities of caraway, coriander, fennel and *porcelic* (perhaps referring to parsley or parsnip) appear in the accounts in the later part of the century. The most common imports, however, were leek and onion seeds, which, like other types of foodstuffs, first entered the accounts in the 1540s. By 1600/1 very significant volumes of onion seeds were imported. This is significant since according to Lucas, species of wild onion, leek and garlic were in common use in Ireland from ancient times. As in England, however, imported foreign varieties were probably perceived as superior to domestic and wild varieties by those who could afford them.[99]

Other food fashions relating to the growing status of vegetables in England also seem to have been slow to gain appreciation in Irish households, even those of the upper classes. Sprinkling olive oil in salads, 'a rich man's taste adopted from the Continent at the beginning of the sixteenth century', had spread gradually among the gentry class in England over the course of the century.[100] By 1600, bottles of 'salad oil', often purchased in London, appeared in the household shopping lists of

[95] Ó'Drisceoil, 'Rothe family garden', p. 43.
[96] Apiaceae is a member of the parsley family.
[97] W. Harrison, *The Description of England*, G Edelen (ed.) (New York, 1994), pp. 267–8.
[98] Thirsk, *Food*, p. 41.
[99] Lucas, 'Irish food', pp. 31–3; Thirsk, *Food*, p. 286.
[100] Thirsk, *Food*, p. 31.

Table 8.6 Volume of vegetables imported from Bristol, 1503–1601

| | 1503/4 | 1516/17 | 1525/6 | 1541/2 | 1542/3 | 1545/6 | 1550/1 | 1563/4 | 1575/6 | 1594/5 | 1600/1 |
|---|---|---|---|---|---|---|---|---|---|---|---|
| barley/malt/peas/ beans (wey) | 229 | - | - | 71 | 9 | - | - | - | 3 | - | - |
| beans (wey) | - | 367 | 38 | 13 | - | - | - | - | 3 | - | - |
| beans/malt (wey) | - | 24 | - | - | - | - | - | - | - | - | - |
| beans/peas (wey) | - | - | 7 | - | - | - | - | - | - | - | - |
| onions (barrel) | - | - | - | - | - | - | - | - | - | - | 1 |
| peas (wey) | - | - | 2 | - | - | - | - | - | - | - | - |
| seed, caraway (lb) | - | - | - | - | - | - | - | - | 4 | - | - |
| seed, coriander (lb) | - | - | - | - | - | - | - | - | 2 | - | - |
| seed, fennel (lb) | - | - | - | - | - | - | - | 2 | - | - | 4 |
| seed, leek (lb) | - | - | - | - | 8 | 1 | | 122 | 4 | 18 | 12 |
| seed, onion (lb) | - | - | - | 27 | 75 | 48 | 136 | 110 | 14 | 101 | 682 |
| seed, porcelic (lb) | - | - | - | - | - | - | - | 2 | - | - | - |

English gentlewomen.[101] As tastes developed, consumers became finicky about the quality of oil they used. In the household accounts of the Howards of Naworth, for example, distinctions were made between frying oil and salad oil, both of which at this date would have been olive oil, but clearly of different qualities.[102] There is no indication that this fashion was embraced by the Irish elites before the end of the sixteenth century. Salad oil does not occur amongst imports from Bristol at all. This may, however, be an example of a new food trend that was introduced with the plantations. In 1614, for example, 15 gallons of salad oil valued at £1 5s was shipped to Derry on the *Seaflower* of London.

[101] Ibid.
[102] Thirsk, *Food*, p. 322.

# 9

# *The Grape and the Grain*

## I. Ale, beer and cider

Comparing the dietary components of England and Ireland during the sixteenth and seventeenth centuries, Clarkson and Crawford noted that beer was in short supply in Ireland. Army victuallers apparently found it difficult to buy hopped beer in Ireland, and English soldiers disliked the local unhopped ale.[1] In 1580, for example, Lord Burghley instructed a Bristol Merchant, John Bland, to ship 2,000lb of hops to Ireland, telling him that there was the 'gravest want of hopps in that country'.[2] Bland was also instructed to send brewing equipment and four coopers for a month, at a total cost of £106.[3]

Contemporary evidence also suggests that the taste for hopped beer was slow to develop in Ireland. Fynes Moryson noted that the 'common sort' of 'English-Irish' drink was 'not English beer made of malt and hops, but ale'.[4] While he noted that the Gaelic Irish did not have:

> … any beer made of malt and hops, nor yet any ale – no, not the chief Lords, except it be very rarely; but they drink milk like nectar, warmed with a stone first cast into the fire, or else beef broth mingled with milk.[5]

Nevertheless, Gaelic Irish literature suggests that beer was consumed by the Gaelic Irish elite and was even considered to have restorative properties. In 1592, the *Annals of the Four Masters* record the escape of Hugh Roe and Art and Henry O'Neill from prison in Dublin and their subsequent adventures in the Wicklow mountains, where:

> Fiagh immediately ordered some of his servants of trust to go to them, taking with them a man to carry food, and another to carry ale and beer … As to Hugh, after some time, he retained the beer; and, after drinking it, his energies were restored.[6]

[1] Clarkson and Crawford, *Feast*, p. 18.

[2] B.L., Add MS. 5754, f. 180. Victualling accounts, c.1580–1600, cited in Clarkson and Crawford, *Feast*, p. 18.

[3] B.L., Add MS. 5754, f. 187. Victualling accounts, c.1580–1600, cited in Clarkson and Crawford, *Feast*, p. 18.

[4] Moryson, 'An Itinerary', in Myers (ed.), *Elizabethan Ireland*, p. 186.

[5] Ibid., p. 189.

[6] AFM, 1592.

Clearly then, by the 1590s, the taste for hopped beer had to some extent penetrated even the most 'secure and impregnable' parts of Gaelic Ireland.[7] It is likely, however, that its use was restricted to the upper classes initially. Luke Gernon, writing in 1620, noted a distinction between the drinking habits of different classes in Ireland, remarking that in the 'baser cabins you shall have no drink but bonyclabber, milk that is sowred to the condition of buttermilk'. In the castles, however, 'you shall be presented with all the drinkes in the house, first the ordinary beere, then aquavitae, then sacke, then olde-ale'.[8]

The social and economic significance of beer shortages in Ireland during this period should not be overstated. Wilson noted that, apart from London in the sixteenth century, beer was 'fairly slow to gain ground in many parts of Britain' and that in the north and west the bitter flavour of the hops was not liked. By the Elizabethan period, while bitter well-hopped beer continued as the favourite drink in the south of England, the sweeter, less-hopped ale was 'long preferred' in the north and in Scotland.[9] Antagonism towards the use of hops in England is evident in Andrew Boorde's comments, written in 1548. He claimed that ale was still a 'natural drink' for an Englishman, while beer was 'a natural drink for a Dutchman' and he further remarked that beer was being used to excess in England to the detriment of many Englishmen, 'for the drynke is a colde drynke: yet it doth make a man fat, & doth inflate the bely, as it doth appere by the dutche mens faces & belyes'.[10] According to Thirsk, even by the eighteenth century local differences in drinking were prevalent in England. In Yorkshire in the 1790s foreign visitors were struck by the fact that they saw ale everywhere but little beer, while in Cheshire and Gloucestershire, cider was the everyday drink.[11]

While brewing 'was not unknown' in Ireland, there was little commercial production outside the Pale, and brewing was an activity undertaken 'principally to supply the great households'.[12] Certainly wills and inventories show a considerable amount of domestic brewing in Cork during this period. Richard Mathew (1582), William Skiddie (1578), Nicholas Faggan (1578) and Edmond Fitznicholls (1580) were all involved in domestic brewing; brewing pans and aqua vitae pots feature as items of both high economic and social value in their wills. Likewise, an inventory of the goods of Andrew Galway, a Cork alderman, taken in 1580, shows that he was in possession of 214lb of hops.[13] As in England, domestic brewing may have been considered the role of the housewife. Brewing equipment was often bequeathed to

[7] AFM, 1592.

[8] Gernon, *Discourse*, p. 360.

[9] Wilson, *Food*, p. 376.

[10] A. Boorde, *A Compendyous Regyment or a Dyetary of Healthe* (London, 1547), p. 18.

[11] Thirsk, *Food*, p. 306.

[12] Clarkson and Crawford, *Feast*, p. 19.

[13] Cork City and County Archives, Caulfield Will Transcripts, U226, pp. 8, 14, 37, 22, 32.

a female relative. In 1578, for example, William Skiddie left his brewing pan to his wife, Ellen, along with a griddle to bake bread.[14]

There is also evidence of what appears to be small-scale commercial brewing in the south-east of the country. John Rothe, a Kilkenny merchant whose activities are recorded in the 1594/5 account, completed the first stage of Rothe House in that year, which, along with a new shop also contained a brew house. Also, Richard Mathew, a Cork merchant whose will was proved in 1582, bequeathed brewing pans and aqua vitae pots to his son and daughters, along with his tavern, which they were to hold for three years each.[15] This again indicates a role played by women in the brewing and drinks-retailing business.

The local and small-scale nature of brewing during this period was again not unique to Ireland. In England also, most beer and ale brewing was carried on by housewives at home or by individual ale-house keepers.[16] This did not change until at least 1637, when a royal edict forbade ale-house keepers, taverners, cooks and victuallers to brew their own beer, and obliged them to obtain supplies from a common brewer, the aim being to make it easier to levy a tax on brewing.[17] Nevertheless, Prussian visitors in Hertfordshire in 1765–66 noted that practically every household there still made its own beer.[18] Also, inventories from Northamptonshire between the 1660s and 1690s show that domestic brewing equipment was still conspicuous at the end of the seventeenth century.[19]

The customs accounts suggest the rising consumption of hopped beer in south-east Ireland in the sixteenth century. Certainly it seems that even very early in the century there was a ready market for this commodity. In 1503/4 and 1516/17, 6,772 and 5,103 gallons of beer were imported from Bristol respectively. This was a fairly low volume of beer, however, given that evidence for England shows relatively heavy alcohol consumption during this period. The account books for the Percy family of Northumberland, for example, show that in 1512 the lord and lady shared a quart of beer and a quart of wine each day for breakfast, while their two children, aged about 8 and 10, shared a quart of beer at breakfast. At the court of Henry VIII, three ladies in waiting shared a gallon of ale between them each day, likewise at breakfast. Also, calculations based on the amount of barley used for brewing in Coventry during the 1520s indicate that the average consumption of ale was 17 pints of strong ale per week for every man, woman and child in the town.[20]

[14] Ibid., p. 8.

[15] Ibid., p. 22.

[16] Wilson, *Food*, p. 384; Thirsk, *Food*, p. 305

[17] Wilson, *Food*, p. 374.

[18] Ibid., p. 304

[19] Ibid.

[20] A. Lynn Martin, 'How much did they drink? The consumption of alcohol in traditional Europe', University of Adelaide, Australia: *Newsletter of the Research Centre on Food and Drink*. Available from: http://www.arts.adelaide.edu.au/centrefooddrink/publications/articles/martinhowmuchdrink0paper.html [accessed 5 January 2009].

Table 9.1
Volume of hops imported, 1503–1601 (lb)

| Year | Vol. (lb) |
|---|---|
| 1503/4 | 36 |
| 1516/17 | 1,498 |
| 1525/6 | 2,931 |
| 1541/2 | 5,908 |
| 1542/3 | 1,890 |
| 1545/6 | 14,220 |
| 1550/1 | 8,470 |
| 1563/4 | 952 |
| 1575/6 | 8,981 |
| 1594/5 | 34,300 |
| 1600/1 | 31,892 |

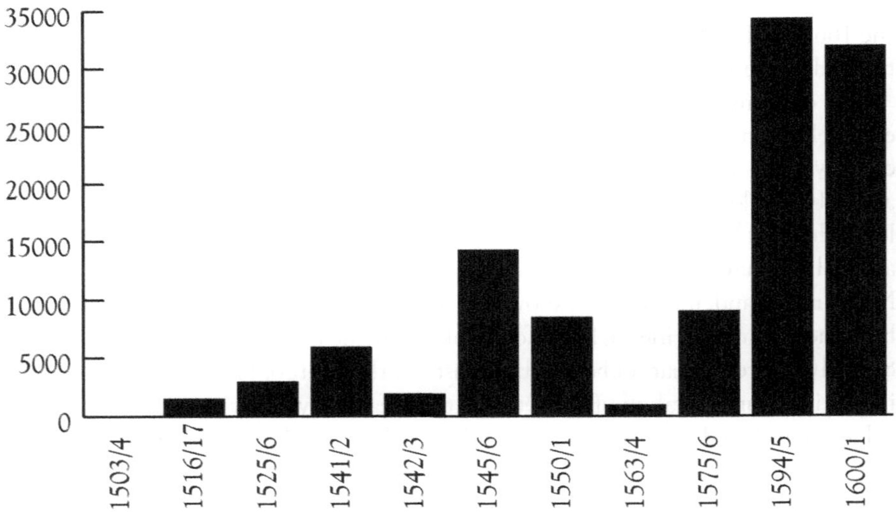


Figure 9.1: Volume of hops imported, 1503–1601 (lb)

After 1516/17 beer was not recorded as an Irish import. On the other hand, as Table 9.1 and Figure 9.1 show, hops became a regular import; an average of 4,987lb per annum was imported in the period 1503–76. Import volumes increased steadily between 1503 and 1542 and then became somewhat erratic until the last decade of the century. In 1594/5, however, there was a massive rise in the volume of hops imported into the region, when 34,300lb was imported, with a similar figure noted for 1600/1.

Table 9.2
Distribution of hops by merchant domicile, 1594/5

| Merchant Domicile | Vol. (lb) |
|---|---|
| Callan | 448 |
| Cashel | 448 |
| Bristol | 560 |
| Clonmel | 1,232 |
| Cork | 3,192 |
| Dungarvan | 112 |
| Fethard-on-Sea | 1,064 |
| Galway | 336 |
| Kilkenny | 6,328 |
| Limerick | 1,512 |
| London | 5,124 |
| New Ross | 2,800 |
| Somerset | 112 |
| Waterford | 8,512 |
| Wexford | 1,232 |
| Youghal | 1,288 |
| Total | 34,300 |

To put these figures in some context in terms of beer consumption, a recipe for beer from 1502 shows that 40lb of hops was used to make 60 barrels of single beer. This, of course, would have varied:

> To brewe beer x. quarters malte. lj. quarters wheet ij. quarters ootos/ xl. ll weight of hoppys.// To make lx barrell[es] of sengyll beer.[21]

The 34,300lb of hops imported in 1594 would therefore have been sufficient to brew approximately 720,216 gallons of single-hopped beer. Table 9.2 shows the probable geographical distribution of hops in that year. It will be noted that the largest volumes were imported by merchants from Waterford, Kilkenny and Cork, but that overall, hops were widely distributed, with small volumes going as far west as Galway.

A possible reason for this increase in beer consumption is that it was driven by economic necessity. The steady acceptance of beer in England in the later sixteenth century was in part due to the fact that it was generally cheaper to produce than ale, since more beer could be made from a given amount of malt.[22] This was of important

[21] R. Arnold, *Customs of London* (1503), p. 247.
[22] P. Hammond, *Food and Feast in Medieval England* (Gloucestershire, 1993), p. 83.

consideration in later sixteenth-century England, a period of inflation. It was no doubt of equal significance in Ireland from the 1580s due to the devastation of Irish land during the Desmond risings and the Nine Years' War, which led to severe grain shortages and dearth. In particular, the year 1600/1 marked a peak in suffering, when severe frost and bad weather compounded the devastation of crops by the English army.[23] On the other hand, it seems that in the early seventeenth century at least, the market value of beer and ale was the same in Ireland. In 1602, the 'rates for victuals' in the corporation book of Irishtown listed 'a quart of the best beer' at 1d, while in the following year 'a quart of the best ale' was valued at the same amount.[24]

It is also likely that the surge in beer production in south-east Ireland in the 1590s was driven, at least initially, by the Munster plantation, and that new settlers, in particular those from southern England, imported with them a taste for hopped beer. It will be noted, however, that the importation of hops remained at a similarly high level after the collapse of the plantation and, therefore, English settlement alone is not a sufficient explanation for this rise. In this regard it is worth thinking about wider European influences on Irish drinking tastes in this period. Certainly the archaeological evidence indicates the extent to which European trends impacted on Irish tastes, and particularly on the material culture of Irish drinking during this period. An excavation at Golden Lane in Dublin unearthed the remains of a number of European-style drinking utensils, including Schnellen drinking tankards from Siegburg in Germany, dating to the 1570s.[25] These were high-status stoneware items used specifically for drinking beer. Also very prominent amongst Irish post-medieval pottery finds are pieces of Westerwald German stoneware, which consisted predominantly of beer tankards, jugs and chamberpots.[26] Westerwald stoneware has been found at various sites in Ireland, in places as far removed as Galway, Kerry, Antrim and Kilkenny.[27] Whatever the main driving force for the demand of hopped beer in Ireland, it is clear that sometime around 1602 it became acknowledged as a staple drink in the south-east of the country. Until 1602, the 'rates for victuals' in the corporation book of Irishtown always listed ale, honeyed ale or aqua vitae, but never beer. In 1602, however, the rates included 'a quart of the best beer', which was listed at 1d.[28]

In addition to beer, another 'new' beverage was consumed in Ireland in the late sixteenth century. In April 1595, 2 tuns of cider was shipped to Sligo by William Hopkins, a Bristol merchant and in May, approximately 168 gallons of cider was shipped to Waterford by a Kilkenny merchant, George St Leger. The St Legers,

[23] Clarkson and Crawford, *Feast*, p. 136.

[24] Ainsworth, 'Corporation book', p. 49.

[25] DIER: Dublin, 2005:442.

[26] Museum of London Catalogue. Available from: http://www.museumoflondon.org.uk/ceramics/pages/subsubcategory.asp?subsubcat_id=839&subsubcat_name=Westerwald&cat_id=714 [accessed 31 December 2010].

[27] DIER: Kilkenny, 2007:970; Kerry, 1997:239; Antrim, 1992:002; Galway, 1992:091.

[28] Ibid.

whose fortunes have been discussed recently by David Edwards,[29] were members of the Kilkenny gentry. Cider was not a fashionable drink in sixteenth-century England and, according to Thirsk, it did not become so until the mid-seventeenth century when it was 'transformed from a poor countryman's taste to a modish urban and upper-class drink'.[30] Thirsk did not make explicit the reason for the mid-seventeenth-century surge in cider drinking but observed that it ceased to be the routine lowly drink of the country folk when it began to be known and consumed in London.[31] This probably related to what has been identified as a transformation in attitudes to fruit in general in the seventeenth century, which was driven by the growing trade in foreign fruit and increasing scientific knowledge, which led to a huge interest in identifying and cultivating new fruits. Seventeenth-century documents from all English counties record many references to the establishment of 'new orchards'.[32] The commonest fruit grown was apples, of which 'innumerable varieties' were produced.[33] The new interest of fruit cultivation no doubt contributed to the growing fashion for cider, which hitherto had been consumed predominantly by the poor in specific regions of the countryside where wild apple trees flourished, including Kent, Sussex, Hertfordshire, Worcestershire and Gloucestershire.[34]

Apple cider, known in Old Irish as *nenadmim*, was drunk by the Gaelic Irish from ancient times. As in England, it was made from wild crab apples that grew in hedgerows and was therefore available to the lower classes. It is surprising, then, that it is not mentioned by any of the English commentators on Gaelic Irish diet, either as a drink of the rich or poor, and it may be that by the sixteenth century it had been supplanted by ale in Ireland.

The importation of cider from England in 1594 is unusual. As a lower-class drink, it may have been imported for the soldiery in Ireland, but this is unlikely given that cider is not recorded in any of the army victualling and purveyancing records between 1566 and 1606.[35] It is more likely, given the very small quantities imported, that the cider was intended for elite consumption, which may perhaps suggest that the drink was becoming modish at an earlier date than that noted by Thirsk. On the other hand, given the volumes under consideration, the imports may just represent an attempt to 'test the market', or to supply an order from a specific household. Archaeological evidence shows that orchards were being planted in Ireland at the end of the century. In Kilkenny, the excavation of Rothe House, completed in 1594, revealed an orchard that was planted with apple and other fruit trees.[36] That this

[29] Edwards, *Ormond Lordship*.
[30] Thirsk, *Food*, p. 18.
[31] Ibid., p. 122.
[32] Ibid., p. 299.
[33] Ibid., p. 299.
[34] Ibid., p. 295.
[35] TNA, E351/148; E351/151; E351/152; E351/157; E351/162; E351/165; E351/170; AO1/292/1095.
[36] Ó'Driscеoil, 'Rothe family garden', p. 44.

was not common practice in Ireland, however, is suggested by the observations of Gernon, who noted that Kilkenny 'is praysed for the wholsom ayer, and delightfull orchards and gardens, which are somewhat rare in Ireland'.[37]

There also appears to have been some demand for imported apples in Ireland. In March 1601 three individual Cork merchants and a merchant from Limerick imported a barrel of apples each into Ireland. That these were not a common variety of apple is indicated by the fact that they were valued at a considerable 3s 4d per barrel. The most expensive variety of apple listed in the 1582 rates book were 'pippins or reinets', which were French dessert apples valued at 3s per barrel.[38] These apples were imported well out of season, suggesting that they may have been a newly introduced longer-lasting variety or that they were preserved in some manner after harvesting. Certainly, the importation of cider and apples for elite consumption in sixteenth-century Ireland suggests that fashion was beginning to change perceptions of fruit in Ireland well before the mid-seventeenth century.

## II. Wine

The Irish wine trade has been discussed in detail elsewhere, particularly in relation to Franco-Irish relations in the late medieval and early modern periods.[39] The vast majority of wine imports were obtained through direct trade with the Continent rather than from England but, unfortunately, most of the surviving evidence about that trade is general in nature, including for example references to the collection of customs in the State Papers and contemporary commentary on the drinking habits of the Irish. In terms of quantitative evidence, only fragmentary records of the accounts of the trade survive.[40] As Longfield has pointed out, this means that any 'definite information' about the trade is 'particularly valuable'.[41]

Certainly, wine seems to have remained the favoured drink of the wealthier Gaelic and Anglo-Irish in the sixteenth century.[42] O'Sullivan remarked that the presence and distribution of wine afforded Irish nobles greater prestige than other beverages

[37] Gernon, *Discourse*, p. 354.

[38] Willan, *Tudor Book*, p. 4.

[39] V. Treadwell, 'The establishment of the Farm of the Irish customs 1603–1613', EHR, 93: 368 (1978), pp. 580–602; M. A. Lyons, 'Maritime relations between Ireland and France, c.1480–c.1630', *Irish Economic and Social History*, 27 (2000), pp. 1–24; M. A. Lyons, *Franco-Irish Relations, 1500–1610: Politics Migration and Trade* (Woodbridge, 2003); T. O'Neill, *Merchants and Mariners in Medieval Ireland* (Dublin, 1987); Longfield, *Anglo-Irish Trade*, pp. 132–46; A. F. O'Brien, 'Commercial relations between Aquitane and Ireland, c.1000 to c.1550' in Jean-Michel Picard (ed.), *Aquitaine and Ireland in the Middle Ages* (Dublin, 1995), pp. 35–87; O' Sullivan, *Hospitality*, pp. 104–5.

[40] The State Papers 23 April 1571 contain 'a briefe note of all suche somes of money as hathe bene reseruede and paiede in readie money to her Majesties's use of the Custome of thimport of wyens'. C.S.P. Ire., xxxii, 14; See also Cal. Carew MSS., ii, p. 27.

[41] Longfield, *Anglo-Irish Trade*, p. 137.

[42] A. Horning, '"The root of all vice and bestiality": exploring the cultural role of the Ulster alehouse', J. Lyttleton and C. Rynn (eds), *Plantation Ireland* (Dublin, 2009), p. 116.

due to its impressive import status.[43] In a sixteenth-century poem addressed to Cú Choigríche Ó Cléirigh it was claimed that 'red wine will not last long in his palace, so abundantly is it drunk'.[44] Likewise another sixteenth-century poem addressed to the same Màg Uidhir chief claimed that 'ships are not sufficient provision for the Màg Uidhir, they do not spare drink; the Màg Uidhir surpass in providing wine, they are not loath to dispense it'.[45] While much of this was probably flattery directed by bards towards their patron, other accounts also suggest the large quantities of wine consumed by Gaelic chiefs. According to Hooker, recorded in Holinshed, Shane O'Neill had 'most commonlie 200 tunnes of wine in his cellar'.[46] While in 1600, when Sir Richard Wingfield raided the home of Phelim McFeagh, he took 600 cows and rifled his house, 'where was great store of wine, aqua vitæ, and other provision for Christmas'.[47]

Although it cannot be quantified, the scale and economic significance of the Hispano-Irish wine trade in the latter part of the century is clear from numerous incidental references in the State Papers. English concern with Spanish and native Irish intrigues meant that Irish merchants returning from Spain were frequently examined by officials. In 1588, lord deputy Perrot forwarded a letter to Walsingham, from Alexander Brywer, mayor of Waterford, in which he noted that 'three ships of our town arrived here who departed Cadiz in Andalucia about the beginning of last month. Their lading is sack and aqua vitae'.[48] Likewise, Patrick Foxe wrote to Walsingham of the intelligence he heard from a Dublin merchant, Herbert, who 'came lately from Spain with a ship laden with wines'.[49]

The Bristol accounts further illuminate the nature and extent of the Irish wine trade in the sixteenth century. First, the accounts confirm that wine was not re-exported from England to Ireland in significant quantities (see Table 9.3 and Figure 9.2). With the exception of 1545/6, the volumes arriving from Bristol were very low and, in some years, particularly towards the end of the century, no wine was recorded among imports. On the other hand, wine did feature as a minor re-export from Ireland to England. Woodward noted this trend in his study of the Chester port books from the later sixteenth century. These showed that re-exports of wine from Dublin to Chester peaked in 1582/3, when 7,119 (28.25 tons) gallons was shipped (Table 9.4). Of this, 189 gallons was French and the remainder Spanish.[50] Woodward suggested that the re-export of Spanish wine to England from Ireland increased during

[43] O'Sullivan, *Hospitality*, p. 104; O'Neill, *Merchants*, pp. 44–8.

[44] D. Greene, (ed. and trans.) *Duanaire Mhéig Uidhir* (Dublin, 1972), poem XX verse 4, cited in O'Sullivan, *Hospitality*, p. 105.

[45] Green, poem XXIV verse 42, cited in O'Sullivan, *Hospitality*, p. 105.

[46] R. Holinshed, *Chronicles of England, Scotland, and Ireland*, vol. III (1587), p. 113. Available from: http://www.english.ox.ac.uk/holinshed/texts.php?text1=1587_0540 [accessed 31 December 2011], cited in Longfield, *Anglo-Irish Trade*, p. 133.

[47] C.S.P. Ire. 1600/1601, pp. v-lxii.

[48] C.S.P Ire., 1586–88, p. 489; cited in Longfield, *Anglo-Irish Trade*, p. 144.

[49] C.S.P *Ire.*, *1588–92*, p. 120; cited in Longfield, *Anglo-Irish Trade*, p. 145.

[50] Woodward, *Trade*, p. 11.

Table 9.3
Volume of wine imported from Bristol, 1503–1601 (gallons)*

| Year | Vol. (gallons) |
|---|---|
| 1503/4 | 756 |
| 1516/17 | 0 |
| 1525/6 | 203 |
| 1541/2 | 126 |
| 1542/3 | 126 |
| 1545/6 | 8,316 |
| 1550/1 | 2,268 |
| 1563/4 | 0 |
| 1575/6 | 0 |
| 1594/5 | 0 |
| 1600/1 | 441 |

*There are 252 gallons to a tun.

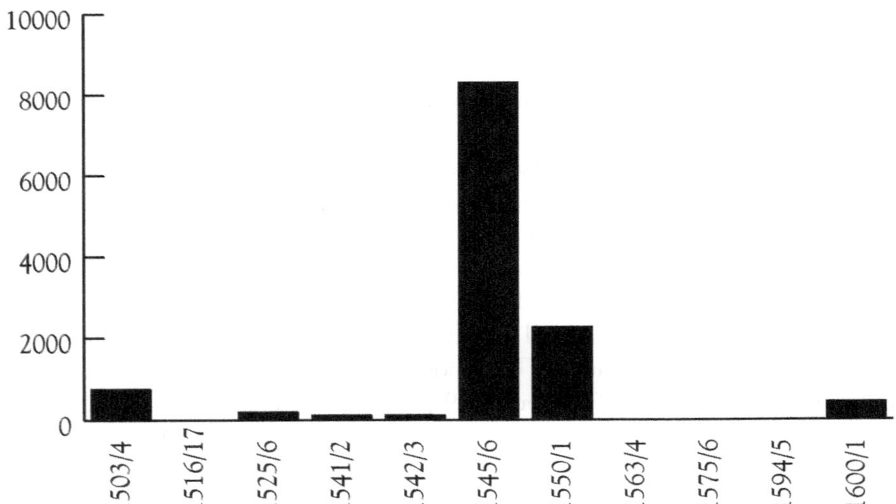


Figure 9.2 Volume of wine imported from Bristol, 1503–1601 (gallons)

the 1580s as tension between England and Spain grew, and that it remained raised until the end of the period.

The Bristol accounts show similar trends to those found by Woodward, with re-exports of Spanish sack from the south-east of Ireland peaking in 1594/5 (Table 9.5). It is also apparent that the volumes exported from this region in some years far exceeded the volumes shipped from Dublin. Indeed, comparing the peak volumes exported from both regions shows that the amount of wine re-exported to England

Table 9.4 Volume of wine re-exported from Ireland to Chester, 1576–1666 (gallons)

| | French | Spanish | Total |
|---|---|---|---|
| 1576/7 | 6300 | 378 | 6,678 |
| 1582/3 | 189 | 6,930 | 7,119 |
| 1584/5 | 756 | 3,402 | 4,158 |
| 1592/3 | 0 | 4,032 | 4,032 |
| 1600/1 (6 months) | 0 | 5,040 | 5,040 |
| 1602/3 | 0 | 4,851 | 4,851 |
| 1665/6 | 0 | 1,890 | 1,890 |

*Source*: Woodward, *Trade*, p. 11

Table 9.5
Volume of wine re-exported from Ireland to Bristol, 1503–1601 (gallons)*

| Year | Vol. (gallons) |
|---|---|
| 1503/4 | 3,780 |
| 1516/17 | 9,072 |
| 1525/6 | 8,442 |
| 1541/2 | 2,173 |
| 1542/3 | 504 |
| 1545/6 | 0 |
| 1550/1 | 7,560 |
| 1563/4 | 252 |
| 1575/6 | 0 |
| 1594/5 | 24,759 |
| 1600/1 | 3,654 |

*In 1594/5 this comprised 5,607 gallons of French wine and 19,152 gallons of Spanish sack; in 1600/1 all of the exports were of Spanish sack.

from the south-east of Ireland was up to 250 per cent greater than from Dublin. While such findings suggest increasing trade between south-east Ireland and Spain, which was of fundamental importance to the economic prosperity of the region during this period, it must be remembered that in the context of Bristol's wine trade, the figures for wine sent from Ireland to Bristol were tiny, both in relative and absolute terms. On an absolute level, declared wine imports to Bristol from the Continent (large volumes were smuggled after the 1558 rates increase) were approximately 1,400 tuns (352,800 gallons) per annum. In relative terms, it might be noted that throughout the sixteenth century wine accounted for around 40 per cent of Bristol's import trade, which made it by far the most important branch of Bristol's overseas trade. Wine alone accounted for about twice the value of *all* Bristol's imports from Ireland. While it is impossible to compare the volumes of wine imported to Ireland and Bristol from the Continent, these figures give a sense of just how important wine was in England at this time and, as such, provide a starting point for thinking about the economic and social significance of wine, and its relative importance with regards to other luxury produce, among the Irish elite at this time.

# 10

# *Cooking and Dining*

## I. Cooking equipment

Very little is currently known about the processes of cooking or food technology in sixteenth-century Ireland. The absence of surviving recipe books, household accounts, probate inventories and physical evidence of everyday domestic utensils makes it extremely difficult to assess what changes, if any, occurred in Irish kitchens in this period. Contemporary references to cooking practices are plentiful but largely unhelpful, being intended to denigrate the practices of both the 'wild' and 'English-Irish', whose cooking practices, according to Moryson, had 'little by little been affected with Irish filthiness'.[1] Nevertheless, it is possible to piece together at least some aspects of the material culture of food preparation in this period, and to compare them with contemporary practices in England.

Documentary evidence suggests that in the wealthier households, cooks in Ireland, as elsewhere, had a significant range of cooking paraphernalia at their disposal – and this gives us some indication of the type of cookery carried out and also of the methods of provisioning a large household in the sixteenth century. An inventory of the household at Castleisland, County Kerry, for example, shows that like most large households in this period, the castle was still very self-sufficient. The presence of items including meal and malt sieves, tubs to make cheese in, milking pails, butter churns, garden seeds, seed barley and so on, indicate that most of the household's basic provisions were produced on site. Other items, too, were produced at home. The inclusion of mustard seeds, a quern with which to grind them, and mustard pots show that the household produced their own mustard rather than buying ready-made.[2] This was not necessarily because ready-made mustard was not available locally. The Willoughbys at Wollaton Hall, whose dietary practices were investigated recently by Dawson, also produced their own mustard, in addition to buying a

[1] For a detailed example of contemporary attitudes to Irish diet see Moryson, 'The Itinerary of Fynes Moryson', in C. L. Faulkner (ed.), *Illustrations of Irish History and Topography, Mainly of Seventeenth Century* (London, 1904), pp. 225–30. Reprinted in Clarkson and Crawford, *Feast*, p. 12.

[2] K. O'Shea, 'A Castleisland inventory, 1590', *Journal of the Kerry Archaeological and Historical Society*, xv–xvi (1982), pp. 37–46.

pre-prepared variety.[3] Mustard was a very common accompaniment in England and was frequently served with preserved fish, which was eaten during Lent.[4]

In terms of preparing food, the kitchen at Castleisland appears to have been equipped in a similar manner to a comparable sixteenth-century English kitchen.[5] A mortar and pestle, for example, was used to pound herbs and spices and to mix together various ingredients. There was also a grater, which was probably used to make breadcrumbs to thicken sauces.[6] The inventory records three types of knife: a chopping knife, table knives and a cleaver, for dividing up joints of meat. The customs accounts show, however, that a range of other kitchen knives were available to the cook, including paring knives, coarse knives, pairs of knives and fine knives, the last presumably used for shredding ingredients.[7]

With regards to cooking itself, inventories, customs accounts and last wills all show the indispensability of brass pans in this period. These were owned in various weights and sizes, depending on the task for which they were intended and, of course, the size of household they catered for.[8] Nicholas Faggan, a Cork merchant, had one large brass pan valued at 30s and four small brass pans valued collectively at the same.[9] Pans are sometimes recorded with 'pothooks', which were used to hang them over the fire to boil food.[10] In the customs accounts, brass pans were recorded by weight and are found in varying sizes from a modest 20lb to a massive 120lb. For mass catering, cauldrons were used. The Castleisland inventory lists a cauldron, which was probably used to boil large quantities of beef. The inventory also lists a beef fork, which would have been used to remove the joint from the pot, and also a skimmer, which was used to remove any scum that collected on the surface of the water during boiling.[11]

Given their significant second-hand value such pans were regularly bequeathed in wills, sometimes along the female line. Ellyne Ny Connyly, in 1581, bequeathed her two brass pans to her granddaughter Margaret.[12] This was common practice in England and was, as Pennell has suggested, a means of affirming close ties of female friendship as well as providing 'some practical insurance against female economic vulnerability'.[13] Pots and pans were part of a 'predominantly female sphere of operation', and in passing them down from female to female, they became 'invested

[3] Dawson, *Plenti*, p. 169.

[4] Dawson, *Plenti*, p. 169. The Willoughbys also made their own mustard.

[5] Dawson, *Plenti*, p. 191.

[6] See Dawson, *Plenti*, p. 191; O'Shea, 'Castleisland inventory', p. 41.

[7] Dawson, *Plenti*, p. 191.

[8] Brass pans are found in a number of different sizes in the customs accounts, from 20lb to a massive 120lb.

[9] Cork City and County Archives, Caulfield Will Transcripts, U226, p. 32.

[10] For example, O'Shea, 'Castleisland inventory', p. 41.

[11] Dawson, *Plenti*, p. 295.

[12] Cork City and County Archives, Caulfield Will Transcripts, U226, p. 15.

[13] Pennell, 'The material culture of food', p. 43; A.L. Ericson, *Women and Property in Early Modern England* (London, 1993), p. 222.

with personal significance as possessions rather than merely utensils'.[14] Brass pans also featured among bequests from men to their female servants. Edmund White, for example, bequeathed to Anastas Morrice a chest that had belonged to his wife, along with a 'little brass pan' and a handiron.[15]

In addition to boiling in pans, food was cooked in a variety of other ways. Spits, dripping pans, rods, basting ladles and andirons are all found in the records and were used to roast meat over an open fire.[16] The spits rested in front of the fire on a pair of andirons. The meat was basted with sauces facilitated by the use of dripping pans and ladles.[17] Food was also grilled on a gridiron or griddle, which was set over the fire.[18] Andirons and gridirons were regularly bequeathed to family members in wills. Andirons, which were also used to hold burning logs in an open fire, were forged from wrought iron and could be very decorative, bearing a family crest, for example.[19] These were sometimes imported directly from the Low Countries. In 1596, for example, merchants from Cork bought gridirons and andirons in Middelburg for shipment back to Cork, suggesting that there was a market in the city for continental styles of metalwork.[20]

Baking was also a common method of cooking in Irish households. The cook at Castleisland baked pies, as indicated by the inclusion of a pie plate in the inventory. Baking food in a pie was a method of food preservation. Dawson has noted that venison was frequently baked in pies because the meat was a mark of social distinction and was eaten by only a limited number of people. It would therefore be quite some time before a carcass, or even a joint, was fully consumed.[21] This would appear to have also been the case in elite Irish homes. Gernon, writing about his experience of hospitality in Ireland noted: 'neyther shall there be wanting a pasty or two of redd deare – that is more common with us then the fallow'.[22] Contemporary recipes show that melted butter was poured into these pies or pasties to seal the contents from the air; a similar method to potting the food.[23] This method would appear to have been very effective. At Wollaton in 1587, for example, Dawson noted that a loin of veal received into the accounts during the week ending 18 March was eaten in the form of two pies, one eaten the following week and one a month later.[24]

With regards to more delicate or finer styles of cookery, it is interesting to note that some of the implements commonly used by English and continental cooks

[14] Pennell, 'The material culture of food', p. 43.

[15] Cork City and County Archives, Caulfield Will Transcripts, U226, p. 23.

[16] The inventory of Edmund Fitznicholls contains 'spits with their hooks all of iron', and a 'gridiron or roasting iron'. Cork City and County Archives, Caulfield Will Transcripts, U226, p. 14.

[17] For example, TNA, E190113110, f. 49v; O'Shea, 'Castleisland inventory', p. 41.

[18] TNA, E1221994 f22v.

[19] Cork City and County Archives, Caulfield Will Transcripts, U226, pp. 8; 14; 36.

[20] Appleby, *Calendar of Material*, p. 84.

[21] Dawson, *Plenti*, p. 184.

[22] Gernon, *Discourse*, p. 361.

[23] G. Markham, *The English Housewife*, ed. M. Best (Toronto, 1994), p. 96.

[24] Dawson, *Plenti*, p. 184.

are difficult to find in the Irish records before the 1590s. Although a frying pan is listed in the Castleisland inventory, taken in 1590, frying pans did not feature as imports before 1594/5. In that year a significant quantity were imported from Bristol, probably destined for kitchens in Cork and Galway.[25] Frying pans were used to make pancakes and fritters as well as fricassees.[26] Another item found only in the later accounts is the chafing dish. These were small dishes for holding charcoals over which another pan could be set, and were used when fine cooking was required. A recipe in a mid-sixteenth-century cookbook for preparing crab, for example, includes placing the meat with some butter in a dish over a chafing dish and adding cinnamon, sugar and a little vinegar before serving with the heads broken and served at the side.[27] Chafing dishes were imported from Bristol in 1600, which again may suggest a late adoption of this cooking method.[28] On the other hand, of course, it may be that these items were arriving into Ireland on another trade route in this period. Archaeological evidence, for example, suggests that chafing dishes also arrived from France. Excavations in Cork city revealed, amongst a range of imported domestic ware, chafing dishes from La Chapelle des Pots.[29] There is other occasional evidence in the customs accounts to suggest the influence of French cookery on upper-class Irish practices. Boultels, from Beaupreau in France, for example, a kind of cloth used for bolting or sifting flour, were imported by a Kilkenny merchant in 1601.[30]

Most cooking in the sixteenth century, in both Ireland and England, was done over an open hearth. Fires were placed on a base in the centre or back of the dwelling and smoke was removed through holes in or near the roof. One of the most significant technological developments in terms of domestic comfort, heating and food preparation in this period was the evolution of the chimney, which became more common in English homes from the sixteenth century.[31] Over time, methods of smoke removal evolved from the use of a chimney bay, to a smoke hood, and then a chimney. Brick fireplaces and chimneys were built on the central hearth to remove smoke more efficiently, shifting to the flank of the house as the chimney became important structurally in supporting the first floor as well as housing ovens for cooking.[32]

The extent to which Irish housing evolved along these lines is unclear. A map of Cork (Plate 12) made at the end of the sixteenth century suggests that by this time many of the houses in the city – even though they were, as Gernon pointed out,

[25] For example, TNA, E19011310 f32r; f39r; f46v.

[26] Dawson, *Plenti*, p. 191.

[27] A. Ahmed (ed.) *A Proper Newe Booke of Cookerye* (Cambridge, 2002), p. 141. Cited in Dawson, *Plenti*, p. 191.

[28] TNA, E190113211 f35r; DIER Galway 1995:119.

[29] DIER Cork 1974:0010.

[30] TNA, E190113211 f32v.

[31] W. S. Sparrow, *The English House: How to Judge its Periods and Styles* (London, 1908) pp. 85–6.

[32] For a detailed discussion of the evolution of chimneys see, for example: L. A. Shuffrey, *The English Fireplace* (London, 1912).

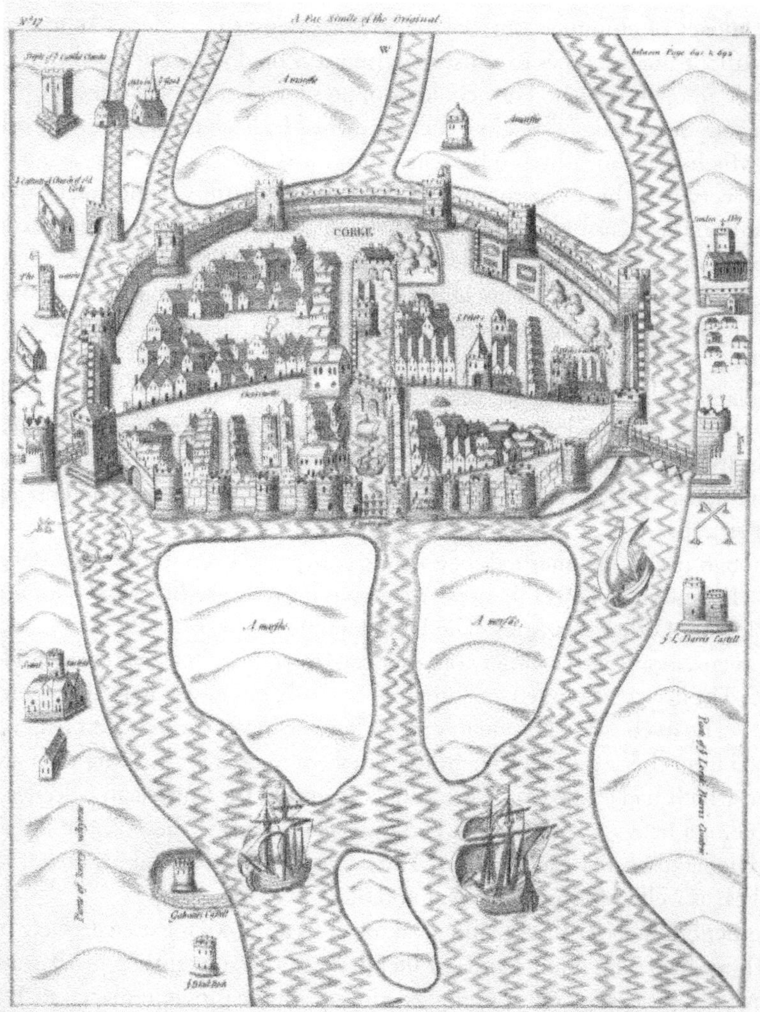

Plate 12 Map showing Cork City, first produced in Pacata Hibernia (London, 1633), but believed to date to c.1585–1600.

built in the 'Irishe forme' – had simple chimneys. Since chimneys were only becoming established in England from the mid-sixteenth century, this does suggest that the more affluent in Irish towns were abreast of current architectural developments and able to afford to implement them. Certainly, the last quarter of the century appears to have been a time of significant house building in Cork. In 1574, William Sarsfield bequeathed a 'newe stone house' in the city to his son, while in 1580 Andrew Galway bequeathed 'newe' stone houses to three of his sons.[33]

[33]Cork City and County Archives, Caulfield Will Transcripts, U226, pp. 6, 37–9.

The impact of chimneys on cooking in Irish houses is unclear. As in England, those without the resources to construct chimneys no doubt continued to cook and bake over an open hearth. They could also, presumably for a small fee, avail of the use of a communal bakehouse, like the one owned by Richard Mathew, a Cork merchant, which he bequeathed to his wife Alison in 1582.[34] It also appears, however, that the very wealthy, even towards the end of the century, continued to bake in the traditional way, using a griddle pan over a fire, rather than in an enclosed oven. William Skiddie, for example, bequeathed his wife 'a gredle with a handiron to bake bred'. Griddle baking was an ancient technique, and was typically associated with the production of oat cakes, which were described by numerous observers as central to the Irish diet. It has been suggested that griddle baking is particularly associated with Ireland and also Scotland, because of the widespread use of peat for fuel. Peat gives a slow, gentle heat unsuited to oven baking. The continuation of this technique in Ireland was probably therefore in part for practical environmental and economic reasons, while also representing the traditional cultural tastes and preferences of Irish citizens.

Although traditional methods of cooking continued even in the more developed parts of Ireland, consumers do appear to have been aware of the developing food technologies of other countries. The best example of this is the lading of two brass Dutch ovens, along with a variety of other cooking related brassware, at Middelburg in 1596. These were intended for shipment to Cork, but never arrived at their destination.[35] The ovens were presumably an earlier version of the cast iron Dutch ovens produced from the seventeenth century, which were used for cooking with an open fire, and which had a huge market in England and in the American colonies. They consisted of a heavy pot with a lid. Food was placed inside the pot, the lid was put on, and hot coals were heaped over it. The ovens were used for baking bread, biscuits and cakes, as well as for roasting meat and other cooking.

Whether boiling, roasting, grilling, baking or frying, cooking utensils were of little use without fuel. The main source of fuel prior to the sixteenth century was wood or charcoal, but as the century progressed it was increasingly replaced in England by coal, or seacoal as it was known, because much of it was mined near the Northumbrian coast.[36] It is not clear when coal became widely used as a cooking fuel, and it probably took some time before it was accepted as a domestic rather than an industrial fuel.[37] In Ireland, coal was shipped to Drogheda in 1576 by a merchant from Workington in Cumberland. This was certainly intended for industrial use, however, since it was described as 'smith coal'.[38]

[34] Cork City and County Archives, Caulfield Will Transcripts, U226, p. 22.
[35] Appleby, *Calendar*, p. 84.
[36] Dawson, *Plenti*, p. 195.
[37] Dawson, *Plenti*, pp. 195–6.
[38] TNA, E190112912 f.18r.

Bristol was also a producer of mineral coal in this period. By 1615 it was noted that:

> the poorer sort of the inhabitants of Bristol do use to burn stone coal alias sea coal in their houses, which coal they have had from Kingswood and other places adjoining the said city … not being able to buy wood which is very dear and scarce to be had.[39]

Certainly from the 1560s onwards, coal was regularly recorded as being exported from Bristol to the Continent. It is instructive, therefore, that it never turns up amongst exports to Ireland on this route before the end of the sixteenth century, suggesting that there was no market for coal in Ireland by this date. This appears to have changed before the middle of the following century. In 1636, gentlemen of London were paying £10,000 per year to lease the administration of coal shipped to Ireland, Guernsey, Jersey and the Isle of Man.[40]

## II. Napery and tableware

Cleanliness was an important feature of good manners when dining in England and, as the sixteenth century progressed, society became more 'civilised', with increasing emphasis placed on dining decorum and standards of behaviour at the table. The development of printing meant that 'manners books' proliferated and became cheaper, making them available to a wider section of society, and there was an increasing emphasis on teaching children how to behave. Erasmus' short treatise, *De Civilitate* (1530), for example, contained such useful advice as 'withdraw when you are going to vomit; vomiting is not shameful, but to have vomited through gluttony is disgusting' and 'Fidgeting in one's seat, shifting side to side, gives the appearance of repeatedly farting, or trying to do so'.[41]

Contemporary manners books were becoming available in Ireland in this period, indicating knowledge of, and perhaps engagement with, evolving attitudes to manners. 'Small books for children', most likely referring to the popular late medieval *The Little Children's Little Book*, and also Francis Seager's manual *The School of Virtue* were imported from at least 1576, and perhaps earlier.[42] Both of these contained specific advice to children regarding table manners and food hygiene, and included detailed instructions on hand washing before and after eating. *The Little Children's Little Book* warned children to:

[39] J. Hatcher, *The History of the British Coal Industry Volume 1, Before 1700: Towards the Age of Coal* (Oxford, 1993) p. 179.

[40] TNA, E 214/725.

[41] Erasmus, *De Civilitate* (1530) cited in M. Visser, *The Rituals of Dinner* (New York, 1992), p. 67.

[42] *The Little Children's Book* MSS. Harl. 541 fol, 210 and Egerton 1995. For imports see, for example, TNA, E190112912 f9v; TNA E190113110 f49r; f50r; TNA, E190113211 f 24 r &v; f26v; f27v; f29r; f 30r; f32r; f 34r & v.

Look thy hands be washed clean,
That no filth on thy nails be seen.
Take thou no meat till grace be said [43]

Children were to keep their cloth clean and to wash their hands again after their meal, taking care to allow their superiors to wash first. They were also advised not to spit in the washing basin. Francis Seager's *School of Virtue* (1557) also directed children with regards to table manners. Children were to bring their parents water to wash in when clearing the table after the meal:

Then on the table attend with all diligence,
It for to void, when done have thy parents.
Each side of the cloth do thou turn in;
Folding it up, at the higher end begin.
A clean towel then on the table spread,
The towel wanting, the cloth take instead.
The basin and ewer to the table then bring,
In place convenient their pleasure abiding.
When thou shalt see them ready to wash,
The ewer take up, and be not too rash
In pouring out water more than will suffice.[44]

The availability of advice, of course, does not necessarily indicate compliance and it is impossible to determine the extent to which the practices of Irish dining incorporated such rituals. Inventories are rare but the occasional surviving example shows that the implements required for hand-washing rituals were certainly present in some Irish homes. Nicholas Faggan's inventory, for example, lists 'two olde hand towels' valued at 4d. These were provided to guests to dry their hands after washing, both before and after meals.[45] The inventory of the castle on Castleisland, unsurprisingly, also listed towels, both old and new, amongst the linen.[46]

Table napkins, used to wipe lips before and after drinking, and tablecloths also feature in records of Irish consumption. Table linen, in the sixteenth century, was used to display wealth and status. According to Visser, by the high Middle Ages tablecloths had become such an essential requirement to the 'beauty of the banquet' that they were 'even more expressive of the community of the diners than the table itself'.[47] She noted that to 'share the cloth' of a nobleman was to be seen and treated as his equal. When a master dined with servants at the same table, either he was the

[43] E. Rickert and L. J. Naylor, *The Babees Book, Medieval Manners for the Young* (Ontario, 2000), p. 9. Available from: http://www.yorku.ca/inpar/babees_rickert.pdf [Accessed 1 January 2014].

[44] Ibid., p. 78.

[45] Dawson, *Plenti*, p. 211; Cork City and County Archives, Caulfield Will Transcripts, U226, p. 32.

[46] O'Shea, 'Castleisland inventory', p. 37.

[47] Visser, *Rituals*, p. 156.

only person with a cloth before him, or the whole table was covered with a cloth but at his place another napkin was laid.[48]

The napkins and tablecloths recorded in customs accounts, in other records of trade and in wills and inventories were generally made of diaper and occasionally of damask.[49] These were self-patterned, fine white linens, the primary difference being the complexity of the pattern. Small repeat patterns, often of a geometrical form, were described as 'diaper', and figurative patterns with longer repeats as 'damasks'.[50] Diaper was made in Italy, Germany and the Low Countries from at least the fourteenth century and subsequently in many other parts of Europe. Linen damask was associated predominantly with the southern Netherlands. There is evidence to suggest that, like other luxury items, these were sourced and imported directly from the Low Countries, which perhaps explains why they are rarely found as imports from England. In 1596, for example, among the luxury items purchased by Cork merchants at Middelburg were five pieces of damask and diaper tablecloths.[51]

Other fabrics were also used to make tablecloths. At Castleisland, two long tables in the parlour, the room most likely to be associated with entertaining in this period, were adorned with calico tablecloths, as were two cupboards used to display the castle's silver and gold.[52] Calico in the sixteenth century referred to a type of heavy cotton fabric, usually decorated with very distinctive and brightly coloured designs. These had been one of the first commodities brought by the Portuguese from Calicut, on the Malabar coast of India. They were very fashionable in the sixteenth century for tablecloths, decorative hangings and window treatments. The castle also contained tablecloths made of dowlas, a coarse linen most often used for cloak bags and the clothing of the lower classes. This suggests that the tables used by the servants of the castle were also covered in this period. Irish tablecloths are also found in the records. Nicholas Faggan owned 'one diaper tablecloth and two olde Irish tablecloths', valued at 13s.[53] They were presumably made of Irish linen, and were considered of sufficient quality to adorn the table of a wealthy merchant. This is interesting as it suggests a specifically Irish table-setting tradition, which may have endured regardless of the increasing availability of luxury imported napery and tableware.

[48] Ibid.

[49] Cork City and County Archives, Caulfield Will Transcripts, U226, pp. 15; 32. O'Shea, 'Castleisland inventory' p. 37; TNA, E190113211 f37v; TNA, E190113110 f46v; f44r; Appleby, *Calendar* pp. 82, 124.

[50] *Oxford Encyclopaedia of Art Materials and Techniques* (Oxford, 2008) Available from: http://www.answers.com/topic/linen-diaper-and-damask [Accessed 1 January 2014].

[51] Appleby, *Calendar*, p. 82.

[52] O'Shea, 'Castleisland inventory, p. 37.

[53] Cork City and County Archives, Caulfield Will Transcripts, U226, P. 32.

### *IIa. The standing salt*

In elite English homes, the table linen was matched by the gold, silver and gilt vessels that adorned it. The first item set on the tablecloth after grace and hand washing was the standing salt, and this remained the principal item of domestic plate in England until the mid-seventeenth century.[54] The standing salt held a prominent position to the right of the host, indicating status and prosperity. The seating placement of other guests in relation to the salt served to identify their social status, and inferior guests were entitled to sit 'below the salt' and at the lower ends of the table only.[55] Families prized their inherited salt cellars, which were passed down in families over generations.[56] It has been suggested that the salt served a primarily decorative function rather than to hold salt for the meal, a supply of which was usually placed near each person's trencher in a smaller salt cellar, called a 'trencher salt'.[57]

The surviving last wills of Cork citizens record frequent bequests of silver salt cellars in the late sixteenth century. In 1580, for example, Andrew Galway bequeathed his son Walter his 'greatest salte of silver gilte with his cover and silver cruse' and to his second son, Patrick, he left his 'seconde salte of silver'. In 1582, Christopher Galway bequeathed his wife a 'silver salt', while an inventory of his goods listed another 'great silver salt', which he held in pledge. In the same year, Maurice Roche Fitzedmund bequeathed to his heir his 'great saltseller gilt with his cover weighinge 33 unces'. In addition to being an item of prestige and status, it seems that the 'salt' may have served an active role at Anglo-Irish tables, since although the customs accounts regularly record the importation of various types of trenchers (wooden platters/plates) towards the end of the century, salt trenchers were never recorded, nor do they occur in any of the wills or inventories, including, for example, the particularly detailed Castleisland inventory of 1590, which records everything from mustard pots to pie plates, and includes 'a bell salt parcel gilt' but no other salt receptacles.[58]

This salt cellar listed in the inventory of the castle of Castleisland, County Kerry is perhaps of further significance. Circular bell-shaped salt cellars or 'spice boxes' were very fashionable at the end of the sixteenth century but, according to Cripps, this was only for a few years.[59] They had three tiered compartments, the upper of which was used as a pepper castor, while the lower compartments formed salt cellars. The ownership of this item is uncertain. The castle and over 13,000 acres of forfeited Fitzgerald lands in Munster was granted to Sir William Herbert, of Monmouthshire, in 1586. Herbert lived in the castle for one year (1586–87) and had the inventory

[54] B. Carver Wees, *English, Irish and Scottish Silver at the Sterling and Francine Clark Art Institute* (New York, 1997), p. 119.

[55] Ibid., pp. 119–20.

[56] Visser, *The Rituals of Dinner*, p. 158.

[57] W. J. Cripps, *Old English Plate* (London, 1899), p. 313.

[58] O'Shea, 'Castleisland inventory', p. 39.

[59] Cripps, *Old English Plate*, p. 20.

of the household goods of the castle made in 1590. It is possible, then, that this apparently fashionable item was of Welsh origin and was brought to Kerry by Herbert to adorn the castle's dining table and display his status and wealth to local visitors.

### *IIb. Plates and dishes*

According to Dawson, for everyday dining the Willoughbys and most of their servants dined off pewter tableware, and indeed, during Elizabeth I's reign, there seems to have been a general increase in the use of pewter tableware in England, with even 'good farmers' of husbandman or yeoman status having a garnish (12 settings) of pewter vessels to furnish their tables.[60] It is difficult to establish whether pewter played a similar role in the dining practices of the Irish and Anglo-Irish in this period. Pewter did not feature at all among Irish imports of tableware from Bristol in the sixteenth century, but there is evidence in the wills and inventories of Cork citizens in this period to show that it was indeed used to make a variety of different items of everyday utensils. In 1582, for instance, Edmund White bequeathed to Margaret White, his 'brass crock and the little spice coffer' and 'all the pewter dishes'.[61] The inventory of Nicholas Faggan, taken in 1578, listed 12 platters of pewter, valued at 8s, 9 pewter trenchers, valued at 2s and 6 'porradgers of pewter' valued at 12d.[62] Pewter was more functional than plate but was still relatively expensive and, as a result, in England it was frequently melted down and refashioned or 'changed' when damaged or worn.[63] This was probably also the case in Ireland, since *The Great Parchment Book* lists 'peutrers' among the artificers living in Waterford in 1577.[64] Along with pewter, brass was commonly used to make cooking pots and pans. It also seems to have furnished sixteenth-century Irish tables and held some status as an item of inheritance and dowry. Henry Verdon, a shop and tavern keeper in Cork, left to his daughter Margaret 'a brasse service towards her marriage' and to his daughter Ellene his 'best service of brass when she is married'.[65]

Unsurprisingly, the wills and inventories do not shed light on the use of tableware made from cheaper materials in this period. It has been widely noted, however, that in the sixteenth century the use of wooden trenchers became increasingly common on English tables.[66] Before about 1500, a trencher was a piece of stale bread, cut into a square shape by a carver and used as a plate.[67] Diners filled their trenchers with food from large platters placed in the centre of the table. By the end of the fifteenth century, particularly in northern Europe, trenchers had evolved into more durable

[60] Dawson, *Plenti*, p. 213; Harrison, *Description of England*, p. 202.
[61] Cork City and County Archives, Caulfield Will Transcripts, U226, p. 23.
[62] Ibid.
[63] Dawson, *Plenti*, p. 214; Barnard, *Making the Grand Figure*, p. 138.
[64] GPB, p. 171.
[65] Cork City and County Archives, Caulfield Will Transcripts, U226, p. 35.
[66] Hammond, *Food*, p. 107; Dawson, *Plenti*, p. 215.
[67] Hammond, *Food*, p. 108.

utensils, made predominantly of wood or pewter.[68] Hammond has implied that this trend may have applied more to the dining habits of the upper and middle classes rather than to peasants, who appear to have been using wooden trenchers since the early fourteenth century. In 1314, for example, in the village of Northcory, the custumal noted that at the Christmas celebration, one villein had to bring with him his own trencher.[69] Since bread was supplied as part of the feast, Hammond suggested that the implication was that the trencher was made of wood.[70]

It is unclear why wooden trenchers became so commonly used in sixteenth-century England. The trend may perhaps relate to the rising price of food in the sixteenth century, which made the daily use of bread trenchers unfeasible, even among the upper classes. Wooden trenchers may have had other practical functions, however. Pewter was an easily damaged metal and wooden trenchers may have been placed in the bottom of pewter dishes in order to protect them.[71] The word trencher was also used in this period to describe small flat wooden platters used to hold suckets and sweetmeats, which were becoming increasingly fashionable in this period. These trenchers were usually decorated with allegorical poesies or poems.[72] Sweets, cheese or fruit were served on the unpainted side of the trencher and when the diner was finished eating the trencher could be turned over to reveal a painted image with a proverb or other such quote, 'like Christmas crackers today'.[73] There are six examples of these painted trenchers at the British Museum, accredited to the court of Henry VIII. Three show flowers with pithy quotes and the other three images of animals.[74] Other examples may be found at the Victoria and Albert Museum, which houses a set of 12 painted trenchers, dated to around 1600, based on the poem 'Yet More Wonders of the World' by Sir John Davies. Each trencher has a verse and image relating to a particular profession, including lawyers, physicians and soldiers. These were made especially for a New Year party given by Thomas Sackville, 1st earl of Dorset, and were published in 1608, when they became available for other trencher makers to copy.[75]

The customs accounts suggest that from 1594/5 wooden trenchers became an item of mass consumption in Ireland. In that year a total of 21,576 trenchers were

[68] Victoria and Albert Museum Collections. Available from: http://collections.vam.ac.uk/item/O131241/trencher/?print=1 [accessed 11 January 2011].

[69] Hammond, *Food*, p. 108.

[70] Ibid.

[71] Dawson, *Plenti*, p. 215.

[72] Ibid.

[73] Victoria and Albert Museum Collections. Available from: http://collections.vam.ac.uk/item/O78997/set-of-roundels-twelve-wonders-of-the-world/ [accessed 1 January 2014].

[74] British Museum Collections. Available from: http://www.britishmuseum.org/research/search_the_collection_database/search_object_details.aspx?objectid=3298028&partid=1&searchText=trenchers&numpages=10&orig=%2fresearch%2fsearch_the_collection_database.aspx&currentPage=1 [accessed 2 January 2011].

[75] Victoria and Albert Museum Collections. Available from: http://collections.vam.ac.uk/item/O78997/set-of-roundels-twelve-wonders-of-the-world/ [accessed 2 January 2011].

imported from Bristol to the south-east of Ireland, with a similar figure noted in 1600/1 (Table 10.1). The vast majority of these were described as 'common' trenchers, which were made from a hardwood such as beech or sycamore that was 'non-porous, did not transmit its taste or odour to the food and turned well'.[76] While small volumes of trenchers were found in the accounts from 1545, the massive increase in the use of this item of tableware may well have been stimulated by the arrival of settlers with the Munster plantation. Certainly, some 36 years later, in 1630, planters intending to go to the New England colonies were advised by Thomas Graves, an 'Engynere' who had gone there with Governor Endecott the previous year, to bring with them 'such needefull things as every Planter doth or ought to provide to go to New-England', including victuals, apparel, arms, tools, spices and various household utensils, in particular 'wooden platters, dishes, spoons and trenchers'. Pewter plates and utensils did not feature in this recommended list of supplies and, according to Dow, wooden trenchers remained the commonest form of dish in 'Old' and 'New' English use until well after 1700.[77]

As noted earlier, however, the plantation added only around 3,000–4,000 settlers to the population of the region, and the fact that such large numbers of trenchers were imported, and continued to be imported after the collapse of the enterprise, suggests that demand for this particular type of wooden dish developed quickly in Ireland. It is difficult to say if this apparent evolution in basic eating utensils signified wider changes in Irish dining practices during this period, since little is known of how food was served or consumed in ordinary households prior to this. Certainly the arrival of fashionable 'painted trenchers' in 1594/5, the significance of which was discussed above, indicates not only the consumption of new types of luxury food types in wealthier Irish households but also the adoption of evolving elite English table rituals.

### *IIc. Cutlery*

During the sixteenth century, the principal eating utensil in England was the knife, which was used to 'cut portions from communal dishes and bring them to the diner's own plate or trencher, when they would be eaten with the fingers'.[78] Spoons were also widely used for soups and semi-liquid dishes, but forks, being an Italian custom, were largely unheard of, at least until the early seventeenth century.[79] In general, hosts did not supply guests with cutlery and it was common practice for guests to bring their own cutlery with them, sometimes carried in a special case or purse.[80]

[76]From: 'Treacle box – Trough', *Dictionary of Traded Goods and Commodities, 1550–1820* (2007). Available from: http://www.british-history.ac.uk/report.aspx?compid=58900 [accessed 12 December 2010].

[77]G. F. Dow, *Every Day Life in the Massachusetts Bay Colony* (Maryland, 2007), p. 84.

[78]Dawson, *Plenti*, p. 218; Hammond, *Food*, pp. 107–9.

[79]Cripps, *Old English Plate*, p. 382; Dawson, *Plenti*, p. 219; Hammond, *Food*, p. 109.

[80]Dawson, *Plenti*, p. 219.

Table 10.1 Volume of domestic utensils and napery imported, 1503–1601 (piece)

| | 1503 | 1516 | 1525 | 1541 | 1542 | 1545 | 1550 | 1563 | 1575 | 1594 | 1600 |
|---|---|---|---|---|---|---|---|---|---|---|---|
| bellows | - | - | - | - | - | - | - | - | - | 16 | - |
| bellows, pairs | - | - | - | - | - | - | - | - | - | 24 | 25 |
| boultel bewpers[1] | - | - | - | - | - | - | - | - | - | - | 1 |
| boxes, black | - | - | - | - | - | - | - | - | - | - | 12 |
| boxes, nest | - | - | - | - | - | - | - | - | - | 24 | 7 |
| boxes, painted | - | - | - | - | - | - | - | - | - | - | 36 |
| boxes, painted, nest | - | - | - | - | - | - | - | - | - | 26 | 14 |
| brushes | - | - | - | - | - | - | - | - | - | 486 | 96 |
| brushes, heath | - | - | - | - | - | - | - | - | - | 90 | - |
| brushes, rubbing | - | - | - | - | - | - | - | - | - | 12 | - |
| brushes, small | - | - | - | - | - | - | - | - | 12 | - | - |
| candlesticks | - | - | - | - | - | - | - | - | 4 | 42 | - |
| candlesticks, brass | - | - | - | - | - | - | - | - | - | 14 | 18 |
| candlesticks, pewter | - | - | - | - | - | - | - | - | 14 | - | - |
| candlesticks, small | - | - | - | - | - | - | - | - | | 138 | 18 |
| cauldrons, brass | - | - | - | - | - | 1 | - | - | - | - | - |
| chafing dishes | - | - | - | - | - | - | - | - | - | 2 | - |
| chest locks | - | - | - | - | - | - | - | - | - | 24 | - |
| chests | - | - | - | 8 | - | - | - | - | - | - | - |
| chests, small painted | - | - | - | - | - | - | - | - | - | - | 3 |

| | | | | | | | | | | | |
|---|---|---|---|---|---|---|---|---|---|---|---|
| cruses, stone | - | - | - | - | - | - | - | - | 12 | 120 | 24 |
| cutts | - | 18,828 | 23,796 | 4,392 | 4,320 | 7,848 | 576 | 17,280 | 17119 | - | 56 |
| cutts (1d) | - | - | - | - | - | - | - | - | - | 240 | - |
| cutts (ob) | - | - | - | - | - | - | - | - | - | 72 | 42 |
| diaper napkins | - | - | - | - | - | - | - | - | - | 6 | - |
| dishes, iron chafing | - | - | - | - | - | - | - | - | - | - | 5 |
| flasket | - | - | - | - | - | - | 92 | - | - | - | - |
| funnels | - | - | - | - | - | - | - | - | 48 | - | - |
| glasses and stone pots | - | - | - | - | - | - | - | - | - | - | 72 |
| graters | - | - | - | - | - | - | - | - | - | - | 60 |
| gridirons | - | - | - | - | 2 | - | - | - | - | - | - |
| knives | 3,708 | 648 | 756 | 45,216 | 31,788 | 24,308 | 39,996 | 12 | 312 | 1,512 | 1,068 |
| knives (1d) | - | - | - | - | - | - | - | - | 348 | 7,788 | 8,280 |
| knives (2d) | - | - | - | - | - | - | - | - | 216 | 1,656 | 72 |
| knives (ob.) | | | | | | | | | | 1,728 | 60 |
| knives, Almaine | | | | | | | 144 | 2,838 | 72 | | |
| knives, Brazil | | | 12 | | | | | | | | |
| knives, bumbard | | | | | | | 360 | 1320 | | | |
| knives, cap[2] | | | | | | | | | 24 | | |
| knives, coarse | | | | | | | | | | 96 | |
| knives, Cullen[3] | | | | | | | | | 216 | | |
| knives, cuttlers | | | | | | | | | | 696 | |

| | | | | | | | | | |
|---|---|---|---|---|---|---|---|---|---|
| knives, fine | | | | | | | | 24 | |
| knives, Flanders | | | | | | | 12 | | |
| knives, Flemish | | | | | | | 120 | | |
| knives, in pairs | 60 | 5,178 | 3,108 | 5,916 | 4,560 | 1,800 | 312 | 192 | |
| knives, in pairs (2d) | | | | | | | 24 | | |
| knives, paring | | | | | | | 6 pair | 48 | |
| knives, pocket | | | | | | | | 2,736 | 696 |
| knives, prage[4] | | | 24 | | | 288 | 12 | 252 | 108 |
| knives, small | 24 | | 30 | | | | | | |
| lanterns | | | | | | | | 31 | 57 |
| mouse snatches | | | | | | | | | 6 |
| pans, brass | | | | | 8 | | 5 | | |
| pans, dripping | | | 2 | | | | | | |
| pans, frying | | | | | | | | 48 | 12lb |
| pans, plate dripping | | | | | | | | 6 | |
| pots, brass | 4 | | | 1 | | | 2.5C, 120lb | 238lb | |
| pots, iron | | | | | | | | 6 | |
| pots, stone uncovered | | | | | | | | | 220 |
| pottle | | | 12 | | 150 | | | | |
| serches[5] | | | | | | | 24 | 12 | 78 |
| setting sticks[6] | | | | | | | | 18 | |

| | | | | | | |
|---|---|---|---|---|---|---|
| skillets, small | | | | | | 6 |
| sleek stone | | | | | | 4 |
| snuffers | | | | | | 24 |
| tablecloths and diapers | | | | | 170 | |
| table napkins | | | | | | 12 |
| tables, pairs | | | | | | 4 |
| taps | 72 | | 216 | | 1,440 | |
| taps and cannells | | | | 1,320 | 2,520 | 11,104 |
| taps, small | | | | | 2,400 | |
| tobacco pipes | | | | | | 756 |
| trenchers | | 2,880 | 648 | | 4,032 | 16,632 |
| trenchers, coarse | | | | 5,568 | | |
| trenchers, common | | | | | 16,512 | 6,264 |
| trenchers, painted | | | | | 24 | |
| trenchers, wooden | | | | | 1,008 | |
| vials | | | | | 288 | |

[1] A boultel was a kind of cloth used for bolting or sifting flour and bewpers probably relates to Beaupreau in France; Willan, Tudor Book, p. 9 and Flavin and Jones, *Bristol's Trade*, *p. 945*.

[2] Possibly means caps for knives.

[3] Cologne.

[4] Perhaps refers to knives from Prague.

[5] Sieves of Spanish origin.

[6] Dibblers.

The positioning of cutlery on the table and its proper use were directed by ritual and etiquette. *The Boke of Kervying* (1508), for example, gave clear instructions to the servitor on where to place specific items on the dining table:

> than take thy salte seller in thy lefte honde and take the ende of the towell in your ryght honde to bere in spones and knyves
> than set your salte on the ryght syde where your soverayne
> shall sytte and on the lefte syde the salte set your tren-
> chours
> than laye your knyves and set your brede on
> lofe by an other
> your spones and your napkyns fayre
> folden besyde your brede
> than cover your brede and trenchoures spones and knyves.[81]

Knives, in particular, played an important role in English medieval and early modern dining rituals. Nobles, for example, employed squire-carvers to cut and serve meat in a ritualised performance. Such carvers used pairs of knives, one to cut the meat, the other to hold it steady, and carry slices to the diners.[82] At the beginning of the meal, the carver laid the knives on the table pointing towards the master and these were covered with a white cloth to symbolically emphasise that this was not a threatening gesture. Owning fine cutlery, like owning plate drinking utensils, was a means of displaying refinement, wealth and elegance, and the use of elaborate carving knives lent 'dignity and splendour' to the serving of food in wealthy and noble households.[83]

A large variety and volume of knives were imported to Ireland from Bristol and also from Chester, indicating, as Woodward pointed out, that Ireland was 'by no means self-sufficient in the manufacture of metal wares' during this period. In the Chester accounts between 1565 and 1603, Woodward identified mincing knives, paring knives, carving knives and pocket knives, and noted that the most commonly imported knives were 'cutts' or more specifically 'Hallamshire cutts', which were knives from the Sheffield region.[84] A similar picture emerges from the Bristol accounts. As in the Chester accounts, 'cutts' were imported in very large quantities in the first three-quarters of the century. Based on their value, these appear specifically to have been small penknives.[85] Unspecified, inexpensive knives and 'knives in pairs', perhaps of the sort used in the ritualised English dining practices noted above, were also regular imports from Bristol (Table 10.1). In the latter part of the century, the range of knives imported diversified further to include continental knives from Germany, France and Flanders. Also, it is significant to note that in the last quarter

[81] Wynken de Worde, *The Boke of Kervynge* (1508)

[82] Victoria and Albert Museum Collections. Available from: http://collections.vam.ac.uk/item/O127799/pair-of-knives/ [accessed 4 January 2011].

[83] Ibid.

[84] Woodward, *Trade*, p. 18.

[85] Flavin and Jones, *Bristol's Trade*, p. 22.

of the century imported knives became increasingly differentiated by price and quality. From 1575, both 'cutts' and knives were differentiated as halfpenny, penny and twopenny varieties. This trend is of particular significance with regards to cutlery, since these were items intended for mass consumption and were not exclusively for the rich.

A number of points can be made about trends in Irish knife imports from England. First, where figures can be roughly correlated, it appears that the quantity of knives recorded as imports to the south-east of Ireland from Bristol was in general far greater than the amounts imported to Dublin from Chester. In 1563/4, for example, 23,538 knives were imported from Bristol, whereas in 1565/6, only 648 were recorded on the Chester route. Similarly in 1575/6, 18,787 were shipped from Bristol, while the following year only 5,760 were shipped from Chester, and again in 1592/3, 17,040 arrived from Bristol while only 12,240 were shipped from Chester. This is surprising given Chester's proximity to south Yorkshire and Sheffield itself, which was one of the principal knife-manufacturing centres in England in this period.[86]

What is also notable is that, despite the increasing diversification of knives, the Bristol accounts show a major overall decline in the volumes imported to Ireland. Imports of knives peaked in 1541/2, when almost 55,000 knives were imported, and then fell steadily from the middle of the century until by 1600/1, they had fallen to around 10,000 knives, a decrease of 81 per cent of the peak volume (see Table 10.2 and Figure 10.1). Knives were an essential commodity, and since there is no evidence that they were manufactured in Ireland or that there was any increase in the volumes imported on the Chester–Dublin route, it seems likely that Irish merchants were obtaining increasing volumes via direct continental trade (see Table 10.3 and Figure 10.2).

Certainly in the 1540s, when Irish imports from England peaked, English merchants were still relying predominantly on foreign imports to meet consumer demand. Like pins, discussed earlier, English projectors bemoaned the fact that knives and daggers were brought into England from abroad, rather than being manufactured at home, and knives appeared in the *Discourse of the Commonweal*, in 1549, as one of the items that Englishmen should make for themselves.[87] Thirsk has noted that foreign knives filled the windows of fashionable shops in London and that 'even the poorest country folk insisted on buying foreign makes'.[88] As such, it is likely that a large proportion of the knives imported from Bristol in the first half of the century were re-exported from the Continent. From the 1560s, however, significant developments occurred in the English knife and edge-tool industry. Improved techniques were actively sought, grinding machines were introduced and foreign cutlers were

[86] Thirsk, *Economic Policy*, p. 108.

[87] Lammond (ed.), *Discourse of the Common Weal*, pp. 16–17, 64, 125, 127; Thirsk, *Economic Policy*, p. 127.

[88] Thirsk, *Economic Policy*, p. 127.

Table 10.2
Volume of knives imported from Bristol 1503–1601 (piece)

| Year | Vol. (piece) |
|---|---|
| 1503/4 | 3,708 |
| 1516/17 | 19,440 |
| 1525/6 | 24,648 |
| 1541/2 | 54,768 |
| 1542/3 | 39,270 |
| 1545/6 | 38,072 |
| 1550/1 | 45,636 |
| 1563/4 | 23,538 |
| 1575/6 | 18,787 |
| 1594/5 | 17,040 |
| 1600/1 | 10,382 |

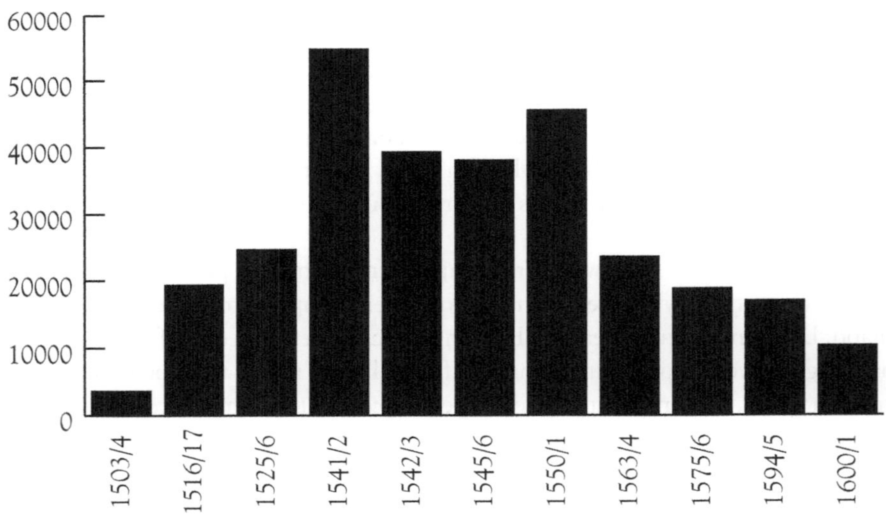


Figure 10.1 Volume of knives imported from Bristol 1503–1601 (piece)

recruited to introduce new skills.[89] Certainly, by 1615, English and in particular London knives had advanced significantly in reputation. In that year, Edmund Howes, in his revision of Stow's *Annales*, wrote that 'there were made in diverse parts of

[89] Ibid.

Table 10.3
Volume of knives imported from Chester, 1565–1603 (piece)

| Year | Vol. (piece) |
|---|---|
| 1565/6 | 648 |
| 1576/7 | 5,760 |
| 1582/3 | 3,600 |
| 1584/5 | 144 |
| 1592/3 | 12,240 |
| 1602/3 | 14,544 |

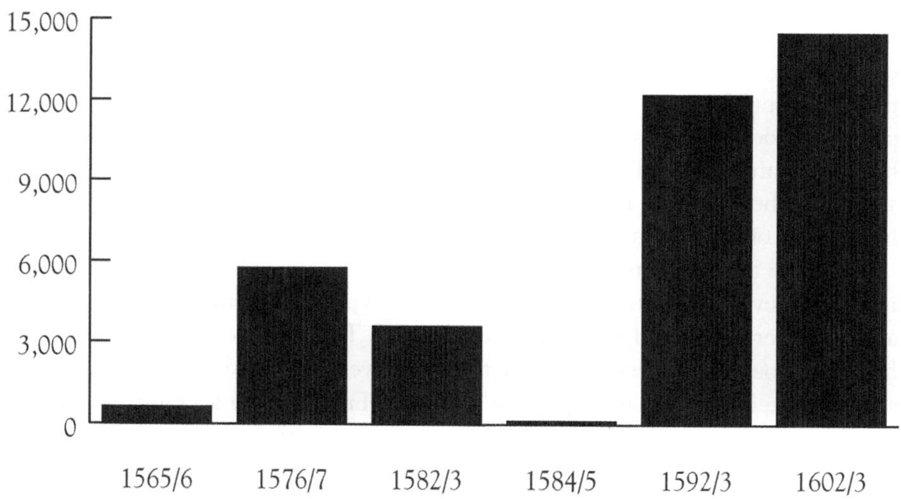

Figure 10.2 Volume of knives imported from Chester 1565–1603 (piece)

this kingdom many coarse and uncomely knives', whereas 'at this day the best and finest knives in the world are made in London'.[90]

Why, then, did Irish knife imports from England decline at a time when English domestic production increased in volume and improved in quality? As with pins, it may be that Irish consumers continued to favour 'foreign' varieties of knife over new domestically produced English versions. Irish consumers were not the only 'reluctant converts' to the English product. Thirsk noted that a textbook of French translation, written by a Huguenot school master for his English pupils between 1566 and 1597, included a gibe at one of his Flemish pupils who had no knife, though he

[90] J. Stow, *Annales of England … Continued by Edmund Howes* (London, 1615) p. 948, cited in Thirsk, *Economic Policy*, p. 128.

came from the country 'where the best knives are made'.[91] It may also be that European – and in particular Dutch – knives, like pins, were more competitively priced than English versions, particularly in the early days of English production. Either way, the falling importation of this essential commodity from England is yet further evidence of Irish reliance on continental imports for everyday items. This trend is of both economic and cultural significance, indicating again the well-developed trade networks of Irish merchants and raising questions, in this case, about the extent to which such foreign rather than English connections influenced Irish table manners and perceptions of 'civility' during this period.

### *IId. Other cutlery*

In describing the 'barbarous and most filthy' nature of Irish eating habits, Fynes Moryson remarked that the Irish 'desire no broth, nor have any use of a spoon'.[92] Certainly, in England during this period, before the introduction of the fork, spoons played a central role at meals 'and persons of every rank seem to have striven to possess a spoon, if only a single one, of silver'.[93] Cripps further noted that 'it would be difficult any time for the last six hundred years to find a man, of however humble station, without a spoon to bequeath to his widow or his son', and that the wills and inventories of the rich mentioned them in great quantities.[94]

Although the accounts show that Ireland remained almost entirely dependent on imports for everyday metalware such as knives and pins, not a single spoon was listed among imports in any of the accounts examined. The absence of imported spoons, however, does not necessarily imply that they were not used in Ireland. If silver spoons were indeed the most popular variety in England, the accounts are not an appropriate source to establish comparisons in consumption. As already noted, the accounts tended to record the consumption of less durable, cheaper items – those intended for fairly immediate consumption. As a valuable item, chiefly acquired through gifts and legacies, spoons are more likely to turn up in wills and inventories, rather than as imported wares.

By the eighteenth century silver teaspoons, in particular, appear to have been an item to which 'contemporaries sneaking into the gentry' aspired to own.[95] Barnard has noted that by this time spoons were by far the most common utensils to be fashioned from silver.[96] The wills of Cork citizens suggest, however, that while silver spoons did feature as an item of bequest among the wealthy, this was not as common an occurrence in sixteenth-century Ireland as it was in England. Indeed, only one of the wills, that of Andrew Galway (Andrewe Galwey) proved in 1580, recorded

[91] M. St. Clare Byrne, *The Elizabethan Home* (London, 1949), p. 10, cited in Thirsk, *Economic Policy*, p. 128.

[92] Moryson, 'An Itinerary' in Myers (ed.) *Elizabethan Ireland*, pp. 188–9.

[93] Cripps, *Old English Plate*, p. 281.

[94] Ibid.

[95] Barnard, *Making the Grand Figure*, p. 136.

[96] Ibid.

the bequest of spoons. Galway bequeathed to his eldest son, Walter, his 'best duson of spoones', while five of his other sons were each left 'three silver spoones'. This was not an unconditional bequest, however, since Richard, his third son, was not to inherit his spoons should he 'enter in religion or become a prieste'.[97]

Spoons do survive as archaeological evidence in Ireland, although the examples found may indicate that spoons were an item of predominantly ceremonial, rather than utilitarian function during this period. The excavation of the garden at Rothe House in Kilkenny, for example, revealed the handle of an 'Apostles' spoon'.[98] These were popular in England in the sixteenth century and were a customary gift from sponsors to their godchildren at christenings. Also dated to this period is a pewter spoon handle with a 'female figure at the end', found at Kilmore Castle in Leitrim.[99] This is most likely a 'maidenhead spoon', so-called in a Bristol Orphan Book will of 1493, which according to Cripps were also common in the late sixteenth century, the female figure being an image of the Virgin Mary.[100] 'Maidenhead' spoons have also been discovered in the archaeology of North Devon for this period.[101]

It is difficult to establish if spoons had a role in everyday consumption at Irish tables. It may be that the poorer Irish continued to use basic, domestically produced wooden spoons for everyday use. Wooden spoons have indeed been found in the medieval archaeology of Dublin and Cork and, certainly in England, wooden or pewter were used as a cheaper alternative to silver spoons.[102] On the other hand, the general lack of evidence for the use of this commodity may indicate a fundamental difference in taste in Irish and English societies, probably in this case relating to basic food preferences and, as Moryson pointed out, the ambivalence towards liquid foods in Ireland.

## III. Drinking vessels and curiosities

### *IIIa. Plate*

Surviving wills and inventories tell much about the manner in which drink was served after its production or purchase, and on the social and economic significance of drinking vessels in affluent sixteenth-century households. The wills of Cork citizens show that drinking vessels were among the most common items of bequest in Cork during the late century. The most frequently occurring items in the wills are 'silver tasters' and 'silver cups'. A taster was 'a small shallow cup of silver, often with an embossed or corrugated bottom which reflected the light through the liquor, for

[97] Cork City and County Archives, Caulfield Will Transcripts, U226, p. 38.

[98] DIER, Kilkenny, 2007:970.

[99] DIER, Leitrim, 1972:0022.

[100] Cripps, *Old English Plate*, p. 282.

[101] British Portable Antiquities Scheme website. Available from: http://www.finds.org.uk/database/artefacts/record/id/216041 [accessed 6 January 2011]

[102] DIER: Dublin, 1972:0014; Cork, 1975:10.

tasting wines'.[103] James Fitzandrew Brown, a Cork merchant who made his will in 1582, being 'now bound for Bourdeaux', bequeathed to Michael Tyrry 'three cups of silver and another which I have in pledge of nyne cowe hides and half of James Galwey' and 'my best tastor of silver'. To his second son he left 'two cups of silver, not the best' and to his third son, John, a 'tastor of silver'.[104]

Silver cups were not usually described in detail in the wills, but a number of varieties are nevertheless distinguishable. Of particular importance were 'standing cups', which are found in several wills. Andrew Galway, a Cork alderman whose will was proved in 1580, bequeathed to his eldest son, Walter, his 'bigg standing cupp of silver gilt' and his 'big cupp of silver'. To his second son, Patrick, he left a silver taster and to his third son, Richard, 'the other two standing gobletts'. Among his other bequests was a 'standing goblet and his cover that my son Walter brought me out of England'.[105] Likewise, Maurice Roche Fitzedmunde, whose will was proved in 1582, bequeathed to his son David the 'remnante of a pledge of 15 li upon a great standing cupp of Margaret Roche that Maurice of Desmonde had in marriage'.[106] He also left to his son Patrick 'a silver cupp that Vincent White hath in pledge of xix s', and to his son Edward a 'silver cupp weighing xii unces which the Archdeacon left said Edward in his will'.[107]

While these standing cups were not described in detail, there is some evidence of the level of workmanship and style of such items. Maurice Roche Fitzedmunde, for example, left his son a 'yallowe bell piece for cupp duble gilt and graven descended to me from my father'.[108] Inverted bell-shaped cups on spreading stems with conical covers, presumably similar to the cup described above, were popular in the late fifteenth and early sixteenth centuries and were used for formal and ceremonial purposes in England.[109] A surviving example of such a 'standing cup' is currently in the possession of the corporation of King's Lynn and consists of an inverted bell-shaped bowl on top of a tall columnar stem with a pronounced knopp and a cinquefoil base.[110]

The complex social and ritual functions of standing cups in England have been discussed elsewhere.[111] The predominant role of these particular vessels was as sideboard display plate and, in contrast to smaller silver cups, they were not intended for everyday use, but rather to impress visitors with their owner's wealth. It has been noted that while many standing cups are today preserved in churches, their original

[103] OED.
[104] Cork City and County Archives, Caulfield Will Transcripts, U226, p. 9.
[105] Ibid., p. 38.
[106] Ibid., p. 28.
[107] Ibid.
[108] Ibid., p. 27.
[109] Carver Wees, *English, Irish and Scottish Silver*, p. 42.
[110] Ibid.
[111] See for example: E. Wenham, 'English Standing Cups', *American Collector* (February, 1947); Cripps, *Old English Plate*.

purpose was secular and they had distinctive ceremonial functions, being associated with a number of social customs.[112]

One such custom was observed at corporation dinners in Lichfield, England, where the two toasts, 'The Queen' and 'Weale and Worship', were drunk from a massive embossed silver cup holding three or four quarts, which was given to the corporation in 1666 by Elias Ashmole, founder of the Ashmolean Museum at Oxford. An account by a Lichfield resident noted that: 'The mayor drinks first and, on his rising, the persons on his right and left also rise. He then hands the cup to the person on his right when the one next to him rises, the one on the left of the mayor still standing. Then the cup is passed across the table to him when *his* left hand neighbour rises; so that, there are always three standing at the same time.'[113] This ceremony was also observed at parish meetings and churchwarden's dinners at St Margaret's, Westminster. Here the cover of the standing cup was held over the head of the person drinking by his neighbours on the right and left of him.[114]

The extent to which ownership of standing cups in Ireland implies engagement with such typically English customs is unclear. Andrew Galway's standing goblet was 'brought to him from England', however, and it therefore seems likely that he would have been aware of the item's wider functions and symbolic significance.[115] It certainly appears that the status attached to silver cups in England, which extended to their role as objects of presentation, was common to Anglo-Ireland also.[116] In addition to their obvious function as items of bequest, standing cups were also considered suitable wedding gifts among the Anglo-Irish elite, as indicated by the last will of Maurice Roche Fitzedmunde.

Dawson has noted the economic value of plate drinking vessels in sixteenth-century England, which were seen as an investment that could be melted down or exchanged for ready cash.[117] The complex economic function of drinking vessels in Anglo-Ireland during this period is made clear by an inventory of the goods of Christopher Galway, an alderman of Cork in 1582, which shows the use of cups and cup components as security for loans and pledges:

> Such plate of myne own and as much as I have in pawn:
> From David Barrayes wife a silver cupp in pawne of 3 li.; from Patrick Gold Fitzgold a silver cupp in pawn of fortie shillings; A silver cupp belonging to John Oge Hodnet which oweth nothing; A goblet for aquavita belonging to myself; and a goblet with his cover which my father left me; a great silver salt belonging to … Galway which I have of him in pledge; a small tastor of mine owne; a big silver cupp which I bought of Alexander Gogh; Two silver cups belonging to my bretherne Stephen and Domynick which my father left with them.

112 Carver Wees, *English, Irish and Scottish Silver*, p. 43.

113 R. Chambers (ed.), *The Book of Days*, ii (London, 1906), p. 531, cited in Wenham, 'English Standing Cups'.

114 Chambers, *Book of Days*, p. 531.

115 Cork City and County Archives, Caulfield Will Transcripts, U226, p. 38.

116 Carver Wees, *English, Irish and Scottish Silver*, p. 42.

117 Dawson, *Plenti*, p. 213.

> Certain pledges which I did deliver in pawn as following:
> To Ballive Creaghe a silver cupp. To Joan Watter a goblet pertaining to Andrew Skiddy and a silver cup belonging to Barnabe Daly I delivered in pawn as then bills do testifie. Walter Copinger hath the cover of my small cup in pawne of three yards of bayes, John Watter hath the bottom of Andrew Skiddy's cupp in pawne of 6s. 8d. old money which my man William Barrett oweth.[118]

While standing cups were reserved for special use, small cups, similar in form but plainer and reserved for everyday use, were fashionable among the wealthy in Tudor England.[119] The frequency with which these occur in the surviving Irish wills and inventories suggests that this would also have been the case in Ireland. It is noteworthy that while small amounts of pewter and brass vessels were listed amongst bequests, items made of silver very much predominated. The use of silver wine cups and goblets was perhaps supported by the belief that precious metals promoted better health than did base metals or wood. In 1602, Dr Vaughan in his *Fifteen Directions for Health* advised: 'The cups whereof you drink should be of silver or silver and gilt.'[120]

Other items of plate drinking vessels listed in Irish wills from this period include gilt and double-gilt tankards and bowls, flagons, porringers, pewter bottles and 'parcel gilt' goblets. As in England, it is clear that different types of vessels were used for different drinks. An inventory of the goods of Christopher Galway, of Cork, compiled in 1582, for example, listed a 'goblet for aquavita' while Robert Fitzsimons, a Dublin merchant, had an 'aquavitae cup' amongst his possessions.[121]

Carver Wees has noted that silver tankards appeared only around the middle of the sixteenth century in England, being adapted from continental examples, and that the term, although recorded in the 1574 inventory of the Royal Jewel House, is found only rarely in sixteenth-century documents.[122] Elite Irish fashions possibly followed a similar trend. Tankards are not found amongst the surviving sixteenth-century Cork wills. They do occur, however, in the inventory of the household goods of the castle on Castleisland in 1590, which records 'two tankers gilt', valued at a substantial £10. As already noted in relation to salt cellars, however, the plate at the castle seems to have been very 'up to date' in fashion. Likewise, the inventory of a sixteenth-century Dublin merchant, Robert Fitzsimons, lists '1 silver tankard, double gilt' and '1 small tankard'.[123] It is also notable that in Derricke's well-known woodcut image of the Gaelic Irish MacSweynes seated at dinner, the only drinking vessel depicted is a large, covered and probably gilded tankard, perhaps indicating a shared Gaelic and Anglo-Irish appreciation of this particular style of drinking vessel.

[118] Cork City and County Archives, Caulfield Will Transcripts, U226, p. 26.

[119] Carver Wees, *English, Irish, and Scottish Silver*, p. 43.

[120] G. Bernard Hughes, 'When wine was drunk from silver', *Country Life* 138 (12 November, 1965), cited in Carver Wees, *English, Irish, and Scottish Silver*, p. 43.

[121] Fenlon, *Goods*, p.13.

[122] Carver Wees, *English, Irish, and Scottish Silver*, p. 42.

[123] Fenlon, *Goods*, pp. 13–14.

Another emerging fashion in late sixteenth-century England was for two-handled cups with covers, known as 'porringers' or 'posset pots', which gained in popularity and status as standing cups began to wane. These were used for 'various spiced alcohol and gruel concoctions'.[124] The inventory of Nicholas Faggan listed amongst his plate, '6 porradgers of pewter price 12d'.[125] While the Castleisland inventory records 'six newe potingers' valued at 6s and 'six elder potingers' valued at 4s.[126]

Although it appears that the wealthy Anglo-Irish owned similar types of plate vessels to their English contemporaries, it is unclear whether they embraced the ritualised domestic etiquette surrounding their use in English households. In English households, display plate was arranged on a buffet or cupboard that also served as a sideboard from which the vessels could be removed when needed. Drinks were not placed on the table but were served to diners on request.[127] In 1587 William Harrison described the social ritual by which beverages were served to diners in an affluent English home. He noted that drinking vessels:

> Are seldom set on the table, but each one, as necessity urgeth, calleth for a cup of such drink as him listeth to have, so that when he hath tasteth of it, he delivered the cup again to some one of the standersby, who making it clean by pouring out the drink remaineth, restoeth him to the cupboard from whence he fetched the same.[128]

Such cupboards were certainly a feature of Anglo-Irish furnishings during this period. In 1595, John White, a Clonmel merchant, imported a dozen cupboard locks from Bristol.[129] Also, an inventory of the goods of Robert Fitzsimons, a Dublin merchant, lists that he had cupboard cloths made of green saye and of linen.[130] Saye was a fine woollen cloth, resembling serge, which, at this date, was often partly made of silk. Cupboard cloths are also recorded in the Castleisland inventory, which lists nine cupboard cloths, including two made of calico. Both of these inventories also list a considerable amount of display plate.

### *IIIb. Glass*

Surviving Irish wills and inventories shed considerable light on the ownership and use of drinking vessels in affluent sixteenth-century Anglo-Irish households. The nature of these sources, however, means that they only record the ownership of durable drinking vessels that had a second-hand value and were chiefly acquired through inheritance. As such, they say little about current demands and fashions or items

[124] Carver Wees, *English, Irish, and Scottish Silver*, p. 42.

[125] Cork City and County Archives, Caulfield Will Transcripts, U226, p. 32. The OED notes various spelling variations for this item, including: paroger, poreger, porrager, porreger and porringer.

[126] O'Shea, 'Castleisland inventory', p. 40.

[127] Carver Wees, *English, Irish, and Scottish Silver*, p. 41.

[128] Harrison, *Description of England*, p. 127.

[129] TNA, E190/1131/10 f53v.

[130] Fenlon, *Goods*, p. 13.

that were produced for more immediate consumption. This is a particular issue with regards to drinking vessels since the newer sorts of vessels appearing on the market in the early modern period tended to be semi-durable.

In particular, according to Harrison, drinking glasses were becoming increasingly popular in the sixteenth century, and were used for the consumption of both beer and wine. He noted that many gentlemen had switched from using gold or silver cups to Venetian glass, or home-produced versions if Venetian was too expensive.[131] Dawson has noted that increased demand for drinking glasses had prompted some continental glassmakers to settle in England.[132] The earliest evidence of an attempt to manufacture fine-quality glass in England is a petition dating from 1550, addressed from London by eight Murano glassmakers to the Council of Ten at Venice, asking to be excused from the penalties decreed in 1549 by that body against Venetian subjects who taught glassmaking to foreigners.[133]

If the interest of foreign glassmakers in developing their trade in England can be taken as an indication of increasing consumer demand for high-quality glasses, there is sufficient evidence to suggest such demand in Ireland also. In 1575, Giacomo Verzelini, the Venetian glassmaker, obtained a patent from Elizabeth I to make Murano-style glass in England and Ireland for 21 years.[134] Likewise, in 1618, John Boyle wrote to his brother Richard Boyle, the 1st earl of Cork, mentioning a Venetian who wanted to set up a glassworks in the south of Ireland.[135] In 1634, Sir Percival Hart obtained a licence for the sole making of black-glass drinking vessels and pots in Ireland, similar to those made in Murano, and commonly called Venice drinking glasses.[136] As in England, however, not all attempts to set up glassworks in this period were successful and there is no evidence, at present, to suggest that any of these individuals ever manufactured glass in Ireland.[137]

Using the household accounts of the Willoughbys, Dawson has shown that drinking glasses began to be purchased in small quantities in the 1520s. In 1522, a single drinking glass was purchased for 2d in London; six were purchased in 1524 for 12d; and a further six were purchased in 1527 for 12d. There was a considerable price disparity noted in the entries. Four glasses purchased for Francis Willoughby in 1584 cost 3s 4d, while in 1599, seven glasses cost just 12d. This, Dawson suggested, reflected the different origins and quality of glass.

[131] Harrison, *Description of England*, p. 128, cited in Dawson, *Plenti*, p. 217.

[132] Dawson, *Plenti*, p. 215.

[133] *Calendar of State Papers Relating to English Affairs in the Archives of Venice*, v: 1534–1554 (1873), pp. 306–12; M. S. Westropp, *Irish Glass: An Account of Glass-Making in Ireland from the XVIth Century to the Present Day* (Ireland and US, 2012), p. 19.

[134] Westropp, *Irish Glass*, p. 25.

[135] A. B. Grosart (ed.), *The Lismore Papers of Richard Boyle, First and 'Great' Earl of Cork*, ii, p. 121; Westropp, *Irish Glass*, p. 25.

[136] Westropp, *Irish Glass*, p. 24.

[137] Dawson noted an unsuccessful attempt by continental glassworkers to establish works at Wollaton in the early seventeenth century. See Dawson, *Plenti*, p. 215.

Domestic accounts of this type do not survive for Irish households in any region during this period and it is therefore impossible to compare trends in consumption in individual Irish and English households. Nevertheless, the customs accounts provide a sense of the development of the fashion in Ireland during this period (see Table 10.4). Drinking glasses are not found in the Bristol accounts until 1541/2, some 20 years after they were first recorded in the English household accounts examined by Dawson. In that year, 1,872 glasses of unspecified variety were imported from Bristol. The customs values ascribed to the glasses – 6d, 4d and 2d per dozen respectively – suggest that three different varieties of glasses were imported. Since superior glass was not manufactured in England by this date, these were probably inferior home-produced varieties but may also have included some re-exported continental glasses. Woodward has noted that in addition to the coarse English glasses sent to Dublin from Chester at the end of the sixteenth century, some of the glass was specifically stated as being from Normandy and Burgundy.[138]

The trade in drinking glasses to south-east Ireland remained rather erratic until the last decade of the century. It is likely that, as in England, the fragility of drinking glasses were 'a bar to their wider adoption'.[139] Small volumes of glasses, of unspecified variety, were recorded in the 1542/3 and 1545/6 accounts but glasses are entirely absent in 1550/1 and 1563/4. In 1595/6, however, 2,766 glasses were shipped to Ireland, by merchants from all the main south-eastern towns in Ireland. In that year, 71 per cent of imported glasses were of inferior quality, comprising of coarse, green, penny and halfpenny glasses. Of the other types, 6 per cent were of unspecified variety and 22 per cent are described as 'French drinking glasses', which at this date may refer to re-exported French glasses or English versions of French styles. There were no imports of fine-quality or luxurious glasses, or Venice glasses, which are found in the 1582 rates book at the very expensive value of 4s per dozen. Woodward has noted a similar trend in the Chester accounts. In 1602/3, 1,968 drinking glasses were shipped to Dublin, along with 60 '"bunches" of glasses'.[140] The latter most likely refers to window glass rather than drinking glasses, since this was sometimes measured by the 'bunch', which was equal to 1/60 of a wey.[141]

It is likely that by the end of the century, the demand for drinking glasses in Ireland, and indeed perhaps in England, was being met in part by Irish domestic production. In the archive at Hatfield House, in a petition of about 1597, George Longe noted that strangers were making glass in England and exporting it unlicensed and without paying duty, while also wasting wood in large parts of the realm. He suggested that by making glass in Ireland and transporting it to England, it would yield custom, preserve English forests, destroy the hiding places of Irish rebels and

[138] Woodward, *Trade*, p. 20.
[139] Dawson, *Plenti*, p. 216.
[140] Woodward, *Trade*, p. 20
[141] R. E. Zupko, *A Dictionary of Weights and Measures for the British Isles* (Philadelphia, 1985) p. 53.

Table 10.4 Volume of drinking vessels imported, 1503–1601 (piece)

| | 1503 | 1516 | 1525 | 1541 | 1542 | 1545 | 1550 | 1563 | 1575 | 1594 | 1600 |
|---|---|---|---|---|---|---|---|---|---|---|---|
| bottles, glass | - | - | - | - | - | - | - | - | - | 36 | 36 |
| bottles, leather small | - | - | - | - | - | - | - | - | - | 18 | - |
| bottles, pewter | - | - | - | - | - | - | - | - | 12 | | - |
| bottles, sucking | - | - | - | - | - | - | - | - | - | 36 | - |
| canikine | - | - | - | | | - | - | - | - | 1 | - |
| cups | - | - | - | | 12 | - | - | - | - | - | - |
| cups, earthen | - | - | - | - | - | - | - | - | - | - | 48 |
| cups, wooden | - | - | - | - | - | - | - | - | - | 624 | 564 |
| drinking cans | - | - | - | - | - | - | - | - | - | - | 12 |
| horns, rough | - | - | - | - | - | - | - | 2,000 | | 120 | |
| glasses (1d) | - | - | - | - | - | - | - | - | - | | 804 |
| glasses (ob) | - | - | - | - | - | - | - | - | - | 48 | - |
| glasses and stone pots | - | - | - | - | - | - | - | - | - | - | 72 |
| glasses, coarse drinking | - | - | - | - | - | - | - | - | - | 1,638 | 1,410 |
| glasses, French drinking | - | - | - | - | - | - | - | - | - | 624 | - |
| glasses, green | - | - | - | - | - | - | - | - | - | 288 | - |
| glasses, unspecified | - | - | - | 1,872 | 552 | 684 | - | - | 54 | 168 | 456 |

generate employment for 'idle men' in Ireland. It would also serve England with cheaper glass, which could be made in Ireland at a lower price because of the difference of the price of victuals and wood. He noted that he had successfully kept one glass house in Drumfenning woods for 10 years.[142] Westropp has suggested that this was probably in County Cork and that, with the exception of the mention of this glass house, nothing more is known about any glass being manufactured in Ireland during this period.[143]

The customs accounts confirm that glass was indeed produced and exported from southern Ireland in the sixteenth century. In 1594/5, 44 cases, or approximately 3,912kg, of glass was exported to Bristol by merchants from Bristol, London and Youghal. The largest volume was exported by London merchants.[144] As it was shipped by the caseload, this was again most likely window glass, rather than drinking glasses but, in the same year, 36 coloured glass bottles, valued at £1 10s, were also sent to Bristol, indicating the development of further skill specialisation and diversification in the industry.[145]

### *IIIc. Wooden and earthenware*

In addition to glass, the customs accounts show the importation of small quantities of other types of drinking vessels, including rough horns, leather bottles, and wooden and earthen cups. The leather bottles, which are found in small quantities in the 1594/5 account, perhaps refer to leather jacks, which were tall toughened-leather serving jugs coated on the inside with pitch to make them watertight and that were used for serving ale and beer.[146] The wooden cups, which are not described in detail, were possibly mazer bowls: turned wooden bowls, usually made of maple wood and sometimes embellished with gold, silver or silver-gilt mounts or fashioned with feet or stems.[147] These were very popular in England from the early Middle Ages into the sixteenth century and later, and were sometimes engraved or enamelled with a personal or religious emblem. Samuel Pepys, for example, drank from a mazer cup in 1660 while on a visit to the King Edward VI alms-houses at Saffron Walden, which had a picture of 'the Virgin and the child in her arms, done in silver'.[148] Wooden cups or bowls were used for everyday drinking and for lower-status drinkers in England. Dawson remarked that at Hampton Court, in the reign of Henry VIII, for example, the servants dining in the great hall were provided with wooden drinking bowls, which were shared between the four men of a mess.[149]

[142] Westropp, *Irish Glass*, pp. 23–4; H.M.C., Salisbury MSS, viii (London, 1899), pp. 530.

[143] Westropp, *Irish Glass*, p. 24.

[144] Zupko's dictionary of weights has a case of glass at 1.75cwt or 88.903kg.

[145] TNA, E190/1131/10.

[146] Dawson, *Plenti*, p. 217.

[147] Carver Wees, *English, Irish and Scottish Silver*, p. 41.

[148] R. Latham and W. Mathews (eds) *The Diary of Samuel Pepys*, 11 vols (Los Angeles, 1970), vol. 1, p. 70; cited in Carver Wees, *English, Irish and Scottish Silver*, p. 44.

[149] Dawson, *Plenti*, p. 216.

Wooden cups were also in use in Ireland from at least the early Middle Ages.[150] A number of cups survive as archaeological evidence from various parts of the country, including for example, 16 lathe-turned bowls found at Waterford, dating from the middle of the thirteenth century.[151] These are not found as imports from Bristol before 1594/5, however, probably because the imports represent a style of cup popular in England and not available in Ireland. This suggests the introduction of non-elite English styles of tableware into Irish usage, most likely due to the new settlement resulting from the Munster plantation. Woodward has noted a similar increase in the importation of wooden ware into Dublin, which peaked in 1602–03, when some 2,294 wooden or treen cups and 300 cups and saucers were imported.[152]

In addition to wooden vessels, earthenware items were also popular in England during this period.[153] Earthenware, however, was a very rare import into Ireland from Bristol and not a single piece is found in the customs accounts prior to 1600/1, and then only 48 cups. This is particularly surprising since the evidence from medieval and early modern archaeological sites frequently includes examples of south-western English pottery, along with a very wide variety of continental, and in particular, French wares. An excavation of Oyster Lane in Wexford town, for example, revealed examples of medieval Bristol and flint-tempered Wiltshire ware, along with Gloucester and Scarborough wares.[154] At Church Street in Wicklow, imported pottery finds included Redcliffe and Minety wares.[155] While at Cork, imported pottery included North Devon sgraffito and gravel-tempered wares and Staffordshire comb wares, along with a remarkable variety of wares from France, Spain, Holland and Germany.[156]

The reason for the near absence of earthenware amongst Bristol's exports to Ireland may be at least partly explained by a recent examination of the role of minor ports in the regional economy of the Bristol Channel during the sixteenth century.[157] This study, undertaken by Duncan Taylor, argued that the development of trade conducted through the minor ports suggests that they were moving towards more specialised and diversified roles in marketing and manufacture, in the same way as has been recognised for their inland counterparts, and that the specialisation and growth of domestic trade facilitated the development of the port towns since it provided new opportunities for local and regional trade.[158] He noted that 'Gloucester

[150] O'Sullivan, *Hospitality*, p. 236.
[151] DIER: Waterford, 1987:51.
[152] Woodward, *Trade*, p. 20.
[153] Dawson, *Plenti*, p. 216
[154] DIER: Wexford, 1974:0041.
[155] DIER: Wicklow, 1997:621.
[156] DIER: Cork, 1974:0010.
[157] A. Dyer, *Decline and Growth in English towns, 1400–1600* (Basingstoke, 1991), p. 48; D. Taylor, 'The maritime trade of the smaller Bristol Channel ports in the sixteenth century' (University of Bristol Thesis, 2010); D. Taylor, 'Somerset's sixteenth-century maritime trade' in A. J. Webb (ed.), *A Maritime History of Somerset*, Vol. 1, Trade and Commerce (Taunton, 2010) , pp. 1–27.
[158] Taylor, 'Maritime trade', p. 239.

developed new trades and markets in the manufacture of linen, in leather production, and in the development of its fishing fleet'; the 'North Devon ports increasingly specialised in the export of kerseys and lighter cloths'; while 'Bridgwater developed the manufacture of felt and pottery ware as late century industries'.[159]

Certainly, an examination of the Bridgwater customs accounts shows a total of 17 entries recording the export of 2,244 pieces of earthenware to Ireland, predominantly by Wexford merchants, between 1590 and 1598.[160] The very fragmented nature of these accounts makes it impossible to gauge the volume of earthenware exported to Ireland in any given year, or indeed the type of earthenware vessels in demand, but the appearance of earthenware as a new export from the port in 1590 perhaps confirms the findings of J. R. L Allen, who noted the expansion of the south Somerset earthenware industry towards the end of the century.[161] The near absence of this item from the Bristol accounts, therefore, is likely to have been a function of the trade and marketing strategies of the port of Bridgwater during this period, rather than a lack of demand for such goods in Ireland.

It is difficult to say whether overlaps occurred between Anglo-Irish and Gaelic Irish choice and use of drinking vessels during this period. O'Sullivan discussed in some detail the drinking feasts of the Gaelic Irish elite, which involved the 'circling of goblets' and other drinking vessels around the great halls, so that they might be admired by guests and show the superiority of the owner, a ritual perhaps not entirely dissimilar to the passing of standing cups at English gatherings.[162] One of the most important vessels in Gaelic Irish use was the ceremonial 'drinking horn', frequently referred to in bardic praise poetry, which had heroic and mythical associations.[163] These vessels were commissioned from the country's best artificers and were highly distinctive and personalised objects, symbolising wealth, power and authority. Significantly, drinking horns are not found in any of the Anglo-Irish wills or inventories for this period. In 1563, however, the customs accounts recorded the importation of 2,000 horns, valued at £3, on a Liverpool vessel. The 1582 rates book lists 'rough horns' at this value.[164] These were probably drinking horns, however, since other types of horns are clearly distinguished in the rates book, which has 'hornes for lanthornes' and 'hornes called blowing horns' and 'ink-hornes' valued at 20s per M, 13s 4d per dozen and 10s per gross respectively.[165] On the other hand, since these were clearly of a coarse variety, they may have served purposes other than drinking, such as holding oil or powder, for example.[166]

[159] Ibid.

[160] My thanks to Duncan Taylor for providing me with these figures.

[161] J. Allen, 'Post-medieval pottery studies in Somerset'. Available from: http://www1.somerset.gov.uk/archives/hes/downloads/HES_150_Years_Chapter_20.pdf [accessed 11 January 2011].

[162] O'Sullivan, *Hospitality*, p. 110.

[163] Ibid., pp. 105–12.

[164] Willan, *Tudor Book*, p. 67.

[165] Ibid., pp. 33–4.

[166] OED.

Whether or not similarities existed in the types of objects traditionally favoured by both societies, Anglo-Irish and English-style drinking vessels and other precious objects certainly entered Gaelic Irish usage. The annals make frequent references to items taken from the English in battle, including: clothing, food, precious goods and battle apparel. One account is particularly notable, recording that in 1579:

> They encamped before Youghal, and finally took that town, which at that time was full of riches and goods. The Geraldines seized upon all the riches they found in this town, excepting such gold and silver as the merchants and burgesses had sent away in ships before the town was taken. Many a poor, indigent person became rich and affluent by the spoils of this town.[167]

O'Sullivan has noted a link between the stolen wealth accrued from militaristic expeditions and Irish hospitality. The distribution of newly won wealth by a victorious chief was a means of supporting his reputation as a 'generous man who was given to largesse, confirming his claim as a true leader'.[168] Spoils were often used in the preparation of lavish feasts and were customarily distributed to guests. A passage in Derricke's *Image of Ireland*, for example, states that the 'captive beaste [s]' taken during predatory incursions were 'knocked doune to make ... a feaste'.[169] This also applied to precious commodities, in particular drinking vessels. In 1522, for example, an annal entry noted that 'the Cinel-Conall seized upon [the Cinel-Owens] ... store of provisions, strong liquors ... both *eiscras* (a brazen vessel for measuring wine) and *bleidh* (drinking cups or goblets)', which O'Sullivan noted were the 'trappings of an ostentatious drinking feast'.[170] This was a method of acquisition that should not be overlooked with regards to the diffusion of new types of goods beyond the towns to the farthest reaches of the country and below the level of elite consumption.

### *IIId. Sucking bottles*

A final utensil worth noting amongst Irish imports was 'sucking' or infant feeding bottles. William Halley, a Limerick merchant, imported 36 of these in 1594.[171] The history of infant feeding and nutrition in Ireland and England is little known. Haskell and Lewis have noted that there was little mention of artificial feeding in the medieval period, babies being suckled by either their mother or a wet nurse for up to the first three years of life. Furthermore, as late as Tudor times, specially designed feeding bottles were not known in England: cow's milk was considered unsuitable for infants, partly due to superstition and partly because of the 'high degree of contamination in an unsanitary world'.[172]

167 AFM, 1579.
168 O'Sullivan, *Hospitality*, p. 110.
169 Derricke, *Image of Irelande* (1581), cited in O'Sullivan, *Hospitality*, p. 111.
170 AFM, 1522; cited in O'Sullivan, *Hospitality*, p. 111.
171 Flavin and Jones, *Bristol's Trade*, p. 785.
172 A. Haskell and M. Lewis (eds), *Infantilia-the Archaeology of the Nursery* (London, 1971), p. 30.

Plate 13 Woodcut illustration showing a child feeding from a bottle, in *Artzneybuch Köstlich für Mancherley Kranckheit des Gantzen Leibs* (1546).

Evidence suggests, however, that hand-feeding utensils were indeed known and used in sixteenth-century Europe. Simon de Vallambert's *Cinq Livres* (1565), the first French book on children's diseases, indicated that it was customary to give other foods in addition to breast milk from the age of three months or even earlier. He suggested cow's milk, or preferably goat's milk boiled with semolina or flour or white breadcrumbs, and described a feeding vessel in the shape of a horn, with the narrow end shaped like a teat.[173] Earlier, European woodcuts from the thirteenth and fourteenth centuries demonstrate the feeding of babies from such cow horns, to which teats made from leather were applied.[174] These vessels may have evolved in structure by the fifteenth century – as a poem on the care of the body, written by Heinrich von Louffenberg in 1429, and printed in 1546 with woodcut illustrations, shows a child feeding from a bottle (see Plate 13).[175] Certainly, by the sixteenth century, especially designed upright 'sucking bottles' made of wood or leather with a small vertical spout were introduced in Germany and Italy and these were soon replaced

[173] S. de Vallambert, *Cinq Livres, de la manière de nourrir et gouverner les enfans dès leur naissance* (1565), ed. C. H. Winn (Geneva, 2005)

[174] Haskell and Lewis, *Infantilia*, p. 33.

[175] Woodcut illustration to poem by Heinrich von Louffenberg, in the *Artzneybuch köstlich für mancherley Kranckheit des gantzen Leibs* (1546).

by pewter flasks, which was a commonly used material for domestic items during this period. These bottles, which as Haskell and Lewis noted sometimes made their way to England from the Continent, co-existed with another feeding device used from the sixteenth to eighteenth centuries in Europe – the *pap-boat*, which was used to feed pap, a semi-solid alternative or supplementary substance to milk.[176]

As in Europe, it is most likely that some form of hand-feeding utensil was known in Ireland before the sixteenth century. An alternative to breastfeeding would have been required for children who were ill, or born with congenital deformities such as cleft lip and palate, and who therefore could not breastfeed effectively. The chronology of imports of 'sucking bottles' into Ireland, however, is highly suggestive. These are not found among imports in any account apart from 1594/5, and then only in a small quantity. As such, their use is very likely to have been a function of new settlement due to the Munster plantation.

This may well reflect broader social and cultural ideologies during the period. *The Boke of Chyldren,* written by Thomas Phaer around 1544, suggests that by this date it was still fashionable and acceptable – for those who could afford to do so – to hire a wet nurse to feed their infants. Phaer preferred that mothers should nurse their own infants, 'Whyche yf it maye be done it shal be most commendable and holsome' but if not: 'ye must be well advised intaking of a nource, not of vil complexion and of worse maners, but such as shal be sobre, honeste and chaste [sic], well fourmed, amyable and chearefull, so that she may accustome the infant unto myrth, no dronkard, vycyous nor sluttyshe, for suche corrupteth the nature of the childe.'[177]

Yet the growing disapproval of the practice of wet nursing is clear in *The Treatise on Children*, published in 1577 by the Italian Omnibonus Ferrarious, who noted that infants would 'savour of the nature of the person by whom they are suckled'.[178] Likewise, the French physician Jacques Guillemeau, whose book on the nursing of children was published in English in 1612, suggested that the wet nurse should be:

> neither squint-ey'd, lame, nor crump shouldred: she must be one that is healthfull, and not subiect to any disease: the complexion and colour of her bodie, must be liuely, and rosie: she must not be spotted with rednesse, and especially she should not haue red haire: and therefore, such as are of a browne complexion, are held to be best, whose haire is of a chestnut colour, betweene yellow and blacke.[179]

He also claimed that the nurse may communicate imperfections of her body or her character into the child and he commented on the loss of affection between the mother and the child sent out to be nursed.[180]

[176]Haskell and Lewis, *Infantilia*, p. 33; E. E. Stevens, 'A history of infant feeding', *Journal of Perinatal Education,* xviii (2009), pp. 32–9.

[177]T. Phaer, *The Boke of Chyldren* (1544).

[178]M. S. Osborn, 'The rent breasts, part II', *Midwife, Health Visitor & Community Nurse*, 1979b, 15, 9, p. 347, cited in Stevens, 'A history of infant feeding', pp. 32–9.

[179]J. Guillemeau, *Child-Birth or, the Happy Deliuerie of Women* (London, 1612).

[180]Ibid.

It is instructive to note the manifestation of similar ideas in Irish colonial discourse during this period. Moryson, discussing the Gaelic Irish practices of fosterage and *gossipred* – which were seen as 'exceedingly evil and full of mischief in this realm … For they made strong parties and factions, whereby the great men were enabled to oppress their inferiors and to oppose their equals' – noted that: 'the children of the nurse and strangers that have sucked her milk, love one another better than natural brothers, and hate them in respect of the other … and some oppose their own brothers to death that they might save their fosterbrothers from dangers thereof'.[181] Likewise, William Good claimed: 'all who have suck'd the same breasts are very kind and loving, and confide more in each other than if they were natural brothers, so that they will have an aversion even to their own brothers for the sake of these'.[182]

The choice between breastfeeding, wet nursing and hand feeding obviously varied over time and between social classes, depending on complex social and economic conditions, and it would therefore be unwise to make any conclusions about the significance of a small quantity of infant feeding bottles in Ireland. Nevertheless, the presence of this commodity raises important questions about the decisions facing English parents arriving in Ireland during this period. Given the prevailing cultural ideas regarding the dangers of wet nurses on infant wellbeing, mothers would perhaps have hesitated to procure a nurse from a race variously described as 'sluttish', 'unclean', 'rude', 'drunken' and 'dull witted'.[183] Edmund Spenser was in no doubt about the dangers of Irish wet nurses:

> The child that sucket the milk of the nurse must of necessity learn his first speech of her, the which being the first that is inured to his tongue is ever after most pleasing to him, insomuch as though he afterwards be taught English, yet the smack of the first will always abide with him and … also of the manners and conditions: for besides that young children be like apes, which will affect and imitate what they see done before them, specially by their nurses whom they love so well, they moreover draw into themselves, together with their suck, even the nature and disposition of their nurses, for the mind followeth much the temperature of the body; and also the words are the image of the mind, so as they, proceeding from the mind, the mind must be needs affected with the words; so that the speech being Irish, the heart must needs be Irish; for out of the abundance of the heart the tongue speaks.[184]

For those English women unable or unwilling to breastfeed their own infants, the risk of illness or infection from artificial feeding was perhaps deemed preferable to the 'dangerous infections' of employing an Irish nurse.[185]

[181] J. Davies, A *Discovery of the True Causes why Ireland was Never Entirely Subdued*, in Myers, (ed.) *Elizabethan Ireland*, p. 161; Moryson, 'An Itinerary', in C. L. Falkiner, *Illustrations of Irish History and Topography* (London, 1904), p. 318.

[182] W. Good, 'Descriptions and Customs of the Wild Irish', in W. Camden, *Britannia* (1586), trans. E. Gibson, vol. ii (London, 1722), p. 1418.

[183] B. Rich and F. Moryson, in Myers (ed.), *Elizabethan Ireland*.

[184] Spenser, 'View', in Myers (ed.), *Elizabethan Ireland*, p. 97.

[185] Ibid., p. 97.

### IIIe. *Curiosities*

Chapter 8 introduced the link between foodstuffs and health in sixteenth-century Ireland. In addition to spices and medicines, however, there is other intriguing evidence of Irish engagement with sixteenth-century medical ideas, in particular alchemical and Hermetic medicine. Barrett, writing in 1815, detailed the rather fantastical story of a shadowy Irish alchemist named Butler, who it was alleged had found the so-called philosopher's stone, an object believed to be able to transmute a lesser substance into a higher form, often lead into gold. Butler, it appears, attracted some attention for his transmutations in London during the reign of King James I. He apparently gained his knowledge in Arabia, when a ship on which he had taken passage was captured by African pirates and he was sold into slavery. His master was an alchemist and Butler assisted him and 'having a perfect knowledge of the importance of the process he bargained with an Irish merchant for his ransom, and made his escape'. Barrett went on to describe how an Irish physician unsuccessfully tried to steal Butler's secrets by disguising himself as a servant, and later how he met and impressed the famous Dutch physiologist, physician and chemical pioneer, Jan Baptist van Helmont. Van Helmont himself provided some fascinating details of Butler's later exploits, whilst a prisoner in the Castle of Vilvord in Flanders. There he apparently performed a number of strange cures using Hermetic medicine. Van Helmont reported his apparent cure of a monk, who was suffering from an acute bacterial infection in his arm, by the administration of almond milk in which he had dipped the philosopher's stone. He also claimed to have witnessed Butler curing an aged woman of migraine by dipping the stone into olive oil and anointing her head, and an abbess who had suffered for 18 years with stiff fingers and a swollen arm, by placing the stone to her tongue.[186]

Beyond such fascinating stories, there is evidence to suggest Irish engagement with contemporary alchemical philosophy. An inventory of the goods of the castle on Castleisland, for example, records a 'Unicornes horn set in golde', valued at £3. A unicorn horn is, of course, a mythical object but one whose reality may have been accepted in Western Europe throughout this period. The actual horns that were used were that of the narwhal, also called the 'Unicorn of the Sea'. These were supposed to possess a range of medical and alchemical properties. When in contact with poison in food or drink, it was believed that the horn would become hot and give off smoke. They could also be consumed in powder form and were believed to cure a range of illnesses as well as purifying contaminated water. Such rare and expensive items were only owned by elite members of society, and were intended to display the owner's status as much as for their medicinal properties.

[186] F. Barrett, *The Lives of Alchemystical Philosophers: With a Critical Catalogue of Books in Occult Chemistry, and a Selection of the Most Celebrated Treatises on the Theory and Practice of the Hermetic Art* (1815) pp. 76–7; Van Helmont, *Ortus Medicinae* (1652) pp. 358–65, and *Oriatrike*, pp. 585–96.

Below the level of the elite, such exotica were also prized. A popular item among the wealthy in sixteenth-century Cork appears to have been the coconut. James Unack, a burgess of Youghal, in 1577, for example, bequeathed a 'nott of silver double gilt' to his son John.[187] Likewise, Andrew Galway, in 1580 bequeathed a 'little black nut covered in silver' and a 'silver nott'.[188] Another 'nott' or 'coconut cup' was bequeathed by Andrew Roche in 1618.[189] Roche's cup was described as a 'small blacke nutt with a faire silver cover and the nutt bound with foure silver bindings and a long silver foot'. Coconuts had been prized by wealthy European collectors since the eighth century. They were originally imported from the south-western coast of the Indian subcontinent by Arab and Jewish traders, but by the sixteenth century Spanish and Portuguese merchants were shipping coconuts to Europe from Central and South America as well. The cups, which were made from a hollowed coconut and mounted in silver, were often elaborately carved with biblical or political imagery. These were fashionable rarities in Western Europe in the late fifteenth century and throughout the sixteenth century, and were valued not only because of their exotic appeal but also because of their purported medical properties. Coconut milk alleviated tapeworm, fever, kidney and bladder afflictions, among other things, and also served as an aphrodisiac. The shell was believed to possess the ability to reveal poisons, a quality that led to its use as the cup element in drinking vessels.

Other items reputed to reveal poisons were also known in Ireland. A deposition of a Bristol merchant in 1595 relates how he bought a 'little bezoar stone' along with 9lb of drugs that were taken off a ship at Baltimore, in West Cork.[190] A bezoar stone is a mass found trapped in the gastrointestinal system of a goat found in the Middle East. These were sought because they were believed to have the power of a universal antidote against any poison. It was thought that a drinking vessel containing a bezoar would neutralise any poison poured into it. The belief in the properties of such objects led to a lively trade in fake objects in this period. A famous case in the common law of England declared the rule of caveat emptor, if the goods purchased were not effective.[191] The particular case concerned a buyer who sued for the return of the price of an allegedly fraudulent bezoar stone. It is unclear how the plaintiff discovered that the bezoar did not work.

The medical effectiveness of such items as unicorn horns and bezoar stones came into question in the late sixteenth century. In 1567, the surgeon Ambroise Paré proved that bezoar stones could not cure all poisons, as was popularly

[187] Cork City and County Archives, Caulfield Will Transcripts, U226, p. 7.

[188] Cork City and County Archives, Caulfield Will Transcripts, U226, P. 39.

[189] R. Caulfield (ed.), 'Wills and inventories, Cork, temp, Elizabeth and James I', in *Gentlemen's Magazine*, April, 1862, p. 441.

[190] Appleby, *Calendar of Material*, p. 81.

[191] Chandelor v Lopus (1603) 79 ER 3.

believed.[192] Likewise, Paré vehemently denied the supposed medicinal effect of unicorn products, arguing that treatments should be based on experimentation and argumentation rather than on superstition and perceived wisdom. His appeal fell largely on deaf ears, probably because the medical establishment was reluctant to give up a rewarding source of income, and 'unicorn' remained in demand as a prescription.

[192] Ambroise Paré, *Apology and Treatise* (1575); C. J. S. Thompson, *Poison Mysteries in History, Romance and Crime* (New York, 1924) pp. 61–2.

# 11

# *Drinking and Entertainment*

## I. Drinking

Audrey Horning recently observed that wine served as a medium of economic exchange in plantation Ireland. In the 1604 leasing arrangements agreed between Thomas Phillips, later one of the chief architects of the Londonderry plantation, and the earl of Tyrone, the timber rights in Killetra County, Londonderry were to be paid for by a rent of one tun of claret and one half-tun of wine.[1] Although the exact role of wine is uncertain, it also seems to have served complex ritual and political functions in Anglo-Irish relations and in the process of negotiation.

In a letter from John Garland to Sir John Perrot in 1589, Garland wrote:

> After the delivery of your Honour's 'scoule,' [scull], to O'Neill, he took it in his hand and kissed it at least half-a-score times, and then presently he sent for two hogsheads of wine and christened your scull, and after he had drunk his fill, and he put on his shirt of mail and his jack, and called for a bowl of wine, and drank it to your Honour's health, withal he put on his scull and drew out his sword with a great oath, and said that Sir John Perrot was the truest man of his word that ever he knew.[2]

The significance of O'Neill's drinking ritual is difficult to determine. There are echoes here, for example, of the ancient practice of Celtic and Scythian head hunting. Scythians, a tribe from which the Irish were believed to be descended, made use of the actual skulls of their enemies so as to drink of their strength and power. There are also religious and liturgical undertones, manifest in the christening of the skull. Whatever the exact significance of the ritual – or, of course, the manner in which Garland chose to report it – it is clear that both the wine and the drinking vessel, in this case Perrot's military helmet, were central to O'Neill's political statement. His actions indeed suggest an overlap between rituals of political and social drinking and the complex procedures of hat etiquette discussed earlier. Certainly, this raises intriguing questions about the extent to which Irish and English drinking practices overlapped, differed and were modified to serve as a point of cultural mediation and commensality between natives and newcomers.

[1] T. W. Moody, 'Sir Thomas Phillips of Limavady, servitor', *Irish Historical Studies*, i (1938–9), p. 254; cited in Horning, 'The root of all vice', p. 116.

[2] C.S. P Ire., 1588–92, p. 234.

Recent historiography has highlighted the importance of the issue of public drinking in the development of elite and popular culture in early modern society. In particular, the study of taverns has been central to the growing interest in the history of consumption and material culture and has contributed to a clearer understanding not only of economic developments but also of issues including sociability and ritual; social regulation; the construction of class distinction; the formation of national identity; and gender and sexual identity.[3]

Drunkenness was a running theme in England throughout the early modern period. In 1576, the English writer George Gascoigne described it as 'a monstrous plant, lately crept into the pleasant orchards of England'.[4] Philip Stubbes, writing in 1586, complained that every town in England hath 'abundance of alehouses, taverns and inns, which are so fraughted with malt-worms, night and day that you would wonder to see them … swilling, gulling and carousing from one to another, till never a one can speak a ready word'.[5] Much of the complaint was centred on two main themes: the rising number of drinking places, and the rituals of drinking, which encouraged heavy consumption and led to drunkenness and disorder.[6] In particular, the drinking of healths came under severe attack from both secular and religious writers in the early seventeenth century. In *Pierce Penilesse*, Thomas Nashe complained that 'now he is a no body that cannot drink *supernagulum*, carouse the hunter's hoop, quaff *upsey freze crosse*, with healths, gloves, mumps, frolics, and a thousand such domineering inventions'.[7] These rituals, Nashe noted, were 'as good as printed precepts, or statutes set down by Act of Parliament'.[8]

James Nicholls has discussed the cultural, religious and social significance of such complaint literature in the sixteenth and seventeenth centuries and has noted that concerns over drinking were 'often overlaid with concerns over national identity'.[9] This, Nicholls argued, was particularly clear in the work of Gascoigne and Nashe. Gascoigne, who blamed English excess on German influences, claimed that drunkenness 'reflected a peculiarly English attitude to foreign fashions; one in which continental vices and foibles were adopted in such an exaggerated way as to render

[3]B. Kümin (ed.) *The World of the Tavern: Public Houses in Early Modern Europe* (Aldershot, 2002);

B. Kümin, *Drinking Matters: Public Houses and Social Exchange in Early Modern Central Europe* (Basingstoke, 2007); P. Clark, *The English Alehouse: A Social History, 1200–1830* (London and New York, 1983); T. Brennan *et al.* (eds), *Public Drinking in the Early Modern World: Voices from the Tavern, 1500–1800* (London, 2011); J. Nicholls, *The Politics of Alcohol: A History of the Drink Question in England* (Manchester, 2009).

[4]G. Gascoigne, *A Delicate Diet for Dainty-mouthed Drunkards* (London, 1576), cited in Nicholls, *Politics*, p. 12.

[5]P. Stubbes, *The Anatomy of Abuses in England in Shakespeares Youth, A.D. 1583* (London, 1879), p. 107.

[6]Nicholls, *Politics*, p. 13.

[7]T. Nashe, *Pierce Penilesse, his Supplication to the Divell* (Edinburgh, 1966) p. 76, cited in Nicholls, *Politics*, p. 22.

[8]Nicholls, *Politics*, p. 22.

[9]Nicholls, *Politics*, p. 12.

them grotesque and absurd'.[10] Of German drinking habits, he wrote, 'we do make banquets and merriments' by which 'we surpass them very far'.[11] Nashe, writing in 1592, 15 years later, noted that 'superfluity in drink' was a sin 'that ever since we have mixed ourselves with the low-countries, is counted honourable: but before we knew their lingering wars, was held in the highest degree of hatred that might be'.[12] Such comments, Nicholls suggested, show a shared sense that drunkenness presented a significant social problem that 'threatened to undermine the nation-building project itself'.[13]

This apparent link between 'nation-building' and excessive consumption can also be extended to English colonial ideology in the late sixteenth century. In 1573, a document entitled 'Offices necessarie in the Colony of the Ardes and orders agreed uppon', listed the qualities required of officials in the colony. Captains were advised not to banquet and feast one another for 'these two years', to consult one another before and after dinner, and not to entertain a stranger, in company with other captains, on grounds of security and expense. These orders were made to avoid 'superfluity of fare or delicatree, and excess of apparel, 'for yow be com to laye the foundation of a good and (as is hoped) an eternall Colony for your posteritie, not a May game or a stage playe'.[14]

Drunkenness was a common charge made by English commentators against Irish men and women during this period. It is clear that the continental drinking rituals that had become established in English popular culture were also embraced by the Anglo-Irish. On the practice of drinking healths, for example, Moryson noted that Irish gentlewomen were 'so free in this excess' that they would 'pledge health after health with men ... till they be drunken, or at least till they void urine in full assemblies of men'.[15] He further noted that he had 'seen virgins ... commanded by their mothers to retire after they had in courtesy pledged one or two healths'.[16]

William Palmer has discussed the political and racist tone of English comments on Irish drinking in the early seventeenth century, in particular with regard to criticism of the drunkenness of Irish women.[17] Discussing the links between gender and disorder in Ireland, he argued that English writers believed that women posed a particular danger to the establishment of order and stability.[18] He suggested that female drunkenness, like promiscuity, was seen as 'the inability to control one's desires' and that the susceptibility of Irish women to alcohol and lewd behaviour meant

[10]Ibid.

[11]Gascoigne, *Delicate Diet*, cited in Nicholls, *Politics*, p. 12.

[12]Nicholls, *Politics*, p. 13; Nashe, *Pierce Penilesse*, p. 76, cited in Nicholls, *Politics*, p. 75.

[13]Nicholls, *Politics*, p. 13.

[14]Essex County Record Office: Hill Hall MSS (D/DSh 01/7), printed in B. Donovan and D. Edwards (eds), *British Sources for Irish History 1485–1641* (Dublin, 1997), p. 50.

[15]Moryson, 'An Itinerary', in Myers (ed.), *Elizabethan Ireland*, p. 187.

[16]Ibid., p. 187.

[17]W. Palmer, 'Gender, violence and rebellion in Tudor and Early Stuart Ireland', *Sixteenth Century Journal*, xxiii, 4 (1992), pp. 699–712.

[18]Ibid.

that they were perceived as 'an obstacle to civil government'.[19] Certainly Moryson's comments, noted above, while not intended, as he put it, 'to excuse the men' were predominantly directed against Irish women.[20] Barnabe Rich also condemned the habits of Irish women and made explicit the link between promiscuity and alcohol when he claimed to have seen in Dublin alehouses 'Huswiues' who were in reality 'filthy and beastly alehouse keepers', and who, he suggested, were capable of 'all manner of idleness, of whoredom and many other abominations'.[21]

Nevertheless, neither the political or gender significance of such comments should be overemphasised, since they clearly reflect popular male discourse, both in England and Europe, during this period. Andrea Snowden Cast has noted that, in early modern England, female drinking was seen as a subversion of patriarchal control and was 'a site of contention between insubordinate women and the dominant paradigm of male expectations about drinking and drunkenness'.[22] Likewise, A. L. Martin noted that stances on female drinking in early modern Europe were decidedly misogynistic. When men drank, the effects of alcohol caused otherwise honourable men to sin, but when women drank the effects of alcohol acted on the already weak nature of women as extolled in the sexual ideology of the day.[23] This view is clear from contemporary English street ballads. In 'Cuckold's Haven', for example, cuckoldry is attributed to the disinhibiting effect of drink:

> Nay you would little think how they will friendly link,
> And how they'll sit and drink till they begin to wink;
> And they if Vulcan will but ride, some cuckold shall be horrified.
> A Woman that will be drunk will easily play the punk;
> For when her wits are sunk, all keys will fit her trunk;
> Then by experience oft' is tried, poor men that way are horrified.[24]

The correlation between prostitutes and alehouses in Dublin, noted by Barnabe Rich, was also a common theme in English, European and American concerns during this period.[25] Indeed, it was not only English settlers who remarked on the problem in Ireland. *The Great Parchment Book of Waterford* discusses in some detail the 'abhomynable trade of horedom'.[26] The chief occasion for this vice was deemed to be the use of women servants in wine taverns. It was noted that certain tavern owners retained 'nawgthie corrupte women by whose procurement and meanes other

[19] Palmer, 'Gender', p. 709.

[20] Moryson, 'An Itinerary', in Myers (ed.), *Elizabethan Ireland*, p. 187.

[21] Rich, *A New Description of Ireland*, pp. 11, 71.

[22] A. Snowden Cast, 'Women drinking in early modern England' (University of Adelaide Ph.D. thesis, 2002), p. vi.

[23] A. L. Martin, *Alcohol, Sex and Gender in Late Medieval and Early Modern Europe* (Basingstoke and New York, 2001).

[24] 'Cuckhold's Haven', *The Roxburghe Ballads* (1638).

[25] See, for example, Martin, 'Alcohol, sex and gender'; T. Brennan *et. al.* (eds), *Public Drinking in the Early Modern World: Voices from the Tavern, 1500–1800* (London, 2011).

[26] GPB, p. 146

honest damsels are often drawn to folly' and it was enacted that 'never more any woman maid wife wench or wyddowe shall be wyne taverner or wyne drawer in any place within the cittie or suburbs upon payne of five powndes in money to be levied of his goodes and cattell'.[27] The failure of this 'holsome remedy' is clear from another enactment made just two years later, which stated that only women of good name and fame could keep a tavern or sell wine, and added that any master or mistress failing to dismiss a servant 'suspected to play the whoore' would have to pay a fine.[28] In 1604, it was again enacted that no woman of any 'qualitie or degree' could retail drink within the city. The law was enacted to avoid 'whordome', the 'consealment of goods stollen' and 'for strenghtning of the Cittie ffor then that all retailers within the Citie must be hereafter men servants and no women servants'.[29] These more expansive aims suggest a perceived link between alcohol, sexual promiscuity and crime in Waterford. They also marry well with Snowden Cast's observations of the tavern as a site of gender contest in early modern England.

Some important points have also been made about the significance of the regulation of public drinking in this period, and these are worth considering in an Irish context.[30] The first attempt in England to co-ordinate the control of drinking establishments was the 1552 Alehouse Act, which sought to regulate all alehouses as a measure against perceived increases in levels of drunkenness and social disorder in England.[31] Under this act no one was allowed to sell beer or ale without the consent of the local justices of the peace. Each person licensed by the justices had to enter into a recognizance, to ensure that good behaviour was maintained in each alehouse. This was followed by an act in 1553 licensing taverns, limiting their number and imposing strict approval processes for becoming a tavern keeper.[32]

James Nicholls argued that the formalisation of distinctions between alehouses and taverns in England was a method of class distinction; one whereby the elite was actively constructed. Taverns, which traditionally sold wine rather than ale or beer, became the most exclusive of the three-tiered system of licensing in England: alehouses, inns and taverns. The purpose of these detailed and exacting regulations, Nicholls argued, was not only to limit drinking and associated social disorder, but to protect the social status of the elite establishments, whose perceived worth was being diminished by proliferation.[33]

In Ireland, taverns were regulated to some extent both locally, as noted in the case of Waterford above, and centrally, before the Elizabethan Conquest. The *Great Parchment Book of Waterford* documents 'pleas of certain writs or acts is enrolled in our Common Bench of Ireland', delivered at Dublin in 1472, which include an

[27] GPB, p. 147.
[28] GPB, p. 152.
[29] GPB, p. 211.
[30] For a recent discussion of drinking in the Ulster Plantation see Horning, 'The root of all vice'.
[31] 5 & 6 Edward. VI, c.25.
[32] 7 Edward VI, c.5.
[33] Nicholls, *Politics* pp. 9–12.

order that no foreigner could 'make a tavern of wines contrary to the will of the chief official and the burgesses of the town'.[34] There is no evidence to suggest, however, that the new licensing laws of the 1550s were enacted or enforced in Ireland, and it is likely that the tiered system of drinking establishments that emerged in England from the middle of the sixteenth century was not as evident in Ireland during this period.

Despite Moryson's comment that 'they have no taverns with ivy bushes or signs hung out, save only some few in Dublin', taverns do seem to have been a distinct feature of the south-eastern port towns. In Cork, Richard Mathew, a local merchant whose will was proved in 1582, bequeathed brewing pans and aqua vitae pots to his son and daughters, along with his tavern, which they were to hold for three years each.[35] The fact that a tavern keeper also possessed brewing equipment may indicate that the distinction in the types of drinks served in Irish drinking establishments was less marked than in English ones. Also, Henry Verdon of Cork bequeathed his 'shopp and the taverne and the next cellar to the taverne' to his son, while his wife was to have another cellar.[36] There are also some indications that taverns provided sustenance beyond the provision of alcoholic beverages. In the will of Piers Gold, of Cork, proved in 1610, he left 2s to Gerrat Fitzrichard or his wife 'to have his or her blessing for a pig of his which was killed for his tavern'.[37]

In addition to the taverns, it is likely that wine was sold directly from such cellars. Moryson noted, for example, that some merchants commonly sold wine 'in their own cellars'.[38] What is unclear, however, is the extent to which commercial drinking establishments existed beyond or below the tavern. Commercial alehouses are rarely mentioned in the Irish literature. The corporation book of Irishtown, for example, makes reference to taverns but not to alehouses.[39] Also, English commentators were in agreement that formal inns were a rarity. According to an unknown traveller in Ireland in 1579:

> If you except the port towns, there are no hotels or lodging houses to be found in the island. Every traveller sets up in the first house he meets, and there is provided with whatever he desires, gratuitously. Table is not usually laid until evening, but in the meantime drink is not denied to travellers.[40]

In 1617, Moryson likewise remarked that:

> I did never see any public inns with signs hanged out among the English or the English-Irish, but the officers of cities and villages appoint lodgings to the passengers, and perhaps

[34] GPB, p. 32.
[35] Cork City and County Archives, Caulfield Will Transcripts, U226, p. 22.
[36] Ibid., p. 35.
[37] R. Caulfield (ed.), 'Wills and inventories, Cork, temp, Elizabeth and James I', in *Gentlemen's Magazine*, November, 1861, p. 503.
[38] Moryson, 'An Itinerary', in Myers (ed.) *Elizabethan Ireland*, p. 186.
[39] Ainsworth, 'Corporation book', pp. 25, 29.
[40] 'An unknown traveller's account of Ireland, 1579', in Maxwell, *Irish History*, p. 320.

> in each city they shall find one or two houses where they will dress meat, and these be commonly houses of Englishmen, seldom of the Irish, so as these houses having no signs hung out, a passenger cannot challenge right to be entertained in them, but must have it of courtesy or entreaty.[41]

The apparent lack of such establishments in Ireland, in contrast to England, was probably owing to a number of key social and economic differences. Peter Clark and Keith Wrightson have identified a number of factors that drove the rise of the alehouse as a social institution in England, one of which was the movement of itinerant workers from their home towns in search of work during periods of low employment. Such workers relied on alehouses to provide rudimentary lodgings and a place to find out what work might be available locally.[42] In Ireland, on the other hand, there existed a comprehensive 'social institution' of hospitality, which has been discussed by Katherine Simms,[43] and, more recently, in a detailed study by Catherine O'Sullivan.[44] The ritualised customs of Irish hospitality, which were enshrined in Brehon law, entitled travellers of any status to receive food and a night's lodging from the road; a lord to receive hospitality from his vassals; and a king to billet his servants on the inhabitants of his kingdom. O'Sullivan has noted that even at the end of the sixteenth century, ordinary householders were still duty bound to practise hospitality, a factor that may well have delayed the development of alehouses and inns.[45]

Economic factors also retarded the growth of commercial drinking establishments in Ireland. Nicholls has argued that the commercial growth of hops in England from the 1520s was 'a pivotal moment in the modernisation of brewing'.[46] Hopped beer was more stable than ale and could therefore be produced in greater volumes and stored by sellers for longer. This meant that what had been 'seasonal, local and domestic was set to become mass produced and highly profitable' and this in turn led to a rise in the number of alehouses.[47] The nature of the Irish economy during this period meant that it relied on imports to supply the growing demand for hops and there was therefore probably less incentive to open commercial alehouses.

Nevertheless, despite such social and economic differences, it is clear that by the end of the sixteenth century, and probably earlier, both the elite and common Gaelic and Anglo-Irish did engage in commercialised public drinking in Irish towns. Moryson noted that the 'mere' Irish 'were:

[41] Moryson, 'An Itinerary', in Myers (ed.) *Elizabethan Ireland*, p. 187.

[42] Nicholls, *Politics*, p. 10; P. Clark, 'Alehouses and alternative society', in D. Pennington and K. Thomas (eds), *Puritans and Revolutionaries: Essays in Seventeenth-Century History* (Oxford, 1978), p. 52; K. Wrightson, 'Alehouses, order and Reformation in rural England 1590–1660' in E. and S. Yeo (eds.), *Popular Culture and Class Conflict 1590–1914* (Brighton, 1981), p. 4.

[43] K. Simms, 'Guesting and Feasting in Gaelic Ireland', JRSAI, 108, pp.67–100; Horning, 'The root of all vice', p. 118.

[44] O'Sullivan, *Hospitality*, p. 13.

[45] Ibid., p. 66.

[46] Nicholls, *Politics*, p. 10.

[47] Ibid.

> excessively given to drunkenness. For howsoever while they lived in woods and in cabins with their cattle, they could be content with water and milk, yet when they came to towns nothing was more frequent than to tie their cows at the doors and never part from the taverns till they had drunk them out of sack and strong water, which they call usquebaugh, and this did not only the lords, but the common people, though half naked for want of clothes to cover them.[48]

It may be that owing to the lack of regulation of taverns and the unavailability of alternate commercial venues, public drinking in Ireland was a more socially inclusive practice than in England at the end of the sixteenth century. Moryson certainly seems to imply that both the elite and the commoners drank at the same establishments. A sudden surge in the licensing of taverns in the early seventeenth century probably changed this, however. In 1613 the register of patents and inventions in Ireland records the first Elizabethan licences issued for Irish taverns. In that year, seven taverns were licensed; a further one in 1614; while seven more received licences in 1616, including three in Cork, Mallow and Bantry.[49] This regulation, however, was probably driven more by economic than social factors. Each of the licences to own taverns also included permission to produce aqua vitae, an occupation that had long caused anxiety for the English administration in Ireland.[50] According to the Act of 3 and 4 Philip and Mary, aqua vitae was made universally throughout Ireland 'for the furniture of Irishmen, and thereby much corn, grain and other things are consumed, spent and wasted, to the great hindrance, loss and damage to the poor inhabitants of this realm'.[51]

## II. Smoking

In addition to drinking, taverns were also becoming the site of other forms of consumption at the close of the sixteenth century. Shammas has noted that pipe smoking, from its introduction to England, was closely associated with the alehouse and that publicans were generally the main retailers of both tobacco and tobacco pipes. As a result, the 'pipeful became another of the refreshments connected with alehouse social life'.[52] Using data from the seventeenth-century London port books, Shammas has discussed the rapid diffusion of tobacco, which she argued became a mass consumption item around the middle of the seventeenth century. Certainly, there is evidence to suggest that by the 1670s this was also the case in Ireland. In 1672, Sir William Petty noted that 'tobacco taken in short pipes seldom burnt,

[48]Moryson, 'An Itinerary', in Myers (ed.) *Elizabethan Ireland*, p. 204.

[49]TNA, HO 42/218.

[50]Longfield, *Anglo-Irish Trade*, p. 147.

[51]F. Vesey, *The Statutes at Large, Passed in the Parliaments held in Ireland*, vol. i (1310–1612), p. 251.

[52]Shammas, 'Changes', p. 181.

seems to be the pleasure of their lives, together with sneezing: Insomuch, the 2/7 of their Expence in Food, is Tobacco'.[53]

Little is known about early trends in the consumption of tobacco in England. Unsurprisingly, since the popularisation of tobacco is generally associated with Sir Walter Raleigh after c.1580, it was not recorded amongst imports to London in 1559, but the gap of some 61 years between this and the next available set of customs data for the port means that the date and volumes imported initially are unknown. Tobacco was not recorded amongst Irish imports from Bristol until 1600/1, indicating that it was possibly first introduced to the south-east of the country somewhere between 1594 and 1600. Importation was in very small quantities in 1600/1. In that year William Hallie of Waterford and Edmund Pontche of Cork imported 1lb each of the substance. Shammas has estimated that the annual per capita consumption of tobacco in England in the 1620s was approximately 0.01lb.[54] Based on this estimation 2lb of tobacco would have been enough to supply around 200 people for a year. The volume of tobacco pipes imported in the same year, however, indicates that smoking was a little more widespread. In 1600/1, some 756 tobacco pipes were imported into the region and, therefore, unless tobacco was entering the region by another route, the volume of tobacco smoked by the consumers that was supplied by the trade was considerably less than 0.01lb per year. Woodward has also noted small quantities of tobacco and pipe imports to Dublin from Chester at the end of the century.[55]

Tobacco smoking was beyond any doubt an elite occupation in Ireland at the beginning of the seventeenth century. Pipes were imported almost exclusively by merchants from the Cork area in 1600/1. In that year, 62 per cent of pipes were imported by merchants from Cork itself, 32 per cent by merchants from Kinsale and the remainder by merchants from Waterford. That there was an established market for this item is suggested by the fact that 11 individual merchants imported them. The highly localised nature of this import trade in 1600/1 may indicate either that the fashion for smoking was at this early date centred on Cork and its environs or that, for commercial reasons, Cork merchants dominated the trade in tobacco pipes. That the demand for pipes continued to increase in the early seventeenth century is clear from a monopoly granted to John Cooker on 23 October 1618 to make tobacco pipes in Ireland.[56]

[53] W. Petty, *The Political Anatomy of Ireland*, vol. 1, p. 191, cited in Clarkson and Crawford, *Feast*, p. 15.

[54] Shammas, 'Changes', p. 180.

[55] Woodward, *Trade*, p. 21.

[56] TNA, H.O. 4/2218.

### III. Gambling and games

Gambling was big business in sixteenth-century Ireland, and of universal appeal. Contemporary English writers complained bitterly about itinerant gamblers known as carrows 'that profess to play at cards all the year-long and make it their only occupation'.[57] There was concern that these carrows, who according to Spenser were 'another much like kern', or in other words of the lower classes, were wandering 'up and down gentlemen's houses', drawing them into their 'lewdness and idleness', and then cheating them of their winnings, by conniving through 'stealth' to avoid payment.[58] There is little direct evidence of the nature of Irish gambling in this period, but it is clear that the well-off were partial to the pastime, even without the enticement of the lower orders. In 1580, for example, David Tyrrie Fitz Edmonde of Cork stipulated in his will that Terry Skiddie 'be paid of his olde challenge to me for a blacke clock and olde turned dublet of duble silke'.[59] The upper classes, it would appear, could also be somewhat tardy in paying their gambling debts.

In a similar manner to their comments on Irish drunkenness, writers such as Campion and Spenser made use of the prevalence of gambling in Ireland as a way of illustrating Irish depravity, barbarism, and social and cultural disorder. It is nonetheless enlightening to read these views in the context of broader contemporary concerns in English and European society. Recent work by Enrique García Santo-Tomás, for example, who has explored social and cultural attitudes to gambling in early modern Spain, identified a surge in upper-class gambling in this period. The 'unprecedented popularity' of gambling, he argues, 'occurred in the wider context of the rise of a mercantile society that created a standardized, universal measure of value where the role of gambling was central, as speculation and risk in economic life had their corollary in the speculation and risk of games of chance'.[60] Such economic changes led to a betting frenzy among the upper classes, since:

> betting on anything was a way of injecting value into a social capital that had become unstable in this age of economic upheaval – not so much an extravagance of the Baroque, as Huizinga put it, but rather the result of the insecurities of a class attempting to validate its fragile authority within a new logic of commercial exchange that witnessed the advent of a competing bourgeois economy.[61]

[57] E. Campion, 'A history of Ireland' (1571), in Myers (ed.), *Elizabethan Ireland*, p. 78.

[58] Spenser, 'View', in Myers (ed.), *Elizabethan Ireland*, p. 104.

[59] Caulfield Will Transcripts, p. 9. The mention of a clock at this early date is very interesting. This was probably an iron chamber clock of Flemish origin, which at this date had painted iron dials. My thanks to Brian Loomes for sharing his expertise on the matter.

[60] Enrique García Santo-Tomás, 'Outside bets: disciplining gamblers in early modern Spain', in *Hispanic Review*, 77, 1, Re-Envisioning Early Modern Iberia: Visuality, Materiality, History (2009), pp. 147–64.

[61] Ibid, p. 154.

This perhaps oversimplifies elite responses to economic and social change, but there is little doubt that upper-class gambling was of great concern to secular and religious authorities. Chance, as Santo-Tomás puts it, was considered a 'type of unnatural equalizer that dissolved boundaries and rank'.[62] Reformers who worried about the dissolution of social hierarchy were less concerned about rowdy players than the possibility that card games might turn society upside-down by transferring capital from the rich to the hands of the undeserving.[63] These broader social fears are certainly present in Spenser's comments about the nature of Irish gambling.

The language used by English commentators to describe the social evils of gambling in Ireland also finds parallels in European discourse. Examining Spanish tracts, Santo-Tomás argued that gambling was viewed in symbolic terms as a disease of the body politic. The gambler embodied a wasted body and symbolised disease through 'pollution, clogging, and putrefaction', antithetic to the structure of a healthy nation.[64] Pedro de Guzman, for example, wrote that the gaming table had made Spaniards 'achacosos y enfermizos', or sickly and infirm, sapping their strength and virility.[65] Likewise, Francisco de Navarrete y Ribera described men who went without food and sleep, lacking the energy to support their families; men who had to flee their towns because of unpaid debts; men who were expelled from their homes, thereby joining the increasing number of vagabonds and criminals, and so on.[66] This symbolic emasculation of the male body through gambling is clearly manifest in Campion's description of the Irish carrow, who pawned away portions of his glib, the nails of his fingers and toes, and even metaphorically lost his privy member to the sport; emphasising perhaps the perceived weakness and instability of Irish social structures.[67]

On another level, gambling was viewed as morally and ethically reprehensible in a reformed society. As Spenser pointed out, gambling was wasteful, dishonest and inherently corrupting. It was also sinful. Religious reformers viewed gamblers as 'thieves before God', whose gains were won out of self-interest and sinfulness.[68] Gambling was also seen as a source of social disorder, and, during the sixteenth century, the English government adopted a policy of prohibition towards the pastime in England. An act passed in 1541, for example, stipulated:

> that no manner of artificer or craftsman of any handicraft or occupation, husbandman, apprentice, labourer, servant at husbandry, journeyman, or servant of artificer, mariners,

[62] Ibid., p. 158. See also Laura A. Smoller, 'Playing cards and popular culture in sixteenth-century Nuremburg', *The Sixteenth Century Journal*, xvii (1986), p. 183. Smoller argues that, in Nuremberg, gambling transcended class and represented a shared popular culture.

[63] Ibid., p. 158.

[64] Ibid., p. 156.

[65] Ibid, p. 156.

[66] Ibid., p. 156.

[67] Campion, 'A history of Ireland' (1571) in Myers (ed.), *Elizabethan Ireland*, p. 78.

[68] Smoller, 'Playing cards', p. 189.

> fishermen, watermen, or any serving-man shall … play at the tables, tennis, dice, cards, bowls, clash, coyting, logating, or any other unlawful game out of Christmas.[69]

The application of this legislation exclusively to the lower orders suggests that, like the control of alehouses discussed earlier, the regulation of gambling was seen as a means of controlling the poor: of preventing large numbers of 'idle' and potentially disorderly people from gathering together to play games, cards or dice.[70] Additional laws were passed during the seventeenth and eighteenth centuries targeting particular games – regardless of social status – and imposing penalties for cheating and limits on the amount of money that players could stake at any one time.[71] Such wide-ranging legislation was, of course, impossible to enforce. Prosecutions were sporadic and only tended to occur during times of moral panic, when illegal gaming houses were causing disorder, or when reforming individuals or groups took a concerted stand against illegal gaming.[72] Given the perceived links between idleness, gambling and disorder, it is hardly surprising that itinerant Irish gamblers were seen as a problem for the English administration in Ireland. Not only were they 'idle losers', as Spenser put it, but their mobility meant that their activities were impossible to regulate and control.

Apart from the odd survival of bone dice or gaming pieces among archaeological finds, little evidence exists of the material culture of games and gambling in medieval or early modern Ireland.[73] Playing cards, due to their fragility, do not survive at all for this period in Ireland, and only very rarely in England. The customs records, however, reveal some interesting trends in the importation of cards and other gaming paraphernalia that sheds some light on Irish gambling in this period. First, it is notable that playing cards do not feature among imports to Ireland in the accounts from the early century. This may well be a function of production costs and the nature of early production of playing cards. The 1507 book of rates, for example, values playing cards at a staggering £4 per gross, or 6d per card, about six times the price of a whole primer. In the early years of European production, cards were made by engraving or woodcutting. Engraving was a much more expensive production technique, but cards made by either method could be finished to a very luxurious standard, including embellishments such as hand-painted images, or gilding with gold or silver. It is likely that the cards referred to in the 1507 book of rates were of a particularly elaborate and luxurious variety, rather than the mass-produced varieties that appeared later in the century. It is hardly surprising, then, given their cost, that

[69] 33 Hen. VIII, c. 9, s. 16.

[70] 33 Hen. VIII, c. 9, s. 11.

[71] N. Tosney, 'Gaming in England, c.1540–1760' (Ph.D. thesis, University of York, 2008) and also Tosney, 'Gaming in Britain and America: some historical comparisons', Center for Gaming Research Occasional Paper Series, University of Nevada, December 2010. Available from: http://gaming.unlv.edu/papers/cgr_op08_tosney.pdf [accessed 9 September 2013].

[72] Tosney, 'Gaming in England', chapter 2.

[73] DIER, Laois, 1994:144; Kildare, 2007:737.

Table 11.1
Volume of playing cards imported, 1503–1601 (pack/deck)

| Year | Packs of cards |
|---|---|
| 1503/4 | 0 |
| 1516/17 | 0 |
| 1525/6 | 54 |
| 1541/2 | 2,292 |
| 1542/3 | 1,176 |
| 1545/6 | 1,806 |
| 1550/1 | 682 |
| 1563/4 | 1,140 |
| 1575/6 | 1,344 |
| 1594/5 | 471 |
| 1600/1 | 426 |

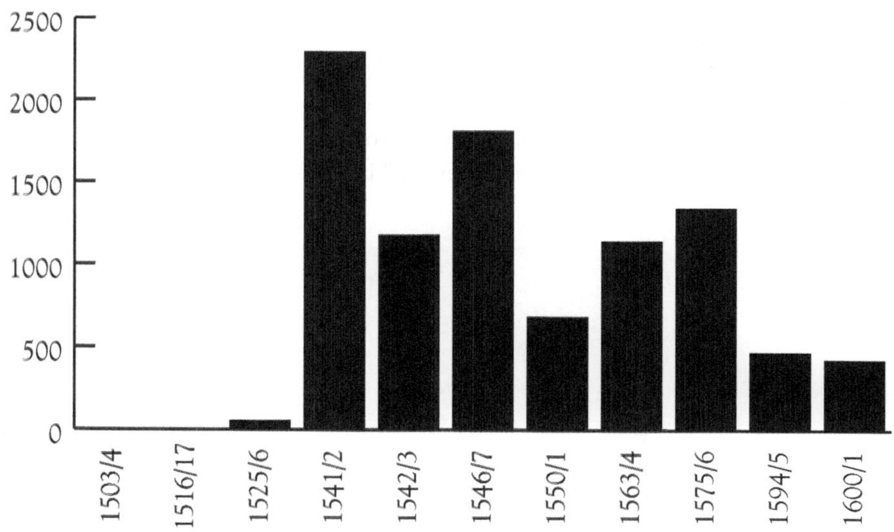


Figure 11.1 Volume of playing cards imported, 1503–1601 (pack/deck)

playing cards do not feature among Irish imports in the earliest part of the sixteenth century. Those able to afford such luxury cards would no doubt have commissioned them privately from artisans and craftsmen rather than purchasing them on the market.

By the mid-sixteenth century, however, it is clear that imported playing cards had become available, affordable and very popular in Irish towns. Cards are listed at 10d to 1s 3d per dozen in the 1540s customs accounts, more than six times cheaper than in the 1507 rates book, and imports increased very dramatically in this period, suggesting that the availability of cheaper versions stimulated their use. It is also of note that the peak in imports of playing cards corresponds directly with the peak in values for Anglo-Irish trade overall, perhaps indicating that gambling in Ireland was linked to improving economic conditions and increasing trade, in line with Enrique García Santo-Tomás' findings for early modern Spain, noted above. See Table 11.1 and Figure 11.1.

Aside from card playing, other games were also known in Ireland. In 1595, 12 pairs of 'playing tables' were imported to Waterford by merchants from Limerick and Fethard-on-Sea.[74] 'Tables' was a general name given in this period to a variety of board games similar to backgammon, and these items, valued at only 5s per dozen, must refer to the playing boards used for these games. Dice, which were used to play at 'tables', are also found in the later accounts. The most common game at tables was 'Ticktack', and all such games, with the exception of chess, had gambling built into the rules.[75] Other board games were also played in Ireland. In the later century 'Merels', or 'Nine Men's Morris', appears to have been particularly popular. In 1575, for example, almost 5,000 game pieces for the game were imported from Bristol. Merels is a strategy board game of ancient origin that was very popular in medieval and sixteenth-century England.[76] Large outdoor boards were sometimes cut into village greens. In Shakespeare's *A Midsummer Night's Dream*, Titania refers to such a board: 'The Nine Men's Morris is filled up with mud'.[77] Boards have also been found carved into the cloister seats at the English cathedrals at Canterbury, Gloucester, Norwich and Salisbury, Westminster Abbey, and into the base of a pillar in Chester Cathedral.[78]

[74]TNA, E190113110 f49v; Tables also feature in the 1600–1 account: E190113211 f26r.

[75]J. L. Forgeng, *Daily Life in Stuart England* (Greenwood, 2007) p. 177.

[76]Merel derives from the Latin word *merellus*, which means a counter or gaming piece. M. Simonds Mohr, *The New Games Treasury* (1997), pp. 30–2.

[77]Shakespeare, *A Midsummer Night's Dream*, Act II, Scene I.

[78]R. C. Bell, *Board and Table Games from Many Civilizations*, Volume 1 (New York, 1979), pp. 90–2.

# *Part III – Summary*

Part 3 has examined the extent to which south-east Ireland was integrated into the 'widening world' of sixteenth-century food, drink and entertainment, and has considered the social, cultural and economic significance of changes in this area of Irish consumption and material culture. As in the other sections of this book, it has questioned the impact of colonisation on the acquisition and interpretation of everyday items and has examined the extent to which changing Irish patterns of consumption indicate the social and cultural assimilation of 'English' habits in the sixteenth century.

Despite contemporary references to the 'filthy' dietary habits of the Anglo and Gaelic Irish, it is clear that significant areas of affinity existed in the material culture and consumption of food and drink in England and Ireland in the sixteenth century. This includes the range of items consumed; the pace and chronology of change; and also, to a certain extent, the interpretation of material culture. Examining the variety of exotic spices imported to Ireland, for example, reveals a similar range of spices to those being used by the citizens of Southampton in the same period, a town that, due to its position on the route of all sea traffic from the Mediterranean to the Netherlands and northern Europe, was very much up-to-date with current food fashions.[79] In addition, both elite and, to some extent, non-elite trends in the use of domestic utensils evolved along similar lines in England and Ireland. New types of items such as beer tankards, porradgers, drinking glasses and specific styles of salt cellars, for example, entered English and Irish use around the same time. Similarities also existed in the interpretation of such objects and it is clear that certain rituals of the table were shared in Anglo-Irish and English societies. Both English and Irish used specific drinking vessels for different types of drink, and drinking vessels and cutlery served similar symbolic functions in both societies: they displayed the wealth and social status of their owners; they had ritual ceremonial functions and were given as items of commemoration, such as at weddings and christenings; and they were regular items of bequest. Such items may also have had other shared symbolic associations, being used in the evolving rituals of public drinking in sixteenth-century society.

[79] Thirsk, *Food*.

Nevertheless, as with the consumption of dress during this period, there is little evidence to indicate the slavish emulation of 'English' modes and manners in south-east Ireland. Consumption was selective, even among the elite who could afford to indulge in new food fashions and trends. Obviously, economic and social conditions imposed limitations on participation. As with dress, lack of skill specialisation may, in particular, have retarded Irish participation in new trends. The shortage of skilled apothecaries, for example, meant that the Irish could not fully embrace the sort of complex experimentation in distillation that was in vogue in England and Europe in the sixteenth century. Again, as with dress, practicality was a considerable factor in determining choice. Drinking glasses, probably owing to their expense and fragility, were slow to find a market in Ireland, whereas durable and practical wooden trenchers became an item of mass consumption within a relatively short period of time.

It also seems that fundamental differences in taste persisted in Ireland and England, even by the end of the century. Spoons – an item of everyday use in England regardless of social status – do not seem to have featured prominently at Irish tables, indicating a persistent difference in food consumption. There was also an apparent preference in Ireland for everyday manufactured items produced on the Continent over those produced in England. Trends in the importation of knives, for example, indicate that Irish consumers – whether due to conservatism, a sense of snobbery, or for economic reasons – continued to favour continental knives, even after English commercial production began in earnest.

With regard to the impact of colonisation and conquest on the consumption of food and drink, the Munster plantation had little or no direct impact on Irish trends. Most of the changes noted had occurred prior to the influx of 'New English' settlers, and the quantitative and qualitative evidence suggests considerable elements of overlap in English and Irish food consumption and material culture, well before the Munster plantation. Certainly, some luxury items appearing in the accounts after 1594 were probably initially intended for English rather than Irish consumption. The importation of sugar, in particular, increased very significantly in 1594/5. On the other hand, rather than relating simply to the importation of new tastes by English settlers, this trend may be due to developing commercial interests in Bristol, and the possible materialisation of a sugar-refining industry in the city, which may well have had an impact on the Irish market. Overall changes in Irish attitudes to food and drink were predominantly rooted in Ireland's society and economy, rather than being imposed by external factors such as colonisation and militarisation.

While the material culture of food and drink had a comparable role in the construction and expression of identity in England and Ireland, major differences existed. In particular, the formalisation of drinking establishments in England in this period, which was an important method of class distinction, was not a feature of Irish society. It is likely that public drinking was a far more socially inclusive practice in Ireland. As a site of social interaction and class convergence, Irish drinking establishments may indeed have had an important function in the spread of new fashions and elite tastes to the lower classes.

If many of the items examined here suggest comparable consumption practices and rituals of domestic etiquette, which perhaps served in the integration of English and Irish societies, others represent the differentiation of social groups in Ireland. The importation of infant feeding bottles, in 1594/5, in light of changing contemporary attitudes to wet nursing in England and Europe, is suggestive of deep social and cultural divisions in colonial Ireland. While attitudes to food and drink may have been shared on a superficial level, prejudice towards the native population meant that more intimate and symbolically charged methods of food-related consumption were rejected. Colonists perhaps discovered similar and acceptable types of inanimate drinking utensils in Ireland, but the employment of the breasts of native Irish wet nurses to nourish their offspring remained anathema, for some.

Finally, some points can be made regarding the regionality of dietary changes in the sixteenth century. In general terms, and within the context of a rapidly changing economic, social and political world, the food scene in England was fundamentally altered in the sixteenth century.[80] Nevertheless, changes to English dietary regimes were regionally distinctive, and the picture emerging from recent English historiography is one of strong local diversity based on regional cultural differences.[81] Examining regional and social patterns of diet, Thirsk noted that natural conditions such as climate and soil, and the varying impact of overseas trade, had a major impact on the pace and extent of change in various regions. As a result, distinct differences existed in the diet of those in the north and south of the country, and diet in coastal areas was qualitatively different from those inland.[82] According to Thirsk, it is indeed impossible to define a typical 'English' diet during this period.

There is little doubt that this was also the case in Ireland, and that foreign luxuries and food flavours probably came the way of the citizens of the south-eastern port towns, and their hinterlands, 'long before they reached places inland'.[83] Indeed, areas remote from the main Irish commercial centres may have seen little overall change to their habits and food customs in this period. This, however, does not indicate general social 'backwardness' or economic stagnation in Ireland. Nor does it make Irish development particularly different to that of England in this period. Thirsk observed that in parts of England, as in Ireland, long-established provincial tastes and cooking practices were often very slow to give way to new fashions, and were only gradually altered by novelties.[84] It must be remembered, therefore, that a visitor to parts of England as diverse as Cornwall and Lincolnshire, in the late

[80] Ibid., p. xi.
[81] Ibid., p. 196.
[82] Ibid.
[83] Ibid.
[84] Ibid.

sixteenth century, would have found commodities such as hopped beer and sugar in as short supply as visitors to Irish regions that were remote from the commerce of the major port towns.[85]

[85] For a detailed discussion of regional and social patterns of diet in England see Thirsk, *Food*, pp. 196–228.

# *Conclusion*

In the sixteenth century, south-east Ireland and its extensive hinterland witnessed significant changes in consumption. These mirrored, in many ways, the sorts of changes occurring in the Pale, in England and across Europe during the period. While not vast in term of value, the progressively complex range of goods imported into Ireland demonstrates that, whether or not Ireland was as 'backwards' as many contemporaries felt, it was gaining access to the increasingly sophisticated and diversified range of consumer goods being produced and traded in England and mainland Europe at this time. Ireland was able to participate in an evolving European consumer culture during this period, even if it was not at the forefront of it.

This book has questioned the impact of a number of broad economic, social and political factors on the growing consumption of luxury goods in Ireland, particularly in the last quarter of the century. Of particular significance in this context has been the extent to which rising consumer imports were a function of English colonialism, as suggested by Thirsk. It would appear, however, that immigration from England was not the chief driving force of these changes, since the increasing diversification of commodity types does not map on to the chief periods of Elizabethan colonisation and conquest. The new ranges of items imported were predominantly for the use of pre-existing Irish 'consumers', rather than the settler population, and the factors driving these changes were rooted in the Irish economy and society.

Unfortunately, the dearth of evidence for this period in Ireland's history makes the specific identification of these Irish 'consumer' groups almost impossible. Without detailed and reliable evidence for demographic change, wages, prices, ownership of goods, mercantile marketing strategies, credit arrangements, and so on, it is difficult to assess the extent and significance of this apparent 'consumer boom'. It is certainly clear, however, that interest in new consumer goods extended beyond the elite in Irish society. The surviving wills and inventories of Cork citizens clearly show that the better-off townspeople, below the level of elite, could aspire to the ownership of very luxurious apparel and domestic furnishing and wares, but there is evidence that the demand for new goods in this period was beginning to extend even further down the social scale. The introduction of sumptuary laws regulating the apparel of the lower classes, the increasing demand for cheaper versions of 'luxury' goods, the widespread geographical spread of items, the diffusion of luxury apparel to servants and maids in wills, and the mass consumption of newly introduced 'lower class' items such as 'common' trenchers – these all suggest that the trends noted by historians of consumption for the seventeenth and eighteenth centuries were emergent as early as the mid-sixteenth century in the more commercialised parts of Ireland.

Much work remains to be done on the nature of the Irish economy in the sixteenth century, but two key broad developments have been identified in this study: the expansion of local industries and the integration of Irish merchants in growing European markets. It appears that these were key factors in stimulating the supply of and demand for new goods in this period. With regards to the former, although Irish 'consumers' remained dependent for the most part on imports for everyday manufactured goods, many of their increasing needs were now met by domestic production. Indeed, it has been seen here that numerous local industries developed in south-east Ireland from the mid-sixteenth century, including stocking knitting, glassmaking, hat making, girdle and garter making, starching, small-scale commercial beer brewing and fine cloth production. All of these industries were stimulated by wider changes in European and English production techniques and fashions, and their development shows attempts to develop new skills in the region, despite the limitations of the Irish economy in this period. Perhaps the most important development, with regards to Irish domestic production in this period, however, was the major increase in the output of cloth and clothing, the export of which increased from about one-tenth of total exports in the late fifteenth century, to half by the 1540s.[1] By the 1540s the majority of Ireland's foreign trade consisted of manufactured goods. This was a state of affairs that Ireland would not enjoy again until modern times.[2] There was a strong correlation between the growth in Irish exports of manufactured goods, and the increasing importation of new consumer goods, since this suggests a dynamic link between increasing domestic production and increasing consumption in sixteenth-century Ireland. Work on the Irish export trade is still in progress, but it is expected that this will shed further light on the connection between the development of industry and the economic integration and prosperity of the south-east region in this period.

The second major development, and a central theme of this book, has been the extent to which continental trade networks influenced trends in Irish consumption. It has been suggested that the growing participation of Irish merchants in European markets was a fundamental force in the evolution of Irish material culture and in changing consumption patterns, creating economic prosperity in the port towns and their hinterlands, and also stimulating and satisfying the desire for new tastes and fashions. Longfield noted that in the sixteenth century, 'the great quantities of fish and hides sold to Spain, when not exchanged for arms, were largely paid

[1] See the 'Ireland–Bristol Project' research page. Available from: http://www.bris.ac.uk/Depts/History/Ireland/research.htm

[2] Ibid.

for in wines'.[3] Although the extent of the wine trade can never be quantified, it is clear from the official records that it was indeed immense and, no doubt, in terms of gross value, dwarfed any other Hiberno-continental trade. Ireland's continental commerce, however, was of vital importance beyond the exchange of Irish raw materials for wine. While lack of skill specialisation in Ireland may have retarded direct participation in many of the developing markets of Europe and Britain in this period, dynamic Irish merchants capitalised on new industries in other ways – supplying fashion-conscious English consumers with re-exported Spanish hat felt and New World Brazilwood, for example, particularly during periods when English access to continental commodities was limited due to war. Indeed it seems that there was a major shift in the relative importance of Ireland's trading partners in the later century, when Irish merchants were apparently sourcing a far greater proportion of everyday items directly from the Continent. Examining the importation of specific commodities has lent weight to this theory, and has shed new light on the role of Ireland's continental commerce in supplying the daily needs of Irish consumers. The absence of pins amongst Irish imports before 1594 and the declining volume of knives imported from England at the end of the century, for example, illustrate an Irish preference for Dutch- and Spanish-produced varieties of essential manufactured items, even after such commodities began to be commercially produced in England.

These findings are of vital importance when approaching the wider significance of evolving material culture in Ireland during this period. Martyn Powell has recently observed that 'as with many other areas of Irish culture and society, consumption cannot be separated from the problems of Anglo-Irish relations'.[4] Certainly, a major question addressed by historians of eighteenth-century Irish material culture is the extent to which the assimilation of 'English' habits by the Irish reveals dependence on or independence from Britain. Barnard has noted, for example, that the 'deeper and wider circulation of the "baubles of empire", if traced, may show Ireland being subordinated and assimilated to British standards'.[5]

Examining trends in Irish consumption as a by-product of, or reaction to, wider British developments is a valid concept for studies of eighteenth-century Ireland. By this time, the island was fully under English rule, firmly integrated into the mercantilist English economy and any potential for independent economic growth was stunted by trade restrictions and competition from English industries. Given the economic, social and political nature of Anglo-Irish relations in this period, there was probably little opportunity for the development of Irish tastes and fashions entirely independent of British influences. The picture emerging from the exploration

[3] Longfield, *Anglo-Irish Trade*, p. 134.

[4] Powell, *Politics*, p. 3.

[5] T. Barnard, 'Integration or separation? Hospitality and display in Protestant Ireland, 1660–1800', in L. Brockliss and D. Eastwood (eds), *A Union of Multiple Identities: The British Isles, c.1750-c.1850* (Manchester, 1997), p. 128; Powell, *Politics*, p. 2.

of sixteenth-century conditions, even after the initial plantation of the region, is very different. In this period, Ireland was not isolated from wider European developments and, indeed, the foregoing analysis suggests that the south-east, at least, played an active, independent part in the early expansion of the European Atlantic economy. While these findings may seem surprising in the context of the existing studies of the Irish economy and society, they marry well with David Edwards' recent study of County Kilkenny in this period, which revealed that the region was becoming more politically and economically integrated during the early sixteenth century.[6] England, then, was just one of the countries whose tastes and manners influenced Irish material culture in the sixteenth century. Indeed, it appears that certain types of continental goods – fine cloths, spectacles and sweets for example – arrived in Ireland directly from the Continent, years before they featured as imports from England. There is also abundant evidence of the independent incorporation of continental dress styles into Irish fashion, and of the use of very expensive foreign commodities, such as saffron, for example, in unique and distinctive ways.

A further point, when considering the influence of 'English' habits and fashions on Irish society, is that the notion of what it meant to be 'English', and how this might be defined by and expressed through material culture, was a fluid concept in the sixteenth century. Regional variation was a distinct feature of English material culture. In addition, major social and political changes, stimulated by the ideology of Renaissance Humanism and the Reformation, were beginning to impact on attitudes to consumption and material culture. The growing emphasis on propriety, authority, repression of individualism, and the development of the nation state, led to major debates in this period regarding the appropriateness or 'naturalness' of various commodities – from beer to padded codpieces – for the 'Englishman'.[7] There was an ever-growing suspicion of items perceived as 'foreign'; and flamboyant foreign fashions were becoming increasingly offensive to the evolving English sense of order and reason.[8] Stallybrass and Jones' discussion of dress in early modern England clearly illustrates the impact of evolving ideas on attitudes to material culture in this period. The major debate surrounding the use of yellow starch, alone, embodied changing attitudes to the expression of gender and sexuality, religious ideology and national identity.[9]

Understanding the crucial and heightened role played by material culture in the development of English national identity helps to contextualise contemporary attitudes to Irish tastes and habits, and makes some sense of the apparent dichotomy between the 'barbarous' and 'filthy' Irish habits described by English writers, and the apparent progressiveness and integration of Irish material culture, implied by the customs accounts. Descriptions of the 'filthy' cheese-making and butter-making

[6] Edwards, *Ormond Lordship*, pp. 42–9.

[7] A. Boorde, A *Compendyous Regyment or a Dyetary of Healthe* (London, 1547), p. 18.

[8] Raffield, 'Sumptuary legislation', p. 147.

[9] Jones and Stallybrass, *Renaissance Clothing*, pp. 59–86.

practices of Irish housewives, for example, should be read alongside English comments on continental practices. Boorde, for example, viewed cheese production methods in High Germany as proof of how 'grossly' the Germans ate, while in 1633 Hart described German cheese as being 'greedily gaped after by gluttons'.[10] Likewise, the Welsh taste for toasted cheese was viewed as disgusting by English observers and, according to Thirsk, confirmed the view of the Welsh as a 'rude, ignorant peasantry'.[11] Comments on Irish drunkenness also reflect wider English concerns regarding the adoption of continental and, in particular, German drinking habits and rituals and, according to Nicholls, the negative impact of such excess on the 'nation building project'.[12] Similarly, English attacks on the bright colours worn by the Irish, and the links made between the use of saffron and Irish cultural debasement, reflect deep-seated associations between the colour yellow and England's traditional enemies: France, Scotland, Spain and Ireland, whose use of the colour yellow was viewed as effeminate, demonic, 'foreign' and symbolically antithetic to the values of the emerging Protestant nation state.[13]

The wider influences on English attitudes to Irish habits and manners do not excuse, of course, the racist tenets of writers such as Moryson, Spenser, Davies and Rich. In many cases, English observations about the 'incivility' of the Irish seem to have been pure fabrication or, at least, gross overgeneralisations. The suggestion that the Irish did not wear hats or caps, for example, is contradicted by the quantitative and qualitative evidence, which suggest not only that headwear was regularly worn in Ireland, but that it evolved in line with continental and English fashions. Nevertheless, English attitudes to Irish habits and customs, as well as actual changes to Irish consumption, were driven by factors beyond colonisation and Anglo-Irish relations. Overall, it seems appropriate for future studies of Irish material culture in this period to widen the frame of reference, to consider not the extent to which Irish 'consumers' emulated 'English' practices, but rather, how individual regions within the British Isles assimilated and interpreted changing European trends in consumption, and what this suggests about their comparative economies and societies.[14]

While major changes in Irish consumption must be considered in the wider context of European developments in this period, it is clear that Irish attitudes to material culture were shaped by the complex, semi-colonised nature of Irish society in this period. Quentin Bell, discussing 'theories of fashion', wrote that 'wherever

[10] Thirsk, *Food*, p. 279; J. Hart, *Klinike or the Diet of the Diseased* (1633).

[11] Thirsk, *Food*, p. 279.

[12] Nicholls, *Politics*, p. 167.

[13] Jones and Stallybrass, *Renaissance Clothing*, p. 67.

[14] This approach has already begun to gain ground in other historiographical fields. Brendan Smith, for example, emphasised the importance of a regional approach to the politics of the British Isles in the late Middle Ages. See: B. Smith, 'The British Isles in the late Middle Ages: shaping the regions', in B. Smith (ed.), *Ireland and English World in the Late Middle Ages: Essays in Honour of Robin Frame* (Basingstoke, 2009), pp. 7–19.

a more sumptuous style is encountered it tends to be imitated'.[15] Irish consumers, however, despite political pressure to conform to English tastes, followed outside fashions discriminately and independently – and growing consumption in Ireland, in large part, served to further the expression of cultural individuality and independence. Nevertheless, such expression was highly self-conscious; material culture played a complex role in the construction of social, cultural and political identity in Ireland. Dress and diet distinguished and identified political allegiance. The ritualised and customary use of objects, including hats and drinking vessels, were often modified and hybridised in order to mediate political and social boundaries. Dress, in particular, was used as a tool of symbolic disempowerment and political propaganda. Most importantly, it functioned as a symbol of resistance, and a continuation of Irish heritage in the face of English attempts to standardise Irish habits. The effigies of the gentry, displaying archaic dress styles, immortalised their elite and traditional position in a declining and contested social order. Likewise, at the lower social levels, the persistence of elaborate linen headwear and the use of saffron dye functioned in the resistance to deculturation and the loss of self-definition in parts of Ireland.

The function of consumption in the formation of colonial identity requires further work. Breen, discussing the 'meaning of things' in eighteenth-century America, argued that colonists and 'even Native Americans' readily embraced the flood of British consumer goods that entered the market and that the 'sudden incorporation into a colonial imagination of an unprecedented quantity of consumer goods' enabled ordinary Americans to 'shape new identities and to fashion themselves in exciting ways'.[16] Other historians, however, have noted more complex responses to material culture in colonial societies. The findings of Kupperman for sixteenth-century America, and Buckridge for eighteenth-century Jamaica, share some interesting broad similarities with Irish trends. This is relevant in view of recent endeavours to establish a comparative historiography of colonialism in the Atlantic World, which has begun to consider the role of consumption and material culture in the formation of colonial identity.[17] From this point of view, the changes in Irish consumption noted here are very significant, since, at least according to the revisionist historiography, Ireland was England's *Terra Florida*, a model for England's later management of its transatlantic plantations and the place where its attitudes to colonisation were first formed.[18]

Finally, while the focus of this study has been on the use of the customs accounts as a source for understanding Irish consumption in the sixteenth century, a major

[15] Bell, *Human Finery*, p. 96.

[16] Breen, 'Meanings of things', pp. 252–3.

[17] N. Canny and A. Pagden (eds) *Colonial Identity in the Atlantic World, 1500–1800* (Princeton, 1989). For an Irish perspective see N. Canny, *Kingdom and Colony: Ireland in the Atlantic World, 1560–1800* (London, 1988); N. Canny, 'Identity formation in Ireland, the emergence of the Anglo-Irish', in Canny and Pagden, *Colonial Identity*, pp. 159–212; A. Horning and N. Brannon (eds), *Ireland and Britain in the Atlantic World. Irish Post Medieval Group Proceedings 2*, (Dublin, 2010).

[18] Canny, *Kingdom and Colony*.

aim has been to reveal the potential value of this source for historians of consumption more generally; and to begin to bridge the divide between purely economic and cultural projects, which has become a defining trend in the current field of consumption historiography. There is no doubt that the counting of goods alone does not produce a sophisticated picture of changing consumption patterns and material culture. But neither do rigid dichotomies in approach or methodology. This study, it is hoped, shows the value of a balanced approach to consumption studies. In this case, integrating quantitative and qualitative evidence, within a meaningful framework of analysis, has opened a window on changing consumption patterns in sixteenth-century Ireland, which provides very significant insights into the Irish economy, culture and society. At the very least, it will hopefully encourage more multidisciplinary studies of Irish social and economic development and its integration with the wider world in this period.

# *Appendices*

## Appendix 1

Range of commodities imported from Bristol: 1503/4, 1545/6, 1594/5

| | 1503–4 | 1545–6 | 1594–5 |
|---|---|---|---|
| 1 | Almonds | Alum/Aniseed | Almonds |
| 2 | Alum | Aniseed | Alum |
| 3 | Aniseed | Assicul | Aniseed |
| 4 | Ashes, Lye | Barrels, Lear | Apothecary Wares |
| 5 | Bacon | Beads | Arridence? |
| 6 | Barley | Books, Primers | Arrow Heads |
| 7 | Battery | Borax | Awl Blades |
| 8 | Beans | Bowstrings | Awl Hafts |
| 9 | Beer | Bristol Frieze Cloth | Balances, Small |
| 10 | Boras | Buttons, Unspecified | Balches |
| 11 | Cards | Cable/Ropes | Bands Plain |
| 12 | Cinnamon | Canvas Cloth | Bands, Coarse Cyprus |
| 13 | Cloth of Assize | Caps | Bands, Falling |
| 14 | Cloth of Assize, Dozen | Cards, Playing | Battery |
| 15 | Cloth of Assize, Dozen Strait | Cauldrons, Brass | Battery/Brass |
| 16 | Cloth of Assize, Dozen Welsh | Cinnamon | Bay Cloth |
| 17 | Cloth of Assize, Kersey | Cloth of Assize | Beads, Bugle |
| 18 | Coal | Cloth of Assize, Dozen | Bed Cords, Small |
| 19 | Combs | Cloth of Assize, Dozen Strait | Bellows |
| 20 | Cord | Cloves | Belts |
| 21 | Cork, Red | Combs | Bibs |
| 22 | Cushions | Cumin | Bits |
| 23 | Fruit | Cutts | Blockwood |

| | | | |
|---|---|---|---|
| 24 | Fustian Cloth | Drugs, miscellaneous | Bologna Sarcenet Cloth |
| 25 | Ginger | Felts | Bombas |
| 26 | Girdles | Fish-Hooks | Books |
| 27 | Hemp | Frankincense | Books, Fable |
| 28 | Honey | Fustian Cloth | Books, Grammar |
| 29 | Hops | Game-birds | Books, Horn |
| 30 | Iron | Ginger | Books, School of Virtue |
| 31 | Kermes | Girdles | Books, Small |
| 32 | Knives | Girdles, Caddis | Bottles, Glass |
| 33 | Lead, Worked | Girdles, Leather | Bottles, Leather small |
| 34 | Liquorice | Girdles, Ribbon | Bottles, Sucking |
| 35 | Mace | Girdles, Silk | Boxes, Unspecified |
| 36 | Malt | Glasses | Boxes, Painted |
| 37 | Mutton Fat | Glue | Bracelets |
| 38 | Needles | Hanging locks | Bristol Frieze Cloth |
| 39 | Orchil, Worked | Hats | Bristol Pairs (? Knives) |
| 40 | Paper | Hemp | Broad Taffeta Cloth |
| 41 | Peas | Holland Cloth | Brushes, Unspecified |
| 42 | Penners | Honey | Brushes, Coarse Heath |
| 43 | Pepper | Hooks | Brushes, Heath |
| 44 | Pilores Tinct | Hooks, Small | Brushes, Rubbing |
| 45 | Pitch | Hops | Buckles |
| 46 | Points | Inkhorns | Buckram Cloth |
| 47 | Porteos | Iron | Buffin Cloth |
| 48 | Red Leather | Kermes | Buttons, Copper |
| 49 | Rosin | Knives | Buttons, Crewel and Silk |
| 50 | Saffron | Knives, in Pairs | Buttons, Glass |
| 51 | Salt | Lacquer | Buttons, Hair |
| 52 | Silk, Worked | Lead | Buttons, Pewter |
| 53 | Skins, Calf Tanned | Liquorice | Buttons, Scottish |
| 54 | Smigmates | Mace | Buttons, Shell |
| 55 | Stock-Cards | Mail | Buttons, Silk |
| 56 | Thimbles | Marmalade | Buttons, Thread |
| 57 | Thread | Mercury | Buttons, Tin |
| 58 | Verdegris | Millstones | Cadows |

| | | | |
|---|---|---|---|
| 59 | Welsh Cloth | Needles | Calico Cloth |
| 60 | Wine | Nightcaps | Candles, Wax |
| 61 | Wine, Corrupt | Nightcaps, Satin | Candlesticks, Brass |
| 62 | Wood, Brazil | Nightcaps, Velvet | Candlesticks, Small |
| 63 | | Nightcaps, Woollen | Candlesticks, Small Brass |
| 64 | | Nutmeg | Canvas Cloth, Striped |
| 65 | | Oleron Cloth | Canykine |
| 66 | | Orchil | Cap Hooks |
| 67 | | Pans, Brass | Cap-Case Locks |
| 68 | | Paper | Cap-Cases |
| 69 | | Payn? | Cards, Hand |
| 70 | | Pepper | Cauls, for Children |
| 71 | | Percular | Chafing Dishes |
| 72 | | Pins | Chalk |
| 73 | | Pitch | Chest locks |
| 74 | | Points | Cider |
| 75 | | Points, Silk | Cloth of Assize |
| 76 | | Poldavis Cloth | Cloth of Assize, Dozen Northern Single |
| 77 | | Purses | Cloth of Assize, Green Kersey |
| 78 | | Purses, belt | Cloth of Assize, Kersey |
| 79 | | Quadrear | Cloth of Assize, Northern Dozen |
| 80 | | Ribbons, Saye | Cloves |
| 81 | | Ropes | Coal |
| 82 | | Rosin | Combs, Bone |
| 83 | | Saffron | Combs, Ivory |
| 84 | | Salt | Combs, Marie |
| 85 | | Scythes | Combs, Light Wooden |
| 86 | | Seed, Leek | Combs, Wooden |
| 87 | | Seed, Onion | Comfits |
| 88 | | Senna | Copperas |
| 89 | | Silk, Worked | Cotton Cloth |
| 90 | | Skins, Calf | Counters |
| 91 | | Skins, Golden | Coarse Cyprus Cloth |

| | | |
|---|---|---|
| 92 | Skins, Red | Coarse Holland Cloth |
| 93 | Soap | Cox Lace |
| 94 | Spectacles | Crab- Locks |
| 95 | Spectacles, Pocket | Crest Cloth |
| 96 | Stecull | Crewel, French |
| 97 | Steel | Cruses, Stone |
| 98 | Stock-Cards | Cruses, Stone Uncovered |
| 99 | Sugar | Cups, Wooden |
| 100 | Sugar-Candy | Currants |
| 101 | Sulpher | Cutts (1d) |
| 102 | Tar | Cutts (ob) |
| 103 | Teazells | Dials |
| 104 | Thread | Diaper Napkins |
| 105 | Thread, Blue | Dice |
| 106 | Trenchers | Dice & small ropes for scales |
| 107 | Turpentine | Dornick Cloth |
| 108 | Twine, for Nets | Drinking Horns |
| 109 | Velvet Cloth | Earthen Ware |
| 110 | Verdigris | Felts |
| 111 | Vials | Felts, Black |
| 112 | Vinegar | Felts, Children's |
| 113 | Wax, Red | Figs |
| 114 | Wine | Files |
| 115 | Wine, Corrupt | Flannel Cloth |
| 116 | Woad Ashes | Flax |
| 117 | Wood, Brazil | Frankinsense |
| 118 | Wood, Laths | Fringe, Crewel and Silk |
| 119 | Wool-Cards | Fustian Cloth |
| 120 | Worsted Russett Cloth | Galer |
| 121 | | Gales |
| 122 | | Gartering |
| 123 | | Gartering, Coarse |
| 124 | | Gartering, Crewel |
| 125 | | Gartering, Norwich |
| 126 | | Garters, Broad |

| | |
|---|---|
| 127 | Garters, Coarse |
| 128 | Gentish Carpen Cloth |
| 129 | Ginger |
| 130 | Girdles (1d) |
| 131 | Girdles (2d) |
| 132 | Girdles (ob) |
| 133 | Girdles, Crewel |
| 134 | Girdles, Leather |
| 135 | Girdles, Leather (1d) |
| 136 | Girdles, Leather (ob) |
| 137 | Girdles, Nobs Silk |
| 138 | Girdles, Round silk |
| 139 | Girdles, Silk |
| 140 | Girdles, Waist |
| 141 | Girth Buckles |
| 142 | Girth- Web |
| 143 | Girths |
| 144 | Glasses, Unspecified |
| 145 | Glasses (1d) |
| 146 | Glasses (ob) |
| 147 | Glasses, Brace |
| 148 | Glasses, Coarse Drinking |
| 149 | Glasses, Drinking |
| 150 | Glasses, French Drinking |
| 151 | Glasses, Green |
| 152 | Glasses, Hour |
| 153 | Glasses, Looking |
| 154 | Glasses, Looking (1d) |
| 155 | Glasses, Looking (ob) |
| 156 | Glasses, Looking small |
| 157 | Gloves, Coarse |
| 158 | Gloves, Pairs |
| 159 | Glue |
| 160 | Gold Paper |
| 161 | Gouge and Formes |

| | |
|---|---|
| 162 | Grainte? |
| 163 | Green Silk Lace |
| 164 | Grind- Stones |
| 165 | Gun Powder |
| 166 | Hair Cloth |
| 167 | Halberts, Ungilted |
| 168 | Hat Bands |
| 169 | Hats, Unspecified |
| 170 | Hats, Children's |
| 171 | Hats, Coarse |
| 172 | Hats, Women's |
| 173 | Hawk Hoods |
| 174 | Hawser? |
| 175 | Headstalls |
| 176 | Hinges |
| 177 | Holland Cloth |
| 178 | Holmes Fustian Cloth |
| 179 | Honey |
| 180 | Hooks, Fish |
| 181 | Hops |
| 182 | Horse Bells, Coarse |
| 183 | Horse Combs |
| 184 | Hose, Women's |
| 185 | Indigo |
| 186 | Ink Horns |
| 187 | Inkle |
| 188 | Iron |
| 189 | Iron Work |
| 190 | Isinglass |
| 191 | Ivory |
| 192 | Jeane Fustian Cloth |
| 193 | Kermes |
| 194 | Knives (1d) |
| 195 | Knives (2d) |
| 196 | Knives (ob) |

| | |
|---|---|
| 197 | Knives, Coarse |
| 198 | Knives, Cuttlers |
| 199 | Knives, Fine |
| 200 | Knives, in Pairs |
| 201 | Knives, Pocket |
| 202 | Knives, Prage |
| 203 | Knives, Shoemaker |
| 204 | Lace (2d) |
| 205 | Lace, Chain |
| 206 | Lace, Statute |
| 207 | Laces for Knives |
| 208 | Laces, Coarse for knives |
| 209 | Lanterns |
| 210 | Lath Nails |
| 211 | Lead |
| 212 | Lead, Red |
| 213 | Levant Taffata Cloth |
| 214 | Lime |
| 215 | Liquorice |
| 216 | Locks Hanging, Small |
| 217 | Locks, Cap Cases |
| 218 | Locks, Cupboard |
| 219 | Locks, Hanging |
| 220 | Locks, Plate |
| 221 | Locks, Small |
| 222 | Mail |
| 223 | Mail, Red |
| 224 | Mantles |
| 225 | Match Cords |
| 226 | Matches |
| 227 | Mercury |
| 228 | Milan Fustian Cloth |
| 229 | Millstones, called Dogstones |
| 230 | Morions Plain |
| 231 | N[]ptmicks? |

| | |
|---|---|
| 232 | Nails (2d) |
| 233 | Nails, Board |
| 234 | Nails, Daysy? |
| 235 | Nails, Lath |
| 236 | Nails, Scopp |
| 237 | Nails, Small |
| 238 | Nails, Yellow |
| 239 | Neckbands/Necklaces |
| 240 | Neck Bracelets |
| 241 | Necklaces |
| 242 | Needles |
| 243 | New Cloth |
| 244 | Nickel |
| 245 | Nutmeg |
| 246 | Orchil |
| 247 | Osborne Fustian Cloth |
| 248 | Pans, Frying |
| 249 | Pans, Plate Dripping |
| 250 | Paper |
| 251 | Paper Brown |
| 252 | Paper, Gold |
| 253 | Paper, Painted |
| 254 | Parchment Skins |
| 255 | Peeres? |
| 256 | Penners |
| 257 | Penners and Inkhorns |
| 258 | Pepper |
| 259 | Pewter |
| 260 | Pile Weights |
| 261 | Pin Purses |
| 262 | Pins |
| 263 | Playing Cards |
| 264 | Playing Tables |
| 265 | Points |
| 266 | Points, Broad (1d) |

| | |
|---|---|
| 267 | Points, Broad (lace) |
| 268 | Points, Bugle |
| 269 | Points, Coarse (lace) |
| 270 | Points, Crewel |
| 271 | Points, Green (green lace) |
| 272 | Points, Inkle |
| 273 | Points, Leather |
| 274 | Points, Red |
| 275 | Points, Saye (lace) |
| 276 | Points, Small Silk |
| 277 | Points, Thread |
| 278 | Points, Thread and Leather |
| 279 | Points, White and Red |
| 280 | Points, White Leather |
| 281 | Portmanteau |
| 282 | Pots, Brass |
| 283 | Pots, Iron |
| 284 | Prunes |
| 285 | Purses |
| 286 | Purses, Taffeta |
| 287 | Quern-Stones |
| 288 | Quern-Stones, Small |
| 289 | Raisins, Great |
| 290 | Ribbon, Unspecified |
| 291 | Ribbon, Broad (1d) |
| 292 | Ribbon, Silk |
| 293 | Rice |
| 294 | Ropes |
| 295 | Ropes, White |
| 296 | Sack Cloth |
| 297 | Saffron |
| 298 | Sandlewood |
| 299 | Sarcenet Cloth |
| 300 | Saws, Hand |

| | |
|---|---|
| 301 | Saye Cloth |
| 302 | Scissors |
| 303 | Scythes |
| 304 | Seed, Cumin |
| 305 | Seed, Leek |
| 306 | Seed, Onion |
| 307 | Senna |
| 308 | Serches |
| 309 | Setting Sticks |
| 310 | Shewers? |
| 311 | Shoe Horns |
| 312 | Silk Cyprus Cloth |
| 313 | Silk, Black |
| 314 | Silk, Coloured |
| 315 | Silk, Ferett |
| 316 | Silk, Nobs |
| 317 | Silk, Paris |
| 318 | Silk, Raw |
| 319 | Silk, Slewe |
| 320 | Skins, Budge |
| 321 | Skins, Parchment |
| 322 | Small Wares |
| 323 | Snaffles |
| 324 | Snuffers |
| 325 | Soap, |
| 326 | Soap, Black |
| 327 | Soap, Castile |
| 328 | Soap, White |
| 329 | Spectacles |
| 330 | Spurs, Unspecified |
| 331 | Spurs, Coarse |
| 332 | Spurs, Small |
| 333 | Starces? |
| 334 | Starch |
| 335 | Steel |

| | |
|---|---|
| 336 | Stirrups, Iron |
| 337 | Stock Locks |
| 338 | Stock-Cards |
| 339 | Stockings, Unspecified |
| 340 | Stockings, Short |
| 341 | Stockings, Short Knit |
| 342 | Stockings, Short Women's |
| 343 | Stockings, Short Woollen |
| 344 | Stockings, Short Worsted |
| 345 | Stockings, Woollen |
| 346 | Stockings, Worsted |
| 347 | Stone Inges? |
| 348 | Striapes |
| 349 | Succado and Marmalade |
| 350 | Sugar |
| 351 | Sugar Candy |
| 352 | Sulpher |
| 353 | Swords |
| 354 | Table Cloths and Diapers |
| 355 | Taffeta Cloth |
| 356 | Tape, Small |
| 357 | Taps |
| 358 | Taps and Cannells |
| 359 | Taps, Small |
| 360 | Thimbles |
| 361 | Thread |
| 362 | Thread, Black |
| 363 | Thread, Blue |
| 364 | Thread, Brown |
| 365 | Thread, Coloured |
| 366 | Thread, Fibulor? |
| 367 | Thread, Inkle |
| 368 | Thread, Packet |
| 369 | Thread, Piecing |

| | |
|---|---|
| 370 | Thread, Sisters |
| 371 | Tin |
| 372 | Towe |
| 373 | Treacle |
| 374 | Trenchers, Unspecified |
| 375 | Trenchers, Common |
| 376 | Trenchers, Painted |
| 377 | Trenchers, Wooden |
| 378 | Trifles |
| 379 | Turnsole |
| 380 | Turpentine |
| 382 | Urinals |
| 383 | Verdegris |
| 385 | Vice, Hand |
| 386 | Vinegar |
| 387 | Violles* |
| 388 | Violles, Square |
| 389 | Visors |
| 390 | Wax |
| 391 | Welsh Frieze Cloth |
| 392 | White Cyprus Cloth |
| 393 | Wine, Rob Davy Corrupt |
| 394 | Wire |
| 395 | Wood, Brazil |
| 396 | Wool-Cards |
| 397 | Wool-Cards, Old |
| 398 | Wormseed |

*Source*: Flavin and Jones, *Bristol's Trade*, pp. 1–102; 457–545; 731–848

*vials

## Appendix 2

Tables A–F provide a detailed breakdown of the percentage of trade owned by merchants from each town for six individual years between 1575 and 1601.

A) Distribution of import commodities in 1575/6 by value, based on port of arrival and merchant domicile.

| Port of Arrival | Value £ | % Imports | Mer. Dom. | Value £ | % Imports to Port |
|---|---|---|---|---|---|
| Cork | 78.11 | 9.31 | Cork | 56.71 | 72.6 |
| | | | Limerick | 21.4 | 27.39 |
| Drogheda | 80.38 | 9.59 | Drogheda | 72.55 | 90.25 |
| | | | Cumbria | 7.83 | 9.74 |
| Dublin | 113.17 | 13.5 | Dublin | 113.17 | 100 |
| Dungarvan | 11.47 | 1.36 | Dungarvan | 3.5 | 30.51 |
| | | | Waterford | 7.97 | 69.48 |
| Fethard-on-Sea | 1.08 | 0.12 | Fethard on Sea | 1.08 | 100 |
| Galway | 27.58 | 3.29 | Galway | 27.58 | 100 |
| Kinsale | 12.93 | 1.54 | Kinsale | 12.93 | 100 |
| New Ross | 11.28 | 1.34 | New Ross | 10.73 | 95.12 |
| | | | Waterford | 0.55 | 4.87 |
| Waterford | 357.09 | 42.6 | London | 19.83 | 5.55 |
| | | | Clonmel | 12.36 | 3.46 |
| | | | Kilkenny | 94.51 | 26.46 |
| | | | Kinsale | 10.17 | 2.84 |
| | | | Limerick | 25.05 | 7.01 |
| | | | New Ross | 23.25 | 6.51 |
| | | | Waterford | 171.92 | 48.14 |
| Wexford | 144.26 | 17.21 | Bristol | 6 | 0.71 |
| | | | Gloucestershire | 6 | 0.71 |
| | | | New Ross | 17.03 | 2.03 |
| | | | Wexford | 115.24 | 13.75 |
| Youghal | 0.75 | 0 | Youghal | 0.75 | 100 |
| Total | 838.1 | 100 | | 838.1 | - |

Source: Flavin and Jones, *Bristol's Trade*, pp. 672–726

B) Distribution of import commodities in 1576/7 by value, based on port of arrival and merchant domicile.

| Port of Arrival | Value £ | % Imports | Mer. Dom. | Value £ | % Imports to Port |
|---|---|---|---|---|---|
| Cork | 13.5 | 2.69 | Cork | 13.5 | 100 |
| Drogheda | 41.75 | 8.32 | Drogheda | 41.75 | 100 |
| Dublin | 20.9 | 4 | Dublin | 14.9 | 71.29 |
| | | | Monmouthshire | 6 | 28.7 |
| Dungarvan | 12.94 | 2.57 | Cork | 12.94 | 100 |
| Fethard-on-Sea | 6.4 | 1.27 | Fethard-on-Sea | 6.4 | 100 |
| Galway | 26.93 | 5.36 | Galway | 26.93 | 100 |
| Kinsale | 5.21 | 1.03 | Kinsale | 5.21 | 100 |
| New Ross | 10.55 | 2.1 | New Ross | 6.2 | 58.76 |
| | | | Waterford | 4.35 | 3.31 |
| Waterford | 335.03 | 66.78 | Bristol | 4 | 1.19 |
| | | | Cashel | 8.58 | 2.56 |
| | | | Callan | 11 | 3.28 |
| | | | Clonmel | 8.6 | 2.56 |
| | | | Cork | 4.63 | 1.38 |
| | | | Kilkenny | 100.57 | 30.01 |
| | | | Limerick | 24.76 | 7.39 |
| | | | London | 3.73 | 1.11 |
| | | | Waterford | 151.69 | 45.27 |
| Wexford | 25.69 | 5.12 | Wexford | 25.69 | 100 |
| Youghal | 2.81 | 0.56 | Youghal | 2.81 | 0.56 |
| Total | 1,859.11 | 100 | 0 | 1,859.11 | |

Source: TNA E190/1129/23

C) Distribution of import commodities in 1591/2 by value, based on port of arrival and merchant domicile

| Port of Arrival | Value £ | % Imports | Mer. Dom. | Value £ | % Imports to Port |
|---|---|---|---|---|---|
| Cork | 291.7 | 10.45 | Bristol | 5.5 | 1.8 |
| | | | Cork | 253.87 | 87.03 |
| | | | Limerick | 24.67 | 8.45 |
| | | | London | 4 | 1.37 |
| | | | Newbury | 3.67 | 1.25 |
| Dungarvan | 68.08 | 2.43 | Dungarvan | 32.08 | 47.12 |
| | | | Limerick | 36 | 52.87 |
| Fethard-on-Sea | 31.92 | 1.14 | Hampshire | 6 | 18.79 |
| | | | New Ross | 25.92 | 81.2 |
| Kinsale | 7 | 0.25 | Kinsale | 7 | 100 |
| Waterford | 2,136.49 | 76.56 | Acton? | 15 | 0.7 |
| | | | Bristol | 115.63 | 5.41 |
| | | | Cashel | 45.75 | 2.14 |
| | | | Clonmel | 36.17 | 1.69 |
| | | | Galway | 22.17 | 1.03 |
| | | | Kilkenny | 220.79 | 10.33 |
| | | | Kinsale | 1.82 | 0.085 |
| | | | Limerick | 186.63 | 8.73 |
| | | | London | 72.17 | 3.37 |
| | | | Salisbury | 9.17 | 0.42 |
| | | | Waterford | 1,411.18 | 66.05 |
| Wexford | 38.08 | 1.36 | Wexford | 38.08 | 100 |
| Youghal | 216.98 | 7.77 | Cork | 13.23 | 6.09 |
| | | | Kilkenny | 24.58 | 11.32 |
| | | | Kilcolman | 4 | 1.84 |
| | | | London | 160.17 | 73.8 |
| | | | Youghal | 15 | 6.91 |
| Total | 2,790.25 | | | 2,790.25 | |

Source: TNA, E190/1131/4, E190/1131/8

D) Distribution of import commodities in 1594/5 by value, based on port of arrival and merchant domicilemerchant domicile

| Port of Arrival | Value £ | % Imports | Mer. Dom. | Value £ | % Imports to Port |
|---|---|---|---|---|---|
| Cork | 207.48 | 11.16 | Bristol | 25 | 12 |
| | | | Cork | 161.5 | 78 |
| | | | Limerick | 15.98 | 8 |
| | | | Youghal | 5 | 2 |
| Drogheda | 16 | 0.86 | Drogheda | 16 | 100 |
| Dublin | 14.17 | 0.76 | Somerset | 4.17 | 28 |
| | | | Gloucestershire | 10 | 72 |
| Dungarvan | 4.63 | 0.24 | Dungarvan | 4.63 | 100 |
| Dundalk | 12 | 0.64 | Dundalk | 12 | 100 |
| New Ross | 116.55 | 6.26 | Kilkenny | 36.07 | 31 |
| | | | New Ross | 80.48 | 69 |
| Sligo | 15.65 | 0.84 | Bristol | 15.65 | 100 |
| Waterford | 1238.91 | 66.63 | Bristol | 38.5 | 3 |
| | | | Callan | 2 | >1 |
| | | | Cashel | 20.08 | 2 |
| | | | London | 197.64 | 15.9 |
| | | | Clonmel | 78.72 | 6 |
| | | | Fethard-on-Sea | 41.73 | 3 |
| | | | Galway | 118.92 | 10 |
| | | | Kilkenny | 226.21 | 18 |
| | | | Limerick | 162.63 | 13 |
| | | | Waterford | 352.48 | 28.45 |
| Wexford | 78.97 | 4.24 | Kilkenny | 8.72 | 29 |
| | | | Wexford | 70.25 | 71 |
| Youghal | 154.75 | 8.32 | Bristol | 12.17 | 8 |
| | | | London | 79.67 | 52 |
| | | | Cork | 15.65 | 10 |
| | | | Limerick | 6.67 | 4 |
| | | | Kerry | 18.6 | 12 |
| | | | Waterford | 6.29 | 4 |
| | | | Youghal | 15.71 | 10 |
| Total | 1859.11 | 100 | | 1,859.11 | |

Source: Flavin and Jones, *Bristol's Trade*, pp. 731–848

E) Distribution of import commodities in 1598/9 by value, based on port of arrival and merchant domicile.

| Port of Arrival | Value £ | % Imports | Mer. Dom. | Value £ | % Imports to Port |
|---|---|---|---|---|---|
| Cork | 198.77 | 28.23 | Bristol | 23 | 11.57 |
| | | | Cork | 142.92 | 71.9 |
| | | | Kinsale | 10.56 | 5.31 |
| | | | Limerick | 22.29 | 11.21 |
| New Ross | 64.46 | 9.15 | New Ross | 64.46 | 100 |
| Waterford | 386.58 | 54.09 | Bristol | 4.33 | 1.12 |
| | | | Cashel | 9.56 | 2.47 |
| | | | Clonmel | 5.44 | 1.4 |
| | | | Fethard | 11.33 | 2.93 |
| | | | Kilkenny | 147.05 | 38.03 |
| | | | Unknown | 6.49 | 1.67 |
| | | | Waterford | 192.38 | 49.76 |
| | | | Wexford | 10 | 2.58 |
| Wexford | 54.27 | 9.12 | Waterford | 12.92 | 20.1 |
| | | | Wexford | 41.35 | 64.33 |
| Total | 704.08 | 100 | | 704.08 | |

Source: TNA, E190/1132/8

F) Distribution of import commodities in 1600/1 by value, based on port of arrival and merchant domicile.

| Port of Arrival | Value £ | % Imports | Mer. Dom. | Value £ | % Imports to Port |
|---|---|---|---|---|---|
| Cork | 568.80 | 31.94 | Berkeley | 2.42 | .42 |
| | | | Bristol | 232.08 | 40.80 |
| | | | Cork | 199.38 | 35.05 |
| | | | Kilmallock | 8.00 | 1.40 |
| | | | Kinsale | 37.83 | 6.65 |
| | | | Limerick | 60.29 | 10.59 |
| | | | London | 7.50 | 1.31 |
| | | | Gloucestershire | 7.00 | 1.23 |
| | | | Waterford | 10.88 | 1.91 |
| | | | Youghal | 3.42 | .60 |
| Dublin | 210.81 | 11.84 | Bristol | 77.64 | 36.82 |
| | | | Dublin | 69.67 | 33.04 |
| | | | Unknown | 50.00 | 23.71 |
| | | | Gloucestershire | 13.50 | 6.40 |
| Limerick | 17.19 | 0.96 | Limerick | 17.19 | 100 |
| New Ross | 118.75 | 6.67 | Cashel | 12.21 | 10.28 |
| | | | New Ross | 73.58 | 61.97 |
| | | | Waterford | 32.93 | 27.73 |
| Unknown | 166.50 | 9.35 | Kilkenny | 152.36 | 91.51 |
| | | | Limerick | 14.15 | 8.49 |
| Waterford | 680.01 | 38.19 | Bristol | 14.50 | 2.13 |
| | | | Cashel | 42.39 | 6.23 |
| | | | Kilkenny | 47.75 | 7.01 |
| | | | Limerick | 44.83 | 6.58 |
| | | | London | 62.24 | 9.14 |
| | | | Unknown | 114.69 | 16.85 |
| | | | Waterford | 353.98 | 52.02 |
| Wexford | 18.29 | 1.02 | Wexford | 18.29 | 100 |
| Total | 1,780.35 | 100 | | | |

Source: Flavin and Jones, *Bristol's Trade*, pp. 849–942

# Appendix 3

Monthly breakdown import commodities by gross value, 1503 and 1550

**1503/4**

| | Oct | Nov | Dec | Jan | Feb | Mar | Apr | May | June | Jul | Aug | Sept |
|---|---|---|---|---|---|---|---|---|---|---|---|---|
| Alum | 1.69 | | 0.13 | | | | | | | | | |
| Aniseed | 0.17 | 0.5 | 2 | | | | | | | 1.4 | 0.49 | 0.15 |
| Bacon | | | | | | 0.25 | | | | | | |
| Barley & Malt | | | | | 1.33 | | | | | | | |
| Battery | | | | | 4.25 | 4.43 | | 2 | | 1 | | |
| Beans | | 6.67 | | 3.66 | 10.67 | 22.83 | | | 8 | 8 | 3.33 | 1.33 |
| Beans & Barley | | | | | | 1.33 | | | | | | |
| Beans & Malt | | | | 29.17 | 14.33 | | | 6.67 | | | | |
| Beans & Peas | | | | | 9.33 | | | | | | | |
| Beans, Barley & Malt | | | | | 8 | | | | | | | |
| Beer | 6 | | | | | 5.69 | 3 | 1.5 | | 5.25 | 1.75 | 3.75 |
| Boras | | | | | | | | | | 0.01 | | |
| Caps | 1.33 | 0.5 | | 0.33 | 0.83 | 3 | | 0.33 | | 2 | 3.17 | |
| Cards, Unspecified | | | | | | 0.75 | | | | 0.2 | 0.2 | |
| Cinnamon | | | | | 0.13 | | | | | 0.13 | 0.39 | |
| Cloth of Assize | 76 | 19 | 26 | 26 | 227 | 135.83 | 4.5 | 31 | 24 | 52 | 178.29 | 16 |
| Cloth of Assize, Dozen | 4 | | | 31 | 10 | 2 | | 32 | | 14 | 19 | |

| | | | | | | | | | | | | |
|---|---|---|---|---|---|---|---|---|---|---|---|---|
| Cloth of Assize, Dozen Strait | 0.5 | | | | 1 | 2 | | 0.5 | | | 2 | |
| Cloth of Assize, Dozen Welsh | | | | | 0.42 | 0.1 | | | | | | |
| Cloth of Assize, Kersey | | | | 2 | 1 | 2.67 | | | | | 0.67 | |
| Coal | 0.67 | | | | | 0.67 | | | | | | |
| Combs | | | | | 0.03 | | | | | | 0.05 | |
| Cord | | | | | | 1 | | | | | | |
| Cork, Red | | | | | | 2 | | | | | | |
| Cushions | | | | | | 0.5 | | | | | | |
| Fruit | | | | | | 0.38 | | | | | | |
| Fustian Cloth | | | | | | 0.25 | | | | | | |
| Ginger | | | | | | 0.13 | | | | 0.05 | 0.1 | |
| Girdles | | | | | | 0.08 | | | | | | |
| Hemp | | | | | | 0.13 | | | | | | |
| Honey | | | 1.17 | | 5.83 | | | | | | | |
| Hops | | | | | | 0.76 | | | | | | |
| Iron | | | | | 12 | 2.5 | | | | | | |
| Kermes | | | | | | | | | | | 0.04 | 0.04 |
| Knives | 0.21 | 1.05 | | 1.33 | 0.17 | 1 | | 0.08 | | 1.33 | 3.5 | |
| Lead, Worked | | | | | 10 | | | | | | | |
| Liquorice | | | | | | 0.25 | | | | | | |
| Mace | | | | | | | | | | | 0.03 | 0.1 |

| | | | | | | | | | | | | |
|---|---|---|---|---|---|---|---|---|---|---|---|---|
| Malt | | | | 5.33 | 0.33 | 0.17 | | | | | 4.67 | |
| Mutton Fat | | | | | | | | | | | 2 | |
| Needles | | | | | | | | | | 0.05 | | |
| Orchil, Worked | | | 1 | | 8.67 | 16.75 | 0.75 | 1.42 | | 0.17 | 3.46 | |
| Paper | 0.05 | | | | | | | | | | 0.05 | |
| Penners | | | | | | | | | | | 0.05 | |
| Pepper | 0.26 | | | | 0.05 | 0.1 | | 0.1 | | 0.1 | 0.2 | |
| Pilus Tinctus | 0.67 | 13.15 | 0.33 | 6.23 | 7.45 | 25.08 | 3.43 | 0.67 | 0.2 | 12.63 | 23.52 | 9.78 |
| Pitch | | | | | | 0.17 | | | | | | |
| Points | 1.25 | 1.55 | | | 0.15 | 2.9 | 0.45 | 0.6 | | 2.83 | 3.6 | |
| Porteos | | 1.9 | | | | | | | | | | |
| Red Leather | | | | | | 0.75 | | | | | | |
| Rosin | | | | | | 0.27 | | | | | | |
| Saffron | 88.67 | 48.67 | | 2.82 | 10.17 | 22 | 4 | 2.66 | | 15.92 | 16.33 | 1 |
| Salt | | | 2.5 | | 0.84 | | | 3.75 | | 6.25 | 10.13 | 2.5 |
| Silk, Worked | 30.67 | 37.67 | 8 | 2.67 | 34.33 | 13.67 | 0.67 | 4 | | 11.33 | 16.67 | 0.67 |
| Skins, Calf Tanned | | | | | 1.88 | 0.42 | | | | | 1.25 | |
| Smigmates | | 0.12 | | | | 0.15 | | | | 0.15 | 0.1 | |
| Stock-Cards | | | | | | | | | | 0.05 | | |
| Thimbles | | | | | | | | | | | | |
| Thread | | 0.04 | | | 0.02 | 0.04 | | | | 0.02 | 0.06 | |
| Verdigris | 0.05 | | | | | | | | | 0.07 | 0.15 | |
| Welsh Cloth | | | | | | | | | | | 8 | |

| | Oct | Nov | Dec | Jan | Feb | Mar | Apr | May | June | July | Aug | Sept |
|---|---|---|---|---|---|---|---|---|---|---|---|---|
| Welsh Cloth, Dozen Strait | | | | | | | | | | 0.21 | 0.83 | |
| Wine | | | | | 2 | | | | | | | 10 |
| Wine, Corrupt | 5.63 | | 9 | | 7.5 | 20.25 | | 12 | | 5.25 | 22.5 | 13.13 |
| Wood, Brazil | | | | | | 0.1 | | | | | 0.23 | |

**1550/1**

| | Oct | Nov | Dec | Jan | Feb | Mar | Apr | May | June | July | Aug | Sept |
|---|---|---|---|---|---|---|---|---|---|---|---|---|
| Alum | | 0.67 | 1.74 | | 1.29 | 0.63 | 2.66 | 0.33 | | | | |
| Aniseed | | 0.08 | 0.28 | | 0.58 | 0.4 | 1.42 | | | | | |
| Battery | | 6.5 | 4 | | 21.93 | 16.83 | | 2 | | | | |
| Books | | | | | | | 0.13 | | | | | |
| Bristol Frieze | | | | | | | 9.33 | | | | | |
| Buttons | | | | | | 0.08 | | 0.13 | | | | |
| Caps | | 3 | 2.67 | 1.25 | 3.71 | 1.33 | 0.25 | | 1.75 | | | |
| Cinnamon | | 0.6 | 0.31 | | 0.63 | | | | 0.5 | | | |
| Cloth of Assize | 11.83 | 85.66 | 22.67 | 0.5 | 34 | 57.16 | 41 | 0.5 | 32.5 | 21 | 81 | |
| Cloves | | 1 | | | 0.13 | | | 0.38 | 0.26 | | | |
| Combs | | 0.36 | 0.05 | | 0.28 | 0.17 | 0.07 | 0.23 | | | | |
| Crab lock | | | 0.08 | | | | | | | | | |
| Cumin | | 0.18 | | | 0.34 | 0.32 | | | | | | |
| Cutts | | 0.5 | | | 0.17 | | | | | | | |
| Figs | | | | | | 1.2 | | | | | | |
| Flax | | 3.65 | 0.33 | | 2.78 | 8.78 | | | | | | 1.5 |

| | | | | | | | | | | | | |
|---|---|---|---|---|---|---|---|---|---|---|---|---|
| Girdles | | 3.61 | 0.36 | | 1.95 | 0.07 | | 0.38 | 0.5 | | 1.71 | |
| Glasses, Looking | | 0.34 | | | | 0.15 | | | 0.1 | | | |
| Gunpowder | | 0.1 | | | | | | | | | | |
| Hats | | 0.58 | 0.21 | | | 0.5 | | | | | | |
| Hemp | | | | | | 0.45 | | | | | | |
| Honey | | 6.68 | 8.33 | | | | | | | | | |
| Hops | | 1.13 | 4.75 | | 3.5 | 11.63 | 4.75 | 1.25 | | | 1 | 6 |
| Hose | 4 | 0.5 | | | | | | | | | | |
| Iron | | 0.5 | | | 0.6 | 0.88 | 1.25 | | | | 19 | |
| Knives | 3.04 | 48.92 | 12.48 | 1.33 | 23.92 | 24.5 | 0.5 | 1.79 | 8.83 | 0.63 | 0.33 | |
| Lacquor | | 3.54 | 1.49 | | 0.12 | 1.79 | 0.08 | 0.08 | | | | |
| Lead | 24 | | 0.91 | | | | | | | | | |
| Liquorice | | 0.04 | | | 0.08 | 0.08 | | | | | | |
| Madder | | | | | | 0.25 | 1.34 | | | | | |
| Mercury | | 0.04 | 0.02 | | | | | | | | | |
| Millstones | 9 | 11 | 12 | | 1 | | | 8 | | | | |
| Needles | | | 0.1 | | 0.1 | | | 0.08 | | | | |
| Nightcaps | | 0.5 | | | | | | | | | | |
| Nutmeg | | 0.05 | | | 0.08 | | | | 0.1 | | | |
| Oil, Bay | | 0.04 | | | | | | | | | | |
| Oil, Olive | | | | | 115 | | | | | | | |
| Orchil | | | | | 0.92 | 4.33 | 20 | 0.5 | | | 1.08 | |
| Pans | | | | | 2.1 | 0.17 | | | | | | |

| | | | | | | | | | | | | |
|---|---|---|---|---|---|---|---|---|---|---|---|---|
| Paper | | 0.32 | 0.12 | | 0.08 | | | | | | | |
| Pepper | | 0.48 | | | | | | | 0.55 | | | 1.5 |
| Pitch & Tar | | | | | 0.58 | | | | | | | |
| Playing Cards | | 1.4 | 0.19 | | 0.65 | 0.3 | 0.06 | 0.26 | 0.12 | | | |
| Points | 1.4 | 26.4 | 5.9 | 0.8 | 11.5 | 5.77 | 0.9 | 1.3 | 3.6 | | | |
| Raisins, Great | | | | | | 22.17 | | | | | | |
| Saffron | 7.5 | 203.5 | 20.5 | 10.03 | 23.5 | 23.5 | 76.25 | 1 | 3 | | 1.5 | |
| Salt | | | | | | | 5 | | | | | |
| Seed, Onion | | 1.38 | 0.28 | | 0.5 | | | | | | | |
| Silk, Worked | 1.33 | 210.27 | 24 | | 16.67 | 18 | 67.35 | 7.33 | 19.33 | | 4.67 | |
| Skins, Golden | | 2.92 | 0.84 | | 1.15 | 0.42 | 16.66 | | 0.62 | | | |
| Soap | | 0.56 | 0.58 | | | 24.25 | | 0.19 | 0.75 | | | 3 |
| Spert | | | 0.07 | | 0.08 | 0.45 | | | | | | |
| Spurs | | | | | | 0.13 | | | | | | |
| Starch | | | | | | 0.03 | | | | | | |
| Steel | | | 0.08 | 0.08 | 0.13 | 0.41 | | | | | | |
| Stock-Cards | | 1.3 | 1.85 | | | 1.75 | | 0.9 | | | | |
| Thread | | 1.67 | 0.32 | | 0.77 | 1.02 | | 0.06 | 0.82 | | | 1.44 |
| Verdigris | | 0.32 | | | 0.02 | | | 0.05 | | | | |
| Wine | | | | | | 36 | | | | | | |
| Wine, Corrupt | | | | | | 22.5 | 27 | | | | 5.75 | |
| Woad, Azores | | | | | 0.33 | | | | | | | |
| Wool-Cards | | | | | 0.2 | 0.1 | | 0.2 | 0.2 | | | |

## Appendix 4

Monthly breakdown of gross value imports, ship movements and merchants – 1503/4

| Month | Value £ | Ship Movements | Merchants |
|---|---|---|---|
| Oct | 219.61 | 4 | 20 |
| Nov | 132.5 | 3 | 14 |
| Dec | 50 | 1 | 2 |
| Jan | 110.69 | 7 | 12 |
| Feb | 397.03 | 12 | 37 |
| Mar | 293.33 | 16 | 65 |
| Apr | 16.8 | 3 | 4 |
| May | 99.49 | 4 | 14 |
| Jun | 32.2 | 2 | 3 |
| Jul | 140.3 | 6 | 26 |
| Aug | 326.85 | 14 | 56 |
| Sept | 61.31 | 4 | 8 |

Monthly breakdown of gross value imports; ship movements and merchants – 1516/17

| Month | Value £ | Ship Movements | Merchants |
|---|---|---|---|
| Oct | 56.01 | 1 | 5 |
| Nov | 217.58 | 4 | 21 |
| Dec | 48.43 | 4 | 8 |
| Jan | 134.6 | 3 | 8 |
| Feb | 55.57 | 6 | 8 |
| Mar | 343.12 | 24 | 46 |
| Apr | 193.94 | 9 | 18 |
| May | 205.57 | 7 | 10 |
| Jun | 139.51 | 5 | 15 |
| Jul | 143.22 | 5 | 16 |
| Aug | 560.63 | 11 | 43 |
| Sept | 0 | 0 | 0 |

Monthly breakdown of gross value imports; ship movements and merchants – 1525/6

| Month | Value £ | Ship Movements | Merchants |
|---|---|---|---|
| Sept | 6.25 | 1 | 1 |
| Oct | 46.72 | 1 | 5 |
| Nov | 99.09 | 2 | 7 |

| | | | |
|---|---|---|---|
| Dec | 12 | 1 | 1 |
| Jan | 0 | 0 | 0 |
| Feb | 535.58 | 32 | 61 |
| Mar | 38.35 | 6 | 10 |
| Apr | 98.94 | 7 | 8 |
| May | 190.78 | 12 | 22 |
| Jun | 331.71 | 15 | 26 |
| Jul | 418.67 | 11 | 29 |
| Aug | 163.93 | 4 | 14 |
| Sept | 16.25 | 2 | 3 |

Monthly breakdown of gross value imports; ship movements and merchants – 1541/2

| Month | Value £ | Ship Movements | Merchants |
|---|---|---|---|
| Sept | 0 | 0 | 0 |
| Oct | 0 | 0 | 0 |
| Nov | 337.83 | 3 | 34 |
| Dec | 10.98 | 4 | 5 |
| Jan | 20.19 | 1 | 3 |
| Feb | 309.06 | 14 | 57 |
| Mar | 335.3 | 14 | 25 |
| Apr | 113.27 | 5 | 10 |
| May | 2 | 1 | 1 |
| Jun | 168.19 | 6 | 13 |
| Jul | 320.12 | 9 | 61 |
| Aug | 71.35 | 5 | 15 |
| Sept | 30.5 | 1 | 1 |

Monthly breakdown of gross value imports; ship movements and merchants – 1542/3

| Month | Value £ | Ship Movements | Merchants |
|---|---|---|---|
| Oct | 201.54 | 9 | 19 |
| Nov | 157.15 | 3 | 22 |
| Dec | 5 | 1 | 1 |
| Jan | 11.2 | 1 | 1 |
| Feb | 312.52 | 21 | 63 |
| Mar | 159.88 | 3 | 12 |
| Apr | 4.33 | 1 | 3 |

| | | | |
|---|---|---|---|
| May | 151.42 | 7 | 8 |
| Jun | 75.29 | 2 | 9 |
| Jul | 162.32 | 3 | 15 |
| Aug | 317.6 | 6 | 28 |
| Sept | 14 | 2 | 2 |

Monthly breakdown of gross value imports; ship movements and merchants – 1545/6

| Month | Value £ | Ship Movements | Merchants |
|---|---|---|---|
| Oct | 34.3 | 1 | 3 |
| Nov | 380.5 | 7 | 36 |
| Dec | 23.07 | 2 | 4 |
| Jan | 109.27 | 3 | 6 |
| Feb | 0 | 0 | 0 |
| Mar | 600.02 | 14 | 66 |
| Apr | 172.41 | 4 | 3 |
| May | 125.08 | 1 | 5 |
| Jun | 52.33 | 5 | 9 |
| Jul | 74.16 | 4 | 11 |
| Aug | 615.15 | 6 | 59 |
| Sept | 0 | 0 | 0 |

Monthly breakdown of gross value imports; ship movements and merchants – 1550/1

| Month | Value £ | Ship Movements | Merchants |
|---|---|---|---|
| Oct | 62.1 | 5 | 7 |
| Nov | 734.72 | 6 | 41 |
| Dec | 130.02 | 3 | 16 |
| Jan | 13.99 | 1 | 1 |
| Feb | 160.59 | 9 | 26 |
| Mar | 410.92 | 9 | 17 |
| Apr | 278.1 | 6 | 11 |
| May | 27.37 | 3 | 4 |
| Jun | 73.53 | 2 | 4 |
| Jul | 69.08 | 3 | 3 |
| Aug | 403.24 | 8 | 7 |
| Sept | 13.44 | 1 | 1 |

Monthly breakdown of gross value imports; ship movements and merchants – 1563/4

| Month | Value £ | Ship Movements | Merchants |
|---|---|---|---|
| Oct | 101.27 | 2 | 5 |
| Nov | 210.43 | 4 | 20 |
| Dec | 0 | 0 | 0 |
| Jan | 4.33 | 1 | 1 |
| Feb | 39.43 | 5 | 11 |
| Mar | 11.58 | 2 | 4 |
| Apr | 100.48 | 6 | 14 |
| May | 29.41 | 2 | 7 |
| Jun | 57.96 | 4 | 9 |
| Jul | 79.85 | 1 | 7 |
| Aug | 253.71 | 4 | 17 |
| Sept | 57.29 | 3 | 5 |

Monthly breakdown of gross value imports; ship movements and merchants – 1575/6

| Month | Value £ | Ship Movements | Merchants |
|---|---|---|---|
| Oct | 0 | 0 | 0 |
| Nov | 0 | 0 | 0 |
| Dec | 0 | 0 | 0 |
| Jan | 7.52 | 1 | 1 |
| Feb | 0 | 0 | 0 |
| Mar | 125.86 | 6 | 13 |
| Apr | 184.4 | 14 | 17 |
| May | 50.83 | 2 | 9 |
| Jun | 56.18 | 4 | 6 |
| Jul | 55.9 | 2 | 3 |
| Aug | 357.41 | 14 | 33 |
| Sept | 0 | 0 | 0 |

Monthly breakdown of gross value imports; ship movements and merchants – 1594/5

| Month | Value £ | Ship Movements | Merchants |
|---|---|---|---|
| Oct | 6.08 | 1 | 2 |
| Nov | 8.29 | 1 | 1 |
| Dec | 53.98 | 2 | 5 |

| | | | |
|---|---|---|---|
| Jan | 38.99 | 2 | 4 |
| Feb | 46.85 | 4 | 4 |
| Mar | 114.7 | 5 | 10 |
| Apr | 123.15 | 3 | 4 |
| May | 222.98 | 5 | 12 |
| Jun | 309.32 | 7 | 19 |
| Jul | 126.64 | 3 | 9 |
| Aug | 720.89 | 11 | 51 |
| Sept | 87.22 | 3 | 3 |

Monthly breakdown of gross value imports; ship movements and merchants – 1600/1

| **Month** | **Value £** | **Ship Movements** | **Merchants** |
|---|---|---|---|
| Oct | 61.58 | 2 | 2 |
| Nov | 36.6 | 3 | 4 |
| Dec | 23.5 | 1 | 1 |
| Jan | 14.86 | 0 | 1 |
| Feb | 24.37 | 3 | 6 |
| Mar | 177.57 | 5 | 13 |
| Apr | 11.5 | 1 | 1 |
| May | 82.6 | 4 | 9 |
| Jun | 95.38 | 1 | 6 |
| Jul | 236.6 | 8 | 11 |
| Aug | 705.82 | 9 | 40 |
| Sept | 257.45 | 9 | 19 |

Source: Flavin and Jones, Bristol's Trade, pp. 1–942

# *Bibliography*

## Primary sources

### *British Library*


Add MSS. 5754, fol. 180: Victualling accounts, c.1580–1600

Add MSS. 5754, fol. 187: Victualling accounts, c.1580–1600


### *Cork City and County Archives*


U226: Caulfield Will Transcripts


### *The National Archives (Kew)*


E122/199/1: Port: Bristol account of John Butteler & William Grene, collectors of customs & subsidies. Covering dates: 19–20 Hen. VII

E122/21/2: Port: Bristol controlment by John Lloyd. Covering dates: 8–9 Hen.VIII

E122/21/5: Port: Bristol ledger of John Bartholomew & William Goodwyn, collectors of customs & subsidies. Covering dates: 17–18 Hen.VIII

E122/1994: Port: Bristol particulars of account of William Goodwyn and Richard Watkyns, collectors of customs & subsidies on exports. Covering dates: 34–35 Hen. VIII

E122/21/10: Port: Bristol ledger of W. Goodwyn & R. Watkyns, collectors. Covering dates: 33–34 Hen.VIII

E122/21/15: Port: Bristol controlment of customs & subsidies by John Wyke. Covering dates: 37–38 Hen.VIII

E122/22/4: Port: Bristol ledger of Thomas Kelke & Henry Pomerey, collectors of customs & subsidies 4–5. Covering dates: Edw.VI

E122/199/9: Port: Bristol particulars of account of Thomas Robertes, collector of customs & subsidies on exports. Covering dates: 5–6 Eliz.

E122/24/12: Port: Bristol controlment of import duties by G. Jones. Covering dates: 5–6 Eliz.

E190/1129/11: Port: Bristol official: controller overseas inwards. Covering dates: Mich. 1575–Mich. 1576

E190/1129/12: Port: Bristol official: controller overseas outwards. Covering dates: Mich. 1575–Mich. 1576

E190/1129/23: Port: Bristol official: controller overseas outwards. Covering dates: Mich. 1576–Mich. 1577

E190/1131/4: Port: Bristol official: customer overseas outwards. Covering dates: Mich. 1591–Eas. 1592

E190/1131/8: Port: Bristol official: surveyor overseas. Covering dates: Eas. 1592–Mich. 1592

E190/1131/10: Port: Bristol official: surveyor overseas. Covering dates: Mich. 1594–Mich. 1595

E190/1132/11: Port: Bristol official: surveyor overseas. Covering dates: Mich. 1600–Mich. 1601

E190/1132/8: Port: Bristol official: surveyor overseas. Covering dates: Mich. 1598–Mich. 1599

HO 42/218: Henry VIII–Geo. III Register of patents, inventions etc. in Ireland

E351/148: 24 June 1566–1 Aug. 1567: army: contractors, purveyors: W. Winter and E. Baeshe. Victualling the army in Ireland

E351/151: 12 Aug.–13 Oct 1578: army: contractors, purveyors: E. Baeshe (per Executrix), surveyor general of victuals for marine affairs. Victualling 200 soldiers for two months and transport of the same into Ireland

E351/152: 13 Aug. 1579–8 Aug. 1580: army: contractors, purveyors: W. Glasier. Victualling and shipping to Ireland 600 soldiers levied in Yorkshire and North Wales

E351/157: 30 July 1580–7 Feb: 1580/1: army: contractors, purveyors: W. Glasyer. Victualling the troops in Ireland

E351/162: 1 Oct. 1588–30 Sept. 1594: army: contractors, purveyors: G. Beverley. Victualling the garrisons of Cork, Limerick, Waterford and Galway

E351/165: 1 Oct. 1598–30 Apr. 1601: army: contractors, purveyors: M. Darrell and J. Jolles. Victualling the troops in Ireland

E351/170: 30 Sept. 1603–1 Apr. 1606: army: contractors, purveyors: U. Babington (per Executrix) and R. Bromley. Contractors for clothing the troops in Ireland

AO1/292/1095: 14 June–7 Oct. 1574: Roll 1095 E. Earl of Bedford. Victualling and transporting 1,000 men from Dorset, Devon and Cornwall for the army in Ireland; also charges of two vessels sent out for the discovery of the Spanish Fleet

**Printed primary sources**

Ainsworth, J. (ed.), 'Corporation book of the Irishtown of Kilkenny, 1537–1628', *Analecta Hibernica*, xxviii (1978), pp. 3–78

Byrne, N. J. (ed.), *The Great Parchment Book of Waterford* (Dublin, 2007)

Chambers, R. (ed.), *The Book of Days*, ii (London, 1906)

Davies, J., 'A discovery of the true causes why Ireland was never entirely subdued', in Myers, J. P. (ed.), *Elizabethan Ireland: A Selection of Writings by Elizabethan Writers on Ireland* (Connecticut, 1983)

Fenlon, J., *Goods & Chattels: A Survey of Early Household Inventories in Ireland* (Kilkenny, 2003)

Harrison, W., *The Description of England* (New York, 1994)

Greene, D. (ed. and trans.) *Duanaire Mhéig Uidhir* (Dublin, 1972)

Grosart, A. B. (ed.), *The Lismore Papers* (1887)

Lamond, E. and Cunningham, W., *A Discourse of the Common Weal of this Realm of England* (Cambridge, 1893)

Mac Cuarta, B., 'A planter's funeral, legacies, and inventory: Sir Matthew De Renzy (1577–1634)', *Journal of the Royal Society of Antiquaries of Ireland*, cxxvii (1996), pp. 18–33

Maxwell, C., *Irish History from Contemporary Sources 1509–1610* (Dublin, 1923)

Moryson, F., 'An Itinerary', in Myers, J. P. (ed.), *Elizabethan Ireland: A Selection of Writings by Elizabethan Writers on Ireland* (Connecticut, 1983)

O'Shea, K., 'A Castleisland inventory, 1590', *Journal of the Kerry Archaeological and Historical Society*, 15–16 (1982), pp. 37–46

Spenser, E., 'A view of the present state of Ireland', in Myers, J. P. (ed.), *Elizabethan Ireland: A Selection of Writings by Elizabethan Writers on Ireland* (Connecticut, 1983)

Stewart, J. I. M. (ed.) *Montaigne's Essays: John Florio's Translation*, 2 vols (London, 1931)

de Vallambert, S., *Cinq Livres, de la Manière de Nourrir et Gouverner les Enfans dès leur Naissance* (1565), ed. C. H. Winn (Geneva, 2005)

### Printed primary sources (contemporary)

Arnold, R., *Customs of London* (1503)
Boorde, A., *A Compendyous Regyment or a Dyetary of Healthe* (London, 1547). (EEBO)
Camden, W., *Britannia* (1607)
Gascoigne, G., *A Delicate Diet for Dainty-mouthed Drunkards* (London, 1576). (EEBO)
Guillemeau, J., *Child-birth or, the Happy Deliuerie of Women* (London, 1612). (EEBO)
Fitzherbert, J., *The Boke of Husbandrie* (London, 1598). (EEBO)
Hester, J., *The True and Perfect Order to Distill Oyles* ... (London, 1575). (EEBO)
Hester, J., *A Joyfull Jewell* ... (London, 1579). (EEBO)
Holinshed, R., *Chronicles of England, Scotland, and Ireland* (1587)
Legh, G., *The Accedens of Armorie* (London, 1591). (EEBO)
Phaer, T., *The Boke of Chyldren* (1544)
Platt, *Sundrie New and Artificiall Remedies Against Famine* (London, 1596). (EEBO)
Platt, *Delightes for Ladies* (London, 1602). (EEBO)
Rich, B., *A New Description of Ireland (London, 1610)*. (EEBO)
Rich, B. *True and Kinde Excuse Written in Defence of That Booke (1612)*. (EEBO)
Stow, J., *Annales of England ... Continued by Edmund Howes* (London, 1615). (EEBO)
Stubbes, P., *The Anatomy of Abuses in England in Shakespeare's Youth, A.D. 1583* (London, 1583)

### Printed Official Documents and Calendars

Appleby, J. C. (ed.) *A Calendar Material Relating to Ireland: From the High Court of Admiralty Examinations, 1536–1641* (Dublin, 1992)
Brewer, J. S., and Bullen, W. (eds), *Calendar of the Carew Manuscripts Preserved in the Archiepiscopal Library at Lambeth*, 6 vols. (London, 1867–73)
*Calendar of State Papers Ireland*, 1509–1603, 11 vols. (London, 1860–1912)
Gilbert, J. T. (ed.), *Calendar of Ancient Records of Dublin*, i (1889)
Hughes, P. L., and Larkin, J. F., *Tudor Royal Proclamations* (New Haven, 1969)
*Journal of the House of Commons*, 1547–1629 (1802)
*Reports of the Deputy Keeper of the Public Records, Ireland* (Dublin, 1869)
*Statutes of the Realm*, 1628–80 (1819)
Vesey, F. (ed.), *Statutes at Large passed in the Parliaments Held in Ireland*, i (Dublin, 1876)

### Historical Manuscripts Commission

*Calendar* of the *Manuscripts* of the Most Honourable The *Marquess* of *Salisbury Preserved at Hatfield House, Hertfordshire*, Commission on Historical Manuscripts, 24 vols., viii (London 1899)
*Report on the Manuscripts of Lord de L'Isle and Dudley Preserved at Penhurst Place*, i, Commission on Historical Manuscripts (1925)

### Electronic sources

Brewer, J., 'The error of our ways: historians and the birth of consumer society', Lecture to the Cultures of Consumption Programme, The Royal Society, 23 September 2003, working paper no. 12., pp. 2–19. Available from: http://www.consume.bbk.ac.uk/publications.html [accessed 2 December 2013]

Lynn, Martin A., 'How much did they drink? the consumption of alcohol in traditional Europe', University of Adelaide, Australia: *Newsletter of the Research Centre on Food and Drink* (2004). Available from: http://www.arts.adelaide.edu.au/centrefooddrink/publications/articles/martinhowmuchdrink0paper.html [accessed 5 January 2011]

### *Databases/ museum catalogues*

Database of Irish excavation reports (DIER):
http://www.excavations.ie
British portable antiquities scheme:
http://www.finds.org.uk/database/artefacts/record/id/216041
Museum of London ceramics and glass catalogue:
http://www.museumoflondon.org.uk/ceramics/index.asp
Victoria and Albert Museum collections:
http://www.collections.vam.ac.uk/

### *Dictionaries/ glossaries:*

Dictionary of traded goods and commodities, 1550/1820 (2007):
Available from: http://www.britishhistory.ac.uk/report.aspx?compid=58700
'Renaissance Tailor' glossary:
Available from: http://www.renaissancetailor.com/research_vocabulary.htm#p

### *University College Cork – Corpus of Electronic Texts (CELT):*

Ryan., E. (ed.), *Annals of the Four Masters* (Corpus of Electronic Texts; a project of University College, Cork, 2002). Available from: http://www.ucc.ie/celt/published/T100005A/index.html. [accessed 13 January 2011]

Gernon, L., A *Discourse of Ireland* (1620). Available from: http://www.ucc.ie/celt/published/E620001/index.html accessed 11 January 2011]

### Secondary literature: general

Archer, I., *History of the Haberdashers' Company* (Chichester, 1991)

Ashenburg, K., Clean: An Unsanitised History of Washing (London, 2009)

Baldwin, F. E., 'Sumptuary legislation and personal legislation in England', in *Johns Hopkins University Studies in Historical and Political Science*, Series 44, No. 1 (Baltimore, 1923)

Balfour-Paul, J., *Indigo in the Arab World* (London, 1997)

Barrett, F., *The Lives of Alchemystical Philosophers: With a Critical Catalogue of Books in Occult Chemistry, and a Selection of the Most Celebrated Treatises on the Theory and Practice of the Hermetic Art* (London, 1815)

Bell, Q., *On Human Finery* (London, 1976)

Berg, M. and Clifford, H., *Consumers and Luxury: Consumer Culture in Europe, 1650–1850* (Manchester and New York, 1999)

Berg, M., *Luxury and Pleasure in Eighteenth-Century Britain* (Oxford, 2005)

Braudel, F., *The Mediterranean and the Mediterranean World in the Age of Philip II*, vol. 1 (Oakland, 1995)
Braudel, F. *Civilization and Capitalism, 15th–18th Century: The Perspective of the World* (Oakland, 1992)
Breen, T. H., 'An empire of goods: the Anglicisation of colonial America, 1690–1776', *Journal of British Studies*, 25 (1986), pp. 468–99
Breen, T. H., '"Baubles of Britain": the American and consumer revolutions of the eighteenth century', *Past and Present*, 119 (1988), pp. 73–104
Breen, T. H., 'The meanings of things: interpreting the consumer economy in the eighteenth century', in Brewer, J. and Porter, R. (eds), *Consumption and the World of Goods* (London, 1993), pp. 249–260
Breen, T. H., 'The marketplace of revolution: how consumer politics shaped American independence', *Reviews in American History*, 32, 3 (2004), pp. 329–40
Brennan, T., *et al.* (eds), *Public Drinking in the Early Modern World: Voices from the Tavern, 1500–1800* (London, 2011)
Brenner, Y. S., 'The inflation of prices in early sixteenth-century England', *Economic History Review*, 2nd ser., xiv, pp. 225–39
Breward, C., *The Culture of Fashion: A New History of Fashionable Dress* (Manchester, 1995)
Brewer, J. and Bermingham, A. (eds), *The Consumption of Culture, 1600/1800: Image, Object, Text*, (London, 1995)
Buck, A., 'Clothing and textiles in Bedfordshire inventories, 1617–1620', *Costume*, 34 (2000), pp. 25–38
Buck, A., *Clothes and the Child* (Bedford, 1996)
Buckland, K., 'The Monmouth cap', *Costume*, 13 (1979), pp. 23–37
Buckridge, S. O., *The Language of Dress, Resistance and Accommodation in Jamaica*, 1790–1890 (Kingston, 2004)
Byrne, M. St. Clare, *The Elizabethan Home* (London, 1949)
Carus-Wilson, E. M., 'The overseas trade of Bristol', in Power, E. E. and Postan, M. M. (eds), *Studies in English Trade in the Fifteenth Century* (1933), pp. 183–246
Carus-Wilson, E. M. (ed.), *The Overseas Trade of Bristol in the Later Middle Ages* (Bristol Record Society Publications, 7 (1937)
Chaudhuri, K. N., *The Trading World of Asia and the English East India Company, 1660–1760* (Cambridge, 1978)
Clark, P., *The English Alehouse: A Social History, 1200–1830* (London and New York, 1983)
Cobb, H. S. (ed.), *The Overseas Trade of London: Exchequer Customs Accounts: 1480–1* (London, 1990)
Coleman, D. C., *The Economy of England 1450–1750* (Oxford, 1977)
Corfield, P., 'Dress for deference and dissent: hats and the decline of hat honour', *Costume*, 23 (1989), pp. 64–79
Crane, D., *Fashion and its Social Agendas* (London, 2000)
Cripps, W. J., *Old English Plate* (London, 1967)
Croft, P., 'Trading with the enemy', *The Historical Journal*, 32, 2 (June, 1989), pp. 281–302
Dawson, M., *Plenti and Grase: Food and Drink in a Sixteenth-Century Household* (Totnes, 2009)
Dyer, A., *Decline and Growth in English Towns, 1400–1600* (Basingstoke, 1991)
Farmer, D. L., 'Prices and Wages 1300–1500', in Miller, E. (ed.), *The Agrarian History of England and Wales, vol. III, 1348–1500* (Cambridge, 1991)
Fryer, C. B., 'Ophthalmics in the reign of Henry VIII', *Ophthalmic Antiques*, 47 (April, 1994)
Gras, N. S. B., *The Early English Customs System* (Cambridge, 1918)

Hammond, P., *Food and Feast in Medieval England* (Gloucestershire, 1993)

Harte, N. B., 'State control of dress and social change in pre-industrial England', in Coleman, D. C. and John, A. H. (eds), *Trade, Government and Economy in Pre-Industrial England, Essays Presented to F. J. Fisher* (London, 1976), pp. 132–65

Haskell, A. and Lewis, M. (eds), *Infantilia – The Archaeology of the Nursery* (London, 1971)

Hayward, M., 'Fashion, finance, foreign politics and the wardrobe of Henry VIII', in Richardson, C. (ed.), *Clothing Culture 1350–1650* (Hampshire, 2004), pp. 165–77

Hayward, M., *Rich Apparel: Clothing and the Law in Henry VIII's England* (Aldershot, 2009)

Heal, F., *Hospitality in Early Modern England* (Oxford, 1990)

Hentschell, R., 'A question of nation: foreign clothes on the English subject', in Richardson, C. (ed.), *Clothing Culture 1350–1650* (Hampshire, 2004), pp. 49–62

Hentschell, R., 'Treasonous textiles: foreign cloth and the construction of Englishness', *Journal of Medieval and Early Modern Studies*, 32, pp. 543–70

Hinton, A. P., *The Port Books of Boston, 1601–1640* (Lincoln Record Society, 1956)

Hooper, W., 'The Tudor sumptuary laws', *English History Review*, 30, 119, pp. 433–49

Hughes, G. B., 'When wine was drunk from silver', *Country Life*, 138 (12 November, 1965)

Hunt, A., *Governance of Consuming Passions: A History of Sumptuary Law* (London, 1996)

Ilardi, V., *Renaissance Vision from Spectacles to Telescopes* (Philadelphia, 2007)

Jacoby, D., 'Silk economics and cross-cultural artistic interaction: Byzantium, the Muslim world, and the Christian West', *Dumbarton Oaks Papers*, 58 (2004), pp. 197–240

Jardine, L., *Worldly Goods: A New History of the Renaissance* (New York, 1996)

Jones, E. T., 'Illicit business: accounting for smuggling in mid-sixteenth century Bristol', *Economic History Review*, 54 (2001), pp. 17–38

Jones, A. and Stallybrass, P., *Renaissance Clothing and the Materials of Memory* (Cambridge, 2001)

Kok, Annette; 'A short history of the orchil dyes', *Lichenologist*, 3, 248 (1966), pp. 248–72

Koweleski, M., 'A consumer economy' in Horrox, R. and Ormrod, W. (eds), *The Social History of England 1200–1500* (Cambridge, 2006), pp. 238–59

Kümin, B. (ed.), *The World of the Tavern: Public Houses in Early Modern Europe* (Aldershot, 2002)

Kümin, B. (ed.), *Drinking Matters: Public Houses and Social Exchange in Early Modern Central Europe* (Basingstoke, 2007)

Latham, R. and Mathews, W. (eds) *The Diary of Samuel Pepys*, 11 vols (Los Angeles, 1970)

Lemire, B., *Fashions Favourite: The Cotton Trade and the Consumer in Britain, 1660–1800* (Oxford, 1991)

Lemire, B., *Dress, Culture and Commerce: The English Clothing Trade before the Factory, 1660–1800* (Basingstoke, 1997)

McKendrick, N., Brewer, J. and Plumb, J. H. (eds), *The Birth of a Consumer Society: The Commercialization of Eighteenth-Century England* (Indiana, 1985)

Melchoir-Bonnet, S., *The Mirror – A History* (New York, 2002)

Muir, E., *Ritual in Early Modern Europe* (Cambridge, 2005)

Munro, J. H., 'The anti-red shift – to the dark side: colour changes in Flemish luxury woollens, 1300–1550', in Netherton, R. and Owen-Crocker, G. R. (eds), *Medieval Clothing and Textiles*, vol. 3 (Woodbridge, 2007), pp. 55–95

Nicholls, J., *The Politics of Alcohol: A History of the Drink Question in England* (Manchester, 2009)

Pennell, S., 'Consumption and consumerism in early-modern England', *Historical Journal*, 42 (1999), pp. 549–64

Pennell, S., '"Pots and pans history": the material culture of the kitchen in early modern England', *Journal of Design History*, 11, 3 (1998), pp. 201–16

Pennell, S., 'The material culture of food in early modern England, circa 1650–1750', in Taylor, S. and West, S. (eds), *The Familiar Past? Archaeologies of Britain, 1550/1950* (London, 1999), pp. 35–50

Raffield, P., 'Reformation, regulation and the image: sumptuary legislation and the subject of law', *Law and Critique*, 13, 2 (2002) pp. 127–50

Ramsey, P. H. (ed.) *The Price Revolution in Sixteenth Century England* (1971)

Rhodes, M., 'A pair of fifteenth-century spectacle frames from the city of London', *Antiquaries Journal*, 62 (1982), pp. 57–73

Richardson, C., *Clothing Culture 1350–1650* (Hampshire, 2004)

Sacks, D. H., *Trade, Society and Politics in Bristol, 1500–1640*, 2 vols (New York, 1985)

Sekatcheva, O., 'The formation of Russian women's costume at the time before the reforms of Peter the Great', in Richardson, C. (ed.) *Clothing Culture 1350–1650* (Hampshire, 2004), pp. 77–94

Shammas, C., 'Changes in English and Anglo-American consumption from 1550 to 1800', in Brewer, J. and Porter, R. (eds), *Consumption and the World of Goods* (London, 1993), pp. 177–205

Shammas, C., *The Pre-Industrial Consumer in England and America* (Oxford, 1990)

Sherratt, A., 'Alcohol and its alternatives', in Goodman, J., *et al.* (eds), *Consuming Habits, Global and Historical Perspectives on How Cultures Define Drugs* (Oxford, 1995), pp. 11–46

Shuffrey, L. A., *The English Fireplace: A History of the Development of the Chimney, Chimney-piece and Firegrate with their Accessories, From the Earliest Times to the Beginning of the XIXth Century* (London, 1912)

Sparrow, W. S., *The English House: How to Judge its Periods and Styles* (London, 1908)

Steensgaard, N., 'The growth and composition of the long-distance trade of England and the Dutch before 1750', in Tracy, J. D. (ed.), *The Rise of Merchant Empires* (Cambridge, 1990), pp. 102–52

Stevens, E. E., 'A history of infant feeding', *Journal of Perinatal Education*, 18 (2009), pp. 32–9

Stephens, W. B., *Seventeenth-century Exeter* (Exeter, 1958)

Taylor, D., 'Somerset's sixteenth-century maritime trade' in Webb, A. J. (ed.), *A Maritime History of Somerset, vol. 1, Trade and Commerce* (Taunton, 2010)

Thirsk, J., *Economic Policy and Projects* (Oxford, 1978)

Thirsk, J., *Food in Early Modern England: Phases, Fads, fashions 1500–1760* (London, 2007)

Thompson, C. J. S., *Poison Mysteries in History, Romance and Crime* (New York, 1924)

Vincent, S., *Dressing the Elite: Clothing, Culture and Identity in Early Modern England* (Oxford, 2003)

de Vries, J., 'Purchasing power and the world of goods', in Brewer, J. and Porter, R. (eds), *Consumption and the World of Goods* (London, 1993), pp. 85–132

Visser, M., *The Rituals of Dinner* (New York, 1992)

Wake, C. H. H., 'The changing pattern of Europe's pepper and spice imports, ca 1400–1700', *Journal of European Economic History*, 8, 2 (1979), pp. 361–403

Walsh, G., 'Spectacles through the ages and period inaccuracies', *Optometry Today* (December, 2001)

Weatherill, L., 'The meaning of consumer behaviour in late seventeenth and early eighteenth-century England' in Brewer, J. and Porter, R. (eds), *Consumption and the World of Goods* (London, 1993), pp. 206–27

Weatherill, L., *Consumer Behaviour and Material Culture in Britain 1660–1760* (London, 1988)

Webb, A. J. (ed.), *A Maritime History of Somerset*, vol. 1 (Taunton, 2010)
Wenham, E., 'English standing cups', *American Collector* (February, 1947)
Wilson, C. A., *Food and Drink in Britain* (London, 1973)
Willan, T. S., *A Tudor Book of Rates* (Manchester, 1962)
Williamson, E., 'The domestication of religious objects in The White Devil', *SEL Studies in English Literature 1500–1900*, 47 (2007)
Wilson, E., *Adorned in Dreams* (London, 1985)
Wood, A. C., *History of the Levant* Company (London, 1964)
Woodward, D., *The Trade of Elizabethan Chester* (Hull, 1970)
Zupko, R. E., *A Dictionary of Weights and Measures for the British Isles* (Philadelphia, 1985)

**Secondary literature on Ireland**

Barnard, T., *A New Anatomy of Ireland: The Irish Protestants, 1649–1770* (London, 2003)
Barnard, T., *Making the Grand Figure: Lives and Possessions in Ireland, 1641–1770* (London, 2004)
Barnard, T., *A Guide to the Sources for the History of Material Culture in Ireland, 1500–2000* (Dublin, 2005)
Breen, C., 'The maritime cultural landscape in medieval Ireland', in Duffy, P., Edwards, D. and Fitzpatrick, E. (eds), *Gaelic Ireland* (Dublin, 2001), pp. 418–35
Burke, H., 'Putting on Irish "stuff": the politics of Irish cross-dressing', in Munns, J. and Richards, P. (eds), *The Clothes that Wear Us: Essays on Dressing and Transgressing in Eighteenth-Century Culture* (Newark, 1999), pp. 233–49
Childs, W. R., 'Ireland's trade with England in the later Middle Ages', *Irish Economic & Social History*, 9 (1982), pp. 5–33
Clarkson, L. A. and Crawford, E. M., *Feast and Famine: A History of Food and Nutrition in Ireland 1500–1920* (Oxford, 2001)
Connell, K. H., *The Population of Ireland 1750–1845* (Oxford, 1950)
Cullen, L. M., *Life in Ireland* (Dublin, 1968)
Cullen, L. M., *The Emergence of Modern Ireland 1600/1900* (London, 1981)
Cullen, L. M. (ed), *Cities and Merchants: French and Irish Perspectives on Urban Development, 1500–1900* (Dublin, 1986), pp. 190–2
Cullen, L., Smout, T. C. and Gibson, A., 'Wages and comparative development in Ireland and Scotland, 1565–1780', in Mitchison, R. and Roebuck, P. (eds), *Economy and Society in Scotland and Ireland, 1500–1939* (Edinburgh, 1988), pp.105–16
Dunlevy, M., *Dress in Ireland* (London, 1989)
Edwards, D., The *Ormond Lordship in County Kilkenny, 1515–1642: The Rise and Fall of Butler Feudal Power* (Dublin, 2002)
Ellis, S. G., 'More Irish than the Irish themselves? – the 'Anglo-Irish' in Tudor Ireland', *History Ireland*, 1 (1999), pp. 22–6
Ellis, S. G., 'Historical revision xix: the Irish customs administration under the early Tudors', *Irish Historical Studies*, 22 (1980–81), pp. 271–7
Ellis, S. G., *Ireland in the Age of the Tudors 1447–1603: English Expansion and the End of Gaelic Rule* (London, 1998)
Flavin, S. and Jones, E. T. (eds), *Bristols' Trade with Ireland and the Continent 1503–1601: The Evidence of the Exchequer Customs Accounts* (Dublin, 2009)
Flavin, S., 'Consumption and material culture in sixteenth-century Ireland', *Economic History Review*, 64, 4 (February, 2011)
Gillespie, R., *The Transformation of the Irish Economy, 1500–1700* (Dundalk, 1991)

Gillespie, R., 'Funerals and society in early seventeenth-century Ireland, *Journal of the Royal Society of Antiquaries of Ireland*, 115 (1985), pp. 86–91

Heckett, E. W., 'Town and country: an overview of Irish archaeological cloth and clothing, 1550–1850', in Horning *et al.* (eds), *The Post-Medieval Archaeology of Ireland, 1550–1850. Papers Presented at the 1st Annual Conference of the Irish Post-Medieval Archaeology Group* (Dublin, 2007)

Heckett, E. W., 'Tomb effigies and archaic dress in sixteenth-century Ireland', in Richardson, C. (ed.), *Clothing Culture 1350–1650* (Hampshire, 2004), pp. 63–76

Horning, A., *et al.* (eds), *The Post-Medieval Archaeology of Ireland, 1550–1850. Papers Presented at the 1st Annual Conference of the Irish Post-Medieval Archaeology Group* (Dublin, 2007)

Horning, A., '"The root of all vice and bestiality": exploring the cultural role of the Ulster alehouse', in Lyttleton, J. and Rynn C. (eds) *Plantation Ireland* (Dublin, 2009), pp. 113–31

Huck, C., 'Clothes make the Irish: Irish dressing and the question of identity', *Irish Studies Review*, 11, 3 (2003), pp. 273–84

Hunt, J., *Irish Medieval Figure Sculpture 1200–1600* (Dublin and London, 1974)

Joyce, P. W., *A Social History of Ancient Ireland* (London, 1903)

Kinmonth, C., *Irish Country Furniture, 1700–1950* (New Haven, 1995)

Lennon, C., *Sixteenth-century Ireland: The Incomplete Conquest* (Dublin, 1994)

Longfield, A. K., *Anglo-Irish Trade in the Sixteenth Century* (London, 1929)

Longfield, A. K., *Irish Lace* (Dublin, 1978)

Lucas, A. T., 'Irish food before the potato', *Gwerin*, 3 (1960), pp. 8–43

Lyons, M. A., 'Maritime relations between Ireland and France, c.1480–c.1630', *Irish Economic and Social History*, 27 (2000), pp. 1–24

Lyons, M. A., *Franco-Irish Relations, 1500–1610: Politics Migration and Trade* (Woodbridge, 2003)

MacCarthy Morrogh, M., *The Munster Plantation: English Migration to Southern Ireland, 1583–1641* (Oxford, 1986)

Mahony, R., 'Protestant dependence and consumption in Swift's Irish writings', in Connolly, S. J. (ed.), *Political Ideas in Eighteenth-Century Ireland* (Dublin, 2000), pp. 83–104

McClintock, H. F., *Old Irish and Highland Dress* (Dundalk, 1950)

Moody, T. W., 'Sir Thomas Phillips of Limavady, Servitor', *Irish Historical Studies*, i (1938–9), pp. 251–72

O'Brien, A. F., 'Commercial relations between Aquitane and Ireland, c.1000 to c.1550', in Picard, J. M. (ed.), *Aquitaine and Ireland in the Middle Ages* (Dublin, 1995), pp. 35–87

Ó'Drisceoil, C., 'The Rothe family garden rediscovered: an interim report on the 2007 archaeological excavation project', *Old Kilkenny Review*, lx (2008), pp. 34–46

O'Neill, T., *Merchants and Mariners in Medieval Ireland* (Dublin, 1987)

O'Sullivan, W., *The Economic History of Cork City to 1800* (Cork, 1937)

O'Sullivan, C. M., *Hospitality in Medieval Ireland, 900–1500* (Dublin, 2004)

Powell, M., *The Politics of Consumption in Eighteenth-Century Ireland* (Hampshire, 2005)

Quinn, D. B., *The Elizabethans and the Irish* (New York, 1966)

Tait, C., 'Colonising memory: manipulations of burial and commemoration in the career of the "great" earl of Cork', *Proceedings of the Royal Irish Academy*, 101 (2001), pp. 107–34

Tait, C., *Death, Burial and Commemoration in Ireland, 1550–1650* (Basingstoke, 2002)

Treadwell, T., 'The establishment of the farm of the Irish customs 1603–1613', *English Historical Review*, 93, 368 (1978), pp. 580–602

Walton, J., 'The merchant community of Waterford in the 16th and 17th Centuries', in Butel, P. and Cullen, L. M., *Cities and Merchants: French and Irish Perspectives on Urban Development, 1500–1900* (Dublin, 1986), pp. 183–92

### Theses

Cast, A Snowden, 'Women drinking in early modern England' (University of Adelaide Ph.D. thesis, 2002)

Flavin, S., 'The development of Anglo-Irish trade in the sixteenth century' (University of Bristol MA thesis, 2004)

Flavin, S., 'Consumption and material culture in sixteenth-century Ireland' (University of Bristol Ph.D. thesis, 2011)

Jones, E. T., 'The Bristol shipping industry in the sixteenth century' (University of Edinburgh Ph.D. thesis, 1998)

Millard, A. M., 'The import trade of London, 1600–40' (London University Ph.D. thesis, 1956)

Taylor, D., 'The maritime trade of the smaller Bristol channel ports in the sixteenth century' (University of Bristol Ph.D. thesis, 2009)

Tosney, N., 'Gaming in England, c.1540–1760' (University of York Ph.D. thesis, 2008)

# *Index*

Page numbers in *italics* denote illustrations. The letter n following a page number indicates that the reference will be found in a note.

Printed and bound by CPI Group (UK) Ltd, Croydon, CR0 4YY

13/09/2026

14961003-0006